THE CAMBRIDGE COMPANION TO
THE AMERICAN MODERNIST NOVEL

The Cambridge Companion to the American Modernist Novel offers a comprehensive analysis of U.S. modernism as part of a wider, global literature. Both modernist and American literary studies have been reshaped by waves of scholarship that unsettled prior consensuses regarding America's relation to transnational, diasporic, and indigenous identities and aesthetics; the role of visual and musical arts in narrative experimentation; science and technology studies; and allegiances across racial, ethnic, gendered, and sexual social groups. Recent writing on U.S. immigration, imperialism, and territorial expansion has generated fresh and exciting reasons to read – or reread – modernist novelists, both prominent and forgotten. Written by a host of leading scholars, this *Companion* provides unique interpretations and approaches to modernist themes, techniques, and texts.

Joshua L. Miller is Associate Professor of English at the University of Michigan. His first book, *Accented America: The Cultural Politics of Multilingual Modernism*, analyzed the mixed languages of interwar U.S. literary modernism. He is the coeditor of the forthcoming book *Languages of Modern Jewish Cultures: Comparative Perspectives*.

A list of titles in the series is at the end of the book.

CAMBRIDGE
COMPANIONS TO
LITERATURE

THE CAMBRIDGE
COMPANION TO

THE AMERICAN
MODERNIST NOVEL

EDITED BY
JOSHUA L. MILLER
University of Michigan

CAMBRIDGE
UNIVERSITY PRESS

CAMBRIDGE
UNIVERSITY PRESS

32 Avenue of the Americas, New York, NY 10013–2473, USA

Cambridge University Press is part of the University of Cambridge.

It furthers the University's mission by disseminating knowledge in the pursuit of education, learning, and research at the highest international levels of excellence.

www.cambridge.org
Information on this title: www.cambridge.org/9781107445895

© Cambridge University Press 2015

First published 2015

Printed in the United Kingdom by Clays, St Ives plc

A catalog record for this publication is available from the British Library.

Library of Congress Cataloging in Publication Data
The Cambridge companion to the American modernist novel /
[edited by] Joshua Miller, University of Michigan.
pages   cm. – (Cambridge companions to literature)
Includes bibliographical references and index.
1. Modernism (Literature) – United States.   2. American fiction – 20th century – History
and criticism.   3. Modernism (Aesthetics) – United States.   4. Ethnic groups in
literature.   5. Cultural pluralism in literature.   6. Transnationalism in
literature.   7. Literature and globalization.   I. Miller, Joshua (Joshua L.) editor.
PS374.M535C36   2015
813'.5209112–dc23
2015011158

ISBN 978-1-107-08895-0 Hardback
ISBN 978-1-107-44589-5 Paperback

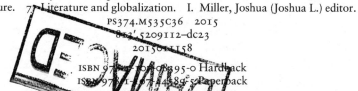

CONTENTS

ILLUSTRATIONS

CONTRIBUTORS

JEFF ALLRED is Associate Professor of English and Codirector of the Academic Center for Excellence in Research and Teaching (ACERT) at Hunter College/ CUNY. He is the author of *American Modernism and Depression Documentary* (Oxford, 2010) and is currently working on a book manuscript on interwar literature and pedagogy, *ABC of Modernism*.

KEVIN BELL is Associate Professor of English and African American Studies at Pennsylvania State University. He is the author of *Ashes Taken for Fire: Aesthetic Modernism and the Critique of Identity* (Minnesota, 2007) and has published essays in such journals as *boundary 2*, *Modern Fiction Studies*, and *The Global South*. He is currently completing a study of postanthropocentric logics and materialities in radical black film and literature since the mid-1960s.

MARY PAT BRADY teaches at Cornell University. She is the author of *Extinct Lands, Temporal Geographies: Chicana Literature and the Urgency of Space* (Duke, 2002) and an associate editor of the seventh edition of *The Heath Anthology of American Literature* (Cengage, 2012).

DENISE CRUZ is Assistant Professor of English at the University of Toronto. She is the author of *Transpacific Femininities: The Making of the Modern Filipina* (Duke, 2012) and the editor of Yay Panlilio's *The Crucible: An Autobiography of Colonel Yay, Filipina American Guerrilla* (Rutgers, 2009). Her articles have appeared (or are forthcoming) in *American Quarterly*, *PMLA*, *Modern Fiction Studies*, *American Literature*, *American Literary History*, and the collection *Eating Asian America: A Food Studies Reader*. Her research centers on the use of spatial and geographic frameworks to analyze gender and sexuality in national and transnational cultures.

YOGITA GOYAL is Associate Professor of English at the University of California, Los Angeles, and Associate Editor of *Contemporary Literature*. She is the author of *Romance, Diaspora, and Black Atlantic Literature* (2010) and the editor of the forthcoming *Cambridge Companion to Transnational American Literature*. Her next book explores the afterlives of slavery in contemporary fiction.

SCOTT HERRING is Professor of English at Indiana University, Bloomington. He is the author of three books, including *The Hoarders: Material Deviance in Modern American Culture* (Chicago, 2014) and *Another Country: Queer Anti-Urbanism* (NYU, 2010).

DANIEL KATZ is Professor of English and Comparative Literary Studies at the University of Warwick. He is the author of *Saying I No More: Subjectivity and Consciousness in the Prose of Samuel Beckett* (Northwestern, 1999), *American Modernism's Expatriate Scene: The Labour of Translation* (Edinburgh, 2007; paperback reissue, 2014), and *The Poetry of Jack Spicer* (Edinburgh, 2013).

EMILY J. LORDI is Assistant Professor of English at the University of Massachusetts, Amherst, and the author of *Black Resonance: Iconic Women Singers and African American Literature* (Rutgers, 2013). She is writing a musical-literary history of the concept of "soul" in African American culture.

STEVEN MEYER teaches intellectual history and modern literature at Washington University in St. Louis. He is the author of *Irresistible Dictation: Gertrude Stein and the Correlations of Writing and Science* (Stanford, 2001), which seeks to establish the interdisciplinary contours of Stein's writing: philosophical, psychological, neurophysiological, literary. He is currently completing *Robust Empiricisms: Jamesian Modernism between the Disciplines, 1878 to the Present*, a cross-disciplinary account of investigations in literature, literary criticism, philosophy, science studies, and the life sciences that involve the development of techniques for eliciting something where, from the perspective of more traditional empiricisms, there is nothing. He is also the editor of the forthcoming *Cambridge Companion to Literature and Science*.

CATHERINE MORLEY is Senior Lecturer in American Literature at the University of Leicester. She has published numerous articles and chapters, as well as two monographs: *The Quest for Epic in Contemporary American Fiction* (Routledge, 2009) and *Modern American Literature* (Edinburgh, 2012). She is the editor of *American Writing after 9/11* (Bloomsbury, 2015) and the coeditor of *American Thought and Culture in the 21st Century* (Edinburgh, 2008) and *American Modernism: Cultural Transactions* (Cambridge Scholars, 2009).

JULIAN MURPHET is Professor in Modern Film and Literature at the School of the Arts and Media as well as Director of the Centre for Modernism Studies in Australia at UNSW, where he edits the journal *Affirmations: of the modern*. He is the author of *Literature and Race in Los Angeles* (Cambridge, 2001) and *Multimedia Modernism* (Cambridge, 2009).

GAYLE ROGERS is Associate Professor of English at the University of Pittsburgh, where he teaches courses in modernism, world literature, translation theory, and archival research methods. He is the author of *Modernism and the New Spain: Britain, Cosmopolitan Europe, and Literary History* (Oxford, 2012) and of publications in *PMLA*, *Modernism/modernity*, *Comparative Literature*, *Journal of Modern Literature*, *James Joyce Quarterly*, *TransLatin Joyce: Global Transmissions in Ibero American Literature*, *Oxford Handbook of Global Modernisms*, *Revista de Estudios Orteguianos*, and *100 Escritores del Siglo XX*. His current book projects are *Modernism: Evolution of an Idea*, coauthored with Sean Latham (Bloomsbury, 2015), and *Between Literary Empires: Translation and the International Emergence of Modernism*, a study of English/Spanish translation practices from the Spanish-American War of 1898 through the modernist era.

HARILAOS STECOPOULOS is Associate Professor of English at the University of Iowa and the editor of *The Iowa Review*. He is the author of *Reconstructing the World: Southern Fictions and U.S. Imperialisms, 1898–1976* (Cornell, 2008).

CHRONOLOGY

1877   Thomas A. Edison invents the phonograph

1879   Henry James, *Daisy Miller: A Study*

1880   George Washington Cable, *The Grandissimes: A Story of Creole Life*

1881   Henry James, *The Portrait of a Lady*

1882   Chinese Exclusion Act
            The Edison Illuminating Company opens the first U.S. central power plant in New York City

1884   Ten-story Home Insurance Building in Chicago is the first "skyscraper"
            Henry James, "The Art of Fiction"

1886   Haymarket Affair in Chicago

1887   Thibodaux (LA) Massacre

1888   Edison and Eadweard Muybridge meet to discuss development of a device to exhibit motion pictures
            First Kodak box cameras sold

1890   Sherman Antitrust Act
            First U.S. census utilizing machine tabulation with data punch cards
            National Afro-American League founded
            Battle of Wounded Knee
            Henry James, *The Tragic Muse*
            William James, *The Principles of Psychology*
            Sarah Orne Jewett, *Tales of New England*
            Mary E. Bradley (Lane), *Mizora*

Jacob Riis, *How the Other Half Lives*
Oscar Wilde, *Picture of Dorian Gray*, published in
Lippincott's Monthly Magazine (Philadelphia)

1891   International Copyright Act
The kineograph and kinetoscope, early motion picture devices
attributed to Edison and W.K.L. Dickson, are exhibited
Henry Ford hired as engineer at Edison Illuminating Company

1892   Francis E.W. Harper, *Iola Leroy*

1893   World's Columbian Exposition in Chicago
Financial panic of 1893

1894   Mark Twain, *The Tragedy of Pudd'nhead Wilson and the
Comedy of Those Extraordinary Twins*
Kate Chopin, *Bayou Folk*

1896   Financial panic of 1896
U.S. Supreme Court upholds "separate but equal" doctrine of
racial segregation in *Plessy v. Ferguson*
Abraham Cahan, *Yekl*
Sarah Orne Jewett, *The Country of the Pointed Firs*

1897   Henry James, *What Maisie Knew*

1898   Sinking of USS *Maine* in Havana, Cuba
Wars with Spain over Cuba, Puerto Rico, Philippines, and
Guam
Hawai'i annexed
Wilmington (NC) coup d'état
United States v. Wong Kim Ark Supreme Court case

1899   Samoa occupied
American Anti-Imperialist League formed
Kate Chopin, *The Awakening*

1900   Pauline Hopkins, *Contending Forces: A Romance*

1901   Pan-American Exposition held in Buffalo, NY
President William McKinley is shot by Leon Czolgosz at the
Pan-American Exposition and dies eight days later; Vice
President Theodore Roosevelt succeeds McKinley
Charles Chesnutt, *The Marrow of Tradition*
Booker T. Washington, *Up from Slavery*

1902   Pauline Hopkins, *Of One Blood,* published serially through
        1903
        William James, *The Varieties of Religious Experience*

1903   Immigration Act of 1903 (Anarchist Exclusion Act)
        W.E.B. Du Bois, *Souls of Black Folk*
        Charlotte Perkins Gilman, *The Home: Its Work and
        Influence*
        Henry James, *The Ambassadors*
        Jack London, *The Call of the Wild*
        Gertrude Stein, *Q.E.D.* composed

1904   Henry James, *The Golden Bowl*

1905   Niagara Movement formed
        Edith Wharton, *The House of Mirth*

1906   Atlanta race riots
        President Theodore Roosevelt receives the Nobel Peace
        Prize
        Meat Inspection Act and Pure Food and Drug Act
        San Francisco earthquake
        Picasso completes his portrait of Gertrude Stein in Paris

1907   Immigration Act of 1907
        Financial panic leads to creation of Federal Reserve System
        Henry Adams, *The Education of Henry Adams*
        Henry James, *The American Scene*
        William James, *Pragmatism: A New Name for Some Old
        Ways of Thinking*

1908   "Gentleman's agreement" with Japan
        Ford Motor Company introduces the Model T automobile
        Jack London, *The Iron Heel*

1909   National Association for the Advancement of Colored People
        (NAACP) founded
        Gertrude Stein, *Three Lives*

1910   Mexican Revolution
        Mann Act ("White-Slave Traffic Act")

1911   Triangle Shirtwaist Company fire
        Dillingham Commission Report

Frederick Winslow Taylor, *The Principles of Scientific Management*

Charlotte Perkins Gilman, *Moving the Mountain*

1912   Mary Antin, *The Promised Land*

Edith Eaton (Sui-Sin Far), *Mrs. Spring Fragrance*

James W. Johnson, *Autobiography of an Ex-Colored Man*

1913   The New York Armory Show

California enacts Alien Land Law

Willa Cather, *O Pioneers!*

1914   Archduke Franz Ferdinand of Austria assassinated in Sarajevo

Panama Canal completed

Tampico Affair and six-month occupation of Veracruz, Mexico

Ludlow Massacre

Henry Ford introduces "Five Dollar Day"

American Society of Composers, Authors and Publishers is established to protect copyrighted music

1915   German U-boat sinks ocean liner *Lusitania*

U.S. occupation of Haiti

Mariano Azuela, *Los de abajo* published serially in *El Paso del Norte* (revised and republished in 1920)

Willa Cather, *The Song of the Lark*

Charlie Chaplin, *The Tramp*

Winnifred Eaton (Onoto Watanna), *Me: A Book of Remembrance*

Charlotte Perkins Gilman, *Herland*

D.W. Griffith, *The Birth of a Nation*

1916   Margaret Sanger, Ethel Byrne, and Fanny Mindell open first U. S. birth control clinic

John Dewey, *Democracy and Education*

W.C. Handy, "Beale Street Blues"

Rabindranath Tagore, *At Home in the World*

1917   United States enters World War I

Russian Revolution

East St. Louis race riot (others in Chester, PA; Philadelphia, PA; and Houston, TX)

Immigration Act of 1917

1918   Influenza epidemic
        Dillingham-Hardwick Act
        Henry Adams, *The Education of Henry Adams*
        Willa Cather, *My Ántonia*
        Olga Beatriz Torres, *Memorias de mi viaje*
        Ralph Werther, *Autobiography of an Androgyne*

1919   Treaty of Versailles
        18th Amendment to the Constitution prohibits alcohol;
            National Prohibition (Volstead) Act
        "Red Summer" of race riots in more than 25 cities, including
            Chicago, IL; Washington, DC; and Elaine, AR
        Palmer Raids
        Sherwood Anderson, *Winesburg, Ohio*
        H.L. Mencken, *The American Language*

1920   F. Scott Fitzgerald, *This Side of Paradise*
        Anzia Yezierska, *Hungry Hearts*

1921   Tulsa race riot
        Emergency Quota Act

1922   Cable Act
        Willa Cather, *One of Ours*
        F. Scott Fitzgerald, *The Beautiful and Damned*
        Waldo Frank, *City Block*
        Anzia Yezierska, *Salome of the Tenements*

1923   Rosewood (FL) Massacre
        United States v. Bhagat Singh Thind Supreme Court decision
            declaring Native Americans nonwhite in the "common
            understanding" of the nation
        Willa Cather, *A Lost Lady*
        Jean Toomer, *Cane*

1924   Johnson-Reed Immigration Act
        Walter White, *The Fire in the Flint*

1925   Scopes trial
        Sherwood Anderson, *Dark Laughter*
        Willa Cather, *The Professor's House*
        John Dos Passos, *Manhattan Transfer*
        F. Scott Fitzgerald, *The Great Gatsby*
        Ernest Hemingway, *In Our Time*
        Alain Locke, *The New Negro*

Anita Loos, *Gentlemen Prefer Blondes*
Gertrude Stein, *The Making of Americans*
Anzia Yezierska, *Bread Givers*

1926   Hilda Doolittle, *Palimpsest*
Ernest Hemingway, *The Sun Also Rises*
Langston Hughes, "The Negro Artist and the Racial
Mountain"

1927   Nicola Sacco and Bartolomeo Vanzetti executed
Willa Cather, *Death Comes for the Archbishop*
Ernest Hemingway, *Men without Women*
V.L. Parrington, *Main Currents in American Thought*
Bessie Smith, "Backwater Blues"

1928   Djuna Barnes, *Ryder* and *Ladies' Almanack*
W.E.B. Du Bois, *Dark Princess: A Romance*
Dashiell Hammett, *Red Harvest*
Nella Larsen, *Quicksand*
Claude McKay, *Home to Harlem*

1929   Stock Market crashes on "Black Thursday"
William Faulkner, *The Sound and the Fury*
Alyse Gregory, *King Log and Lady Lea*
Ernest Hemingway, *A Farewell to Arms*
Nella Larsen, *Passing*
Oliver La Farge, *Laughing Boy*
Claude McKay, *Banjo*

1930   Sinclair Lewis is the first U.S. writer to win the Nobel Prize in
Literature
Watsonville (CA) riots
John Dos Passos, *42nd Parallel*
William Faulkner, *As I Lay Dying*
Michael Gold, *Jews without Money*
Langston Hughes, *Not without Laughter*

1931   Pearl S. Buck, *The Good Earth*
William Faulkner, *Sanctuary*
George Schuyler, *Black No More*
Edmund Wilson, *Axel's Castle*

1932   John Dos Passos, *1919*
William Faulkner, *Light in August*

Kathleen Tamagawa, *Holy Prayers in a Horse's Ear*
Wallace Thurman, *Infants of the Spring*

1933 21st Amendment to the Constitution repeals Prohibition
Gertrude Stein, *Autobiography of Alice B. Toklas*
Nathanael West, *Miss Lonelyhearts*

1934 Gertrude Stein and Alice Toklas tour United States
James M. Cain, *The Postman Always Rings Twice*
F. Scott Fitzgerald, *Tender Is the Night*
Henry Miller, *Tropic of Cancer*
Henry Roth, *Call It Sleep*
Nathanael West, *A Cool Million, or, the Dismantling of
Lemuel Pitkin*

1935 Harlem race riot
James M. Cain, *Double Indemnity*
W.E.B. Du Bois, *Black Reconstruction in America*
*Jovita González, "Shades of the Tenth Muses" completed
Horace McCoy, *They Shoot Horses, Don't They?*
Gertrude Stein, *Lectures in America* and *Narration*
H.T. Tsiang, *The Hanging on Union Square*

1936 Djuna Barnes, *Nightwood*
John Dos Passos, *The Big Money*
William Faulkner, *Absalom, Absalom!*
D'Arcy McNickle, *The Surrounded*
George Santayana, *The Last Puritan: A Memoir in the Form of
a Novel*

1937 Ernest Hemingway, *To Have and Have Not*
Zora Neale Hurston, *Their Eyes Were Watching God*
Younghill Kang, *East Goes West*
Claude McKay, *A Long Way from Home*
H.T. Tsiang, *And China Has Hands*

1938 Pearl Buck receives Nobel Prize
Zora Neale Hurston, *Tell My Horse*

1939 World's Fair in New York City
Golden Gate Exposition in San Francisco
Raymond Chandler, *The Big Sleep*

* NB: An asterisk denotes uncertain date of composition or completion of a work.

John Fante, *Ask the Dust*
William Faulkner, *The Wild Palms* [*If I Forget Thee, Jerusalem*]
Zora Neale Hurston, *Moses, Man of the Mountain*
John Steinbeck, *The Grapes of Wrath*
Nathanael West, *The Day of the Locust*

1940   James Agee and Walker Evans, *Let Us Now Praise Famous Men*
Willa Cather, *Sapphira and the Slave Girl*
Raymond Chandler, *Farewell, My Lovely*
Ernest Hemingway, *For Whom the Bell Tolls*
Langston Hughes, *The Big Sea*
*Américo Paredes, *George Washington Gómez* completed
Richard Wright, *Native Son*

1941   F. Scott Fitzgerald, *The Last Tycoon*
Lin Yutang, *A Leaf in the Storm*
Richard Wright, *12 Million Black Voices*

1942   Alfred Kazin, *On Native Grounds*

1943   Magnuson Act repeals the Chinese Exclusion Act of 1882
Race riots in Detroit, MI; New York, NY; and Los Angeles, CA (Zoot Suit Riots)
*Jovita González and Margaret Elmer [Eve Raleigh], *Caballero: A Historical Novel* completed

1945   Chester Himes, *If He Hollers, Let Him Go*

1946   Carlos Bulosan, *America Is in the Heart*
Gertrude Stein, *Wars I Have Seen*

1948   Zora Neale Hurston, *Seraph on the Suwanee*
Lin Yutang, *Chinatown Family*

1950   William Faulkner receives Nobel Prize
Jade Snow Wong, *Fifth Chinese Daughter*

1952   Ralph Ellison, *Invisible Man*
Ernest Hemingway, *The Old Man and the Sea*

1953   Raymond Chandler, *The Long Goodbye*

---

* NB: An asterisk denotes uncertain date of composition or completion of a work.

I

JOSHUA L. MILLER

Introduction

The twenty-first century's second decade is awash with centennials, including those of the New York Armory Show (1913), the assassination of the Archduke Franz Ferdinand, the completion of the Panama Canal, the Ford "Five Dollar Day" (1914), the first transcontinental telephone call, the sinking of the ocean liner *Lusitania* (1915), the opening of the first birth control clinic (1916), and U.S. entry into World War I (1917).

In the midst of such commemorations, however, we may overlook signal moments 75 and 125 years ago that bookend the cultural and political ferment of U.S. literary modernism. In 1890, literary works that would become important forerunners of modernism were published in the United States by Mary E. Bradley (Lane), Henry James, William James, Sarah Orne Jewett, Jacob Riis, and Oscar Wilde. That eventful year saw statehood for Idaho and Wyoming, the Sherman Antitrust Act, a national census (the first to be machine tabulated) declaring the closing of the Western frontier, and the Wounded Knee Massacre. The same year, Chicago was selected as the site of the World's Columbian Exposition, the first major American imperial spectacle of civilizational progress. In the midst of a national economic recession, the exposition was a commemoration itself of Columbus' arrival in the Americas, a commercial opportunity, and an assertion of U.S. prominence in the world. The spectacular, ephemeral, and aptly named "White City" opened to the public in 1893, powered by Westinghouse Electric (chosen over rival Thomas Edison's General Electric), with buildings dedicated to mining, electricity, fine arts, administration, technology, agriculture, and women. The latter building was designed by twenty-one-year-old Sophia Hayden and introduced with an address by Susan B. Anthony.[1] Organizers' reluctance to include exhibits of African American contributions led to protests and calls for a boycott. Frederick Douglass served as Haiti's representative and also contributed an introduction to Ida B. Wells' pamphlet *The Reason Why the Colored American Is Not in the World's Columbian Exposition*. The first Parliament of the World's Religions was held at the exhibition to bring into dialogue leaders of varied faiths throughout the world; it is considered the earliest large-scale gathering of figures representing Eastern and Western religions. Frederick Jackson Turner presented his "frontier thesis" based on 1890 census data. A visiting Henry Ford first saw a one-cylinder, gas-powered engine developed by Gottlieb Daimler on a platform quadricycle, though it was overshadowed by a large display of steam locomotives and other transportational technologies. Visitors were introduced to an amusement park with the first moving walkway, the original Ferris wheel, and the first commercial movie theater, where Eadweard Muybridge gave lectures and demonstrated his zoopraxiscope. Scott Joplin made a name for himself and early ragtime.

The United States was a particularly active participant during this era of public celebrations of empire and globalist progress at the 1901 Pan-American Exposition (Buffalo), where President William McKinley was fatally shot; the 1904 Louisiana Purchase Exposition (St. Louis); the 1907 Jamestown Exposition (Norfolk); the 1915 Panama-Pacific International Exposition (San Francisco); the 1918 Bronx International Exposition of Science, Arts, and Industries (New York); and the 1933–1934 Century of Progress International Exposition (Chicago).

The events that took place three-quarters of a century ago in the hinge years of 1939 and 1940, situated between the Depression and U.S. entry into armed conflict in World War II, are similarly indicative of ongoing U.S. collective preoccupations with the country's place in the world. Notable literary works appeared in those years, authored by James Agee and Walker Evans, Willa Cather, Raymond Chandler, John Fante, William Faulkner, Ernest Hemingway, Langston Hughes, Zora Neale Hurston, John Steinbeck, Nathanael West, and Richard Wright. The year 1939 also saw the openings of the New York World's Fair and the Golden Gate International Exposition in San Francisco, the "Pageant of the Pacific." The latter's aim of centralizing Asian Pacific peoples required some creative balancing of primitivist nostalgia and techno-futurism in its architecture, exhibitions, and events. Diego Rivera foregrounded this tension in the mural he contributed to the Exposition, *Pan-American Unity*. Describing its themes, he wrote: "My mural ... is about the marriage of the artistic expression of the North and of the South on this continent, that is all. I believe in order to make an American art, a real American art, this will be necessary, this blending of the art of the Indian, the Mexican, the Eskimo, with this kind of urge which makes the machine, the invention in the material side of life, which is also an artistic urge, the same urge primarily but in a different form of expression."[2] In contrast to the dynamic fusions in Rivera's painting, the Exposition's photographic exhibition was more protective of what curator Ansel Adams declared "a decisive American art."[3]

FIGURE I.I: Stuart Davis, "Study for *History of Communication* Mural," 1939.
9 5/8 × 29 7/8 in. image; 14 7/8 × 34 in. sheet.
Collection Minnesota Museum of American Art, St. Paul. Art © Estate of Stuart
Davis/Licensed by VAGA, New York, NY.

The New York World's Fair claimed futurism as its theme, "Building the World of Tomorrow with the Tools of Today." The temporal shift away from rescripting the present (as the apogee of progress) to projecting the future suited the gloomy global outlook of the late 1930s, but it also conveyed popular understandings of the cultural momentum of literary modernism's long-standing vanguardisms. As in previous fairs, corporate, commercial, scientific, and technological priorities prevailed – in sleek exhibits featuring General Motors' "Futurama"; AT&T and RCA's demonstrations of long-distance telephone calls, tape recorders, FM radio, and a television studio; Goodrich's "tire guillotine," demonstrating rubber's durability; the railroads pavilion; Democracity, the metropolis to be; and Elektro, a seven-foot-tall robot – though cultural expression also played a prominent role, particularly visual culture, in architecture, design, lighting, exhibits, and murals.

Modernist painter Stuart Davis, whose early work appeared in the Armory Show, contributed the mural *History of Communication*, which survives today only in a study (Figure I.I).[4] An artist influenced by (and influencing) abstraction, pop art, and cross-media experimentation, Davis incorporated elements of language and photographic images throughout his career. His *History* mural recontextualizes familiar iconography (based on photographs from the New York Public Library's Print and Photography Division) within a blurred timeline that evokes contiguities and transformations in the historical relations between technology and expressive media.[5] The stark white-on-black composition, too, implies affinities with earlier modes of visual expression, while repurposing corporate logos from an advertising industry dependent on the sophisticated deployment of visual signs. Davis' mural runs on a leftward continuum from gestural and alphabetic communication to electronic and visual forms. The icons of modernity's mechanized devices are cluttered, overlapping, and self-reflexive (as in a letter addressed to the New York World's Fair postmarked "SF CAL," perhaps sent by the Golden Gate Exposition planners), narrating the increasing massification of communication, which culminates in cinema and television, new cultural platforms with the global reach of visual transmission. Davis' expansive, antididactic *History* does not provide a univocal assessment of the modernist American mediascape, but rather invites further interrogation. For our purposes, we might ask: Where in his scheme would Davis fit the modernist novel? And how did awareness of the newly global scope of U.S. art affect the production and reception of those novels?

The history of U.S. World's Fairs offers vivid snapshots of popular, technological, scientific, commercial, and artistic projections of Americanist engagements with the world. Rather than operating in a void, U.S. modernist authors wrote with these contemporary developments in mind, though they set them in rather different contexts in crafting juxtapositional forms and techniques within experimental novels that critiqued central tenets of expansionist modernity. As one example, we might relate Konrad Bercovici's account of New York City as "not a city but a world" – a modern, immigrant-surcharged successor to the "world cities" of London, Paris, and Rome in *Around the World in New York* (1924) – to John Dos Passos' *Manhattan Transfer* (1925), whose textual cacophony includes newspaper and song fragments, vernacular and multilingual dialogue, hairpin perspectival shifts, and the clatter of mechanized urbanity.[6] W.E.B. Du Bois, Gertrude Stein, and Zora Neale Hurston drew on emergent and shifting paradigms in sociology, anthropology, and medicine in their narrative representations of gendered and racialized interior experience and collective im/migration. Meanwhile, visual art depicting intranational and international tensions intervenes in mixed-media modernism by varied novelists, such as Julian Benda's illustrations in Willa Cather's *My Ántonia* (1918), Milt Gross' and Miné Okubo's graphic novels, Works Progress Administration collaborations between photographers and authors, and Djuna Barnes' illustrations. Dos Passos' grandiose, centrifugal narrative, like the World's Fairs themselves, attempts to discern patterns formed across the era's movements of thought and bodies.

Reverberations of these concurrent social and cultural trends continue to resonate in studies of what Marjorie Perloff has called "21st Century Modernism," as well as in what other scholars have termed "alternative modernities," "digital modernism," "global modernism," "pop modernism," "ethnic modernism," "Afromodernism," "virtual modernism," and "geomodernism."[7] The field of modernist studies has been greatly enriched in the past two decades by new methodologies informed by studies of transnational/global and hemispheric cultures, new media, race and gender, science and technology, visual culture, translation and multilingualism, sexualities, and many others. *The Cambridge Companion to the American Modernist Novel* draws on each of these ongoing scholarly trends, with particular emphasis on how they generate fresh insights for investigations into the transnational substrates and superstrates of national literary movements.

As many have documented, the era of modernism was one in which nationalisms coincided with varied, clashing, and parallel internationalisms: immigration, Marxism, aesthetic movements, hemispheric expansionism, consumerism, anarchism, mass culture, and so on. Not unrelatedly, the decades between the 1890s and the 1940s bore witness to unprecedentedly rapid and diverse demographic changes to the composition of the United States and an extraordinary economic expansion. Consequently, U.S. cultural trends were infused by alternating tensions of inward incorporation and outward expansion; discursive homogeneity and alterity; institutions of order and celebrations of eccentricity/individualism; tourism and impoverishment; and structures of formal and informal border surveillance, segregation, imprisonment, exclusion, and banishment. Modernist novels of the United States drew upon these varied vectors of movement through formal experiments with narratorial perspective, genre blurring, linguistic code-switching and translation, mixed media, and synesthesia, among other forms.

The institutional establishment of university programs of study in American Literature (and those of writing/composition and descriptivist linguistics) coincided with the emergence of experimental modernist narratives, a paradox that the chapters in this volume use to convey a sense of the period's complex affinities for chaos/fragmentation/mixture on the one hand and order/wholeness/purity on the other. Recent scholarship on U.S. literary modernism has prioritized the cultural implications of trends in immigration, expatriation, and imperial expansion as they intensified the anxieties, fantasies, pleasures, terrors, and grandiosity coursing through the novels of the age. Such work has complicated high/low, inside/outside, timeless/ephemeral binaries and demonstrated that a diverse range of authors navigated both sides of the mixture/purity and chaos/order dynamics. Rather than viewing authors in one context (as radical, fascist, ethnically or sexually other, expatriate, nationalist, etc.), this volume's contributors offer conceptually nuanced and historically sensitive perspectives on both the novels and the era from which they issued.

Scholarship on and compendia of both world and comparative literature have offered reconsiderations of literary genealogies from the nineteenth century onward, frequently (in the United States) posing challenges to the primacy of English departments. One such salvo, written in 1949 by

W.P. Friederich and Clarence Gohdes, called for establishing a "Department of American and Comparative Literature," since U.S. literature was at least as influenced by French, German, Scandinavian, and Russian sources as English ones. Moreover, "modern America is what it is" because of its "rich mixture" of immigrants' cultural traditions.[8] The literature of the United States ought to be read as a part of world literature, they contend, and thus be paired methodologically with comparative literature. Quixotic as this particular proposal may have been, its authorship by two distinguished scholars (who later served as editors of the journals *American Literature* and *Comparative Literature*) conveys the significance of efforts then and afterward to engage "the new internationalism of our post-war world" through a new field of study that "represents America as a whole in its relationship to the outer world as a whole."

Literary criticism since the 1980s has undertaken systematic reconsiderations of national(ist) traditions it once presumed. Multidisciplinary investigations of nationalism have been both extended and interrogated by treatments of inter-, trans-, and post-national relations. Subsequently, the currents of both modernist and Americanist literary studies were redirected by waves of scholarship that unsettled prior consensuses regarding transnational, diasporic, and indigenous aesthetics and temporalities; the role of visual and musical arts in narrative experimentation; media paradigm shifts; allegiances among and across racial, ethnic, gendered, and sexual social groups; and reception (translations, adaptations, intertextuality). Since assertions of autonomy from history through the artistically "new" are themselves famously part of both modernist and Americanist self-fashioning rhetorics, the academic work of "New Americanists" (as in the Duke University Press series launched in 1993) and that on "New Modernisms" (the initial Modernist Studies Association annual conferences starting in 1999) has scrutinized the boundaries of inherited binaries of new/old, core/periphery, domestic/foreign, and so on, in order to reconsider the New Critical and Cold War frameworks that shaped both areas of study in the 1950s.[9]

Scholars in each field have challenged presumed boundaries in time (when modernism began and when, or if, it ended), space (whether and how American studies should encompass the Caribbean, Asia-Pacific, and/or Latin America), language (to include U.S. works written in non-English or mixed languages and modernist works written in non-European languages), and media (unconventionally published works and those drawing on visual and musical forms). Efforts to comprehend the lived experience of social heterogeneity in nuanced, inclusive, and historically illuminating studies have led to efforts at pluralizing Americas studies and modernisms, as in the formation of the International American Studies Association and the journal *Comparative American Studies* (founded 2003). As is already evident, the notions of U.S. literature as part of world cultures and of modernism as a global set of phenomena are not in themselves new, but the implications drawn, the range of literary works considered, the methods of critical interpretation, and the conceptions of transnational cultural crossings are all twenty-first-century contributions to these long-standing conversations.[10] In these ways, modernist studies and American studies, though very different fields methodologically, have supported pathbreaking cross-field comparative conversations.

What, then, does it mean to read U.S. modernism in relation to something called world or global cultures? As in any emergent area with broad scholarly interest, widely varying and, at times, incompatible approaches have emerged. Scholars have argued for increased attention to undervalued texts or traditions; distinctively comparative methodologies; alternative periodizations or temporal models; and new genealogies of formal techniques, cultural practices, or concepts derived from multiple national traditions. Reparative, comparative, revisionary, and recontextualizing projects have arisen under the aegis of global, hemispheric, and postcolonial modernist studies. But, as Mark Wollaeger notes, this diversity of approaches need not be reconciled, and he argues for a self-aware, decentered "perspective [that] must be mobile and continuously provisional," not a classificatory scheme, but sets of "polythetic" family resemblances.[11] Paul Saint-Amour suggests that scholars moved away from a singular, static Modernism in favor of those that are "pluralized, adjectivalized, decoupled from high culture, and rethought as a transnational and transhistorical phenomenon." This "general weakening of the theory of modernism" has "strengthened" the field by becoming "less axiomatic, more conjectural, more conjunctural."[12] Saint-Amour's arguments regarding weak theory and modernism both explain and exemplify the virtues of methodological and perspectival pluralism.

As the foregoing discussion suggests, the *Cambridge Companion to the American Modernist Novel* provides a wide range of perspectives by eminent scholars in the field, reflecting innovative work on novels crucial to twenty-first-century U.S. modernist studies. It is designed to supplement and extend Walter Kalaidjian's *Cambridge Companion to American Modernism* (2005) by focusing on narrative experimentation during the half-century-plus between the 1890s and the 1940s.

This *Companion* is organized into three parts, each of which highlights a particular domain of research: historical, methodological, and generic. Attentive readers will note that some of the chapters share common thematic and methodological engagements. This reflects a salutary development of the conceptual contributions of interdisciplinary, comparative, and theoretical studies. Rather than treating literary domains as separate silos (for example, restricting analysis of gender, race, or region to one chapter), the chapters in this *Companion* draw different implications from some of the same critical terms or authors. The collective effort is to pursue the ambitious goal of distinguishing among coeval modernities and modernisms while attending to the structural forces they share.[13] For example, African American modernism, frequently called the Harlem Renaissance, has been reconsidered as a global constellation taking shape in multiple nodes of translation networked across numerous cultural centers writing to and about transnational black communities.[14] The themes and techniques of African American modernists are significant to a range of scholarly approaches and thus are referenced in multiple chapters. Blurred boundaries in novels that defy discrete categorical divisions – between formal experimentalism and putatively conventional realism as well as among generic distinctions of prose, poetry, and drama – are important themes of multiple chapters as well.[15] Mixed, impure, and "mongrel" modernisms have been crucial sites of research since Michael North, Ann Douglas, George Hutchinson, Andreas Huyssen, and others demonstrated the many ways in which literary modernism was characterized by inter- and cross-racial, generic, sexual, media, and other mixtures rather than purist or elitist binaries, even as U.S. society at large steadfastly sought to uphold nationalist, hierarchical, and segregated boundaries.[16]

The first part, "Movements," contextualizes novelistic experimentation in interwar U.S. novels by examining historical trends spurred on by movements of bodies and of ideas: industrialization, nationalism, geopolitical expansion, regional integration, immigration, and internationalist movements (Marxist, cosmopolitan, tourist, lumpen, anarchist, émigré, and many others). Urbanization has long been a topos of modernist studies, which deemed literature of rural and provincial life un-, anti-, or a-modern. However, Harilaos Stecopoulos argues that such long-standing assumptions obscured vital and distinctive critiques of modernity within regionalist narrative experiments with form. The complexity of modernists' engagements with place and locally situated perspectives unearths what he calls "radical localism," intense and ambivalent engagements with modernism's prioritization of the disjunctive new/now by representing communities whose present day has complex links to its past(s). In an era of nationalist standardization, regionally specific contexts and features recur significantly in literary works from early detective noir to expatriate fiction and throughout interwar modernism. Stecopoulos suggests that these critical insights regarding place, temporality, environment, language, and narrative form can be brought to bear on the work of authors who have not traditionally been described as regionalists, such as Nathanael West, Ralph Ellison, and F. Scott Fitzgerald. Their works respond to the normative pressures to standardize and homogenize through their representations of distinctive features of place: urban neighborhoods, architecture, antiuniversalist politics, vernacular speech forms, and so on. Stecopoulos' reading of localist elements of *The Great Gatsby* demonstrates that Fitzgerald's critique of modernity depends on its representation of place, specifically its regional, rather than urban or cosmopolitan, features.

Narratives that employ subtle modes of formal experimentation are also central to the next chapter, "Transpacific Modernisms." Denise Cruz points out that Asian American modernists embedded formally self-reflexive, psychologically complex, and genre-mixing narratives within seemingly conventional realist narratives. Her chapter brings critical considerations of place, history, immigration, race, and identity to novels of transpacific crossings. Early twentieth-century Asian American authors, she claims, sought out narrative forms that could be simultaneously realist and experimental, autobiographical and inventional, in efforts to render the fraught interstitial experience of U.S. life during the era of anti-Asian citizenship restriction; racialized, gendered, and sexualized stereotypes; everyday violence; oppressive labor conditions; exoticization; and silencing. From the 1882 Exclusion Act to Japanese American internment during World War II, Asian American novelists treated modernist themes while facing distinctive denials of their humanity and limits on their movement, belonging, and expression. Included in this analysis are Kathleen Tamagawa, H.T. Tsiang, Younghill Kang, Lin Yutang, Winnifred Eaton, and Carlos Bulosan, who composed narratives in which protagonists struggle with multiple forms of nonbeing: unwelcome in their countries of origin and noncitizens in the United States. In scenes depicting literacy, labor, exile, and romance, their works draw on techniques of fiction, life-writing, and performance to develop political and aesthetic engagements that register resistance even to norms they avow.

In her chapter on transatlantic "Ethnic American Modernisms," Catherine Morley considers the range of literary efforts to represent mass immigration in U.S. narratives as negotiations of gender and space. She points out that awareness of the demographic changes in U.S. cities and towns during these decades stoked interest in novels that represented both urban and rural communities transformed by the visibility of ethnic others. Morley demonstrates that authors as diverse as John Dos Passos, Henry Roth, John Steinbeck, and Michael Gold experimented with novelistic conventions to prioritize the representation of nonnative Americans' psyches as what Priscilla Wald has termed "selves in transit."[17] In the works of Anzia Yezierska, as well as Willa Cather, Morley locates important instances of the gendered mastery of space – characters marked as ethnically other and female who encounter both domestic and social/national constraints on selfhood and who struggle to define and defend Woolfian rooms of their own. Possession of spaces of selfhood and development are both literal and conceptual; the physical cultivation and management of tenement interiors and prairie exteriors represent the emergence of new ethnic femininities.

The author most frequently associated with meditations on modernist self-reflexivity, W.E.B. Du Bois, reemerges in Kevin Bell's chapter on "The Worlds of Black Literary Modernism" as a theorist and historian of the tradition of aesthetic creativity surfacing from the ongoing dehumanization of Afro-diasporic subjectivity. Bell puts Du Bois' famous formulation of double consciousness in dialogue with transnational U.S. novelists of black personhood and dislocation in an era shaped by the flow of global economic expansion. When viewed from this Du Boisian perspective, the ontological challenges that emerge in the experimental prose narratives of James Weldon Johnson, Claude McKay, Nella Larsen, Zora Neale Hurston, Ralph Ellison, and Chester Himes, among others, have newly urgent implications for understandings of literary modernism, subjectivity, genre, labor, gender, and community. Aesthetics of decadence, propriety, musical innovation, disposability, hyper- and in-visibility, psychic rupture, revision, exoticism, and deep interiority run through African American novels from the late nineteenth century through the middle of the twentieth.

The second part, "Methodologies," brings together chapters mapping current approaches to analyzing modernist novelistic themes and techniques. These chapters draw on recent scholarship on distant geographies and temporalities, sexualities studies, empiricism and science/technology studies, objects and material cultures, imperialism and transborder identities, rural and nonurban modernisms, and popular culture. Yogita Goyal's chapter on "Gender and Geomodernisms" demonstrates that comparative studies of gender, genre, and geography have informed one another in crucial ways throughout early twenty-first-century scholarship. She points out that the historical periodization, canon formation, and epistemologies of literary modernism have been under discussion since its inception, but the complexity of the locations and sites within narratives have only recently received significant attention. As empire, nation/nationalism, race, and gender have come to the fore in the present age of globalization, literary studies have found new implications of the transnational movement of peoples, ideas, capital, and objects. Goyal brings the concept of "geomodernism" – the term Laura Doyle and Laura Winkiel coined to identify cultural works that complicate setting, place, and locality by representing transborder and transoceanic crossings and histories – to discussions of works by Pauline Hopkins,

W.E.B. Du Bois, and Rabindranath Tagore. Hopkins' *Of One Blood* complicates the intersections of feminism, internationalism, and historicity through its interracial revision of the conventions of sentimental fiction and imperial romance. Goyal's comparative analysis recasts the romance plots in Du Bois and Tagore's novels as political allegories of ambivalent modernisms that critique discourses of biology, culture, and nation as each constructs "a poetics of internationalism" that traces the potential for anticolonial thought in response to "the lure of the universal."

Productive tensions across and between national divides also infuse "Border Modernism" with distinctive textual and lexical features, as Mary Pat Brady demonstrates. These decentered, nonurban narratives represent lives situated within U.S. and Mexican modernities through a wide range of techniques drawn from Latin American, European, and North American literary traditions. Drawing on and critical of dominant modes of both *modernismo* and modernism, Mariano Azuela, Olga Beatriz Torres, Jovita González, and Américo Paredes revise existing forms – the *crónica*, the *corrido*, ethnography, photographic realism, romance, epistolary novels, and historical fiction, among others – to represent situated scenes of binational subjectivity, post-Mexican Revolution émigré communities, lost or hidden histories, same-sex desire, multilingual expression, and border violence. In considering works such as *Los de abajo* that were published and widely circulated at the time of their composition, influencing Ernest Hemingway and other contemporaries, and those that were unpublished until decades later, Brady points to border modernism's complex intertextual history, some of which has come into focus only recently through the excavation of print cultures, unpublished manuscripts, and archival documents.

The recovery of lost, hidden, or forgotten lives and texts has proven crucial to sexualities studies scholars of literary modernism as well. Whether authors were relatively overt in their portrayals of same-sex desire, as in the fiction of Gertrude Stein, Claude McKay, and Djuna Barnes, or implicit, as in works by Willa Cather and Nella Larsen, attentive readings have identified a rich literary archive of complex portraits of sexuality. As Scott Herring argues, queer narratives and literary modernism shared the aim of fashioning antinormative experimentation that pulled the rug out from beneath established social conventions and expectations. Consequently, scholars have argued recently for expanded conceptions of both modernism and queerness in discussions of aesthetics, affect, temporality, politics, geography, and vernaculars, among other areas. Herring brings this capacious perspective to consider the queer roles of childhood, region, and property in novels that undermine desires for standardization and normalization. His close readings of Henry James and Ernest Hemingway present their narratives of youth as stalled, perverted, or ruined – the very antithesis to conventionalist paradigms of childhood. Nonprogressive and nonstandard representations of bodies, region, childhood, and property similarly queer novels by Cather, Nathanael West, and Zora Neale Hurston, among others.

Another kind of literary historical absence forms the subject of Steven Meyer's chapter on the U.S. modernist novel of science. Noting the prominence of scientific thought in the modernist era and the presence of modernist authors with scientific training, Meyer argues that the surprising dearth of experimental modernist novels that explicitly engage scientific principles and professions derives from critiques of perceived determinism in their literary naturalist predecessors. Expanding the category to "novels informed by science," Meyer identifies a fascinating tradition of novels that trouble the relationship between science and modernity as well as those that sidestep naturalism by drawing on romance techniques and themes. Meyer's distinction between rigid and robust empiricisms as formulated by Alfred North Whitehead and William James, among others, illuminates the scientific and speculative engagements of authors from Mark Twain and Gertrude Stein to Willa Cather, Ernest Hemingway, John Dos Passos, Djuna Barnes, and Zora Neale Hurston. Moreover, Meyer argues that these authors' representational and compositional studies of consciousness, interiority, landscape, medicine, technology, race, and family remain influential beyond the decades usually ascribed to U.S. modernism. He cites Thomas Pyncheon's early twenty-first-century work as emerging from modernist robust empiricists' problematizations of mechanized modernity.

The third part, "Textualities," expands existing perspectives on modernist genres and media by considering novels that engage contemporary visual cultures, musical forms, vernacular/multilingual expressive cultures, mixed- and new media art, and global and transnational contexts. Many narratives discussed in the chapters of this part experiment with the very notion of textuality, asking how a novel can respond to a jazz riff, a photograph, or a plurilingual urban neighborhood. Jeff Allred's chapter considers the distinctively American modernist interactivity between visual and verbal artists. He assesses the antagonistic, mistrustful, and collaborative relations among writers and painters, filmmakers, and photographers around the emergent power of iconography. Allred's attentive reading of Henry James' *The American Scene* finds in the travel narrative of an exile's return a key problematic of the era: that literary narrative and visual representation were each undergoing a shift in which artists and readers/viewers were confronting their disdain for and identification with subaltern subjects. James thus confronts the Du Boisian problematic of determining how to represent the experience of both seeing (to be "one of the people on whom nothing is lost") and being seen.[18] Other authors, such as Gertrude Stein and William Carlos Williams, develop their aesthetics in relation to painters and photographers, while John Dos Passos' *U.S.A.* trilogy forms an extended meditation on the interrelations between narrative and early cinema, experimental painters, and the image fashioning of journalism and advertising. Allred reads Richard Wright's *12 Million Black Voices* (1941) as a work that counters the visual violence of racialized iconography through a canny first-person-plural narrative instructing readers to adopt new ways of seeing African American history, labor, domesticity, literacy, and everyday life within U.S. modernity.

Just as some modernist novels trouble the distinction between image and word in order to pursue aesthetic and political imperatives, others interrogate the role of music in narrative and vice versa. Emily J. Lordi's chapter "Jazz and Blues Modernisms" demonstrates the remarkable flourishing of novelistic representations of African American musical forms, representing the geographical dynamism of both the Great Migration and exile/émigré influences abroad. Although these were present in nineteenth-century works as well, music and song – popular and vanguard, performance and text, forward-looking and nostalgic – become especially generative sources for modernist literary cultures that innovate novelistic forms for new readerships and diasporic communities. Moreover, as the musical forms of blues and jazz extend outward, novels not explicitly about music also follow their increasingly pervasive logics. Lordi's close readings of Nella Larsen, Ernest Hemingway, F. Scott Fitzgerald, and Zora Neale Hurston identify their novels' easily overlooked formal and affective musical affinities. Moreover, she points out that works by James Weldon Johnson, Jean Toomer, Langston Hughes, Claude McKay, and others ought to be reread for their nuanced attention to complex local, regional, national, and global musical sources.

Translation and multilingualism constitute another mode of artistic exchange across putative divides, as Daniel Katz's chapter shows. Resistance to mixture – racial, sexual, national, and linguistic – is especially charged in the history of modernist novels, from Henry James' fear that U.S. English was descending into a disordered Esperanto to H.L. Mencken's upbeat, if ironic, narration of the "American language" as an increasingly interlingual, global phenomenon reflecting U.S. cultural sway. Linguistically complex modernist novels confront the varied meanings attributed to scenes of literary multilingualism and translation. Katz reads Stein's prose aesthetic as both nonmimetic and resistant to the universalist dream of unmediated translation. Instead, he argues, Stein's antinormative style generates an idiom overlayered by multiple speech forms. Immigrant novels, such as Henry Roth's *Call It Sleep*, push translation modernism into new arenas as they represent plurilingual communities undergoing collective linguistic change. Meanwhile, a novel of global dispersion, such as Claude McKay's *Banjo*, stresses increasingly multilingual and vernacular voices, unlike Roth's, which moves more toward shared speech forms. Ernest Hemingway's narratives prove to be a rich site of linguistic experimentation in which many of the previously discussed techniques and attitudes toward linguistic mixture and translation resurface to form a paradoxical idiom that Katz calls a "deterritorialized colloquial."

As in the other chapters of this part, mixed textualities are central to Julian Murphet's account of "New Media Modernism." He argues that the emergent cultural primacy of media and communications inventions in the United States constituted a distinctive rupture between the printed novel and its multimedia competitors (the phonograph, photograph, radio, cinema, advertising, etc.), a "psychic trauma" that constitutes modernism itself. In light of the cultural politics of new and mixed media, he reads Stein's *The Making of Americans* as a literary response to standardization of labor, mass culture, and national-political discourse. Murphet posits Hemingway as a prime example of the literary inhabitation of the "inhumanism" of modernity's media. Similarly, "hard-boiled" crime fiction and noir aesthetics extend posthuman modernism into the realms of absurdism, abstraction, detachment, paranoia, emptiness, and speedup. Novelists from a wide range of backgrounds were employed by the nascent film industry, which coopted literary innovation and entwined it within cinematic adaptation. Murphet's readings of Fitzgerald, Faulkner, and Dos Passos proceed from the insight that their formal innovations in narrative prose emerge from preoccupations with new media devices – particularly film, radio, journalism, and advertising.

Gayle Rogers' concluding chapter brings the insights of comparative and world literature to considerations of U.S. literature's place in studies of global modernisms. What does it mean to read U.S. novels within histories of world literatures? Drawing on postcolonial, New Americanist, Black Atlantic, and hemispheric studies, Rogers argues for a heterodox and decentered U.S. modernism shaped by what Alain Locke called a "new internationalism." In surveying worldly U.S. novelists, Rogers demonstrates the manifold ways in which globalist thematics – empire, travel, slavery, Marxism, translation, im/migration, Classicism, and so on – complicate the Americanisms of U.S. modernism. His chapter takes up William Faulkner as a case study of a global modernist – a paradoxical choice, since he is best known for writing intensively about a single fictional southern county. However, as many scholars have documented, Faulkner's Yoknapatawpha is not a delimited territory, but rather a portal through space, time, and language to the Caribbean, Latin America, Africa, and Europe. The Caribbean and Pan-American reverberations of Faulkner's novels include

Jorge Luis Borges' stories, intertextual references, and translations, which constituted one part of a deep engagement among Hispanophone writers prior to, during, and following the Latin American Boom. Faulkner's mode of novelistic worldliness differs substantially from the others discussed in the rest of this volume, but the depth and diversity of the chapters of the *Companion to the American Modernist Novel* demonstrate that they share complex engagements with social, philosophical, political, technological, and cultural trends emerging from and leading to other parts of an increasingly interconnected globe.

Two notes on terminology: The keyword "modernism" is used in both the plural and singular forms throughout. Invocations of one or the other are not designed to indicate a programmatic distinction, since an awareness of the multiplicity (and, indeed, incompatibility) among many coeval narrative modernisms is shared by all the contributors of this volume. However, restricting usage to only the plural form throughout would have been stylistically unwieldy, so both are in play here. Similarly, "American," as a descriptor of the United States, has a long and contentious history. Some scholars eschew it in favor of "U.S." when referring to one nation as opposed to the hemisphere of the Americas. Since U.S. nationalism and its rhetorical coding of Americanism are explicit engagements in the following chapters, both terms are employed.

NOTES

I am grateful to Gayle Rogers and Ruby C. Tapia for their comments and suggestions.

1. Enid Yandell, Jean Loughborough, and Laura Hayes, *Three Girls in a Flat* (Chicago: Knight, Leonard & Co., 1892), 53–82.

2. *Diego Rivera: The Story of His Mural at the 1940 Golden Gate International Exposition* (San Francisco, 1940), n.p. See Anthony W. Lee, *Painting on the Left: Diego Rivera, Radical Politics, and San Francisco's Public Murals* (Berkeley: University of California Press, 1999), 209.

3. Ansel Adams, "Introduction," *A Pageant of Photography* (San Francisco: Crocker-Union for the San Francisco Exposition Co., 1940), n.p. See John Raeburn, *A Staggering Revolution: A Cultural History of Thirties Photography* (Champaign: University of Illinois Press, 2006), 285–292.

4. Ani Boyajian and Mark Rutkoski, eds., *Stuart Davis: A Catalogue Raisonné, Vol. 2* (New Haven, CT: Yale University Press, 2007), 314–319.

5. See Jody Patterson, "Modernism and Murals at the 1939 New York World's Fair," *American Art* 24, no. 2 (Summer 2010): 50–73; Erica Doss, *Benton, Pollock, and the Politics of Modernism: From Regionalism to Abstract Expressionism* (Chicago: University of Chicago Press, 1991), 277–279; and Diane Kelder, "Stuart Davis: Pragmatist of American Modernism," *Art Journal* 39, no. 1 (Autumn 1979): 29–31.

6. Konrad Bercovici, *Around the World in New York* (New York: Century Co., 1924), 4–5.

7. Dilip Parameshwar Gaonkar, ed., *Alternative Modernities* (Durham: Duke University Press, 2001); Marjorie Perloff, *21st Century Modernism: The "New" Poetics* (Oxford: Blackwell, 2002); Laura Doyle and Laura Winkiel, eds., *Geomodernisms: Race, Modernism, Modernity* (Bloomington: Indiana University Press, 2005); Juan A. Suárez, *Pop Modernism: Noise and the Reinvention of the Everyday* (Urbana: University of Illinois Press); Werner Sollors, *Ethnic Modernism* (Cambridge: Harvard University Press, 2008); Mark Wollagaer with Matt Eatough, eds., *The Oxford Handbook of Global Modernisms* (New York: Oxford University Press, 2012); Fionnghuala Sweeney and Kate Marsh, eds., *Afromodernisms* (Edinburgh: Edinburgh University Press, 2013); Katherine Biers, *Virtual Modernism: Writing and Technology in the Progressive Era* (Minneapolis: University of Minnesota Press, 2013); and Jessica Pressman, *Digital Modernism: Making It New in New Media* (New York: Oxford University Press, 2014).
8. W.P. Friederich and Clarence Gohdes, "A Department of American and Comparative Literature," *Modern Language Journal* 33, no. 2 (February 1949): 136.
9. Many scholars (including many contributors to this volume) have discussed the transnational turn with regard to U.S. modernist studies. See, for example, the special issue "Modernism and Transnationalisms," *Modernism/modernity* 13, no. 3 (Sept 2006); Mary Ann Gillies, Helen Sword, and Steven Yao, eds., *Pacific Rim Modernisms* (Toronto: University of Toronto Press, 2009); Susan Stanford Friedman, "Planetarity: Musing Modernist Studies," *Modernism/modernity* 17, no. 3 (September 2010): 471–499; Douglas Mao and Rebecca Walkowitz, "The New Modernist Studies," *PMLA* 123, no. 3 (May 2008): 737–748; Joshua L. Miller, "American Languages," in *A Concise Companion to American Studies*, ed. John Carlos Rowe (Malden, MA: Blackwell, 2010), 124–149; John Carlos Rowe, *Afterlives of Modernism: Liberalism, Transnationalism, Political Critique* (Hanover: Dartmouth College Press, 2011); and Robyn Wiegman, "The Ends of New Americanism," *New Literary History* 42, no. 3 (Summer 2011): 385–407.
10. See, for example, Ali Behdad, "What Can American Studies and Comparative Literature Learn from Each Other?" *American Literary History* 24, no. 3 (Fall 2012): 608–617.
11. Mark Wollaeger, "Introduction," *Global Modernisms*, 5, 12.
12. Paul K. Saint-Amour, *Tense Future: Modernism, Total War, Encyclopedic Form* (New York: Oxford University Press, 2015), 41.
13. Many have discussed the challenges inherent to conceptualizing global modernities as plural (alternate and heterogeneous) or singular (emerging from a capitalist world system of uneven development). For an influential formulation of "modernity's singularity and global simultaneity," see Fredric Jameson, *A Singular Modernity* (New York: Verso, 2002), and also Neil Lazarus, "Modernism and African Literatures," *Global Modernisms*, 233.
14. See, for example, Kate Baldwin, *Beyond the Color Line and the Iron Curtain: Reading Encounters between Black and Red, 1922–1963* (Durham: Duke University Press, 2002); Brent Hayes Edwards, *The Practice of Diaspora: Literature, Translation, and the Rise of Black Internationalism* (Cambridge: Harvard University Press, 2003); and the special issue "In Conversation: The

Harlem Renaissance and the New Modernist Studies," *Modernism/modernity* 20, no. 3 (Summer 2013).

15. For a reconsideration of realism and modernism in light of transnational modernist studies, see Jed Esty and Colleen Lye, "Peripheral Realisms Now," *Modern Language Quarterly* 73, no. 3 (September 2012): 269–288.

16. Michael North, *The Dialect of Modernism: Race, Language, and Twentieth-Century Literature* (New York: Oxford University Press, 1994); Ann Douglas, *Terrible Honesty* (New York: Farrar, Straus and Giroux, 1995); George Hutchinson, *Harlem Renaissance in Black and White* (Cambridge: Harvard University Press, 1995); Andreas Huyssen, "High/Low in an Expanded Field," *Modernism/modernity* 9, no. 3 (2002), 363–374.

17. Priscilla Wald, *Constituting Americans: Cultural Anxiety and Narrative Form* (Durham: Duke University Press, 1995), 238.

18. Henry James, "The Art of Fiction," in *Literary Criticism* (New York: Library of America), 53.

PART I

Movements

2

HARILAOS STECOPOULOS

Regionalism in the American Modernist Novel

Van Doren's Legacies

Of the many arguments about U.S. literary regionalism, one of the most significant has been Carl Van Doren's claim that Edgar Lee Masters, Sinclair Lewis, Edith Wharton, and other modern writers rejected the Victorian era's approving representation of the village and the farm.[1] According to Van Doren, Masters and Lewis found anathema the regionalist endorsement of provincial community, and sought to depict local life in far more negative terms. For these modern litterateurs, small towns and rural homesteads didn't so much evoke exemplary American values of church and family as suggest an oppressive investment in homogeneous tradition. Rather than sustaining a vital sense of community, regionalism encouraged conformity and intolerance. One only has to remember how Sinclair Lewis' Carol Kennicott cannot abide Gopher Prairie (*Main Street* [1920]) or how Ernest Hemingway's Harold Krebs finds intolerable his hometown ("Soldier's Home" [1925]) to appreciate the power of Van Doren's thesis.

The corollary to this argument about modern novelists is that even as they rejected the stultification of the provincial, they also embraced the stimulation of the urban. In Raymond Williams' famous formulation, "the key cultural factor of the modernist shift is the metropolis" not only because the metropolis offered heterotopic possibilities, but also because it opposed and supplanted the region.[2] Whether focused on New York or Paris, Chicago or Berlin, modernists found in the provocative diversity of the city a means of escaping the suffocating traditionalism of small-town existence. In their efforts to chronicle the complex meaning of modern life, they turned from the local to a *Manhattan Transfer*. The American modernist novel emerges from – and depends upon – a hierarchical geography that brooks little or no dialogue between city and country, urban art and local color.

Or so the older school of modernist studies would have it. Yet contemporary scholars have come to challenge traditional modernism's geographic

21

imperatives in two complementary ways: by demonstrating that the exclusionary and prejudicial qualities so often ascribed to local writing could also be located in modernism, and by showing that the generative critical function frequently assigned to the avant-garde could be identified in certain types of regionalism. For some time now, the critique of the avant-garde has played an important role in challenging both the canon and the methodology of traditional modernist studies. In the aftermath of the 1960s, feminist, African Americanist, postcolonial, and other scholars questioned whether that diversity of the metropole necessarily inspired a productive conjunction of experimental art and progressive politics.[3] They argued that T.S. Eliot, Ernest Hemingway, William Faulkner, and other U.S. high modernists were, for all their cosmopolitan predilections and innovative aesthetics, quite comfortable expressing racist sentiments. Eliot's use of ethnic and racial stereotypes in the King Bolo poems, "Burbank with a Baedeker: Bleistein with a Cigar" (1920) and *Sweeney Agonistes* (1932); Hemingway's anti-Semitic portrayal of Robert Cohn in *The Sun Also Rises* (1926) and his reliance on "redface" minstrel discourse in *Torrents of the Spring* (1926); and Faulkner's incapacity to jettison Jim Crow ideology even when addressing its contradictions in such works as *Light in August* (1932) amply demonstrated U.S. modernism's acceptance of xenophobia. Within and without the United States, modernism's affinity for intolerance proved as central as its better-known attraction to cutting-edge artistic strategies.

Not surprisingly, the critique of traditional modernism's restrictive covenant inspired scholars to redraw the literary map. Setting aside an earlier generation's biases, these new critics located alternative modernisms in New York's Harlem and the Lower East Side, in sub-Saharan Africa and East Asia, in myriad geographic and literary formations that had previously been ignored and devalued. In the process, these scholars also redefined the meaning of regionalist literary discourse for twentieth-century writers, jettisoning the wholesale demonization of the local for a new awareness of how late nineteenth-century and early twentieth-century regionalism might have preempted the modernists' critique of the status quo and contributed to their rich formal innovations.[4] Thus Marjorie Pryse, Judith Fetterley, Stephanie Foote, and Tom Lutz each demonstrated that certain turn-of-the-century regionalists found in their autochthonous subject matter a rich inspiration for radical political art. In the words of Pryse and Fetterley, "Regionalism marks that point where region becomes mobilized as a tool for critique of hierarchies based on gender as well as race, class, age, and economic resources."[5] These scholars maintained that one could find in the best local color writing evidence of what theorist Kenneth Frampton famously dubbed critical regionalism – a "strategy ... to mediate the impact of universal civilization with elements derived indirectly from the peculiarities of a particular place."[6] By insisting on the preservation of local cultural and social practices, marginalized communities fought against the exploitative standardization and uniformity endemic to the twentieth century. The provincial rootedness or emphasis on traditional folkways often associated with regionalism becomes for this new wave of scholars less a sign of fascistic intolerance than a manifestation of resistance against the totalizing tendencies of capitalist modernity. Rather than represent the urge to stamp out difference in favor of homogeneous community, regionalism names a means of generating political and cultural critique in and through place.

Many of these scholars turned to late nineteenth- and early twentieth-century women writers – Alice Dunbar-Nelson, Kate Chopin, Sarah Orne Jewett – for examples of how local color literature sought to resist a reactionary, if not a commodified, sense of geography. Rejecting the idea that regionalism provided WASP bourgeois readers with a means of either escaping or managing the unsettling presence of urban alterity, these scholars claimed that regional literature adumbrates some of the more radical aspects of U.S. modernism.[7] Jewett's works have proved particularly important to this revised sense of regionalism. When Jewett deployed (and sometimes undercut) her anonymous female narrator in *The Country of the Pointed Firs* (1896), she rendered her novel less a respite for the beleaguered bourgeois reader than a rich engagement with the way in which regional narrative could make and unmake place in modernity. The narrator, a writer of ethnographic bent, unwittingly demonstrates that Dunnet Landing stands in critical relation to a capitalist economy that has destroyed the shipping industry and, with it, the town's cosmopolitan character. In Jewett's hands, local color writing proves less an exercise in reactionary traditionalism than an opportunity to reconsider the shifting spatial scales of modern subjectivity. Jewett's innovative regionalism looks toward Willa Cather's modernist achievement in *My Ántonia* (1918), as well as the work of Zora Neale Hurston, the Harlem Renaissance writer whose classic *Their Eyes Were Watching God* (1937) also draws on humble village materials to fashion a surprisingly modern story. Hurston's Janie may not resemble Jewett's anonymous narrator, but both authors use their outlier main characters to expose the webs of connection and deceit that undergird their respective small communities. For all their seemingly quiet focus on little-known corners of the nation, these female regional writers imagined new forms of storytelling that challenged the status quo.

They were hardly alone in turning to the regional for critical and creative energy. Even as they engaged with the linked historical challenges of tradition and modernity, many modern American writers responded to regionalism with rich explorations of space and place. Some novelists, such as John Dos Passos (*U.S.A.* [1936]), confirmed the Van Doren critique and rejected provincialism for the diverse themes of the cosmopolitan city; others, such as Oliver Lafarge (*Laughing Boy* [1929]), responded to this dismissal of the local with what Robert Dorman has nicely dubbed "the revolt of the provinces"; and still others counterintuitively found in regionalism the inspiration for transnational fiction.[8] The last category has proven of great interest to twenty-first-century scholars of modernism eager to reimagine their field by redefining its geographies. They have pursued this goal by looking at a wide variety of regional texts. Critics of southern literature have demonstrated that from the West Indian plot in Faulkner's *Absalom, Absalom!* (1936) to the Filipino servant theme in Carson McCullers' *Reflections in a Golden Eye* (1940), writers from the U.S. Southeast explored the myriad ways in which narratives of place could subvert the national border and create a new transnational sense of region in the process. Scholars have also identified international emphases in modernist texts associated with other regions: consider the overarching theme of European immigration in Cather's *My Ántonia*, James Farrell's Studs Lonigan trilogy, and other Midwestern novels. The question of regionalism figured in a converse and somewhat counterintuitive manner for more displaced modernists: local themes emerge powerfully at key moments in expatriate novels ostensibly focused on Americans abroad. Fitzgerald's *Tender Is the Night* (1934) ends with Dick Diver moving peripatetically through his native upstate New York, while Gertrude Stein's *The Autobiography of Alice B. Toklas* (1933) attends to the interregional through its interest in Baltimore and Oakland. If European modernism is, as Edward Said has argued, preoccupied with far-flung colonies as much as it is with the proximate metropole, these U.S. modernist novels manifest a similarly bifocal attitude: at once registering the challenge of the universal and worrying about the implications of the local.[9]

One can see that ambivalence at work in the self-consciously geographic works just mentioned, but one can also see it in modernist novels rarely thought of in those terms. Nathanael West's *The Day of the Locust* (1939) engages with the standardization of difference in modern Los Angeles – consider the wonderful account of global architectural styles – and, at the same time, roots itself in a distinctive sense of Southern Californian place. *Invisible Man* (1952) suggests a different strategy as Ralph Ellison plots the emphatically urban clash between the anonymous protagonist's black southern experience and the Brotherhood's universalist conception of proletarian rights. In the remainder of this essay, I turn to *The Great Gatsby* (1925), another text rarely read in provincial terms, to examine how F. Scott Fitzgerald explores regionalism's importance for a critical engagement with modernity. For Fitzgerald, as we shall see, attention to the local inspires unusual configurations of space and identity – configurations that diverge from his better-known transnational themes in *Tender Is the Night* (1934) and Hollywood topoi in *The Last Tycoon* (1941). Casting narrator Nick Carraway in the role of inadvertent geographer, Fitzgerald links the challenge of chronicling Gatsby's story with the equally difficult task of understanding his relationship to place. James Gatz might hail from the Midwest, but as Nick comes to realize, traditional regionalism will hardly prove adequate to mapping Jay Gatsby in a disorienting New York context. The mysterious titular figure both evokes certain unusual geographic associations – particularly with respect to the South and, to a lesser extent, the immigrant slum – and also exists apart from any location at all. Conventional representations of the Midwest dominate the end of the novel, but those images can't completely suppress an alternate geographic discourse that finds in Gatsby the inspiration for a more fluid and disjunctive sense of place. Despite its closing investment in a traditional image of the local, this Jazz Age text doesn't so much privilege the country or the city as richly explore the imaginative uses to which regionalism can be put: that this critical cartography stands in tension with the novel's famed affective rewards testifies all the more to the power of Fitzgerald's distinctive geographic aesthetic.

The Great Gatsby as a Regional Novel

Thanks to *The Great Gatsby*'s explicit engagement with questions of history and memory, loss and reparation, critics have tended to ignore the text's geographic concerns. For most readers, this is a novel about the possibility and consequence of repeating the past: a novel about time, not space. That Fitzgerald largely limits himself to a New York setting only reinforces this impression. Other American modernist novels engage explicitly with exoticized subnational or transnational spaces – the African American South in Jean Toomer's *Cane* (1923), Central America in Jane Bowles' *Two Serious Ladies* (1943) – and thus seem to invite a focus on geography. *Gatsby* does not offer readers so much as an expatriate episode or a southwestern sojourn. For all the references to "Santa Barbara" and "lost Swede towns," to Versailles and Kapiolani, the novel refuses to abandon Manhattan and Long Island.[10] *Gatsby*'s rich engagement with the mnemonic only highlights its seemingly neglectful attitude toward the geographic.

Of course, to separate the two strands does the text a disservice. If *Gatsby* constitutes Nick Carraway's narrative commemoration of a murdered friend, the novel also chronicles the narrator's attempt to place his subject. Deeply invested in Gatsby's romantic self-creation, the narrator works hard to situate the deceased hero in space and, in the process, to explore his own complicated attitude toward the geographic. Nick wrestles with the challenge of mapping Gatsby from his earliest encounter with the fascinating tycoon. "Where is he from?" he demands of Jordan Baker, eager to solve the mystery of their enigmatic host through his location (49). One would expect no less of a narrator who describes himself as "a pathfinder" (4) and provides exacting topographical descriptions of eastern Long Island (4) and of Queens (23). Unwilling to accept Jordan's suggestion that Gatsby might be "an Oxford man" or rumors of Gatsby's German provenance, our skeptical speaker immediately turns to more subaltern spatial possibilities: "I would have accepted without question the information that Gatsby sprang from the swamps of Louisiana or from the lower East Side of New York. That was comprehensible. But young men didn't ... drift coolly out of nowhere and buy a palace on Long Island Sound" (49). Nick finds these locales "comprehensible" because both "the swamps of Louisiana" and "the lower East Side" name dubious environments associated not only with impenetrable mystery, but also with potentially lucrative criminal activity. Neither place denotes a proper and respectable American identity; to the contrary, their association with heterogeneous immigration and diverse populations of color renders them marginal to a normative sense of national belonging. In terms of conventional notions of American place and region, the southern swamp and the urban ghetto are indeed "nowhere."

Nick's background, by contrast, seems as conventionally locatable as it is impeccably white. "Prominent, well-to-do people" in a "Middle Western city," the Carraways recall the WASP Minnesota families satirized by Sinclair Lewis in *Main Street* (1920) and *Babbitt* (1922) (2). Like the scions of such clans, Nick grows up increasingly frustrated with life in a "bored, sprawling, swollen" town "beyond the Ohio" (177). He returns from the Great War only to leave the heartland behind: "instead of being the warm center of the world, the Middle West now seemed like the ragged edge of the universe" (3). The unflattering portrait of a stultifying Midwest recurs in Nick's account of the young James Gatz, aka Jay Gatsby, a North Dakotan dismayed at the region's "ferocious indifference" and eager to make his way in the world (100). Nick escapes through his participation in WWI, while Gatz finds his way out through the *deus ex machina* of Dan Cody's yacht; both men paint the "the Middle West" as a place whose torpor offers few prospects for change (3).

In modern fashion, one might expect Nick's "revolt from the village" to inspire a long-standing attachment to the metropole, but the Minnesotan's experience in New York provokes countervailing feelings. The desire for eastern diversion does not translate into an embrace of heterotopic New

York, but instead reveals Nick's persistent investment in a stable geography. Afflicted from the outset with alienation and anomie – consider the Prufrockian description of lonely clerks haunting restaurants – Nick endures a far greater crisis of location in Gatsby's company (57). The mysterious tycoon evinces an unorthodox conception of space when situating "San Francisco" in "the Middle West," and that strange geography comes to affect Nick's urban experience as well (65). As Nick sees the world through Gatsby's eyes, he grows newly sensitive to an alternative and disjunctive sense of place; a certain spatial "distortion" soon becomes the measure of his New York narrative (177). The novel's modernism often takes the form of a crisis of cognitive mapping that Nick finds difficult to endure. Little wonder, then, that Miss Baedeker is "the most bewildered character in the book."[11]

Consider, for example, how Nick describes the first time he and Gatsby travel together into Manhattan. In this liminal episode, which both fascinates and unsettles the narrator, the New York of "white heaps and sugar lumps," of "non-olfactory" money – no filthy lucre here – suddenly transmutes into something quite different: a space of color, immigration, and subaltern identity (69). While crossing the Queensboro Bridge, the two men espy in a funeral procession mourners "with the tragic eyes and short upper lips of southeastern Europe" and then, soon after, see "a limousine . . . driven by a white chauffeur, in which sat three modish negroes, two bucks and a girl" (69). Fitzgerald's reference to the physiognomy of "southeastern Europe" finds its domestic correlative in the implicitly U.S. southern origin of the offensively dubbed "two bucks." Taken together, the contiguous sentences suggest a variegated population distinctly different from the "clerks and young bond-salesman" that work with Nick in "the white chasms of lower New York" (56). If Nick once understood the East as the Midwest's antithesis – consider how the opposition of East and West Egg resonates throughout the text – traveling in Gatsby's company draws the narrator's attention to how New York resists such comforting regional polarities and signifies in a more expansive and discomfiting manner. Instead of enjoying a predictably cosmopolitan city, Nick finds himself accosted by a "fantastic" and "grotesque" metropolis where "anything can happen," even the South and the immigrant slum (178; 69).[12] To map Gatsby, the narrator must locate himself in a disordered geography.

In the aftermath of the bridge scene, Nick's fleeting encounter with the Lower East Side seems to persist. The two men dine with Jewish gambler Meyer Wolfsheim, and the narrator listens attentively to the latter's account of the titular hero (72–73). Yet this conversation and a late encounter with Wolfsheim are the only sustained interactions Nick has with a Jewish character, and the only significant connection the narrator has with any immigrant. Uneasy in the presence of alterity, Nick finds the Lower East Side disturbing because it seems to replicate in miniature the heterotopic and ungrounded quality of the New York area. Much like the so-called Valley of Ashes, a "nowhere" populated by downtrodden WASPs (the Wilsons), Greek Americans (Michaelis [137]), "scrawny Italian" children (26), and a "pale well-dressed negro" [sic] (140), the Lower East Side signifies for Nick as a strange conflation of otherness and placelessness. That famous immigrant zone is in his view as geographically unstable as the stretch of road that passes before George Wilson's garage. (When, in the aftermath of Myrtle Wilson's death, the policeman asks Michaelis for "the name of this place," the coffee shop owner replies, "Hasn't got any name" [140]. For Carraway, the presence of a multiethnic population exacerbates his crisis of cognitive mapping; only a normative notion of place can restore Nick's sense of spatial coherence.

Unwilling to solve Gatsby's mystery through recourse to immigrant identity and geography, Nick seizes upon what he'd already suggested as one likely point of origin – "the swamps of Louisiana" or, more broadly, the South – and attempts to redefine that place as the means by which he can restore cognitive order to his disorienting New York experience. The rejection of a heterogeneous Lower East Side results in a new valuation of the white South and confirms to some degree Walter Benn Michaels' famous reading of the novel as a nativist and white supremacist text.[13] This regional turn is in part a consequence of narrating Gatsby's Louisville experience with Daisy, a story that, like F. Scott Fitzgerald's Montgomery romance with Zelda Sayre, originates in a southern locale. After limning the lunchtime encounter with Wolfsheim, Nick segues almost immediately to Jordan Baker's story of southern "white girlhood," a gesture that implicitly contrasts Daisy and Jordan to the immigrants and the African Americans on the bridge, and to the Jews of the Metropole restaurant (20). A fellow Kentuckian, Jordan emphasizes Daisy's southern origins by stressing the older girl's love of white clothing (75) and her use of the vernacular ("Daisy's change' her min!" [77]), regional touches that accrue in value when Nick later describes Daisy pining away for Gatsby while listening to W.C. Handy's "Beale Street Blues" (151).

Nick's invocation of the South grows particularly important during his late account of Gatsby's climatic confrontation with Tom – the confrontation that will in its denouement lead to the end of the narrative itself. Fitzgerald first brings together changes in setting and plot through an overweening emphasis on climate. As the novelist turns up the narrative temperature, that is, he also emphasizes the terrible heat of the day. The suburban train conductor repeats the word "hot" (115); Nick imagines that the butler proclaims the master's body "too hot to touch" (115); Tom comments on the rising temperature

(118). However, it is Daisy who reminds the reader that the excruciating climate should be read in terms of the impending clash between Tom and Gatsby. "But it's so hot," she exclaims. "And everything's confused" (118). For Daisy, as for Nick, the blistering summer day captures in climatological terms the impending conflagration: affective and geographic torrid zones prove mutually reinforcing.

Jordan will endorse Daisy's sense of general confusion in more explicitly geographic terms when she registers the change that has transformed the city. As Tom drives through Astoria, in the borough of Queens, Jordan comments that she loves "New York on a summer afternoon. ... There's something very sensuous about it – overripe, as if all sorts of funny fruits were going to fall into your hands" (125). Her sensual account of Manhattan not only prods Tom into troubling thoughts of his wife's resurgent romance with Gatsby, but also calls attention to the regional reterritorialization already under way. And with good reason: Jordan, like Daisy, hails from Louisville, and the heat seems to prompt memories of her natal zone, with its exotic flora and lassitude. The supposedly sober quality of diligent and hard-working Manhattan, a city of bonds and finances, transmutes into a tropical fecundity that threatens to subvert the national borders and push into the hemispheric south. Daisy will later stress again the cross-regional association as she harps on the topic of mint juleps (126, 127, 130), that most stereotypically southern drink, and remembers how she was married in her humid native city (128).

Yet for all the geographic work accomplished by the two Louisville natives, it is Tom Buchanan who makes most palpable the southern aspects of Gatsby's mystery. Prompted by Daisy's vague reference to a man who fainted at their wedding, Tom finds in the heat-stricken figure of "Blocks" Biloxi a means of highlighting Gatsby's lack of definable identity. After establishing that Biloxi hadn't been invited to the nuptials, Tom and Nick recognize as well that the mysterious wedding crasher has falsely claimed a Yale University connection to gain access to their social circle. Tom finds in the imposter's fraudulence an opportunity to interrogate Gatsby about his claim to be "an Oxford man." "You must have gone there about the time Biloxi went to New Haven," Tom exclaims as he begins his verbal attack on Gatsby. Denouncing the adulterous relationship, Tom goes on to name Gatsby a Biloxi-like "Mr. Nobody from Nowhere" who is trying to "make love" to Daisy (130).

Tom's attack would seem to deny both imposters a legitimate identity of any kind. But in drawing a connection between Biloxi and Gatsby, he suggests that "nowhere" has a distinct geographical referent, and that Gatsby might be understood in rather specific regional terms. While the wedding crasher's true identity and background remain unknown, he manifests a powerful connection to the South that redounds to Gatsby. As his surname emphasizes, "Blocks" Biloxi cannot help but suggest a specific region. Daisy states that "Blocks" was from the (fictive) town of Biloxi, Tennessee (128), while Tom says he was raised in Louisville, Kentucky (129) – the Mississippi resonance of Biloxi's moniker notwithstanding. Nick recalls that he "used to know a Bill Biloxi from Memphis," and Jordan claims that the latter was a cousin of "Boxes" (128). From beginning to end, the discussion of "Blocks" Biloxi takes the South as its geographic purview.[14]

For Tom, the confusion over the wedding guest's geographic origin should only signify to the extent that it allows him to connect Biloxi's hoax to Gatsby's fraudulence, a strategy that will eventually lead to the latter's exposure as "a cheap sharper" of dubious background (135). Yet the southern geography crucial to the Biloxi anecdote also proves important; for Tom, a fervent defender of Nordic purity, seems to associate the region with the specter of race mixing. After labeling Gatsby another Biloxi, Tom invokes the threat of interracial union and implies that his wife's ex-lover may be black. "Next they'll throw everything overboard," he declaims, "and have intermarriage between black and white" (130). In Tom's view, we may speculate, to be uncertain of a southern charlatan's birthplace is to be uncertain of his color. The problem of "Blocks" Biloxi necessarily leads to the problem of southern blood, and the challenge of geographic location takes on new racial dimensions.

Fitzgerald doesn't pursue the implications of Tom's indictment in a predictable manner. The novel never identifies Gatsby as a light-skinned African American of southeastern origin. Instead, Fitzgerald uses the "Blocks" Biloxi anecdote to explore a more interesting prospect: that of understanding its titular figure's fantastic imposture as a racially hybrid and loosely southern phenomenon typical of the era's popular culture (148). While we don't know much about Biloxi, there is little doubt that Gatsby, a man of popular music and pink suits, outrageous cars, and effortless "cool," embodies the transgressive racialism of the Jazz Age. Like Jim Powell, the Georgian hero of Fitzgerald's tellingly titled "Dice, Brassknuckles & Guitar" (1923), Gatsby manifests an outrageous and racially suspect cultural style characteristic of the syncopated South's vexed relation to normative, which is to say, white, national identity. That Powell, a self-appointed "jazz master," brings his supposedly African American accouterments and skills to the Northeast only reinforces the parallels with Gatsby, a fellow outlier associated with the new "raced" popular culture.[15]

It cannot be overstated that Fitzgerald's southern-accented invocations of a "white negro" reflect a Jazz Age image of the region. Instead of testifying to a coherent and distinct South, and shoring up the meaning of regionalism, the characters of Biloxi, Gatsby, and Powell inadvertently suggest a jazz geography that connects Georgia, Kentucky, New Jersey, and New York through the mobility of sound itself. *The Great Gatsby*'s musical allusions suggest as much. The "orchestras which set the rhythm of the year, summing up the sadness and suggestiveness of life in new tunes" in Daisy's postwar Louisville, seem to foreshadow the strains of Vladimir Tostoff's "Jazz History of the World" at Gatsby's Long Island party (151; 50). And "The Sheik of Araby," a jazz standard cited during the New York portion of the novel, recalls the earlier Louisville invocation of W.C. Handy's "Beale Street Blues" (83; 151). A jazz refrain reterritorializes region as Fitzgerald struggles to articulate a fluid version of subaltern space that, like the Lower East Side or the nameless Valley of the Ashes, doesn't so much oppose as take shape through heterotopic modernity. "Nowhere" can name a region, but it can also name an improvisational relation to place itself.

To make this point is to suggest that Fitzgerald could at times find in southern regionalism, if not in regionalism itself, the incitement needed to imagine a disjunctive "geomodernism" we rarely associate with his works.[16] A similarly bold, if more palpably racist, deployment of southern regionalism emerges in that portion of *Tender Is the Night* (1934) devoted to Jules Peterson, the black man found dead in the white starlet Rosemary Hoyt's bed. In *Gatsby*, of course, the regionally inspired foray into avant-garde aesthetics doesn't endure. Nick attempts for a time to value such spatial improvisation as the key to understanding and appreciating Gatsby's extraordinary subjectivity; but the narrative's violent denouement prompts the narrator to reject that possibility in favor of a stable sense of cognitive mapping. By the end of the novel, Nick dismisses a mobile notion of region existing in dynamic relation with modernity, and instead yearns for a sense of place where one "is unutterably aware of [his] identity with this country for one strange hour, before" he melts "indistinguishably into it again" (177). Ideally, for Nick, we might say, a region should not mean but be. Rather than imagine Gatsby in and through the syncopated strains of a Jazz Age South, Nick seems to find in the Biloxi anecdote a comforting reminder that traditional regionalism can still order space in a comprehensible manner. The South's capacity to function as a geographic touchstone reminds the midwesterner that even in modernity, an older notion of place might prove a useful guide – that even in the midst of a distorted multiethnic New York, a coherent sense of place might serve to orient those white Americans suffering from alienation and anomie. The quest to locate Gatsby's origins may not have revealed the real story behind a man of glorious self-invention – such a desire is to some degree beside the point in a text Hugh Kenner dubbed a novel of belief – but it has helped Nick recover some small sense of cognitive mapping in a disordered modern world.[17]

It's no accident, then, that after Myrtle's death and Gatsby's murder, after the funeral and the recriminations, Nick not only decides to "come back home" to Minnesota, but also defends the very idea of region that so disturbed Edgar Lee Masters, Sinclair Lewis, and other modern writers (178). Fitzgerald has his narrator claim his natal region ("that's my Middle West") and remember fondly the "street lamps and sleigh bells in the frosty dark and the shadows of holly wreaths thrown by lighted windows on the snow" (177). That promise of regional reparation extends to Nick's closing treatment of his titular subject, another midwesterner who has lost his way in the eastern metropole. Stressing the value of that "vast obscurity," middle America, Nick muses that Gatsby could never grasp his "dream" because "it was already behind him, somewhere back in that vast obscurity beyond the city, where the dark fields of the republic rolled on under the night" (182). Gatsby's rush to urban riches becomes in the narrator's hands an allegory of how the nation has, in speeding toward modernity, abandoned the dream that inspired it in the first place. In this regional epiphany, the provincial regains its traditional valuation and emerges as the place that marks America as exceptional. Fitzgerald's peculiar brand of modernism seems to depend on a return to the farm and the small town. That this lesson seems increasingly untenable in modernity renders the novel's conclusion as quixotic as it is affective. *The Great Gatsby* finds in regionalism both the signs of a neglected past and the makings of an uncertain future.

Conclusion

To take as my main example *The Great Gatsby* is to stress that regionalism may emerge in unexpected places for today's scholars of modernism. And how could it be otherwise? The long-standing association of modernism and the metropole didn't so much eliminate as repress regionalism's import. And, as modernist studies has undergone a spatial turn, regionalism has returned to shape new visions of the field. The focus on such vast formations as the Black Atlantic and the borderlands has urged new sensitivity to lower-scale geographies. One can point to the recent publication of such books as Leigh Anne Duck's *The Nation's Region: Southern Modernism, Segregation, and U.S. Modernism* (2006), Daniel Worden's *Masculine Style: The American West and Literary Modernism* (2013), and Mark Buechsel's *Sacred Land: Sherwood Anderson, Midwestern Modernism, and the Sacramental Vision of Nature* (2014). One can cite as well the emergence of organizations that prioritize a particular region (The Society for the Study of Southern Literature) and the important place of work on regionalism in the various iterations of sustainability studies that have emerged over the past twenty years. But to stress the current scholarly interest in place hardly means we should uncritically celebrate regionalism as modernism's subaltern other; the former doesn't necessarily figure as insurgent radicalism to the latter's hegemonic power, but rather functions as a provocation capable of generating a number of political and cultural effects. Regionalism can validate the existing social and cultural order through geographic means, or it can inspire a critical relationship to the status quo. Most powerfully, perhaps, it can serve as a fluid heuristic through which a novelist may explore the interrelated meanings of particular geographic formations. No less than modernism, its more fashionable relation, regionalism deserves our attention and our analysis. Our understanding of twentieth-century literature remains impoverished without it.

NOTES

1. Carl Van Doren, "The Revolt from the Village," *Contemporary American Novelists 1900–1920* (New York: Macmillan, 1922), 146–157.
2. See Raymond Williams, *The Politics of Modernism: Against the Conformists* (London: Verso, 1989), 45.
3. For some relevant examples, see Shari Benstock, *The Women of the Left Bank: Paris, 1900–1940* (Austin: University of Texas Press, 1987); Edward Said, *Culture and Imperialism* (New York: Vintage, 1994); and Paul Gilroy, *The Black Atlantic: Modernity and Double Consciousness* (London: Verso, 1993).
4. Scott Herring has written brilliantly on these issues. See "Regional Modernism: A Reintroduction," *Modern Fiction Studies* 55.1 (2009): 1–10.
5. *Writing out of Place: Regionalism, Women, and American Literary Culture* (Urbana: University of Illinois Press, 2005), 14.
6. Kenneth Frampton, "Towards a Critical Regionalism: Six Points for an Architecture of Resistance" in *The Anti-Aesthetic: Essays on Postmodern Culture*, ed. Hal Foster (Seattle, WA: Bay Press, 1983), 21.
7. For important arguments on the ameliorative function of regional writing for the nineteenth-century bourgeoisie, see Richard Brodhead, *Cultures of Letters: Scenes of Reading and Writing in 19th Century America* (Chicago: University of Chicago Press, 1993), 107–176; and Amy Kaplan, "Nation, Region, and Empire," in Emory Elliott, *Columbia History of the American Novel* (New York: Columbia University Press, 1991), 240–266.
8. Robert L. Dorman, *Revolt of the Provinces: The Regionalist Movement in America, 1920–1945* (Chapel Hill: University of North Carolina Press, 1993).
9. See Edward Said, *Culture and Imperialism* (New York: Vintage, 1983), 186–190. For an important book-length study of this dynamic in American regionalism, see Tom Lutz, *Cosmopolitan Vistas: American Regionalism and Literary Value* (Ithaca: Cornell University Press, 2004).

10. *The Great Gatsby* (New York: Scribners, 1925), 78, 177, 29, 133; hereafter cited in text.

11. Ronald Berman, *The Great Gatsby and Modern Times* (Urbana: University of Illinois Press, 1996), 42.

12. For two other important readings of this scene, see Jeffrey Louis Decker, "Gatsby's Pristine Dream: The Diminishment of the Self-Made Man in the Tribal Twenties," *Novel: Forum on Fiction* 28.1 (Autumn 1994): 52–71; and Michael North, *Camera Works: Photography and the Twentieth-Century Word* (New York: Oxford, 2005), 109–139.

13. See *Our America: Nativism, Modernism, Pluralism* (Durham: Duke University Press, 1995), 23–28.

14. For an important but very different reading of the "Boxes" Biloxi sequence, see Arnold Weinstein, "Fiction as Greatness: The Case of Gatsby," *Novel: A Forum on Fiction* 19.1 (Autumn 1985): 22–38.

15. "Dice, Brassknuckles & Guitar," in *The Short Stories of F. Scott Fitzgerald: A New Collection*, ed. Matthew Bruccoli (New York: Simon and Schuster, 1995), 251.

16. For an interesting discussion of the term "geomodernism," see Laura Doyle and Laura Winkiel, "Introduction: The Global Horizons of Modernism," in Doyle and Winkiel, eds., *Geomodernisms: Race, Modernism, Modernity* (Bloomington: Indiana University Press, 2005), 1–16.

17. Hugh Kenner, *A Homemade World: The American Modernist Writers* (Alfred A. Knopf, 1975), 20–49.

3

DENISE CRUZ

Transpacific Modernisms

For Asian American authors, the task of capturing transpacific modernity defied realist modes of representation. Chungpa Han, Younghill Kang's narrator and alter ego in *East Goes West: The Making of an Oriental Yankee* (1937), observes as much in a conversation with a ghostwriter about the possibility of her authoring his autobiography. The young white woman "immediately said that she would rather write about America, and realism was the thing." Privately disagreeing, Han confesses, "I forebore to mention that a tenuous life on paper was neither American nor realistic."[1] Han's recognition of transpacific Asian American life as "tenuous" – out of place within the boundaries of the U.S. identity and the genre of literary realism – grafts the national onto the formal. Centering on the difficulties of representing Asian lives and bodies, this observation has multiple valences. During the early twentieth century, the Asian life "on paper" was precarious because of a long history of immigration exclusions; Asian stereotypes in print culture and visual media; and legal and juridical measures that narrowed the definition of citizenship, family formations, and intimacies.[2]

Beginning with the acknowledgment that Asian and Asian American experience and its representation in print escaped the bounds of realism, this chapter analyzes how transpacific authors encountered and produced modernisms in their novels, a category that I employ loosely because of the literary history detailed below. Their strategies and forms (the memoir, the autobiographical novel, and the romance) might initially read as counter to the aesthetic experimentation of other modernisms, but for Asian American authors, the narration of their own lives and intimacies as authentic countered dominant discourses that repeatedly denied them subjectivity.[3] These authors also offer transpacific examinations of issues familiar in other modernist cultural inquiries: difficulties of exile and alienation, reconstructions of modern subjectivity through literary form, critiques of capitalism and materialism, and stagings of new gendered and sexed identities.

Initially, the transpacific novel's representation of tenuous life might seem conversant with "double consciousness," defined by W.E.B. Du Bois as the "sense of always looking at one's self through the eyes of others."[4] But for Asian and Asian American writers, the color line was entangled with increasingly demarcated national and transnational lines. The ever-present feeling of "twoness" so important to double consciousness is complicated by attention to the bounds of national identities and communities, a process catalyzed by U.S. political and economic interactions with Asia. As I discuss in the next section, during the late nineteenth and early twentieth centuries, the migration of Asian laborers shifted the landscape of immigration and the racial makeup of the country. At the same time, the United States continued a long fascination with Asia and the Pacific as key to the nation's global prominence.

Reading modernism within this context builds upon criticism by Asian American and modernist scholars over the past two decades. Working against what David Palumbo-Liu has called the "fetishization of the present," Asian Americanists have recovered authors such as H.T. Tsiang, Onoto Watanna, and Kathleen Tamagawa.[5] Corresponding with global modernist studies, they have extended temporal and geographic boundaries to consider Asian American authors' engagement with modernist imaginaries from the early to mid-twentieth century.[6] These critics have also dismantled the borders between the projects of ethnic cultural nationalism and U.S. canon formation.[7] The term *transpacific modernism* indexes oft-mentioned connections between the white modernist writer's interest in the Orient, such as the speaker's invocation of "Shantih" in the closing lines to T.S. Eliot's *The Waste Land* or Ezra Pound's fascination with the haiku and ideograph. In contrast, Asian and Asian American–authored texts disappeared from the modernist canon even though Younghill Kang, Carlos Bulosan, and José Garcia Villa contributed to mainstream outlets such as *Story*, the *New Yorker*, and *Poetry* and can be glimpsed in black-and-white photographs in the company of Marianne Moore and e.e. cummings.[8]

As Viet Thanh Nguyen, Jinqi Ling, Timothy Yu, and others have asserted, the boundaries of an Asian American literary canon were grounded in the politics of 1960s and 1970s cultural nationalism, which led to the development of "Asian American" as identity and community, field of inquiry, and, in Sau-Ling Wong's term, "textual coalition."[9] Thus while Carlos Bulosan's *America Is in the Heart* (1946) was lionized because of its Marxist critique of race, class, and labor in the United States, scholars dismissed Jade Snow Wong's *Fifth Chinese Daughter* (1950) and Onoto Watanna's popular romances because their authorial and textual politics were uneasy fits within the rubric of resistance. These novels became suspect for their supposed accommodation of white perceptions of Asians or their desire to assimilate to white U.S. cultural and middle-class norms.[10]

The vexed enterprise of applying the term *transpacific modernism* to the work of Asian American authors is exacerbated by what Susan Koshy and others have called the "slow emergence of the category of fiction in Asian American narrative," a "belatedness" shaped not only by the primacy of autobiography, memoir, and the autobiographical novel in early Asian American literature but also by a critical tendency to view these texts as documentary evidence of lived experience.[11] If modernist texts that played with autobiography – from James Weldon Johnson's *The Autobiography of an Ex-Colored Man* (1912) to Gertrude Stein's *The Autobiography of Alice B. Toklas* (1933) – were read as innovative explorations of modern subjectivity, Asian American authors occupied the opposite end of the spectrum. Rather than advancing an aesthetics of difficulty, transpacific texts have been aligned with transparency, a reflection of their presumed ability to represent Asian and American lives and communities with verisimilitude. Thus even though Kang's character does not champion realism as a genre capable of representing Asian American life, his readers praised works such as *East Goes West*, Pardee Lowe's *Father and Glorious Descendant* (1943), Bulosan's *America Is in the Heart*, Lin Yutang's *Chinatown Family* (1948), and Wong's *Fifth Chinese Daughter* for their ability to capture Asian bodies, spaces, and communities for a mainstream U.S. readership.

The remaining sections reconsider Asian and Asian American authors' engagement with transpacific modernisms. Although many of these texts lack the more recognizable forms of aesthetic experimentation that are modernism's key signatures, their representation of transpacific subjectivities and communities differed prominently from nineteenth- and early twentieth-century strategies of racial representation (such as dialect speech or caricatures) that in the guise of realism also ultimately reinforced notions of white superiority. Within a national frame that rendered their bodies unfit for citizenship, threatening to normative sociality, or exoticized objects, transpacific authors used the literary to assert the psychological complexity of Asian and Asian American subjects; expose labor and class oppression; imagine complicated formations of gender and sexuality; and construct intimacies across race and class. As examples of transpacific modernism, their texts defy any easy containment as memoir, autobiography, or romance. More broadly, they offer alternative meditations on the conditions of modernity, shaped by transpacific relations at home and abroad.

Transpacific Contexts

In the first section of Willa Cather's *The Professor's House* (1925), Godfrey St. Peter and his family entertain a visiting scholar of Spanish imperial history. After introductions are made, the men realize that they have mutual connections in Asia and begin to discuss them while the women sit nearby "listening to the talk about China."[12] Framed as a mere, brief recounting of polite party banter, this moment nevertheless illustrates Cather's awareness of ties between "conditions in the Orient" (26) and Western imperial expansion. Cather was not alone in pursuing these links, nor is the dinner conversation about China incidental, for the rise of the American modernist novel coincided with global interest in the Pacific.

Although U.S. modernists looked to Asia for inspiration as they contended with a fallen world, until recently the focus of transnational scholarship on modernism has traveled primarily across and around the Atlantic.[13] During the late nineteenth and twentieth centuries, however, the United States increasingly turned its gaze across the Pacific. If, as Aihwa Ong notes, the prefix *trans* signals change, mobility, exchange, and adaptation, the term *transpacific* emphasizes that throughout this period, U.S.-Asian relations were tied to a web of geopolitical formations in the Pacific region that had repercussions for constructions of Asians and Asian Americans.[14] At various historical moments, depending upon whether or not they were from China, Japan, Korea, the Philippines, or India, various Asian populations were and were not eligible for citizenship. The United States began to consolidate the gendered national subject, and as Lisa Lowe has argued, America's relationship with Asia was critical to this process, for "the American *citizen* has been defined ... against the Asian *immigrant*, legally, economically, and culturally." The racialization of citizenship was also a gendered and sexed process, one that "ascribed 'gender' to the Asian American subject" (by barring Asian women from immigration, for example, or restricting interracial intimacy).[15]

Transpacific chronologies often begin with 1853, the year in which Commodore Matthew Perry famously "opened" the door to trade with Asia. As the United States confronted a disappearing frontier, geopolitical momentum moved westward.[16] During these years, the United States annexed Hawai'i (1898), acquired the Philippines at the end of the Spanish-American War (1898), and established a long-standing presence in the Pacific Islands. Often, these encroachments were cast in familial plots of benevolence. In the Philippines, for example, the U.S. government (which had as part of the same war "liberated" Cuba from Spain) rationalized long-term occupation of the archipelago (1898–1945) with the claim that Filipinos were unfit for self-government. This narrative of expansion as well meaning and morally justified set the stage for later justifications of U.S. wars, violence, and military action in Korea and Vietnam, and for the rhetoric of democratic guardianship that would be critical to the Cold War years.

The temporal period usually associated with the development of the modernist novel overlapped with a discursive cycle of transpacific fascination and fear – what Gina Marchetti calls "romance and the yellow peril."[17] This cycle played out on the pages of travel memoirs, fiction, newspapers, and in visual culture. While the "open door" eventually led to heightened trade regulations monitoring economic exchanges (often in favor of the United States and Europe), it also spurred greater interactions between the United States and Asia. American missionaries and tourists traveled to China and Japan, and they returned to publish travelogues and memoirs. Increased transpacific contact influenced *Japonisme*, a widespread fascination with Japanese culture that was accompanied by a vilification of China and Chinese bodies (especially because of the large numbers of Chinese laborers moving to the United States in the late nineteenth century).[18] The interest in Japan, however, would pivot dramatically in the other direction after Japan's triumphs in the Sino-Japanese (1894–1895) and Russo-Japanese (1907) wars, for Americans began to view Japan's expansion as a "yellow peril" and threat to Western power. This vilification peaked during World War II, when the U.S. government interned over a hundred thousand Japanese Americans.

At the same time, as Sucheng Chan, David Palumbo-Liu, and others have documented, changes in U.S. immigration and inter-Asian politics and economies led to surges in Asian migration to the United States and to the construction of "Asiatic racial forms," Colleen Lye's term for dominant stereotypes that circulated in late nineteenth- and early twentieth-century public discourse.[19] Objectified as exotic or transgressive, Asian bodies exceeded the limits of proper sociality in white mainstream culture. The United States depended upon laborers from China, Japan, Korea, India, and the Philippines in the years following the civil war.[20] Recruited for their labor and then reviled, Asian migrants became a social threat – from the supposedly lecherous Chinese opium dealer, to the hyper-sexed Filipino bachelor, to the construction of Japanese Americans as a danger to national security.[21] As I detail in the section "Transpacific Femininities," while men were suspect, popular typologies reified Asian women as submissive and exotic.[22] These racial forms provide crucial context for the transpacific novel's first-person narration of alternate Asian and Asian American subjectivities, and their imaginings of characters who resisted these representations.

Exile, Alienation, and the Transpacific Elite

Against this backdrop of transpacific relations, Asian American authors take up modernism's preoccupation with exile and alienation and explicitly figured these conditions as products of racism, the exploitation of labor, and the uncertain status of Asians in the wake of immigration regulation. For these authors, exile and alienation are conditions that nation-states and national communities impose upon transpacific, racialized subjects. This section focuses first on Kathleen Tamagawa's memoir *Holy Prayers in a Horse's Ear* (1932). Tamagawa, who has a Japanese father and an Irish American mother, explores the dualities of exile for someone who is legally a nonsubject in the United States yet who is also ostracized in Japan. I then analyze Kang's *East Goes West* through the narrator's recognition of the failed promise of the American dream, the plot that ends with an immigrant's capitalist success and inclusion. Instead, racialized alienation dismantles this fantasy, as Han's education and class aspirations do not shield him from injustice. In their play with the form of the memoir and autobiography, both books turn to what Yoon Sun Lee calls a "desire for a new time" in order to disrupt a teleological narrative of racial inclusion.[23]

Tamagawa's uncertain status is written upon her mixed-race body. In the late nineteenth and early twentieth centuries, the definition of "American" was redefined from within and without U.S. borders. Immigration laws determined who was allowed entry to the United States, while miscegenation and citizenship statutes reinforced links between national identity and whiteness. Tamagawa begins *Holy Prayers* with the circumstances of her birth; the opening paragraphs immediately reveal that U.S. law renders her illegitimate. "The trouble with me," she states, "is my ancestry. I really should not have been born; as a matter of fact half of my world declares I never was born. They say, that I am the non-existent daughter of my parents, that I am not their lineal descendant."[24] Here, Tamagawa refers to 1920s and 1930s legislation and court cases that limited U.S. citizenship, such as the 1923 *United States v. Bhagat Singh Thind* decision, in which the Supreme Court ruled that despite the scientific categorization of Indians as Caucasian, they were nevertheless "nonwhite in the 'common understanding.'"[25] These juridical and legislative landmarks were accompanied by antimiscenation legislation that, as Koshy argues, "turned sex acts into race acts and engendered new meanings for both."[26] The combination of the Expatriate Act (1907) and the Cable Act (1922), for example, meant that white women who married "aliens ineligible for citizenship" were no longer considered citizens. Although the United States is the primary site of alienation, Tamagawa also finds no escape when her family moves from the United States to Japan. Her

Japanese father is immediately at ease, but despite their concerted efforts to fit into Japanese society, Tamagawa and her mother remain outsiders.

How do you recount a life that is unrecognized? In a variation of modernist difficulty, both Tamagawa and Kang describe this process as antithetical to the usual forms of self-representation. The erasure of Tamagawa's "lineal heritage" as an "outlawed product of a legal marriage" confounds linearity. Writing is "like grabbing at a whirling circle. There doesn't seem to be any beginning and ... there is no proper end. With frantic gesture, I grab at the circle and whichever way I turn I get no-where" (5). This process of representing hybrid identity is further complicated by her racialized and gendered objectification in both countries. As a "citizen of Nowhere" (158) with "no race, nationality, or home" (38), she becomes a "decoration," "gimcrack," "barbarism and a blemish" (38). Tamagawa ultimately finds no easy way of negotiating this world, and the memoir's final pages are not in her own voice, but rather narrated by her white American husband.[27]

Kang also calls attention to the difficulty of representing alienation in *East Goes West*, which opens with a Faulkner-like rumination on time and temporality. *East Goes West* reverses the Orientalist gaze of the American modernist. Though the book formally recalls realist strategies of representation in its linear progression and detailing of Chungpa Han's encounters with the United States and Canada, the text's recurring interest in displacement questions the triumphant trajectory of Asian immigration. Chungpa Han, "speaking with an Asian's natural bias," exists outside of the linear passage of time: "it seems to me it is wrong to say, time passes. Time never passes. We say that it does, as long as we have a clock to calculate it for us" (3). Like Quentin Compson (whose section in *The Sound and the Fury* begins with a ticking watch and the tyranny of time), Han wrestles with his existence "in time."[28] For Han, however, the difficulty of living in the contemporary moment stems from his Asian body, "alien to the Machine Age and New York" (13). The rest of the novel tracks his peripatetic movements as he attempts to find work, attends university, and gradually becomes aware of the disconnect between the idealized America of his dreams and the country he encounters.

Kang's narrator wrestles with his growing awareness that the "confused racial components" (162) in the United States lead to limitation rather than boundless opportunity. The text as a whole thus questions celebratory plots of migration. As he encounters race and class difference, Han initially clings to his elite cosmopolitanism as much as possible. As Elaine Kim contends, for much of the novel "that there might be a connection between race discrimination and his own dire circumstances never seems to occur to him."[29] He is initially fascinated by the teeming possibilities of the United States – "traditionless, new, almost naïve, ready for anything, with confused unlimited potentialities both of good and bad" (162). Yet Han finally confronts the fact that his education and class status do not translate into an exemption from prejudice. The book ends with a frightening nightmare of racist violence. Trapped on a "hairlike bridge," he watches with dismay as his possessions tumble into an abyss, and he is pushed into a "cryptlike cellar" with some "frightened-looking Negroes." With them, he is burned alive until he "awoke like the phoenix," but this rebirth comes only after he realizes that his racialized status overwrites his class and education (400–401). For Kang, the forward progression of the novel only underscores how the Asian elite remains beyond the dream of immigrant inclusion, and there is no easy resolution for modernist exile.

Of Markets, Systems, and Literary Resistance

The closing moments of *East Goes West* and their disruption of a nationalist American fantasy illustrate a broader trend in many transpacific novels: a suspicion of U.S. capitalism and an interest in laying bare the workings of capitalist labor on gendered Asian bodies through a self-reflexive treatment of the value and forms of literature. Kang's work would famously inspire Carlos Bulosan's *America Is in the Heart* (1946), a novel often read as formally and politically transparent, a primer for a Marxist critique of the grueling conditions of migrant labor and the development of resistant Asian American cultural nationalism. Bulosan has been praised for his mastery of social realism, for in *America*, narrator Carlos witnesses the horrors of racist violence and their perpetration on Filipino bodies. In this section, I examine the ways in which novels by Bulosan and H.T. Tsiang emphasize the literary as producing resistance and critique. While the representation of race and class oppression was critical to the transpacific novel, authors also tied this exposure to literary form in order to counter the market's objectification of Asian bodies and texts.

As others have observed, the political critique of *America Is in the Heart* is made possible by an examination of literature and its resistant potential. Martin Joseph Ponce points out that Carlos reads frequently and widely, and he describes reading itself as a revelation. The global scope of Bulosan's literary appetite is central to a "doubled mode of address" that responds to U.S. racism and criticizes Philippine literature in English as "under-politicized."[30] The text refers to these connections via allusions to figures such as Faulkner, who inspires Carlos to write about "where he lives" (242); Filipino nationalist author José Rizal (266); and American writers Richard Wright, Younghill Kang, and Yone Noguchi (265). These authors serve as Carlos' "intellectual guides through the swamp of a culture based on

42

property" (266). This examination of the politics of literary form, however, also provides a cautionary tale that recognizes the uncertain reception of politicized fiction. In one scene, Carlos recalls the emergence of the proletarian novel as a counter to popular works such as Margaret Mitchell's *Gone with the Wind*; he cites the work of Laura Clarendorn (Clara Weatherwax's *Marching! Marching!*) as an example that notably includes a Filipino character (238) yet also disappears from American literary history.

Bulosan's reference to a forgotten novel illustrates his careful awareness of how literature about racist and capitalist injustice was consumed by U.S. readers. The issue of capitalism and the market was even more vexed for his counterpart, H.T. Tsiang, who also excoriated U.S. classism in his formally experimental *The Hanging on Union Square: An American Epic* (1935). Unlike Bulosan, Tsiang never saw widespread mainstream success. In a note published with the 2013 reprint of *Hanging*, Tsiang explains that he decided to "tak[e] the liberty of asserting his own viewpoint" via self-publication. *Hanging* is a mixed-genre piece in four prose acts that interweave poetry, drama, and parody. Each act is preceded by verse interludes of "poetizing" or "satirizing" that become recurring refrains. "Try my pill," taunts one interlude, "New Deal!/ Hello, /Everybody:/How do you feel?"[31] The novel lambasts the New Deal welfare state and its empty promises, but it also criticizes empty commitments to communism.

Unlike in Tsiang's later *And China Has Hands* (1937), in *Hanging* characters are not explicitly racially marked, and the novel centers instead on class oppression and Popular Front politics. *Hanging* functions in part as a political allegory as its two principal characters become cognizant of their place in an exploitative capitalist system. Mr. Nut, "a worker" (14), loses his job and falls in love with Stubborn, a woman who becomes an outspoken communist voice after her family is evicted and her parents kill themselves in desperation. Although Nut is initially attracted to the beautiful and materialist Miss Digger (who is involved with a bureaucrat, Mr. System), he eventually realizes that he loves Stubborn and resolves to publicly hang himself. Mr. System saves Nut before he dies, so that Mr. System and others might capitalize on the spectacle of death. Thinking of his love for Stubborn, Nut thwarts his exploiters by shooting himself in front of the audience that has gleefully gathered to see his suicide.

Tsiang's elimination of racial and ethnic markers responds to a literary market that eagerly consumed texts authored by white Americans about Asia and Asians, and he was quite aware of the potentially adverse effects of his "experiment" in this context. Moreover, Tsiang's unmarked characters call attention to the subjugation of women within these literary and capitalist markets. In a clear reference to Pearl Buck and her bestselling (and Pulitzer

Prize–winning) novel *The Good Earth* (1931), Stubborn and Miss Digger have an extended conversation about an unnamed female missionary who travels to Asia and authors a memoir. Miss Digger is horrified but intrigued by Buck's model. Early in the novel, Miss Digger earns money by displaying her naked body onstage, and she compares these sexualized exploits to "the woman who made money from her Oriental novels! ... She talks about 'Earth' and 'Soil' a lot, but I think what her publishers gave her as royalties was the same thing that I have received from my customers – dollars" (186). This conversation illustrates Tsiang's critique of women's objectification within a capitalist economy. Stubborn, the novel's catalyst for change, feels uneasy when she thinks of "the tradition that made a woman 'It' and not 'She'" (171). In an epiphany, she recognizes that she must resist her subjugation under capitalism, "overthrow this tradition and stand up and become 'She'" (171). Tsiang thus ties together the marketing of Asian bodies in literature with a broader capitalist objectification of women. This scene clarifies how *Hanging*'s experimentation resists the realist novel and memoir's more easily marketable forms and their commercialization of raced, gendered, and classed oppression. For Tsiang, defying these systems demands a resistant and innovative aesthetic, one that eschews literary, capitalist, and gendered traditions in its blend of genres and political satire, which exposes how the literary marketplace is inextricably connected to other types of capitalist oppression.

Transpacific Femininities

Tsiang's Stubborn has much company in the pages of American modernist novels, which are filled with transgressive women: Djuna Barnes' Robin Vote, William Faulkner's Caddy Compson, Nella Larsen's Irene Redfield, F. Scott Fitzgerald's Daisy Buchanan, and Gertrude Stein's Melanctha, to name a few examples. Often, like Tsiang, these authors used aesthetic experimentation (such as Stein's repetitions or Faulkner's multiple narrators) to craft female characters who resist the bounds of gender and sexuality. But the obsession with modern women also led to novels that do not fit within the usual purview of modernist experimentation. This section considers the vexed construction of transpacific femininity in the romance, from Lin Yutang's exploration of an unruly woman's ties to the nation to Winnifred Eaton's production of multiple female voices over the course of her career.

Transpacific novels responded to the circulation of new women and the intersection of U.S. women's suffrage movements with women's rights movements in Asia. Global women's suffrage initiatives in Japan, China, India, and the Philippines developed rapidly in the early twentieth century. As the

Modern Girl Around the World Research Group has demonstrated, the U.S. flapper and the Gibson girl had their counterparts in the New Filipina, the Chinese *nuxing*, and the Japanese *moga*, who could also be found in university classrooms and jazz clubs, in the pages of newspapers, and on the silver screen.[32] Within the United States, however, these women were not the dominant representation of Asian transpacific femininities. Instead, popular media figured them in reified and exotic terms, encapsulated by the butterfly trope, a "narrative pattern" in which a Western man falls in love with a submissive Asian woman.[33] In the United States, the fascination with the Asian butterfly offered a stark contrast with the public circulation of American flappers and suffragettes. Whereas Asian men in the United States presented a threat to social communities, the Asian butterfly presented the tantalizing promise of a woman who, unlike the unruly Western modern girl, would willingly submit to normative femininity.

Transpacific writers pointed to contact with the West as influencing modern Asian women, though frequently it is these women's hybridity that is at issue (rather than a desire to assimilate to Western notions of femininity). Lin Yutang's *A Leaf in the Storm: A Novel of Warswept China* (1941) is a romance in which a Westernized Asian woman has questionable ties to national communities at home and abroad. The book is set during the guerrilla resistance to Japanese forces in the years before and immediately following the 1937 fall of Nanjing. The heart of Lin's novel is the conversion of the elite Chinese woman, Malin, and her rejection of Western ways (through her rebirth as the guerrilla nationalist Tanni). Like other popular constructions of the flapper or modern girl (often identified by transgressive dress, speech, and mannerisms), Malin's modernity is visible through the flicker of pink French underwear beneath a Chinese dress or in an argument with her lover over how a woman should stand. "The western women all have square shoulders," she protests, when the couple discusses "the *mei-jenchien*, or [sloping] 'beauty's shoulders'" of Chinese women.[34] In a surreal moment at a dance club, "the sight of the foreign naked women turning somersaults" leads to "a profound change in her view of life" (212). She returns home and burns her Western clothing. Lin juxtaposes this moment of revelation with a glimpse of her later role as a guerrilla, when she would see "another vision of naked human bodies in great multitudes" (212) amid poverty, violence, and death inflicted by the Japanese.

In transpacific novels, then, Asian women often figured as symbolic of lost connections to home (such as the suffering mothers in *America Is in the Heart* or John Okada's 1957 novel *No-No Boy*) or as the embodiment of fraught hybridity. Asian women writers were acutely aware of this spectrum, and their texts and authorial performances illustrate their uneasy treatment of these representations. Chinese Canadian author Winnifred Eaton, for example, infamously chose to pass as Japanese: she used Onoto Watanna as her pseudonym, dressed in kimonos, and wrote romances set in Japan that were astoundingly successful commercially. She draws attention to her own construction of transpacific femininity in *Me: A Book of Remembrance* (1915). In *Me*, first-person narrator Nora Ascough reflects upon her success and its troubling repercussions as she looks back with regret over the sentimentality of her work: "founded upon a cheap and popular divide and that jumble of sentimental moonshine that they called my play seem to me the pathetic stamp of my inefficiency. Oh, I had sold my birthright for a mess of potage! [*sic*]."[35] Published in 1915, Eaton's reference to regret here is "an almost eerie echo" of her friend and fellow writer James Weldon Johnson and the closing to *The Autobiography of an Ex-Colored Man* (1912).[36] As Jean Lee Cole argues, both texts are produced under the guise of an autobiography and refer to authorial passing and betrayal through an allusion to the Biblical story of Esau and Jacob, Isaac and Rebecca's twins. (The darker Esau promises his birthright to Jacob in exchange for a bowl of stew; later, Jacob, in the guise of Esau, tricks Isaac into giving him the inheritance.)

Eaton's polyphonic negotiation of racial and gendered performance, authorship, and the literary market was an important feature of her many novels. Her characters and narrators crossed lines of nation, race, and class, and she produced a cast that, in addition to Asian women, also included "Irish maids, a Scottish doctor, an androgynous (and misanthropic) British spinster, naïve Norwegian farm girls, Canadian ranchers, Chinese cooks, 'half-breed' Indians, and headstrong saloon-keeper's daughters."[37] Across a spectrum of fiction, including hundreds of short stories and articles and over a dozen novels, Eaton (who also later published under Winifred Reeve) staged scenes and characters of transpacific or interracial intimacy. Her settings range from Japan to U.S. cities to the Canadian prairie, and her books have been categorized as popular romance, working-girl novel, or prairie literature. In these crossings, as others have claimed, she sometimes subverted popular butterfly tropes of Asian women and at other times reinforced ideals of white bourgeois femininity.[38]

But more often than not, Eaton, her romances, and their complex status in the Asian American and U.S. literary traditions are especially instructive in their defiance of categorization. In a context in which transpacific and interracial lives and intimacies were rigorously policed by the U.S. nation-state, Eaton's multivocal imaginings of U.S., Asian, and Canadian femininities are important precisely because they are uneasy fits within definitions of identity, genre, and canon. In later years, the many voices of Eaton's characters would be diminished, critically sidelined by dismissals of her work. Her interest in racial passing and the middlebrow romance would make her and her works irreconcilable within the contexts of Asian American cultural nationalism or accounts of literary modernism that depended upon formal experimentation.[39] Eaton's exploration of a broad range of female subjectivity should be read in conversation with other modernist texts that imagined alternate versions of gendered, classed, and raced identity through the rubric of passing and polyphony, from Johnson's *Autobiography* to Stein's *Three Lives* (1909). A reconsideration of Eaton's novels offers a different view of this pattern of imagining modern femininity, for these romances are part of a broader spectrum of literary and cultural modernisms that return, again and again, to voicing uncontainable women.

Coda

By the time Jade Snow Wong published her memoir, *Fifth Chinese Daughter*, the conditions of representing transpacific life had altered significantly. These changes created an eager audience for Wong's book, the most widely read work of an Asian American writer during the mid-twentieth century.[40] Spurred by the involvement of nations such as the Philippines and China as allies in the Pacific War, in the 1940s and 1950s the United States began revising immigration and foreign policy. The government repealed Chinese exclusion, recognized Philippine independence, and began closing Japanese internment camps. The development of the Asian American as model minority ostensibly diffused the contrast between America's professed motives of spreading global democracy during the Cold War and the lingering specter of continued racism in the United States. Ellen Wu encapsulates this overlap of racial and transpacific dynamics with the observation that Asian Americans were examples of immigrant potential because they were "definitively not-black."[41] Wong's life and its representation in *Fifth Chinese Daughter* contributed to and was exemplary of this lasting construction. The book tracks her rise in American society through hard work and perseverance. She is from a family of garment workers, and despite her parents' dismissal of her desire for a university education, she persists, earns a degree, and begins her own successful business. There is ample evidence of Wong's acceptance of U.S. racial politics, and she claims that "her knowledge that racial prejudice existed had never interfered with her personal goals."[42]

Asian American scholars initially dismissed *Fifth Chinese Daughter* for its perpetuation of model minority mythologies. But as Leslie Bow and others have observed, this novel, despite its consumption as a realist and idealized account of Chinese American life, is actually quite complicated.[43] In much of the text, Wong reveals that she is well aware of how an American audience views her as a racialized phenomenon. Her character becomes a ceramics artist, and she sets up a window in a Chinatown shop. Members of her community immediately scoff at her ability to earn money by selling her pottery and laugh at the prospect of others watching her as she works. But Wong remains adamant, for prior experience has taught her that "being Chinese had created a great deal of favorable interest" (189). Tourists soon gather to gaze in awe at the woman making pottery, and her creations begin flying off the shelves. Indeed, "Jade Snow had become a wonder in the eyes of the Western world" (244). Like so many transpacific texts, Wong here illustrates her knowledge of the Asian American body as itself a spectacle and her awareness of the fact that her art is marketable in part because it offers a racialized representation that would sit comfortably with a white readership, a construction that absolves them of their guilt and assures them that the responsibility for success lies not in addressing racism in the United States, but rather with Asian American individuals.

The image of Wong molding clay in a window is an apt metaphor of creation and framing that underscores the transpacific writer's self-awareness. And indeed, Wong, Kang, Tamagawa, Bulosan, Tsiang, Lin, and Eaton carefully explore the difficulties of authoring and representing transpacific lives, communities, and relations. Their texts respond to these challenges in form and content: from Kang's disavowal of linear temporality and Tamagawa's swirling circle; to Bulosan's recognition of literary traditions and Tsiang's experimental blurring of genres; to Lin and Eaton's exploration of new femininities. They resist the fantasy of the United States and the celebratory plot attached to migration, even though many of them cling to its potential. They attempt to represent hybrid transpacific lives in flux and rendered nonexistent by U.S. legal, public, and juridical discourse. They turn to literature, performance, and the creation of alternate selves as formal strategies that were essential to how Asian and Asian American authors represented the tenuous life on paper – in all of its complexity.

NOTES

1. Younghill Kang, *East Goes West: The Making of an Oriental Yankee* (New York: Charles Scribner's Sons, 1937), 344. For an extended examination of Kang and realism, see Julia H. Lee, *Interracial Encounters: Reciprocal Representations in African and Asian American Literatures, 1896–1937* (New York: New York University Press, 2011), 138–168.
2. On precarity, see Judith Butler, *Precarious Life: The Powers of Mourning and Violence* (London: Verso, 2004).

3. Delia Konzett makes a similar observation in "The Belated Tradition of Asian-American Modernism," in *A Companion to the Modern American Novel 1900–1950*, ed. John T. Matthews (Malden, MA: Wiley Blackwell, 2009), 496–517. See also Viet Thanh Nguyen, *Race and Resistance: Literature and Politics in Asian America* (New York: Oxford University Press, 2002), and Susan Koshy, "The Rise of the Asian American Novel," in *The Cambridge History of the American Novel*, eds. Leonard Cassuto et al. (Cambridge: Cambridge University Press, 2011), 1046–1063.

4. W.E.B. Du Bois, *The Souls of Black Folk* (1903; New York: Simon and Schuster, 2005), 7.

5. David Palumbo-Liu, "Theory and the Subject of Asian America Studies," *Amerasia Journal* 21, nos. 1–2 (1995): 55–65, 58; quoted in Keith Lawrence and Floyd Cheung, eds., *Recovered Legacies: Authority and Identity in Early Asian American Literature* (Philadelphia: Temple University Press, 2005), 3.

6. See Susan Stanford Friedman, "Periodizing Modernism: Postcolonial Modernities and the Space/Time Borders of Modernist Studies," *Modernism/modernity* 13, no. 3 (2006): 425–453.

7. In addition to the works cited throughout this essay, see Lawrence and Cheung, *Recovered Legacies*; Hsuan Hsu, *Geography and the Production of Space in Nineteenth-Century American Literature* (Cambridge: Cambridge University Press, 2010); Yunte Huang, *Transpacific Imaginations: History, Literature, Counterpoetics* (Cambridge: Harvard University Press, 2008); Christopher Lee, *The Semblance of Identity: Aesthetic Mediation in Asian American Literature* (Stanford, CA: Stanford University Press, 2012); and Josephine Nock-Hee Park, *Apparitions of Asia: Modernist Form and Asian American Poetics* (New York: Oxford University Press, 2008). These conversations have their counterpart in debates over Harlem Renaissance literature and American modernism. See Houston A. Baker Jr., *Modernism and the Harlem Renaissance* (Chicago: Chicago University Press, 1987), and Brent Hayes Edwards, *The Practice of Diaspora: Literature, Translation, and the Rise of Black Internationalism* (Cambridge: Harvard University Press, 2003).

8. Timothy Yu, "'The Hand of a Chinese Master': José Garcia Villa and Modernist Orientalism," *MELUS* 29, no. 1 (Spring 2004): 41–59.

9. Sau-Ling Wong, *Reading Asian American Literature: From Necessity to Extravagance* (Princeton, NJ: Princeton University Press, 1993), 9.

10. Nguyen, *Race and Resistance*, and Jinqi Ling, *Narrating Nationalisms: Ideology and Form in Asian American Literature* (New York: Oxford University Press, 1998).

11. Koshy, "The Rise of the Asian American Novel," 1049; Konzett, "The Belated Tradition."

12. Willa Cather, *The Professor's House* (1925; New York: Vintage, 1990), 26.

13. Scholars of modernism now readily employ circumatlantic and transatlantic frameworks, a critical move indebted to foundational work on African American, diasporic, and global modernisms. See Edwards, *The Practice of Diaspora*; Baker, *Modernism and the Harlem Renaissance*; Michael North, *The Dialect of Modernism: Race, Language, and Twentieth-Century Literature* (New York: Oxford University Press, 1998); Paul Gilroy, *The Black Atlantic: Modernity and Double Consciousness* (Cambridge: Harvard University Press,

1993); Douglas Mao and Rebecca Walkowitz, eds., *Bad Modernisms* (Durham: Duke University Press, 2006); and Laura Doyle and Laura Winkiel, eds., *Geomodernisms: Race, Modernism, Modernity* (Bloomington: Indiana University Press, 2005).

14. Aihwa Ong, *Flexible Citizenship: The Cultural Logic of Transnationality* (Durham: Duke University Press, 1998), 4.

15. Lisa Lowe, *Immigrant Acts: On Asian American Cultural Politics* (Durham: Duke University Press, 1996), 4, 11; see also Rogers M. Smith, *Civic Ideals: Conflicting Visions of Citizenship in US History* (New Haven, CT: Yale University Press, 1999).

16. Sucheng Chan, *Asian Americans: An Interpretive History* (Boston: Twayne, 1991); David Palumbo-Liu, *Asian/American: Historical Crossings of a Racial Frontier* (Stanford, CA: Stanford University Press, 1999); and Rob Wilson, *Reimagining the American Pacific: From* South Pacific *to Bamboo Ridge and Beyond* (Durham: Duke University Press, 2000).

17. Gina Marchetti, *Romance and the Yellow Peril* (Berkeley: University of California Press, 1993).

18. Dominika Ferens, *Edith and Winnifred Eaton: Chinatown Missionaries and Japanese Romances* (Urbana: University of Illinois Press, 2002).

19. Colleen Lye, *America's Asia: Racial Form and American Literature, 1893–1945* (Princeton, NJ: Princeton University Press, 2005).

20. Lisa Lowe, *Immigrant Acts*, and Mae M. Ngai, *Impossible Subjects: Illegal Aliens and the Making of Modern America* (Princeton, NJ: Princeton University Press, 2004).

21. Nayan Shah, *Contagious Divides: Epidemics and Race in San Francisco's Chinatown* (Berkeley: University of California Press, 2001) and Linda España-Maram, *Creating Masculinity in Los Angeles's Little Manila: Working Class Filipinos and Popular Culture* (New York: Columbia University Press, 2006).

22. Marchetti, *Romance and the Yellow Peril*, and Denise Cruz, *Transpacific Femininities: The Making of the Modern Filipina* (Durham: Duke University Press, 2012).

23. Yoon Sun Lee, *Modern Minority: Asian American Literature and Everyday Life* (New York: Oxford University Press, 2013), 27.

24. Kathleen Tamagawa, *Holy Prayers in a Horse's Ear: A Japanese American Memoir*, eds. Greg Robinson and Elena Tajima Creef (New Brunswick: Rutgers University Press, 2008), 5.

25. Susan Koshy, *Sexual Naturalization: Asian Americans and Miscegenation* (Stanford, CA: Stanford University Press, 2004), 9.

26. Ibid., 1, 7.

27. For a reading of this switch, see the introduction to Tamagawa.

28. William Faulkner, *The Sound and the Fury* (1929; New York: Vintage, 1990), 76.

29. Elaine Kim, *Asian American Literature: An Introduction to the Writings and Their Social Context* (Philadelphia: Temple University Press, 1982), 39.

30. Martin Joseph Ponce, "On Becoming Socially Articulate: Transnational Bulosan," *Journal of Asian American Studies* 8, no. 1 (2005): 49–80, 54, 52.

31. H.T. Tsiang, *The Hanging on Union Square: An American Epic*, ed. Floyd T. Cheung (1935; New York: Kaya, 2013), 107.

32. Alys Eve Weinbaum et al., eds., *The Modern Girl around the World: Consumption, Modernity, and Globalization* (Durham: Duke University Press, 2008).

33. Marchetti, *Romance and the Yellow Peril*, 10.

34. Lin Yutang, *A Leaf in the Storm* (New York: John Day Company, 1941), 184.

35. *Me: A Book of Remembrance* (New York: Century Co., 1915).

36. Jean Lee Cole, *The Literary Voices of Winnifred Eaton: Redefining Ethnicity and Authenticity* (New Brunswick: Rutgers University Press, 2002), 100.

37. Cole, *The Literary Voices*, 4.

38. See Cole, *The Literary Voices*; Ferens, *Edith and Winnifred Eaton*; and Lee, *Interracial Encounters*.

39. Nguyen, *Race and Resistance*, 33–59.

40. Lawrence and Cheung, *Recovered Legacies*, 9.

41. Ellen Wu, *The Color of Success: Asian Americans and the Origins of the Model Minority* (Princeton, NJ: Princeton University Press, 2013), 2.

42. Jade Snow Wong, *Fifth Chinese Daughter* (New York: Harper and Brothers, 1950).

43. Leslie Bow, *Betrayal and Other Acts of Subversion: Feminism, Sexual Politics, Asian American Women's Literature* (Princeton, NJ: Princeton University Press, 2001), 70–114; Lawrence and Cheung, *Recovered Legacies*, 10.

4

CATHERINE MORLEY

Ethnic American Modernisms

John Dos Passos' *Manhattan Transfer* (1925) opens with an image of immigrants to the "world's second metropolis" emerging from the dark interior of a sailing vessel, as if born into a vast new space of "opportoonity" as they take their first uncertain steps down to the ferry slip and into the light of the city.[1] This opening moment precedes the birth of one of the novel's protagonists, Elaine Thatcher, an infant likened to a "knot of earthworms" (15) and held aloft by a nurse who regards the child with the disdain usually reserved for the handling of a bedpan. Both "births" are anticipated by an epigraph, almost prophetic in its tone and its depiction of the contemporary urban wasteland, which compares the immigrants' arrival in the city to the processing of apples down a chute – cored, pulped, juiced. These concurrent moments of arrival, the optimism of which is distempered by procedure, ill feeling, and mechanization, indicate the antipathy with which many immigrants to New York City were greeted in the first decade or so of the twentieth century. On board the immigrant-laden ship, those on the lower decks break into an impromptu rendition of "Yankee Doodle" in celebration of Independence Day. Upon dry land, however, the mood is less than celebratory: Bud Korpenning is unable to find the "center of things" (16) that might offer some stability to his situation, Susie Thatcher hysterically rejects her baby as a changeling, Jimmy Herf is disconnected from his mother in meeting the unwelcoming Harlands, and Ed Thatcher is defrauded of the cost of a few drinks by a German New Yorker wetting the head of his newborn baby "poy" (19). Each instance bespeaks a kind of disappointment on the part of the incoming New Yorker, but each moment also depicts a native suspicion of the other, a wariness and distrust of the vulnerable newcomer, who is reduced to a mere quantitative value.

To gauge the quantitative value of the immigrant, one merely needs to look at the hard facts of the United States' population explosion in the late nineteenth and early twentieth centuries. In New York alone, 27 million immigrants arrived between 1880 and 1930. Prior to this, of course, the United

52

States had been a prime destination for European immigrants seeking a better way of life. From 1845 to 1852, for instance, during the years of the Irish Potato Famine, over one million people crossed the Atlantic. By 1850 the Irish represented a quarter of New York's population. Other national groups immigrating to the United States during this time included Germans, French, Italians, and Scandinavians. This wave of immigration reached a peak in the 1850s, although it was curtailed by the American Civil War, which brought further demographic changes. While some of these immigrants moved beyond the cities of their arrival to the West, most stayed in the urban hubs at which they had debarked. New York, in particular, was the metropolitan magnet for immigrants arriving after the war, and it expanded exponentially in the latter decades of the nineteenth century. The United States Census of 1890 revealed the population of the city to be 1.5 million people, with approximately half foreign born; a decade later the figure had leapt to 3.5 million, representing a growth of 126.8 percent. And by 1930 New York was home to just under 7 million inhabitants.[2]

Across the United States as a whole, the foreign-born population exceeded 9 million people (an extraordinary figure given that the overall population was then just 63 million). In 1890 alone almost half a million immigrants entered the United States, with almost a quarter arriving from Eastern and Southern Europe. Thus the types of immigrants entering American ports were no longer primarily Protestant Northern Europeans or Irish Catholics, but Jews, Orthodox Greeks, Italians, and Slavs who brought with them their respective customs and beliefs as well as the idiomatic dialects that would come to characterize the diverse tang of the modern New York cultural scene in the early decades of the twentieth century.[3] The working and living conditions of these immigrants are well known: most came to escape religious persecution and the abject poverty of their homelands only to be confronted by joblessness, overcrowded conditions, and antagonistic landlords. Writers such as Anzia Yezierska, Isaac Bashevis Singer, Henry Roth, and Willa Cather would come to recreate the conditions faced by such people in modernist novels that blend experimentalism with searing social criticism. All in all, migration and immigration had a profound effect on modern American art and literature. They engendered a fusion of cultures and ethnicities that would feed into the dazzling polyphony of modernist experimentalism. Immigrants also contributed to the labor movement and the socialist-inspired art that would be written by the likes of Mike Gold and John Steinbeck. Finally, postbellum migration liberated the African American folk cultures and art forms that would be so crucial to the New Negro Renaissance.

The net result of the unprecedented surge of immigration was a profound reappraisal of American identity. With the ghettoization of many immigrant groups, progressivist notions that new immigrants would adapt and assimilate to the codes of Anglo-Saxon gentility and adopt the lingua franca were not always realized. And large enclaves of immigrant communities, whose values and ambitions could be at odds with those of the nation, caused consternation amongst many of the Anglo-American intelligentsia. In Charles G. Gould's polemic of 1922, *America: A Family Matter*, the author makes the case that immigrants can never be "Americanized," as such qualities could not be taught but "must come to us from the mother's milk, the baby's lisping questions, and grow with our nerves and thews and sinews until they become part and parcel of our very being."[4] For Gould and others of his nativist persuasion, naturalization was an impossibility and the influx of immigrants represented a threat to national "purity." On the other hand, for intellectuals such as Randolph Bourne and Horace Kallen, immigrant communities embodied a cultural pluralism that was true to the original ideals of the nation. Nonetheless, the expansive demography of New York City brought about political changes such as the Emergency Quota Act of 1921, which limited immigration from each nation to the 1910 quotas, and the Johnson-Reed Immigration Act of 1924, which brought quotas back to the 1890 limit. The effect was to lower the number of new arrivals, but by this stage the immigrant stamp had been imprinted indelibly on the city, and it was the very fact of this surge in immigrant communities that contributed to New York's reputation as a center of modernism. As Werner Sollers has observed, "ethnicization and modernization go hand in hand."[5] And, indeed, a novel such as *Manhattan Transfer*, with its deliberate interpolation of the tenets of cubism and Russian constructivism in a text of competing ethnic voices and experiences, perfectly encapsulates this idea. Dos Passos, though not an immigrant writer per se, was fascinated by the immigrant experience – a fascination perhaps attributable to his own "outsider" status as the product of an extra-marital love affair between the wealthy lawyer John Randolph Dos Passos and Lucy Addison Sprigg Madison, and certainly evident in his staunch defense of the executed Italian-American immigrants Nicola Sacco and Bartolomeo Vanzetti. In many ways *Manhattan Transfer* offers a spatial portrait of the ethnic American city, and its presentation of the ways in which newcomers interact with established American families offers a deliberate meditation on contemporary debates about the name and nature of American identity, fears of miscegenation carried over from the antebellum South, and the impact of ethnic communities upon core American values.

Two writers who also address these themes, albeit in very different contexts and from vastly different perspectives, are Willa Cather and Anzia Yezierska: the former a Virginia-born prairie writer of Irish extraction; the latter an Eastern European–born city dweller. What these writers share is an interest in the female immigrant's story, along with the accompanying concerns of gender inequalities, the tug of family and spousal/sibling responsibility (which seems especially relevant to the female immigrant), and, above all, the special relationship between the female immigrant character and geographical space. For each writer, space is particularly pertinent as an entity that can define identity; but it is also something fluid and eventually conquerable. It is in the mastery of space that the female immigrant subject can take control of her identity, rather than having it conferred upon her by an environment shaped by others. For Alexandra Bergson and Sara Smolinsky, of *O Pioneers!* (1913) and *Bread Givers* (1925), respectively, the acquisition of geographical space is not unlike Woolf's notion of the necessary "room of one's own" in which the female subject can create an identity for herself beyond that created by patriarchal representations of womanhood. While admittedly Sara and Alexandra's interest in spatial proprietorship is more prosaic – domestic and entrepreneurial, respectively – than that described by Woolf (since neither demonstrates any literary aspirations), the principle remains that the self can be created and shaped by the attainment and mastery of geographical space. This notion of space as a determinant of identity goes beyond mere notions of ownership conferring power. In the case of each character, there is a clear relationship between the female subject and the space she inhabits. The modern city and the spaces within it are the crucible for Smolinsky's transformation; it seems that there is a symbiotic relationship between the protagonist and the evolving modern space, with the congruity of the Jewish ghetto and the glittering skyscraper engendering the protagonist's social and intellectual ascent. In the case of Bergson, the mere acquisition of the Great Plains landscape is insufficient to her aims. The land must yield to her hand, become fertile and receptive to her inventive agricultural methods: it must engender the future.

Though Anzia Yezierska is rarely celebrated as a modernist writer, her novels and short stories, tracking the lives of young female Jewish immigrants, engage with similar ideas to those tackled by the likes of Dos Passos, Faulkner, Fitzgerald, and Hemingway. Her characters strive to extricate themselves from the social difficulties brought about by poverty, femininity, and their Jewishness. Criticized in her lifetime for a prose style that was unapologetically melodramatic, sentimental, and thin in terms of characterization, Yezierska was also praised for her powerful portrayals of ghetto life, her own personal tenacity to succeed as a writer, and her success in highlighting of the plight of immigrant women on New York's Lower East Side (an area of twenty blocks south of Houston Street and east of Broadway). Above all, the novel *Bread Givers* sealed Yezierska's reputation as a writer devoted to uncovering the complexities of immigrant life in the United States.[6] The story of Sara Smolinsky's rise from the crowded tenement blocks of Jewish New York and her concurrent loss of familial loyalty appeared in an auspicious year for American literary fiction and touched on the themes and issues that preoccupied Yezierska's fellow modernists. These are, namely, the sacrifice of one's individuality in the name of American success, the alienating capacity of the American city, and the social impact of the emerging "New Woman," as well as the modernist literary experiments with verisimilitude.

Yezierska's interest in realistically representing the lives of her immigrant characters in all their ethnic particularities is very obvious to anybody who opens one of her books. For example, she used Yiddish names (for instance, Shprintzeh Gittel in *Bread Givers* and Motkeh Pelz in "Wings"); she inserted transliterated Yiddish, German and Russian phrases throughout ("Oi wei" and "Blut und Eisen" recur frequently throughout *Bread Givers*); and she wrote in an English that is syntactically altered to reproduce the inflections of an immigrant speaking in a second (or third) language. Moreover, her fiction documents the historical conditions endured by the Lower East Side's 135,000 Jews, from the constant threat of eviction to the dank apartments that often sheltered families of ten or more people. These cramped experiences are reflected in *Bread Givers* in terms of the novel's abiding preoccupation with space. Smolinsky's life can, in fact, be mapped out by the gradually more expansive spaces she comes to occupy: from the cluttered tenement room she shares with her family, to finding her voice selling herring in the street, the ghetto, the suburban space of the college, the city, and, finally, the corridor in which she ambivalently agrees to take her antagonistic father back into her life. Sara's quest for an uncluttered room of her own is undoubtedly part of a wider tradition of conquering geographical space in the making of an American identity; furthermore, the upward ascent of New York City, symbolized by the vertical rise of the skyscraper, mirrors Sara's success. However, the acquisition of space is also part of Yezierska's feminist agenda, enabling the female subject to be educated, to think, and to write. Notably, Yezierska emphasizes the small, enclosed, private spaces of feminist discourse rather than the public, architectural spaces associated with American success.

Sara's journey begins in the crowded slums of Hester Street where there is no room for personal expression or for neat American maxims on cleanliness: "The school teacher's rule, 'A place for everything and everything in its place' was no good for us because there weren't enough places."[7] Defying her "Old World" father, who insists on claiming the largest room in the apartment for himself and his religious books, Sara rents a room of her own, a filthy "dark hole" that at least has "a door I could shut" (158). From this room Sara moves to a suburban setting, forsaking the cityscape as she attends college among "quiet streets, shaded with greens" (210). She tries out a number of different rooms in an attempt to fit in with her teachers and fellow students, but all of her choices seem self-negating and ill-fitting, perhaps due to her trying to shape herself into an alien space. It is only upon completion of her college course that Sara finds a room that mirrors her newfound independence and status:

> I had selected a sunny, airy room, the kind of a room I had always wanted ... No carpet on the floor. No pictures on the wall. Nothing but a clean, airy emptiness ... I celebrated it alone with myself. I celebrated it in my room, my first clean, empty room. ... I had achieved that marvelous thing, "a place for everything and everything in its place." (267)

With the acquisition of the new apartment, far removed from the cluttered room on Hester Street in which the novel opens, Sara conquers not only geographical space but at last possesses a room that reflects her own sense of selfhood and her personal achievement.

This strong sense of selfhood is evident from the very outset of the novel. The narrative voice is characterized by an insistence upon an individualistic "I." For instance, in struggling with the family detritus in the kitchen on Hester Street, the narrating "I" battles heroically against the smothering rags, tables, chairs, and unclean windows. For Yezierska the "I" is a site of uncertainty. Traditionally the "I" is hewed to a unified, coherent, male self-hood and manacled to the autobiographical genre. In *Bread Givers*, the "I" is the nexus where real and imagined selves collide, thus opening up a new narrative space between the autobiographical and the fictional. This new narrative space ideally fits Yezierska's hitherto untapped subject: the position of the immigrant woman in an early twentieth-century urban environment.[8] This space, between the autobiographical and the fictional, allows the female subject (and indeed the writer herself) to move into and out of "controlling" generic structures. Thus the invention of this new literary space is a deeply political act of self-expression and self-definition, but it also allows Yezierska to play with the boundaries of genre in exploring both the liminality and the "in between-ness" of her subject – a woman outside both Jewish and American patriarchal cultures yet also caught between them.[9] The final scene of the novel, in which Sara stands in the corridor deciding her father's fate, is a physical, spatial representation of this bind. While this "in between" space can be liberating, allowing the subject to move between worlds and identities without being contained by either, it can also be a site of limbo, a no-man's land in which the subject is locked until she decides which way to turn.

While undoubtedly linked to a feminist tradition in terms of the female subject's relationship with various physical spaces, Yezierska's deceptively simple novel also exhibits an immersion in the debates about ethnicity that permeated early twentieth-century American culture. For many readers, Yezierska's writing actively encourages the assimilation of Yiddish culture into the United States, and there is clearly some truth in this. After all, Yezierska's primary aim in her early life, echoing the aim of most of her characters, was to become a "real" American:

> Then came a light – a great revelation! I saw America – a big idea – a deathless hope – a world still in the making. I saw that it was the glory of America that it was not yet finished. And I, the last comer, had her share to give, small or great, to the making of America, like those Pilgrims who came in the *Mayflower*.[10]

However, Yezierska's work is undeniably critical of the processes of Americanization and assimilation, as exemplified in the subtitle to *Bread Givers: The Struggle between a Father of the Old World and a Daughter of the New*. The relationship between first- and second-generation American Jews is presented as an ordeal, a tortured emotional process for both parties. Ron Ebest convincingly argues that Yezierska's overwrought style and frequent use of what might be construed as anti-Semitic stereotypes (for instance, the selfish scholarly father as personified in Reb Smolinsky) are better understood as the products of the context in which she wrote. For example, Yezierska's stories appeared in periodicals that ran nativist, anti-immigrant articles and ongoing debates on the so-called "Jewish Question." Ebest observes that "Yezierska's stories engaged this debate in the space it was already occupying. . . . Thus the stories may be understood as arguments, offered by one of the Jews under discussion, and interjected into an ongoing, often ugly, frequently nativist, many voiced debate."[11] So while Sara may celebrate the success embodied in her empty female space, her freedom is compromised by her willingness to accept her misogynistic father back into her life after she finds him hawking matches in the ghetto: "I felt the shadow still there, over me. It wasn't just my father, but the generations who made my father whose weight was still upon me" (297). As a result, Sara's independence from the "Old World" remains an unrealized dream, and her articulation of this at the very end of the novel denies the reader the closure or the happy ending one expects of the rags-to-riches story. In a way, therefore, the conclusion depicts a subject in an indeterminate state of limbo. Stuck out in the corridor between rooms, Sara is caught between worlds and learns that she cannot fit into either. But it is a space in which she has finally achieved some mastery in her relationship with the father who once controlled her fate. Here, in this in-between space, she holds the power over his destiny. Whereas once he controlled domestic space with his scholarly books and matchmaking proclivities, now she will decide the space he is to occupy. She will decide his future.

In contrast to Yezierska, Willa Cather often intervened directly in the nativist and political debates of the day. Though she is frequently derided as a curmudgeonly regionalist, her writing exhibits a deep interest in experimenting with representations of the lives of the various immigrant communities that occupy her prairie novels, as well as an abiding concern with geographical space. As for the "regionalist" tag, as Guy Reynolds has observed, Cather was conscious of her reputation and willingly embraced it. Alas, although it was this label that first brought Cather national success, it has also served to restrict her literary reputation. The misconceptions associated with Cather's supposedly nostalgic Nebraska style have often blinded readers to the author's deep immersion in a wider cultural context, both at the national and international levels.[12] Yet scholars have long explored her literary influences, both American and European, her taste in the visual and the culinary arts, and her deployment of Greek and Latin epic conventions and allusions throughout even the earliest of her fiction.[13] Yet the assumption of parochialism persists.[14] One of the reasons, of course, is the success of Cather's earlier fiction, namely, O Pioneers! (1913) and My Ántonia (1918), which were deeply rooted in her Nebraska settings. Another is her fascination with the processes of memory and recovery, as well as her lifelong interest in origin, purity, and identity.[15] However, even in these early novels, Cather's world is much wider than the prairie. Certainly the prairie location and context are cardinal for the stories, and Cather's poetic descriptions of the landscapes her protagonists inhabit are crucial to these novels. However, the world Cather presents in these earlier books is distinctly modern and multicultural, teeming with immigrant voices and stories in all their discordant polyphony.

During Cather's lifetime, one of her most sympathetic reviewers was the antiwar intellectual and sometime writer for The Dial, Randolph Bourne. In his review of My Ántonia in 1918, Bourne described Cather as belonging to the international group of modernist writers – a seemingly curious ascription when one considers that this is supposedly one of the books that most firmly situates Cather in the prairies. However, a closer look at Bourne's writing reveals a conception of region, indeed even of nation, as distinctly cosmopolitan. For Bourne, the term "trans-national America" referred to "a federation of cultures," "a cosmopolitan federation of national colonies, of foreign cultures" with "an intellectual internationalism ... [interested in] different cultural expressions." He envisaged the United States as a nation of immigrants who could "retain that distinctiveness of their native cultures" and hence be "more valuable and interesting to each other for being different," a nation of "cosmopolitan interchange ... in spite of the war and all its national exclusiveness."[16] Indeed, on numerous occasions in the years before World War I, Cather championed immigrants' rights against the forces of Americanization, and, when asked about the importance of immigrant communities in her work in an interview for the *New York Times Book Review* in 1924, she remarked:

> They have come here to live in the sense that they lived in the Old World, and if they were let alone their lives might turn into the beautiful ways of their homeland. But they are not let alone. Social workers, missionaries – call them what you will – go after them, hound them, pursue them and devote their days and nights toward the great task of turning them into stupid replicas of smug American citizens. This passion for Americanizing everything and everybody is a deadly disease with us.[17]

The key term here is "Americanizing," and it is worth reflecting on the author's condemnation of it as a procedure that threatens to iron out the idiosyncrasies of immigrant and, by implication, regional cultures (after all, Cather's prairie fictions are populated by Germans, Scandinavians, and Czechs).[18] Indeed, what have come to be regarded as Cather's mythic pastoral visions of American identity at the beginning of the twentieth century can also be viewed as narratives of dislocation and social isolation, while her regionalist proclivities are no less a social critique than the experiments of the urban avant-garde.[19] For Cather, any kind of Americanization, including the notion of the melting pot, presents precisely the cultural (and racial) homogeneity she abhors. And while certainly elegiac in tone, her novels offer not so much a lament for some stable American or regional identity as a repudiation of an Americanized identity that threatens to eradicate diverse cultures. Indeed, in her 1938 essay "On *The Professor's House*," Cather writes that she deliberately engaged with French and Spanish forms to present an antithesis to the stifling conformity of Godfrey St. Peter's American house: "In my book I tried to make Professor St. Peter's house rather overcrowded and stuffy with new things; American proprieties, clothes, furs, petty ambitions, quivering jealousies – until one got rather stifled."[20] Thus the world of Professor St. Peter and his daughters is less the protected and vulnerable space identified by critics such as Walter Benn Michaels than it is a space that threatens to infect, commodify, and eradicate immigrant and indigenous cultures.[21] Far from being introspective, backward, and parochial, Cather's methodology and her themes reveal a writer attuned to the wider dangers of cultural conformity.

O Pioneers! which takes its title from Whitman's homage to westward expansion, very deliberately focuses on the immigrant experience. Like

Bread Givers, it concentrates on the story of a willful female immigrant within that traditionally male spatial context. Alexandra Bergson is portrayed as a manager of men from the outset of the novel, rounding up Carl Linstrum to rescue her young brother's kitten in the midst of running errands for her dying father. Watched by a traveling salesman as she battles with an inhospitable landscape of "tough prairie sod" and a town "which was trying not to be blown away," Alexandra is a "ray of hope," a purposeful and resolute force.[22] Whereas Yezierska's novel focuses upon the appropriation of urban space in the development of a Jewish-American female subjectivity, *O Pioneers!* ties its heroine to the rural landscape of the Nebraska Divide. Shrewd and resourceful, Alexandra is Cather's heroic woman, dressed "like a young soldier" (5) in a man's ulster and a woman's veil. With her imposing physique and golden plaits, surrounded throughout her life by "little men" (105), she is like a character from an old Scandinavian epic. It is perhaps no coincidence that Alexandra can recite long sections of the Icelandic *Frithjof Saga*, at the heart of which is a heroine, Ingeborg, who is shuttled between "little men" while she awaits the return of her larger-than-life lover, Frithjof. Ingeborg, whose name suggests a stronghold, is certainly a model for Alexandra, the stalwart of the family who too dreams of being "lifted and carried by a strong being who carried from her all her bodily weariness" (102). Much like the Icelandic princess, Alexandra is buffeted by the demands of her brothers and denied her lover. But she resists the pressure exerted by Lou and Oscar Bergson, and by the end of the novel she has maintained her stronghold and the love of Carl. As a result, Cather's intertextual deployment of the saga within that most American of stories, the expansion of the West, reveals an authorial sensibility committed to the preservation and adaptation of myths and stories carried from the Old World. Indeed, Cather's deployment of the Norse epic, alongside the references to Longfellow's "Golden Legend" and *The Swiss Family Robinson*, evokes the "intellectual internationalism" described by Bourne.[23]

The novel reflects at length on language. Alexandra and her brothers maintain their mother tongue, but American-born Emil, the youngest of the Bergson children, understands no Swedish despite speaking (as a child) in an English that bears the hallmarks of a nonnative speaker: "My kitten, oh, my kitten. Her will fweeze" (4). When the children converse with Crazy Ivar, they translate his Norwegian for Emil, while later in the novel Alexandra employs a series of girls from the old country largely because she likes to hear them chatter in their own language while performing household chores. As the Bergson family spreads and marries, the emphasis upon respectability and speaking English becomes more of an issue:

> The conversation at the table was all in English. Oscar's wife, from the malaria district of Missouri, was ashamed of marrying a foreigner, and his boys do not understand a word of Swedish. Annie and Lou sometimes speak Swedish at home, but Annie is . . . afraid of being "caught" at it. . . . Oscar still has a thick accent, but Lou speaks like anybody from Iowa. (59)

Again, Cather makes a subtle appeal for the preservation of immigrant cultures and languages. The un-Americanized world of Alexandra's homestead, filled with Swedish chatter and the nightly Norwegian readings of Old Ivar, is a great deal more interesting and, indeed, liberating than the homes of Oscar and Lou. Mrs. Lee, Lou's mother-in-law, enjoys her annual visits to Alexandra precisely because it "be yust-a like old times":

> She enjoyed the liberty Alexandra gave her, and hearing her old language about her all day long. Here she could wear her nightcap and sleep with all her windows shut, listen to Ivar reading the Bible, and here she could run about among the stables in a pair of Emil's old boots. (110)

For old Mrs. Lee, the freedom to speak in her own tongue and wear her outmoded nightcap is something she associates with the past and with the Old World. The New World and the lifestyle choices of her daughter and son-in-law curtail those liberties and deny the essence of a culture that in its openness and flexibility has, in fact, facilitated their new, modern identities. There is an implicit contrast here, of course, with Americanization programs such as those organized by the Colonial Dames of America or the Sons of the American Revolution, and who can deny that Cather was remarkably prescient in her prediction of the loss of immigrant languages among settlers' descendants? Even so, her portraits of the immigrant communities of the prairies have often been cast as folksy, nostalgic, and, as noted, parochial. A nostalgic streak certainly runs through her work, but, rather like Yezierska, Cather purposefully deploys this to make a fundamental (and eminently modern) point about the curtailment of individual liberties and the possible eradication of ethnic cultures and communities.

By setting a woman at the heart of this pioneer story of conquering the West, at one level at least Cather engages with Frederick Jackson Turner's thesis that the harsh conditions and poverty of the untrammelled landscape and developing towns engendered a kind of necessary equality – in this instance a gender equality.[24] Yet, Alexandra's achievements in spite of her gender are rarely easily won. While her father acknowledges that she is the quickest and the brightest of his children, he wishes that one of her brothers had her attributes. Even when presenting her plans for the development of the farmstead, she is called upon by her mother to complete her domestic chores. Perhaps most significantly, once the family has prospered under her care and management, Alexandra is expected to sacrifice her share of it to her brothers, who have become suspicious of her relationship with Carl Linstrum:

> The property of a family really belongs to the men of the family, no matter about the title. If anything goes wrong, it's the men that are held responsible. . . .
>
> The property of a family belongs to the men of the family, because they are held responsible, and because they do the work. (98)

Indeed, as the farm becomes more successful and the family's material wealth increases, Alexandra finds it even more difficult to maintain her hold on the property and her position as the head of the family. Her brothers invoke the mores of traditional and established communities, assert notions of sexual propriety and female duty, and use the murmurings of the community to cast a pall over her friendship with Carl, urging her to hand the property over to them. Again, the issue comes back to the control and management of space, and the brothers' attempts to seize ownership of the land is coterminous with their attempts to reign in the unruly and expansive female. Alexandra is instrumental to the expansion of the family holdings; she enlarges the farm and makes it work. In doing so, in setting herself out-of-doors, she enters into a traditionally male territory, forsaking the comforts of the narrow domestic spaces that cannot contain her. Yet, having achieved success and facilitated the family's entry into society, she is impelled by the patriarchal rules of society to return to the socially acceptable domestic sphere of the household, indoors. And while she resists the efforts of Lou and Oscar to divest her of her property, the novel concludes on a note of ambiguity implicit in her decision to marry Carl, the man from whom as a girl she had taken the reins in setting out into darkness. Like Yezierska, therefore, Cather offers a portrait of a female immigrant caught between the Old World and the New World, and also between a liberated feminine identity and a selfhood ensnared in a resilient culture of gender conformity.

Alexandra's affinity with the prairie landscape is perhaps the novel's greatest feminist statement.[25] Given charge of the homestead in her father's dying instructions, Cather's heroine is liberated from the usual trappings of domesticity and offered a new spatial framework. Shortly after her father's death, out of an instinctual feeling for the land, she remortgages the homestead to purchase part of the Linstrum, Crow, and Struble farms, making the family prosperous independent landowners. Alexandra's house is described as "curiously unfinished and uneven in comfort" (49); the cooking, cleaning, pickling, and preserving are handled by her three hired Swedish girls. But it is outside that Alexandra's "order and fine arrangement manifest all over the great farm." As the narrator observes, "you feel that, properly, Alexandra's house is the big out-of-doors, and it is in the soil that she expresses herself best" (50). Later, Alexandra recalls "days when she was close to the flat, fallow world about her, and felt, as it were, in her own body the joyous germination of the soil" (118). The convergence of Cather's heroine with the soil presents a vision of ethnic womanhood as the exemplary pioneer; she is the bold and modern entrepreneur experimenting in new farming methods, testing new practices of animal husbandry, and introducing mechanical means of production. It is the immigrant woman who develops and expands the homestead, organizing its growth and wealth. It is she who breaks the land that her father describes as "like a horse that no one knows how to break to harness" (13). Cather offers a portrait not only of a woman who knows how to manage the land, but of a woman who is *of* the land. It is not simply a matter of property, as for her brothers Oscar and Lou, but of unity. Alexandra, the immigrant woman, is *the land itself*. Shaped by her hand and saturated by the blood of her family, the land is locked with Alexandra in a symbiosis of nurture and reproduction:

> Fortunate country, that is one day to receive hearts like Alexandra's into its bosom, to give them out again in the yellow wheat, in the rustling corn . . .
>
> (180)

For Cather, therefore, it is the ethnic American immigrant communities – their stories, their histories, and their languages – that are the true stuff of the nation. Theirs are the stories that demand to be written and rewritten, told and retold. Theirs is the future that lies beneath the ridges of the prairie. It is no accident that Alexandra Bergson's mind is described as a "white book, with clear writing about weather and beasts and growing things" (189). For her mind is the white space of the West that takes shape and develops as we read the book, culminating in the final section, entitled "Alexandra." The "white book" is the land, it is Alexandra, and it is Cather's modern literary experiment: the female pioneer novel.

NOTES

1. John Dos Passos, *Manhattan Transfer* (1925; London: Penguin, 2000), 23.
2. See Campbell Gibson, "Population of the 100 Largest Cities and Other Urban Places in the United States: 1790–1990" (June 1998): http://www.census.gov/po pulation/www/documentation/twps0027/twps0027.html. For more-general historical studies of immigration to the United States, see John E. Bodnar's *The Transplanted: A History of Immigrants in Urban America* (Bloomington: Indiana University Press, 1997) and Oscar Handlin's *The Uprooted* (London: Little, Brown, 1973). See also Robert F. Zeidel's *Immigrants, Progressives and Exclusion Politics: The Dillingham Commission, 1900–1927* (Chicago: Northern Illinois University Press, 2004).

3. For an excellent study of the cultural impact of these immigrants' socioreligious backgrounds, see John E. Bodnar, *Remaking America: Public Memory, Commemoration and Patriotism in the Twentieth Century* (Princeton, NJ: Princeton University Press, 1992).

4. Cited in Walter Benn Michaels, *Our America: Nativism, Modernism and Pluralism* (Durham: Duke University Press, 1995), 8.

5. Werner Sollors, *Beyond Ethnicity: Consent and Descent in American Culture* (New York: Oxford University Press, 1986), 246. Recent studies that have energized debates about the impact of immigration on American modernism include Sarah Wilson's excellent *Melting Pot Modernism* (Ithaca, NY: Cornell University Press, 2010); Werner Sollors' *Ethnic Modernism* (Cambridge: Harvard University Press, 2008); and Rita Keresztesi's *Strangers at Home: Ethnic American Modernism between the World Wars* (Lincoln: University of Nebraska Press, 2009).

6. Indeed, Yezierska's commitment to exploring new cultural modes is evident in her connection with early film history. She sold the rights to her first collection, *Hungry Hearts*, to Samuel Goldwyn. For an excellent appraisal of the commercialization of Jewish identity, see Lisa Botshon, "Anzia Yezierska and the Marketing of the Jewish Immigrant in 1920s Hollywood," *JNT: Journal of Narrative Theory* 30, no. 3 (Fall 2000): 287–312.

7. Anzia Yezierska, *Bread Givers* (1925; New York: Persea, 2003), 10.

8. Priscilla Wald is especially insightful on the anxiety of the self and the conceptualization of identity in literary texts, especially those narratives "suppressed and repressed by the official stories of We the People." See *Constituting Americans: Cultural Anxiety and Narrative Form* (Durham: Duke University Press, 1995). For an interesting discussion of the distinctions among life writing, life narrative, and autobiography, see Sidonie Smith and Julia Watson, *Reading Autobiography: A Guide for Interpreting Life Narratives* (Minneapolis: University of Minnesota Press, 2010).

9. Gay Wilentz makes a similar observation regarding the double bind of the Jewish female protagonist and, indeed, about the plight of the immigrant in the face of Americanization programs in her "Introduction" to *Salome of the Tenements* (1923; Chicago: University of Illinois, 1995), ix–xxiii.

10. Anzia Yezierska, "America and I," *Children of Loneliness: Stories of Immigrant Life in America* (New York: Funk and Wagnalls, 1923), 50.

11. Ron Ebest, "Anzia Yezierska and the Popular Debate over the Jews," *MELUS* 25, no. 1 (2000): 3.

12. As Guy Reynolds, Richard H. Millington, Ian F. A. Bell, and Sharon O'Brien have observed, Cather is often neglected in literary anthologies and rarely considered in most accounts of Anglo-American modernism. During her lifetime, Cather was often the subject of debate in terms of her seeming conservatism and detachment from the modern American scene. Most notable among her contemporary critics were Granville Hicks and Lionel Trilling, who lamented the perceived nostalgia and celebration of rural values within her work. See Hicks, "The Case against Willa Cather," *English Journal* (November 1933), in James Schroeter, ed., *Willa Cather and Her Critics* (Ithaca, NY: Cornell University Press, 1967), 139–147.

13. A wide range of scholarship uncovers Cather's European influences. Some notable examples include: Helen Dennis, ed., *Willa Cather and European Cultural*

Influences (Lewiston: Edwin Mellen Press, 1996); Ian Bell, "Re-Writing America: Origin and Gender in *The Professor's House*," *Yearbook of English Studies* 24 (1994): 12–43; Robert Nelson, *Willa Cather and France: In Search of the Lost Language* (Champaign: University of Illinois Press, 1988); Stéphanie Durrans, *The Influence of French Culture on Willa Cather: Intertextual References and Resonances* (Lewiston: Edwin Mellen Press, 2008); Janis Stout, *Willa Cather: The Writer and Her World* (Charlottesville: University of Virginia Press, 2000); Hermione Lee, *Willa Cather: A Life Saved Up* (London: Virago: 1997); and Mary Ryder, *Willa Cather and the Classical Myth: The Search for a New Parnassus* (Lewiston: Edwin Mellen Press, 1990).

14. Reynolds argues persuasively against the negative and parochial connotations associated with Cather's regionalism, noting her representation of lost communities not as a retreat into the past but as "a form of regionalist commitment (and recommitment) to the 'beloved community' that once existed." Furthermore, Reynolds observes that Cather weaves a progressive reform derived from populism into her characters' lives and stories. See Reynolds, "Willa Cather as Progressive: Politics and the Writer," in *The Cambridge Companion to Willa Cather*, ed. Marilee Lindemann (Cambridge: Cambridge University Press, 2005), 21.

15. Bell makes a compelling argument for Cather as self-consciously and deliberately interested in the purity associated with the primitive in *The Professor's House* (1925), linking Tom Outland's excavations on the Mesa and St. Peter's recollection of Outland's story as "the romance of the elusive, unwritable other as a means of approaching the beginning of things." See Bell, "Origin and Gender in Willa Cather," 24. Millington also observes an interest in the primitive in Cather's writing and describes her interest in immigrant and ancient cultures as animated by the new perspectives offered by Boasian anthropology. See Millington, "Willa Cather's American Modernism," in *The Cambridge Companion to Willa Cather*, ed. Marilee Lindemann (Cambridge: Cambridge University Press, 2005), 57.

16. Randolph Bourne, "Trans-national America" (1916), in *The Heath Anthology of American Literature*, eds. Paul Lauter et al. (New York: Houghton Mifflin, 2006), 1637–1648.

17. See Rose C. Field, "Restlessness Such as Ours Does Not Make for Beauty," *New York Times Book Review*, December 21, 1924, 11.

18. Here Cather's desire to protect regional cultures is borne out of opposition to the perceived monolithic versions of American identity coming from the East, which is linked to the grievances of the populists.

19. For a reappraisal of Cather along these lines, see the authoritative work by Guy Reynolds, "Willa Cather as Progressive," and "*My Ántonia* and the Americanization Debate" in *Willa Cather in Context* (London and Basingstoke: Macmillan, 1996), 73–98.

20. Willa Cather, "On *The Professor's House*" (1938), in *Willa Cather on Writing* (New York: Bison Books, 1988), 31.

21. For an alternative interpretation of Cather as a writer with nativist proclivities, see Walter Benn Michaels' *Our America: Nativism, Modernism and Pluralism* (Durham and London: Duke University Press, 1995).

22. Willa Cather, *O Pioneers!* (1913; New York: Houghton Mifflin, 1995), 3.

23. Susan Rosowski and Hermione Lee have noted the various parallels between Alexandra's story and Virgil's *Eclogues*. Laird points out that Marie and Emil's

story of doomed love is a literary analogue of the Pyramus and Thisbe story of Ovid's *Metamorphoses*.

24. See David Laird, "Willa Cather's Women: Gender Place and Narrativity in *O Pioneers!* and *My Ántonia*," *Great Plains Quarterly* 1, no. 1 (1992): 242–253.

25. It is worth noting that Toni Morrison cites Cather as among those who had tried to counter "a centuries-long, hysterical blindness to feminist discourse and the way in which women and women's issues were read (or unread)." See *Playing in the Dark: Whiteness and the Literary Imagination* (Cambridge: Harvard University Press, 1992), 14.

5

KEVIN BELL

The Worlds of Black Literary Modernism

For the "stupefying frequency"[1] with which scholarly discussions of modern American literature and culture at some point autopilot into obligatory – and usually noninterrogative – reference to the premise of "double-consciousness" in W.E.B. Du Bois' *The Souls of Black Folk* (1903), there is an even more ubiquitous *silence* in critical response to subsequent pronouncements from Du Bois on the relation of black people in the United States to the spectacular wave of post-Enlightenment modernity that was the nineteenth-century hyperindustrialization of global capitalism. The general nonengagement of literary and cultural scholarship that still greets the latter Du Bois of *Black Reconstruction in America 1860–1880* (1935) should be read as only a different mode of the ongoing institutional routinizing of the former.

Double consciousness narrates an inaugurating severance and excess at the historical aperture of black American existence. The severance is from the presumption of humanity in common with the "white" world and from the Enlightenment notion of individual freedom explicit in the discourse of the nation's ideological formation. The excess, or doubling, lies in nearly three centuries of black reflectivity on the contradiction between that discourse and its sustained nonapplication to black people in the United States.

As a condition of black epistemological becoming in an atmosphere largely organized by the presumption and the rhetoric of its nonpossibility, this history has to be absorbed and theorized. The amputation at the root of both its entry into the American social and at that of its own self-assemblage is the point of historical and imaginative genesis in the twentieth-century thinking of a black American literary modernism, diversely inimical, wary, and strategic in its responsiveness to the proliferating economic and cognitive matrices of Euro-American modernity, whose rapid institutionalization and massive global expansion proceed as a direct function of the logics and practices of coloniality, enslavement, and radical underdevelopment of much of the non-European world.

Critical illumination of this "darker side of modernity,"[2] demands a grasping of Afro-diasporic and indigenous American intellectual and aesthetic production in a global context, shaped and reformulated since the fifteenth century by rationalist economic and political imperatives extending in space and time far beyond the self-inaugurating procedures of the later eighteenth-century United States. These imperatives – as Karl Marx noted cursorily in the first volume of *Capital*, and as black scholars such as Du Bois and Afro-Trinidadian intellectuals C.L.R James and Eric Williams demonstrated far more comprehensively in the first half of the twentieth century[3] – appear in the devastations of material culture and massive deletions of indigenous history across the African, Caribbean, Central American, South American, and Asian spheres. And, as subsequent scholarship from such thinkers as Walter Rodney, Eduardo Galeano, Enrique Dussel, Aníbal Quijano, Walter Mignolo, among others, would emphasize, these imperatives were crucial to the entrenchment of Euro-American statist, industrialist, and imperialist enterprise over the next 500 years.[4] Afro-diasporic intellectuals, revolutionaries, and artists such as Frantz Fanon, Amílcar Cabral, Wilson Harris, Édouard Glissant, Sylvia Wynter, and Cedric Robinson would expand these critical investigations, theorizing the necessity to modern epistemological formation throughout the West that the reflective singularity of Afro-diasporic thought – and its capacities to define the intellectual and spiritual dynamics and genealogies of its own production – be converted into the rank deadness of "the Negro." The suddenly ahistorical thing of pure commodity exchangeability that had been cultural blackness was made the measure of depravity and barbarism against which was contoured the very conception of "the human" or of "Man" as the bases of the philosophical and political discourses transforming every dimension of life in the Western hemisphere during the 15th century.

In her 2003 essay "Unsettling the Coloniality of Being," Wynter cites Mignolo's observation that

> in the imaginary of the modern/colonial world system, sustainable knowledge . . . disregarded Amerindian ways of knowing and knowledge production that were reduced to curious practices of strange people and, in another domain were demonized.[5]

But Wynter is ultimately more concerned with the enormity of ambitions intensifying the momentum of European deconstitutings and reconstitutings of the space suddenly reconceived as the New World. Following Jacob Pandian's 1985 *Anthropology and the Western Tradition*, Wynter notes that this epistemological "disregard" was itself part of an even more central imperative – that of the sustainability of the new mode of being human, of its epochal re-description as ... that of the political subject of the state Man. ... Rather than "sustainable knowledge" merely disregarding the "other ways of knowing" of the Amerindian peoples ... instead ... it was to be the discourses of this knowledge, including centrally those of anthropology, that would function to construct all the non-Europeans that (it) encountered ... as the physical referent of ... its irrational or subrational Human Other. ... While the "Indians" were portrayed as the very acme of the savage, irrational Other, the "Negroes" were assimilated to the former's category, represented as its most extreme form and as the ostensible missing link between rational humans and irrational animals. (265–266)

It is not difficult to imagine how such a totalizing disposition forms part of what Wahneema Lubiano has in mind when she writes, in 1991, that "if postmodernism marks an 'incredulity toward metanarratives' it is certainly an appropriate name for African-Americans ... our histories show that we've maintained a fairly consistent level of incredulity; perhaps it is time that the 'West' caught up with us."[6]

So, if black severance from Western imaginings of "humanity" and "rationality" is unavoidable, consciousness of the cut becomes a question of how to process it analytically and reproject it creatively. For such prose modernists as James Weldon Johnson, Jean Toomer, Nella Larsen, Claude McKay, Richard Bruce Nugent, Wallace Thurman, George Schuyler, Zora Neale Hurston, Richard Wright, Ralph Ellison, and Chester Himes, there would be ample opportunity to do so with originality. Each writer would draw not only from literary and philosophic traditions already internalized (and already burdensome) as a condition of professional entry, but would pull just as directly from socio-political formations taking shape in U.S. cities, themselves massively reconstituted by the migration of millions of black people rapidly abandoning the Jim Crow South – and, perhaps even more importantly, from the conceptual resources structuring the formal systems and traditions of modern black musics.

The Reconstructive Pivot of Modern Black Writing

For Afro-modernists working in the cultural contexts of world wars, global economic collapse, and swiftly proliferating aspects of state-sanctioned racialist terrorism and underdevelopment in the United States, creativity would not be separable from critique – and critique would not be able to settle into any stable stance of reactive oppositionality. Alternative materialities would have to emerge by which black aesthetic forms would convene other worlds, but in terms that would first illuminate the violences, social mythologies, and false coherences of this one.

Such explorative means of revisualizing social reality find practical application in Jamaican-born modernist Claude McKay's 1937 memoir *A Long Way from Home* when he suggests that James Joyce's *Ulysses* is "greater as a textbook for modern writers than as a novel for the general public."[7] While McKay finds "more modern" the themes he ascribes to D.H. Lawrence, in whom he hears "confusion – all of the ferment and torment and turmoil, the hesitation and hate and alarm, the sexual inquietude and incertitude of this age" – he finds in Joyce a surer, more playfully opportunistic engagement or reanimation of the social materialities and representations constituting modern existence. At the same time, when McKay writes plainly that European expatriates remain thickly insensate to "the profundity of blackness,"[8] he marks the order of conceptual difference between Afro-diasporic reflectivity *as* a necessarily creative reprojection of lived abjections and a European perspective evidently indifferent to the ways in which its racialism grounds its own epistemic emergence *as such*.

Not only does McKay's formulation revisit the critical resiliency structuring the nomadic sensibility by which he animates the internationalist black "vagabonds" of his 1929 novel *Banjo* (to be revisited momentarily), but it also theorizes the necessarily experimental inhabitation of paradox designated later by Édouard Glissant as being perhaps the unique psychic terrain of the figure of blackness in the modern Americas – "a new man, capable of living the relative after suffering the absolute."[9]

Elsewhere Glissant becomes more specific about the geographies of that terrain:

> the Middle Passage was truly the unknown ... what characterises the Africans' situation in this adventure is the abyss, the abyss of the unknown, the abyss of the ocean floor. ... The Africans in the New World – African-Americans, but also the Antilleans, Brazilians, etc. – escaped the abyss and carry within them the abyss's dimension. ... I believe the arrival of the Africans within the phenomenon of slavery is not about the Atlantic, but the Caribbean. That's where they arrived: in Louisiana, the islands, Cuba, Jamaica, Martinique, and it spread from there across the new continent. And the Caribbean is the source, the origin of the plantation system that began to contain and signify the existence of the Blacks.[10]

In perhaps a less esoteric sense, "the profundity of blackness" had also preoccupied Du Bois, who, two years before McKay published his memoir, attempted in *Black Reconstruction* not only to explain the centrality of the U.S. plantation system's exploitation of blackness to the metastasizing practices of industrial world capitalism, but to mark the relation, within and among the exploited and the enslaved, between self-realization and collective radicalization.

> It was ... the black worker, as founding stone of a new economic system in the nineteenth century and for the modern world, who brought civil war in America. He was its underlying cause, in spite of every effort to base the strife upon union and national power. That dark and vast sea of human labor in China and India, the South Seas and all Africa; in the West Indies and Central America and in the United States – that great majority of mankind, on whose bent and broken backs rest today the founding stones of modern industry – shares a common destiny; it is despised and rejected by race and color; paid a wage below the level of decent living; driven, beaten, prisoned and enslaved in all but name; spawning the world's raw material and luxury—cotton, wool, coffee, tea, cocoa, palm oil, fibers, spices, rubber, silks, lumber, copper, gold, diamonds, leather—how shall we end the list and where? All these are gathered up at prices lowest of the low, manufactured, transformed and transported at fabulous gain; and the resultant wealth is distributed and displayed and made the basis of world power and universal dominion and armed arrogance in London and Paris, Berlin and Rome, New York and Rio de Janeiro.[11]

While Du Bois' change of conceptual focus – from the double consciousness of *The Souls of Black Folk* to the vexed formalization of insurrectionary political consciousness at the heart of *Black Reconstruction* – can be easily imagined as a shift from the ontological domain of black psychic life to an intricate historiographical exhumation of the unique sociopolitical conditions of U.S. slavery's demise, it would be just as precise to describe the movement between the two projects as itself a "doubling" of a signature tendency in Du Bois' work toward the notion of self-transmutation as the only modality within which thinking life can be constituted. It is in this sense that Du Bois can be said to open the meditative context for a discussion of black *aesthetic* modernisms.

In each of the two texts, there remains for Du Bois at least one dimension of black cultural practice by which to document[12] and to reproject, as (self) critique *and* (self) creation, as archive *and* art, the living excess of thought that outlives, even as it endures, its brutalization and ongoing social destitution. This is from the first chapter of *Black Reconstruction*:

> And of all human development, ancient and modern, not the least singular and significant is the philosophy of life and action which slavery bred in the souls of black folk. In most respects its expression was stilted and confused; the rolling periods of Hebrew prophecy and biblical legend furnished inaccurate but splendid words. The subtle folk-lore of Africa, with whimsy and parable, veiled wish and wisdom; and above all fell the anointing chrism of the slave music, the

only gift of pure art in America. . . . Nothing else of art or religion did the slave South give to the world, except the Negro song and story.[13]

The most comprehensive guide to *Black Reconstruction* and its crucial revisions of both Western theoretical Marxism and the critical imagining of blackness in the development of global capitalism is the work of Cedric Robinson. In *Black Marxism: The Making of the Black Radical Tradition* (1983), Robinson examines Du Bois' mammoth 1935 text by the analytic protocols of archival historiography. But it is in *Black Reconstruction*'s brief discussions of black *aesthetic* and affective/cultural production that Robinson discerns the deepest implications of Du Bois' political radicalization.

> The ideology of the Black struggle, the revolutionary consciousness of the slaves, had appeared to [Du Bois'] Westernized eyes, part legend, part whimsy, part art. Yet he realized it had been sufficient to arouse them into mass resistance and had provided them with a vision of the world they preferred. Their collective action had achieved the force of a historical anti-logic to racism, slavery and capitalism.[14]

Robinson's attunement to the scholarly self-adjustment Du Bois makes to clear passage for his own gravitation into the force carried by the "whimsical" errancy of slave art forms helps us grasp the inward turn toward the insubstantial yet transfigurative force of the idioms the enslaved had learned and reconfigured. Imperatives of alterity and futurity torque the slaves' internalizing of this archive of aesthetic forms into the "stilted and confused" reanimation of that material back outward, sounding an exertion of collective pressure in the Civil War South that accelerated political decisiveness. "Freedom for the slave was the logical result of a crazy attempt to wage war in the midst of four million black slaves, and trying . . . to ignore the interests of those slaves in the outcome of the fighting. . . . It was the fugitive slave who made the slaveholders face the alternative of surrendering to the North or surrendering to the Negroes."[15]

Such graphing of political consequence from within the opacities of the figural secures for later scholars such as Robinson, Nikhil Pal Singh, and Robin Kelley the signal value of *Black Reconstruction*'s conceptual horizons – even as these estranged the text from the conventions of historiographic protocol governing its institutional fields at the time. As Singh encapsulates:

> Because Du Bois' critics could only conceive of black modernity as a movement into normalized, institutionalized forms of national belonging, they failed to see what was most profound about Du Bois' reading of slave emancipation – that it was an event that remade the world, "an upheaval of humanity like the Reformation and the French Revolution."[16]

Each contemporary mode of critical deflection of either Du Bois text discussed here articulates the consistency with which the political economy of the U.S. humanities remains, at best, a difficult zone for black writing presented in antagonism to the social order in which it becomes conscious of itself *as* consciousness. Both the customary, perfunctory acknowledgment of the significance of the "double-consciousness" passage in *Souls* – a decisive veering away from what *overflows* the documentary "givenness" of the circumstances of "the Negro" as the focal point of the passage, and therefore a veering away from what compels its composition in the first place – and the general withholding of response to *Black Reconstruction* altogether lend significantly to the contemporary convention of celebrating "one" Du Bois while sidestepping "another." This constitutes a vanished angle of entry onto the critical and creative stakes of black literary modernism.

Double Consciousness and Black Modernism

One provocative interrogation of the notion of double consciousness is opened by R. Radhakrishnan, who reminds us that "the entire elaboration of double consciousness is set in motion by a pathology: a pathology that has been foisted upon the American Negro as a condition for his ontological emergence."[17]

But for Radhakrishnan, Du Bois never emerges fully from the pathology within which he recognizes the "Negro" to be ensnared. Radhakrishnan goes on to argue that Du Bois is ultimately unable to push himself beyond the logic of "race" to which he is opposed and that a more active dismantling of its premises lies before him:

> the racialized double-conscious subject has to achieve a double articulation: proclaim the truth that race is a lie, but at the same time acknowledge as real and consequential the brutal and dehumanizing history of that lie. This has to be a dialectically oriented project where the emerging liberatory truth will have to be seen in process, will have to be seen in emergence as the result of an antagonism. There indeed has been another history than the one engineered by the racial visual machine, and the problem is how to make that other history emerge on its own terms, and not as the "other" of the scopic regime.[18]

For the depth and precision of Radhakrishnan's insight into how double consciousness restructures the psychic apparatus by hegemonic projection and then *appears* to simply inhabit or reproduce (rather than deconstruct) the positions dictated by that pathological discourse, Radhakrishnan seems at the same time not to hear, in black American aesthetic/cultural practice, much reverberation of the "other history," the unhistory, or the other *of* history for which he calls. Such practice, as figuration or art, must take leave of its subject matter in the moment of its enunciation. A look at a different moment from *Souls* might help isolate what is at stake in double consciousness as an idea.

While the double-consciousness passage from *Souls* is found in its first chapter, entitled "Of Our Spiritual Strivings," Ronald A.T. Judy's prescient analysis of Du Boisian double consciousness leads him to the conclusion that it is the book's penultimate thirteenth chapter, the short story entitled "Of the Coming of John," that actually provides *Souls'* "most vivid portrait of double-consciousness."[19] The story enacts Du Bois' sense of what it means to "strive," which in his usage does not denote an acquisitive orientation toward some fantasy continuum of object-fixated comfort and status. Rather, it designates an unrelentingly proleptic disposition, moving away from logics of reproduction, gravitating toward less-traversed zones of problem or experience. At the same time, it is the story of what it means precisely to be barred from pursuit of such internal choreographies of becoming, sparked as these are by resources external to the self.

Du Bois' young protagonist is enraptured while seated in a New York concert hall, immersed in the textures and tensions of the inaugural chords of a performance of Wagner's *Lohengrin*. John Jones, a student from an all-black preparatory school in the Deep South, on a summer sojourn to New York with the school's vocal quartet, feels himself lifted not only out of the "dirt and dust" of the Jim Crow South, but transported altogether out of the anthropomorphic grids of "race" and ideological category that produce it. His sense of personal identity is rematerialized into a wave of sensorial lucidity by which he is freshly attuned to both the singularities of his own temperament and to a sharpened (because belated) awareness of the limitations of his own development under Jim Crow. When his accidental touch of the "white" woman in the adjoining seat results in his being requested to vacate his, John angrily leaves the hall altogether.

Called by the music into the "world beyond men," he is just as suddenly "called outside" by the usher's tap on the shoulder, and he falls from the "free air" of singing birds and setting suns back into the "dirt and dust" of the South. That so transformative an exposure to aesthetico/critical experience can be erased from possibility so arbitrarily introduces John to a deepened understanding of black incapacity to register its legitimacy anywhere in American culture. He realizes that this is only a single instance in a vast, undocumentable history of the systematic predeleting of entire horizons of information and possibility for black people in the United States.

In his 2000 essay "Originary Displacement," Nahum D. Chandler demonstrates greater patience with Du Bois' terms than Radhakrishnan does and perhaps for this reason sees in double consciousness a more productively fluid imagining of black American identity as critical practice rather than mere positionality. Where Radhakrishnan ultimately finds that Du Bois remains entangled in the "either/or" logic of American "race" ideology, Chandler discerns a multiply-strategic thrust in Du Bois' not relinquishing *either the intertwining or the disjunctive force* in the term 'Negro American.' Its reverberations open a zone within which the subject of this history might generate unpredictable cultural accountings of the lived conditions of its emergence – and also, crucially, forestalls the power of "whiteness" to project itself as the normative measure of "wholeness" or coherence by which to assess all "other":

> For Du Bois ... the difficulty of this double reference did not mean that the Negro should reject one term or aspect of its identification for another. Rather, this doubling was the very future or possibility of its becoming. It marked out the very space and possibility of desire and the future ... one can be both a Negro and an American. It confounds the ultimate premise of racial distinction, a categorical or oppositional logic of distinction or identification. On the other hand, it affirms a difference as operative in America, one that Du Bois, perhaps strategically, perhaps anachronistically (and perhaps not), names as "African."[20]

By absorbing as fact the hegemonic imposition of racialism, and somehow processing, without memorializing, the centrality to "white" self-conception of the image of black animality, "Negro American," as Chandler hears Du Bois, would then open the "space and possibility of desire and the future" that Amiri Baraka (then LeRoi Jones) in 1963 recognizes as the simultaneously null and generative "no man's land," in which black people in America "had to make use of other resources, whether African, subcultural or hermetic ... that provided the logic and beauty of (their) music."[21]

Music enables the anonymous protagonist of James Weldon Johnson's *Autobiography of an Ex-Colored Man* (1913) to learn sooner than does Du Bois' John Jones that the play of aesthetic forms can momentarily disjoin the rigid matrix of racialist constraint. In piano study with his mother, he discovers a "fondness" for the "strange harmonies" produced when he finds his hands gravitating toward the black keys and is no less enthralled when, in the course of learning to read with his tutor, he would, from the basis of illustrations in his texts, frequently improvise entire paragraphs of spontaneous fiction whenever he encountered "difficult or unfamiliar" words on the actual page.[22] His musical and linguistic talents enable his continual sidestepping of any pocket of definitional stasis, as the lightness of his skin provides the means by which he is able to crystallize privately the "either/or" absurdity of "race" and deconstruct the ideological bases of its elaboration – but he never takes the risk of doing so publicly, and this aversion hollows out his sense of self-value.

While the new wave of black writing plays out the increasingly familiar modernist protocols of self-attentiveness, dissonance, multiplicity, and self-dissolve, its texts are at the same time underscored by a material threat of pure and arbitrary violence that differentiates them from other modernist traditions. By way of example, in "Kabnis," the concluding section of Jean Toomer's *Cane* (1923), the scene of reading is disrupted by a fall back into a prior textuality that anticipates – indeed, that installs – the unease that the book is supposed to calm or stabilize:

> Ralph Kabnis, propped in his bed tries to read. ... The walls, unpainted are seasoned a rosin yellow. And cracks between the boards are black. These cracks are the lips the night winds use for whispering. Night winds in Georgia are vagrant poets, whispering. Kabnis, against his will, lets his book slip down, and listens to them. The warm whiteness of his bed, the lamp-light, do not protect him from the weird chill of their song:
>
> > White-man's land
> > Niggers, sing
> > Burn, bear black children
> > Till poor rivers bring
> > Rest, and sweet glory
> > In Camp Ground.

Never does Kabnis realize the totality of his immersion within, or penetration by, another text he does not choose, this being the poetry of the night winds engulfing him and overtaking the book. "Vagrant poets" of vanished origin who derive their haunting powers of inhabitation precisely by way of their insubstantiality, the text of night wind displaces the actual text in Kabnis' hands, propelled by its own displacement, which is its own becoming. Ralph's having to divide himself in order to compose himself, having to focus elsewhere – on his chosen text – in order to unify himself in peaceful sleep, is only the first element of a modernist equation in which, once again, whatever is inside develops as a function of what is outside. The equation is repeated when his project of reading is permeated by the wind's poetry whistling through the cracks of his walls and his senses. Its "night song" breaks the imagined consistency of Kabnis' book with the incommensurability of its own elusive whisperings, warping his pursuit of meaning and stability into a scene of racialized anxiety. Such emphasis upon the vivifying (as opposed to representational) dimension of poetic black American prose will probably not reappear until the fiction of Henry Dumas emerges in the

1960s and the experimental series of epistolary music novels of Nathaniel Mackey begin in the late 1970s. These explorative qualities can be discerned in the drifting tonalities of another of their modernist precursors, Richard Bruce Nugent:

> ... he wondered why he couldn't find work ... a job ... when he had first come to New York he had ... and he had only been fourteen then ... was it because he was nineteen now that he felt so idle ... and contented ... he should be ashamed that he didn't work ... but ... was it five years in New York ... or the fact that he was an artist ... when his mother said she couldn't understand him ... why did he vaguely pity her instead of being ashamed ... he ... Alex ... was content to lay and smoke and meet friends at night ... to argue and read Wilde ... Freud ... Boccacio and Schnitzler ... to attend Gurdjieff meetings and know things ... Why did they scoff at him for knowing such people as Carl ... Mencken ... Toomer ... Hughes ... Cullen ... Wood ... Cabell ... oh the whole lot of them ...[23]

Alternative materialities – such as mesh the nets of language, imagery, sound, and reference of Nugent's "Smoke, Lilies and Jade" (1926) – also deviate, in languorous and aristocratic indolence, from the imperative of *work* simultaneously structuring the global exploitation of black and brown people at the basis of both transatlantic industrial capitalism *and* of the "New Negro" middle-class discourse of "achievement" and acquisition in the United States. Indeed, the image of "New Negro" elitism and stiffly starched sobriety, by which both Du Bois and Alain Locke (editor of the influential *The New Negro*) are openly caricatured in the unsparingly brilliant satire *Black No More* (1931) by George S. Schuyler and Wallace Thurman's *Infants of the Spring* (1932), respectively. Whatever "decadence" may drive Nugent's experimental narrative, it presents a creative rejoinder to a compensatory cultural strain of sexual repression and social conservatism that Du Bois himself descries in his 1926 essay "Criteria of Negro Art" but then appears to manifest in his vehemently moralistic dismissal of "drunkenness, fighting and sexual promiscuity" in Claude McKay's "nauseating" *Home to Harlem* (1928).[24]

Nugent's Alex – bisexual, aestheticist, gleefully unemployed – is realized in self-suspending "stream of consciousness" prose, emerging as a paradoxical figure of a sequestered and impoverished excess who quietly revels in his profound uselessness to any of the predominant social advocacy organizations or philosophies of the time. His laconic resistance to work is raised nearly to an ethical principle, striking for its being set, unlike either Toomer's or Du Bois' southern rural narratives, in submerged cloisters of the metropole and for its thematic revolving around the urgency of financial survival.

Nugent's text undermines, even as it installs, Alex's seemingly perfected image of modernist detachment and self-regard, rendering it by way of a tweak in the literary lineage on which it is so heavily modeled. Going up in endless ringlets of blue smoke, ensconced in the dark of his apartment, Alex resides in the cordoned interiors and consuming addictions of consumption of Wilde's *Dorian Gray* or Henry Wotton – or of their own paradigmatically "poisonous" influence, Huysmans' Des Esseintes. Unlike those characters, however, Alex actually does produce the work of writing – the ironic difference being that his work results in material poverty while their refusal to work begets more time in which to luxuriate in inherited opulence and do nothing.[25] In the mid-1960s this thrust of self-conscious, writerly indolence will be emptied of its subjectivist pathos and retextured in the jagged, gallows humor of Charles Wright's postmodern narratives of black, bisexual, and dissipatory brilliance between Harlem and Greenwich Village.

Space beyond Place

By now, as is exemplified in Larsen's 1928 novel *Quicksand*, and in Thurman's iconoclastic but far less accomplished *Infants of the Spring*, the problem of doing nothing occupies a central thematic station in black modernist prose. Whereas the onset of the Depression meant that many Americans would be so reduced, the real question, as writers as disparate as Nugent, Thurman, and Larsen pursued it, was of an entirely different order. When Amiri Baraka muses in 1963 that the end of slavery also meant the end of whatever "place" black people had in American society, the formulation also underscores the negative dynamism of socioeconomic non-situatedness as reflective and private space, revisited more explicitly by such writers as Ralph Ellison, Chester Himes, and Charles Wright, among others in the later twentieth century.[26]

Larsen's novel deconstructs the ways in which black "middle class" valorization of such self-denuding of desire and experience aligns smoothly with the logic of capitalist reproduction, organizing a bloodless machine of functionalist uniformity in which black people mindlessly comply with their reduction to cogs. Anticipating Ellison's depiction in *Invisible Man* of southern, all-black, practical education ("shoes shined, minds laced up"), Larsen's preparatory Naxos Institute is her nightmarishly stifling version of Booker T. Washington's "Tuskegee Machine." Her intelligent and attractive Helga Crane quickly leaves her career as a teacher at Naxos but finds life among the Harlem black bourgeoisie too insistently categorical in its varying obsessions with notions of "race" advance and "uplift" ideology. The daughter of a black American father and a Danish mother, she sails to Denmark to find refuge with relatives. She momentarily senses a freedom from racialized social horizons – only to realize belatedly that she is tolerated as a figure of black sexual exotica whose critical intelligence again constitutes an unacceptable social excess. She comes to find Europe culturally cold, bloodless, and nearly impenetrable, producing in her a degree of nostalgia for the vitality and expressivity of Harlem – the racially circumscribed limits of which so frustrated her in the first place.[27]

> No. She couldn't stay. Nor, she saw now, could she remain away. Leaving, she would have to come back. (96)

This doubly suspended prolepsis, this continual need to flex or move elsewhere is only another iteration of black modernism's agitated disposition toward the terminal character of station in any sociogeographic "place" structured by Euro-capitalist cultural imperatives always already stratified by racialism.

While Larsen's Helga is crushed by the gradual realization that there is no real place in such a sphere for the work or thinking of a black woman, McKay's black international "beachcombers, guides, procurers, prostitutes of both sexes and bistro bandits – all of motley-making Marseilles"[28] find in their social disposability a different horizon of self-contour. Note the sharpness of the difference when McKay's intellectual drifter, Ray, reflects on what might be gained from his association with this improbable lot.

> Ray loved to be with them in constant physical contact. . . . He loved their tricks of language, loved to pick up and feel and taste new words from their rich reservoir of niggerisms . . . he admired the black boys' unconscious artistic capacity for eliminating the rotten-dead stock words of the proletariat and replacing them with startling new ones. . . . He gained from them finer nuances of the necromancy of language and the wisdom that any word may be right and magical in its proper setting.[29]

In such passages, McKay doesn't merely thematize the oscillating distance between Ray's existence and his changing grasp of it – rather, the text's structuring oppositions (which anticipate McKay's critical distinction between Lawrentian and Joycean modernisms) of the primitive to the reflective, the instinctual to the learned, the earthy/sensuous to the cold and theoretical are frequently shown to inform and therefore destabilize the presumptive solidity of "each." The "finer nuances of the necromancy of language" and the "magical" effect of the felicitous word or phrase only underscores the reality of language *as* a formalized discipline to be learned before it can be freely mobilized, the apparently instinctive spontaneity of his counterparts' quicksilver verbal improvisations only the outcome of an antecedent "internalization of a repertoire," as Nathaniel Mackey would designate it, the acutely self-conscious movement of study and experimentation similar to that practiced both musically and linguistically by J.W. Johnson's "ex-colored man" in youth.[30] The paradox, of course, lies in the superfluity of these "colored rogues and vagabonds" to the European society at whose fringe they live – in the capacity of this "internationalism of the defective: the unregistered, the undocumented, the untracked – an ab-nationalism, as it were, of all the Doubtful," as Edwards terms it, to draw greatest strength precisely from their inability "to fit into the grooves of the machines that would work them, above all traveling, elusive, moving on."[31]

Perhaps nowhere so vibrantly or so dissonantly among our considered modernists are both the brutalistic and regenerative aspects of double consciousness worked out with the kind of rhetorical muscularity that structures Zora Neale Hurston's *Their Eyes Were Watching God* (1937). In the cosmogonic reconstruction of a swiftly receding cultural history of similarly "untracked" people, the revisionist perspective of Janie Crawford projects images, ideas, and sounds of black worlds built and sustained in exclusion from the industrial modernity their raw labor had helped produce – even as that modernity imprints itself on them (evidenced by Joe Starks' rapid consolidation of local capital and power).[32] The psychic resourcefulness of Hurston's Janie, who endures largely through a continual relinquishing of idealist constructions of permanence and by making practical use of available forms and materials, presents an aesthetic advance on related themes in *Banjo* and a conceptual alternative to Larsen's ideological critique. The novel unfolds from the perspective of a protagonist who survives and theorizes cultural violence – particularly in its sexual, racialist, and positivist/representational registers – instead of from one who is shut down by them.

Thematizing in order to more thoroughly abandon the principle of subjectivist reconstruction central to Hurston's negotiation of black cultural obliteration, the mid-century novels of Ralph Ellison and Chester Himes explode the boundaries of a double-consciousness model evidently conceived too narrowly to engage a postwar, commercial grid of urban modernity whose triumphalist mediatic discourses of its own necessity to the world are now disseminated and consumed at unprecedented speeds. For the protagonists of Ellison's and Himes' novels, the ungraspability of the spiritual abundance and peace pictured in Hurston's conclusion is made all the more infuriating because it is promised in so many commodity forms from so many material angles of existence – and the competition is fierce. Whereas the novels of each writer unfold biting analyses of U.S. consumerist ideology, their wartime essays reflect not only critical outrage at the gap between American popular rhetorics of democracy mobilized against totalitarian regimes in Europe and the ongoing daily American practices of antiblack segregation, but also occasion intensified renewal of earlier calls from such figures as Du Bois and Langston Hughes for clearer recognition of the global implicatedness of U.S. black radicalism in the organization of insurrection against Euro-colonialist exploitation.[33] Singh writes:

> Rather than assume an uncomplicated standpoint of national unity, black activists used racial division as an interpretive lens upon broader problems of nationality and world order. The war thus sharpened the dialectic of race and nation – color and democracy – as U.S. blacks viewed their own struggles, in Himes' words, as "the very essence of the fight for freedom of all the peoples of all the world."[34]

In the final wave of black American prose modernism, the question becomes one of a liquefied psychic apparatus infused and dispersed by racialist and commercialist pressures. Himes' first three novels, *If He Hollers, Let Him Go* (1945), *Lonely Crusade* (1947), and *The End of a Primitive* (1952), and Ellison's 1952 masterpiece, *Invisible Man*, animate the oscillatory play of internalization and redistribution of these anxieties. This passage is from the opening of *If He Hollers*:

> But I began feeling scared in spite of hiding from the day. It came along with consciousness. It came into my head first, somewhere back of my closed eyes, moved slowly underneath my skull to the base of my brain. It seeped down my spine, into my arms, spread through my groin with an almost sexual torture, settled in my stomach like butterfly wings. For a moment, I felt torn all loose inside, shrivelled, paralysed, as if after a while I'd have to get up and die.[35]

Meanwhile, this is from *Invisible Man*:

> He was a broad man, a man of parts who got around. Rinehart the rounder. . . . His world was possibility and he knew it . . . the world in which we lived was without boundaries. A vast seething, hot world of fluidity, and Rine the rascal was at home.[36]

These are different literary responses to the same orders of pathology that Radhakrishnan identifies as having set the machinery of black American double consciousness into motion. Himes' protagonist Bob Jones – young, fit, and acutely perceptive – is also under physical occupation by a wartime Los Angeles strain of this insistent racialist pathogen. Jones' electrified consciousness is so saturated by the fear and paranoia that are his only defenses against the concrete antagonisms awaiting him in the social that such encounters inhabit and organize his dreams. He sees racism in his sleep – and it looks suspiciously like the racism he endures when he's awake – which suggests that either he doesn't really sleep or that the racism never really stops. He doesn't. It doesn't. His inability to secure external corroboration of his experience or to find allies in challenging this normative field of social violence intensifies an already impressively schooled cynicism.

But Ellison's young counterpart to Bob Jones finds in the street hustler Rinehart a fluid model of subversion by which to at least momentarily disrupt the entire field of accepted power relations. While it's hardly likely that Rinehart entertains intentions any more politically revolutionary than do Claude McKay's Marseille vagabonds, what the Invisible Man realizes (and wants to repress) is that Rinehart may well be the ideal insurrectionist, precisely because he is in such rhythm with the instrumentalist dimension of the ideological networks of relations that organize what we call "everyday life." He appears to have no interest in troubling that matrix, but only in exploiting for his own unnamed purposes the internal relations of desire by which it is structured. What he opens for Invisible Man is a new and discomfiting vantage point from which to assess the structure and how to reenter its frame as differential rather than repetition.

The open conclusions of each novel lead us into reconsideration of what black modernisms foreground as the essential absurdity of a "place" for black people in U.S. civil society after enslavement. The works considered here explore the reflective space in which blackness exceeds the methodologies by which most American representational and scholarly apparatuses would historicize or even comprehend it. Du Bois' *Black Reconstruction* articulates not only the necessity of exposing the impoverishment of such standardized flattenings,[37] but of creating conceptual languages by which to attune critically to the discarded forms vivifying the cultures. Throughout the second half of the century, such explorative literature would be generated by a host of accomplished Afro-diasporic writers and poets, including Mackey, Wilson Harris, Kamau Brathwaite, Gayl Jones, Toni Morrison, and John E. Wideman, each of whom has imagined differently an irreconcilable sense of connectedness to devastated African social space – realizations of which are recast in their works as a channel of psychic, intellectual, and aesthetic genesis.

NOTES

1. Wilson J. Moses, *Afrotopia: The Roots of African American Popular History* (Cambridge: Cambridge University Press 1998), 149. To consider a few of the more sustained and influential analytic exceptions to the "routine" I mark here, see Bernard W. Bell, "Genealogical Shifts in Du Bois' Discourse on Double Consciousness as the Sign of African American Difference," in *W.E.B. Du Bois on Race and Culture*, ed. Bernard W. Bell, Emily R. Grosholz, and James B. Stewart (New York: Routledge, 1996), 87–108; Ronald A.T. Judy, "The New

Black Aesthetic and W.E.B. Du Bois, or Hephaestus, Limping," *Massachusetts Review* 35, no. 2 (Summer 1994): 249–282; Robert Gooding-Williams, *In the Shadow of Du Bois: Afro-Modern Political Thought in America* (Cambridge: Harvard University Press, 2009), 66–129; R. Radhakrishnan, "Race and Double-Consciousness," *Works and Days* 47/48 24, nos. 1–2 (2006): 45–67; Günter Lenz, "Radical Cosmopolitanism: W.E.B. Du Bois, Germany, and African American Pragmatist Visions for Twenty-First Century Europe," *Journal of Transnational American Studies* 4, no. 2 (2012): 65–96; Arnold Rampersad, *The Art and Imagination of W.E.B Du Bois* (Cambridge: Harvard University Press, 1976); Adolph L. Reed Jr., *W.E.B. Du Bois and American Political Thought: Fabianism and the Color Line* (New York: Oxford University Press, 1997), 91–125; Eric Sundquist, *To Wake the Nations: Race in the Making of American Literature* (Cambridge: Harvard University Press, 1993); Paul Gilroy, *The Black Atlantic: Modernity and Double Consciousness* (Cambridge: Harvard University Press, 1993); and Nahum D. Chandler, *X – The Problem of the Negro as a Problem for Thought* (New York: Fordham University Press, 2014).

2. See Walter Mignolo's *The Darker Side of Western Modernity: Global Futures, Decolonial Options* (Durham: Duke University Press, 2011).

3. See Eric Williams, *Capitalism and Slavery* (1944; Chapel Hill: University of North Carolina Press, 1994).

4. See Enrique Dussel, *Invention of the Americas: Eclipse of "the Other" and the Myth of Modernity*, trans. Michael Barber (New York: Continuum, 1995), and *Ethics of Liberation: In the Age of Globalization and Exclusion*, trans. E. Mendieta, ed. Alejandro Vallega (Durham: Duke University Press, 2013); Mignolo, *Darker Side*; Walter Rodney, *How Europe Underdeveloped Africa* (Washington DC, Howard University Press, 1974); Eduardo Galeano, *Open Veins of Latin America: Five Centuries of the Pillage of a Continent*, trans. Cedric Belfrage (1997; New York: Monthly Review Press, 1973); Jacob Pandian, *Anthropology and the Western Tradition: Towards an Authentic Anthropology* (Prospect Heights: Waveland Press, 1985); Aníbal Quijano, "Questioning 'Race,'" *Socialism and Democracy* 21, no. 1 (March 2007): 45–53.

5. Sylvia Wynter, "Unsettling the Coloniality of Being/Power/Truth/Freedom: Towards the Human, after Man, Its Overrepresentation – An Argument," *New Centennial Review* 3, no. 3 (2003): 265.

6. Wahneema Lubiano, "Shuckin' Off the African-American Native Other: What's 'Po-Mo' Got to Do with It," *Cultural Critique* 18 (Spring 1991): 160.

7. Claude McKay, *A Long Way from Home* (1937; New Brunswick: Rutgers University Press, 2007), 190

8. Ibid, 189.

9. Édouard Glissant, *Caribbean Discourse*, trans. J. Michael Dash (Charlottesville: University Press of Virginia, 1989), 147–148.

10. Manthia Diawara, "Édouard Glissant in Conversation with Manthia Diawara," trans. Christopher Winks, *Nka: Journal of Contemporary African Art* 28 (2011): 4–19.

11. W.E.B. Du Bois, *Black Reconstruction in America* (1935; New York: Free Press, 1998), 15–16. See also Karl Marx, "Marx to Annenkov, December 28, 1846," *Collected Works, Volume 38* (New York: Progress Publishers, 1982), 101–102.

12. This emphasis is intensified by Judy, "New Black Aesthetic," 256.
13. Du Bois, *Black Reconstruction*, 14.
14. Cedric Robinson, *Black Marxism: The Making of the Black Radical Tradition* (Chapel Hill: University of North Carolina Press, 1983), 240.
15. Du Bois, *Black Reconstruction*, 121.
16. Nikhil Pal Singh, *Black Is a Country: Race and the Unfinished Struggle for Democracy* (Cambridge: Harvard University Press, 2004), 95–96.
17. Radhakrishnan, "Race and Double-Consciousness," 46.
18. Ibid., 59.
19. Judy, "The New Black Aesthetic," 255.
20. Chandler, "Originary Displacement," *boundary 2* 27, no. 3 (Fall 2000): 274–275.
21. LeRoi Jones (Amiri Baraka), *Blues People: Negro Music in America* (New York: Harper Perennial, 1963), 80.
22. James W. Johnson, *The Autobiography of an Ex-Colored Man* (1912; New York: Vintage, 1989), 8.
23. Richard Bruce [Nugent], "Smoke, Lilies and Jade," *Fire!!* 1, no. 1 (1926): 34. I am grateful to Julie Herrada, curator, Joseph A. Labadie Collection at the University of Michigan Library, for assistance with this citation.
24. W.E.B. Du Bois, "Two Novels," *Crisis* 35 (June 1928): 202
25. For a nice gloss on smoking and commodity consumption in relation to Nugent and Wilde, see Elisa Glick, "Harlem's Queer Dandy: African American Modernism and the Artifice of Blackness," *Modern Fiction Studies* 49, no. 3 (2003): 422.
26. Baraka, *Blues People*, 55.
27. See Patricia E. Chu, *Race, Nationalism and the State in British and American Modernism* (Cambridge: Cambridge University Press 2006), 164–165. Chu saliently notes Larsen's conscious juxtaposing of dissatisfactions with both European- and American-inscribed models of public "blackness," pinpointing not only *Quicksand*'s disparagement of what it presents as a particularly pathetic black mode of American "patriotism," but seeing in this aspect of the novel a strong presaging of more-vituperative critique of such stances in the wartime context of Himes' *If He Hollers Let Him Go*.
28. McKay, *A Long Way from Home*, 277.
29. McKay, *Banjo: A Story without a Plot* (1929; New York: Harcourt Brace, 1957), 321.
30. Nathaniel Mackey, *Paracritical Hinge: Essays, Talks, Notes, Interviews* (Madison: University of Wisconsin Press, 2005), 280.
31. Brent Hayes Edwards, *The Practice of Diaspora: Literature, Translation, and the Rise of Black Internationalism* (Cambridge: Harvard University Press, 2003), 239.
32. Zora Neale Hurston, *Their Eyes Were Watching God* (New York: Harper Perennial, 1998).
33. For a fascinating discussion of Du Bois' evident reticence on the question of the Spanish Civil War, fought during his writing and publication of *Black Reconstruction*, see Kathyrne Lindberg, "W.E.B. Du Bois's *Dusk of Dawn* and James Yates's *Mississippi to Madrid*, Or 'What Goes Around Comes Around and Around and Around' in Autobiography," *Massachusetts Review* 35, no. 2 (Summer 1994): 283–309.

34. Singh, 108. For more-exclusive concentration on Himes' challenges to the racial hypocrisy of wartime American rhetorics of democracy, see Justus Nieland, "Everybody's Noir Humanism: Chester Himes, *Lonely Crusade*, and the Quality of Hurt," *African American Review* 43, nos. 2–3 (Summer/Fall 2009): 277–293.
35. Chester Himes, *If He Hollers Let Him Go* (New York: Thunder's Mouth, 1986), 2.
36. Ralph Ellison, *Invisible Man*, 498.
37. Du Bois, *Black Reconstruction*; see both the concluding chapter, "The Propaganda of History," and the annotated bibliography to the text, 711–739.

PART II

Methodologies

6

YOGITA GOYAL

Gender and Geomodernisms

Although the when, what, and why of modernism has been long debated, recent accounts of the new modernist studies have especially emphasized the *where*, highlighting both place and space as key organizing rubrics for opening up a conventional modernist canon. For Douglas Mao and Rebecca Walkowitz, if there was a single word that could sum up the critical transformation of the field over the last few decades, it would be *expansion*.[1] Rethinking modernism expansively proceeds along three distinct lines. First, scholars reconsider periodization, expanding modernism forward temporally into the late twentieth century and beyond, but also unsettling conventional notions of time and historicity to offer new understandings of modernity itself.[2] Next, the genealogies of modernism are themselves expanding as modernist writing is seen as emerging not fully formed from isolated genius but as part of larger currents of circulation and exchange. Empire, nation, and race thus become central frames for understanding modernist aesthetics and politics, in contrast to older notions of solipsistic or self-contained artists. Whereas themes of exile and expatriation have always been central to the study of modernism, new approaches expand on these themes to explore how modernist writers imagine and represent other worlds in relation to their own, and how tangled lines of connection and disjuncture, locality and global flows, movement and stasis assume form in different places and situations. Finally, the expansion of modernist studies positions it in dialogue – some would say belatedly so – with such fields as postcolonial studies. At least since the early 1990s, following the pioneering scholarship of Edward Said, Fredric Jameson, Paul Gilroy, and Amy Kaplan, questions of empire have become central to discussions of modernism's formal and material praxis.[3]

Relocating Modernism

Coining the term *geomodernisms* to signify place, position, and perspective, Laura Doyle and Laura Winkiel insist that modernism must be understood as truly global, interconnected, worldly, and locational. For them, any under-standing of modernism must inevitably engage with race and place, as what was once thought local turns out to be not only proximate to transnational forces, but indeed constituted by them, because various kinds of modernisms are "made from the *outside in*."[4] Undoing the elitism and ethnocentrism of earlier accounts, geomodernism seeks to broaden the modernist archive, rethinking established canons and including a variety of alternative tradi-tions. Stressing the centrality of circulation and translation in transnational print cultures, geomodernist scholarship explores how modernist writers responded to imperialism and anticolonialism and produced new models of community, modernity, and tradition. Such reconsiderations call for new approaches to space and time, as well as genre and aesthetics, which remain neither native nor exceptional to the United States, but rather born in Atlantic crossings of the slave trade, border modernization projects, or fantasmatic accounts of travel to Asia and Africa.

Part of a wider transnational turn in literary studies, such rethinking illumi-nates the formative role of place in such resonant sites as Willa Cather's New Mexico or Henry James' Europe. It also enables new forms of comparative study, exploring the representation of Haiti in writers as diverse as Zora Neale Hurston and Langston Hughes, or of Paris in Gertrude Stein, Djuna Barnes, and Richard Wright, or Spain in Ernest Hemingway, Hughes, and Wright. William Faulkner is no longer read just for race and region, but as an essential part of a redefined Caribbean frontier, as Édouard Glissant proposes.[5] The relation between genre and nation changes as well when Latin American novelists reinvent James Fenimore Cooper's national romances or when T.S. Eliot turns to India to shore up the ruins of Western civilization. Wai Chee Dimock similarly emphasizes interdependencies between the local and the distant, advocating a planetary perspective that links Asian, Caribbean, and American texts through what she terms "deep time." In Emerson, Dimock shows – through Goethe in eighteenth-century Germany – we find fourteenth-century Persia in Hafiz as each adaptation recreates and proliferates meaning rather than signaling influence or derivation.[6] Instead of tracing borrowings from one context or writer to another, such efforts demonstrate how multiple modernisms exist in a matrix, cross-pollinating each other, with no one formal or ideological note as the dominant one.

Perhaps the first question such perspectives may beg is how conventional notions of modernism as primarily concerned with individual freedom and formal experimentation might be squared with the new emphasis on geopo-litics. Certainly, one of the tasks of the new scholarship is to relate global currents of empire, war, revolution, and resistance to such truisms about modernist fiction as its reconfiguration of time and perspective. In shifting away from omniscient narration and realist construction of familiar worlds, much modernist fiction not only raises questions about how we know what we know, but also shows that such knowledge is incomplete, distorted, and shifting. Although this type of experimentation was once seen as a withdrawal from history and politics, such a binary between aesthetics and ideology is now being dismantled. Repetition, return, or the recursivity of time signals not the disavowal of trauma, but its haunting presence and formal experimentation can be tied to a text's negotiation of history rather than its disavowal. The rethinking of time and space that geomodernism calls for thus offers both formalist and historicist benefits, offering ways to place the two approaches in dialogue, as I suggest below in my discussion of Pauline Hopkins, W.E.B. Du Bois, and Rabindranath Tagore. Rather than viewing modernism as a revolt against realism and romanticism or a self-conscious and introspective exploration of paradox and ambiguity, thinking of modernism as a form characterized by crisis (as Michael Levenson urges) or as centrally concerned with resistance and revolution more clearly situates the contributions of gender and geomodernisms.[7]

Since the last decade of the nineteenth century, as women across the world entered the workplace, agitated for voting rights, and transformed the spaces of cities, the figure of the "New Woman" acquired greater prominence in the novel. The decades of high modernism (1890–1920) were also the heyday of first-wave feminism and the rise of the women's suffrage movement. Such changes in gender relations helped pave the way for the emergence of modernism as the independent, educated, sexually liberated New Woman sought to intervene in the public sphere of nation and empire. Recent scholarship has highlighted how travel shaped the writing of such authors as Gertrude Stein, Djuna Barnes, Nella Larsen, and Zora Neale Hurston, expanding the exclusionary canon of male writers. Andreas Huyssen has influentially shown how a modernist canon was produced by gendering mass culture as feminine.[8] Many of the key symbols of the modern – the dandy, the new woman, the flapper, the vamp, or the flaneur – are clearly gendered and linked to the rise of consumer culture. As Rita Felski demonstrates, woman as sign can indicate a sphere of authenticity untouched by modern alienation, limited to the private domain of home, safe from the contamination of the public sphere. A "striving, competitive masculinity and a nurturant, domestic femininity" serve to create rigid boundaries between public and private worlds.[9] But as consumer culture gained more prominence, women began to be more firmly linked to the contaminated figure of consumption and uncontrolled desire, easily seduced by commercialism and materialism. As consumers and producers of lowbrow or genre fiction, given to sentimentality, melodrama, and romance, women writers could not be thought of as objective, ironic,

self-conscious aesthetic practitioners. Domesticity thus emerges as a contested site of negotiations of gender and of meanings of home and the
world. Stein was famously enamored of domestic objects, as she reimagined
ordinary objects such as tables and chairs, cups and saucers, and food items
such as eggs, coffee, and sugar in *Tender Buttons* (1913), thus fusing the
domestic with the experimental. She also reconceives domesticity itself in
The Autobiography of Alice B. Toklas (1932), channeling the words of her
domestic partner. When domestic space is rendered female and the city
provides a refuge from its suffocation, or when black women writers such
as Pauline Hopkins reimagine domestic fiction, fusing it with the novel of
ideas, as well as the imperial adventure tale, the terrains of gender and
geomodernism take shape.

Not only does gender shape modernism through the visible figures of the
New Woman, it also shapes our understanding of modernist form and genre
itself, because the style of modernism has conventionally been seen as masculine, with an emphasis on difficulty, experimentation, objectivity, and rationality. In contrast, much of women's writing and female characters in fiction
appear in the form of excessive figures, as Felski argues – as the hysteric or the
uncontrolled shopper, the prostitute, or the pervert. To problematize the
conventional distinction between an experimental masculine avant-garde
and a purportedly regressive feminized mass culture, scholars have had to
break down the barriers between high art and popular culture, and direct
serious attention to such degraded genres as popular romance, melodrama,
and sentimental fiction to mine their participation in the cultural, scientific,
and economic ideologies of the day, ranging from eugenics to the new
psychology.[10]

Numerous feminist critics of nationalist discourses have shown how
women are coded as the static carriers of a conservative culture and charged
with the task of preserving tradition in the name of difference. In the postcolonial context, Partha Chatterjee's formulation of nationalism's enabling
division between the home and the world – the former imagined as feminine,
spiritual, and indigenous, the latter its opposite – has been seen as widely
applicable to any number of historical and cultural contexts.[11] Notions of
feminist time and queer time seek to challenge narratives of linear progression, thus also asking for a change in conventional notions of generations and
genealogies evident in the conception of waves of feminism (first wave,
second wave, and so on).[12] In contrast to older concepts of a global sister-
hood, newer frames of transnational feminism emphasize the historical and
continuing impact of imperialism, showing how there is no feminism free of
asymmetrical power or structural inequality. If geomodernism signals a
geopolitical approach, influential critiques of white liberal feminist erasure

of native women by postcolonial feminists Gayatri Spivak and Chandra Mohanty become newly relevant.[13] The geopolitics of war, migration, and terror cannot be understood without attention to gender, as theories of sexuality, corporeality, and intimacy complicate the analysis of the national and the global. Feminist critiques of nationalism, as well as gendered constructions of the foreign, emphasize the intersectionality of race and nation, gender and sexuality, region and class.

Domesticity, Empire, and Genre in Pauline Hopkins

For such rethinking along the lines of gender and geomodernism, the work of Pauline Hopkins offers a remarkable instance. As a writer preceding the more familiar New Negro modernism of Nella Larsen and Zora Neale Hurston, Hopkins bridges the transition between a genteel Victorian tradition to a more complex modernism precisely by drawing on and reformulating imperial ideologies. While her tragic heroines do not offer anything like Larsen's Clare Kendry of *Passing* – a cosmopolitan, nonmaternal woman, "without any proper morals or sense of duty," who can easily slip in and out of a racialized identity – Hopkins also reveals that race is a performance, tied to mobility and geography. She makes it difficult to think race, nation, and gender outside of empire, as seemingly domestic accounts of racial uplift turn out to be firmly entangled with, indeed constituted by, what seems to be their polar opposite: African emigration. Hopkins thus forces a recognition of the mutual constitution of the national and the transnational, rather than an opposition between them. It has not made sense, for a while now, to separate out American from ethnic modernism. Although Henry Louis Gates Jr. and Houston Baker define an autonomous African American literary tradition, recent work has seen the story as more contaminated, more mixed. Geomodernism further layers these debates, because nationalism itself must be seen as constitutively calibrated by both gender and empire. As Kaplan argues, "imperialism does not emanate from the solid center of a fully formed nation; rather, the meaning of the nation itself is both questioned and redefined through the outward reach of empire."[14]

Hopkins has long been celebrated for her powerful focus on the racist violence of lynching and rape, her feminist excavation of maternal genealogies of slavery, and her unsettling of race through fictions of passing. Although she was once dismissed for writing domestic fictions that were just Victorian love stories in blackface, the revisionist criticism of Claudia Tate and Hazel Carby showed that such romances must be read as a studied intervention in the racial conflicts characterizing the post-Reconstruction era.[15] For Tate, the seemingly formulaic use of melodramatic pairs of good and evil, chaste and fallen inscribe the longing for civic order and racial justice through portraits of genteel domesticity. Plots of reunion and estrangement, lost inheritances, and children switched at birth function not just as a nod to sensationalism but as productive of new allegories of the nation as racially hybrid, showing that the domestic is invariably political and that it also carries radically destabilizing potential for narratives of the nation. Reading Hopkins as a geomodernist reveals how she exposes the incoherencies that link together race and gender, nation and empire even if narrative experimentation is not explicit but instead lies beneath the surface.

In *Of One Blood: Or, the Hidden Self* (1902–1903), Hopkins collides the domestic discourse of racial uplift with the diasporic one of Back-to-Africa movements as the novel abruptly splits between two seemingly antithetical genres: sentimental fiction and imperial romance.[16] While earlier novels such as *Contending Forces* (1900), *Winona* (1902), and *Hagar's Daughter* (1901–1902) gesture toward a more inclusive vision of a segregated nation by drawing on the familiar literary trope of the tragic mulatto/mulatta, who stages within a single body the contradictions that plague the body politic at large, *Of One Blood* takes a gothic turn to figure such intermingling as a gruesome incestuous drama, recurring across multiple generations in the form of flashbacks, interpolated tales, and repetition in its plot. The three main characters – Reuel Briggs, the melancholic hero, passing as white, his wife, Dianthe Lusk, unconsciously passing as white, and a villainous white southerner, Aubrey Livingstone – are literally of one blood, born of the same slave master and his female slave. However excessive, such a plot is still recognizable within the script of New Negro modernism, where narratives of passing convey fragmentation, alienation, and liminality. But the novel takes a detour to Africa, seemingly hearkening back to an imperial rather than modern imagining, as Reuel joins a British archaeological expedition in search of ancient Ethiopian cities. The expedition fulfills an important socio-logical function – proving that classical Greek culture was itself derived from Egypt and Ethiopia, which are themselves shown to be distinctly black civilizations – and Reuel also stumbles into an ancient subterranean city, where he is recognized as the royal heir of legend, Ergamenes, the Messiah whose arrival the city has awaited for centuries. As the plot of the novel moves outward, to Africa and beyond, the texture of its New Negro modernism also changes: empire becomes a necessary, albeit unstable, prop to the ideologies of race, gender, and miscegenation.

This aspect is important to recognize because *Of One Blood* differs significantly from Hopkins' earlier impassioned advocacy of equal rights in the United States. Not only is *Of One Blood* one of the first African American novels to be set on African soil and to feature African characters, it also seemingly embeds Africa as homeland for the African American protagonists, far in advance of later efforts to do so, whether in Marcus Garvey's Back-to-Africa movement or mid-twentieth-century emigration to Africa to help in the mission of decolonization. This is why scholars have championed the novel as diasporic or Pan-African, but a closer look at the novel's representation of Africa reveals that it imagines the diasporic realm with the same logic of reproductive determinism that it unravels in the domestic realm. That is to say, the mythical underground city is not a real homeland, but a grave or "magnificent Necropolis."[17] It is thus fitting that the novel ends with a prophecy of a "dark-skinned" (570) dynasty, jettisoning Hopkins' usual argument for the acceptance of racial mixture. Advocating a separatist logic of black nationalism, the novel equates the failure of the romance plot with the failure of the United States to provide a home for Hopkins' mixed-race characters and substitutes the failed domestic romance with the successful union of its light-skinned hero and a virgin African queen, Candace, in the hidden African city of Meroe. It thus shows how race, nation, gender, and empire are invariably mixed up and that the legacy of American slavery and miscegenation cannot be assessed without a turn to Africa.

As Hopkins sutures together uplift and emigration, race mixture and hybridity, and the domestic romance and the imperial tale, her representation of Africa echoes the period's imperial romances by such European writers as H. Rider Haggard, Robert Louis Stevenson, and Joseph Conrad, demonstrating imperial tendencies to instrumentalize Africa as a blank space that can resolve American quandaries. Tapping into contemporaneous accounts of archaeological excavations in Africa, as well as the developments in psychology that rendered woman as a dark continent, Hopkins clearly brings together genres associated with distinct traditions – the feminized sentimental novel and the masculine imperial romance – only to dissolve the binary and show how the domestic and the imperial are mutually constitutive.[18] This is why when Reuel enters the hidden city, it reveals to him not difference but intimacy, as "shadowy images of past scenes flitted across his brain like transient reflections of a past perfectly familiar to him" (551). He remembers rather than learns the wisdom of the ancient Ethiopians, instantiating Hopkins' belief in the existence of an essential racial soul that survives slavery and reemerges in the hidden city of Meroe. Reminiscent of Conrad's *Heart of Darkness*, though inverted to assert African superiority, Hopkins' Africa becomes the staging ground for reclaiming Reuel's mulatto body from the shame associated with black blood and repositioning it as heir to a glorious lineage of kings. Such a conclusion reframes Reuel's earlier experiments at Harvard with hypnosis and trance states, showing that "the dead [may be] brought back to life" and the racial unconscious of the tragic mulatto may be revived, because "life may be recalled when it has become entirely extinct" (467, 468). Hopkins turns to the genre of imperial romance to present Africa as the buried self of her characters, as the journey into the depths of one's own subconscious maps onto the imperial exploration and discovery of unknown worlds.

In doing so, Hopkins suggests that the forbidding exterior of Africa masks an illustrious history and potentiality, inviting her readers to claim a heritage that speaks of an exotic antiquity rather than a commonplace modernity. But to do so, she has to echo the readily available tendencies of her age, which could acknowledge Africa as the origin of humanity, but only by distancing it from modernity itself. This is why Hopkins' Africa remains mystical and supernatural, where specificities of time and place melt away. In part, this is the effect of the generic shift from domestic sentimental melodrama to imperial adventure fiction, as descriptions of leopards, lions, snakes, hidden treasures, and subservient natives abound. But this is also an effect of Hopkins' occlusion of contemporary Africa altogether. As Prime Minister Ai explains, "We are but a remnant, and here we wait behind the protection of our mountains and swamps, secure from the intrusion of a world that has forgotten, for the coming of our king who shall restore to the Ethiopian race its ancient glory" (547). Seeking to escape the brutal failure of the post-Reconstruction era, Talented Tenth intellectuals seek an alternative beyond the American horizon, but end up exporting nostalgic imperial urges along with their diasporic longings. It is precisely these fault lines of Hopkins' novel that are instructive for geomodernism; the novel forces us to recognize the contradictions that attend any quest for a heritage, showing how race writes and unwrites itself variously by location, in Africa and America.

The New Woman in W.E.B. Du Bois and Rabindranath Tagore

Such contradictions were most substantively limned by W.E.B. Du Bois (1868–1963), through his insistence that the "Negro problem" was neither partisan nor provincial but global, as "the problem of the Twentieth Century [was] the problem of the color-line."[19] Du Bois prefigures such currently influential projects as provincializing Europe, defining a Global South, or imagining Afro-Asia, especially in his proleptic 1928 novel, *Dark Princess: A Romance*.[20] This work, which imagines an international council of darker peoples plotting the end of white supremacy, allegorized through a highly embellished romance between an African American member of the Talented Tenth and an Indian princess traveling in Europe and the United States, is often summoned as an exemplar of the global leanings of black modernity, or what Paul Gilroy terms a black Atlantic "counter-culture to modernity."[21] I want to suggest that how we read *Dark Princess* changes if we follow Du Bois' turn to India, in geomodernist fashion, and juxtapose his novel to Nobel Prize–winning poet and philosopher Rabindranath Tagore's (1861–1941) novel *The Home and the World* (1916), an equally foundational account of Indian and Bengali modernity.

Dark Princess stages a whirlwind romance between a New Woman, the princess Kautilya, and a modernist hero, Matthew Towns, who moves through the roles of a medical student hounded by racism, a fashionable exile in Europe as a flaneur, and, following a stint in jail after the lynching of a fellow Pullman porter, a respectable member of the black bourgeoisie. Du Bois thus writes the possible history of a race struggling with modern racism, only to have Matthew walk away from all of these options in favor of an erotic union with the exotic Kautilya and her Council of Darker Races and its aspirations to end global white supremacy. At the novel's core is the relation between love and politics, the private and the public sphere, as the passion for the cause and for the person intertwine to advance solidarity as both an Afrocentric claim (based on race) and an anticolonial one (based on politics).

The Home and the World also has as its protagonist a dark princess of sorts – a dark-skinned woman named Bimala who marries into a princely estate in Bengal. Nikhilesh (Nikhil), her reformist husband, urges her to leave the sphere of the home, the world of *purdah*, evocatively represented by Tagore as a veil, and come out into the world. Sandip, a fiery nationalist, symbolizes the world. The love triangle between the three maps on to political debates about nationalism or universalism, passion or abstraction, symbols or realism, violence or nonviolence. Bimala and Kautilya both serve as figures for India, equally charged by revolutionary enthusiasm for nationalism and serving as emblems of the New Woman.

Both novels represent as inseparable a political consciousness with a sexual awakening – thus offering romance as national allegory, or foundational fiction, as Doris Sommer influentially argues in the Latin American context.[22] Staging the relation between home and world, local and global, and universal and particular, both also probe the meaning of a politics that demands allegory, asking what space exists for the private, for interiority, for "home" as Tagore defines it, for the aesthetic and the erotic, for that which resists simplification or analogy – in other words, for difference, recalcitrance, and incommensurability. In this sense, *The Home and the World* is – to use Claudia Tate's choice phrase – a "domestic allegory of political desire" as much as is *Dark Princess*. Meanwhile, *Dark Princess* is also about the home and the world, as the princess symbolizes the world for Matthew, because Asia is the figure that provincializes U.S. racism.

Much of the criticism that situates *Dark Princess* as the quintessential instance of black Atlantic modernity rests on the novel's conclusion. Gilroy argues that the novel offers a vision of "hybridity and intermixture that is especially valuable" because it ends not with "the fusion of two purified essences but rather a meeting of two heterogeneous multiplicities."[23] In a Marxist reading, Bill Mullen also approves of the ending, arguing that Du Bois "turned further East as he turned deeper Red, and vice versa." But if Du Bois' racial romanticism is taken into account, the novel appears not just as emblematic of black Atlantic hybridity or anticolonial Marxism, but also as a sign of a more complex and conflicted modernism that unevenly navigated the pulls of biology and culture in its definition of race and nation, gender and empire. The novel ends not with revolution, as a precursor to the Afro-Asian alliance imagined by the 1955 Bandung Conference, but an elaborate pageant of the marriage of Matthew and Kautilya that makes no concession to the early twentieth century but hearkens back further, to a mythical Afro-Asian union from antiquity. The wedding moves out of the private sphere as Matthew's southern mother morphs into an Afro-Asian deity and black preachers and high-caste Hindu priests arrive in Virginia to hail the birth of the "Messiah," a royal mixed-race child, prophesying, like Hopkins, the rise of a dark empire.[24]

Reading Tagore's critique of ecstatic nationalism and its need for erotic and gendered symbols in *The Home and the World* radically recasts the ending of *Dark Princess*. Tagore represents the arrival of the *Swadeshi* movement (literally, of one's own country) in Bengal as a new epoch in which all that is solid turns into air. "One day there came the new era of *Swadeshi* in Bengal. . . . There was no gradual scope connecting the past with the present. For that reason, I imagine, the new epoch came in like a flood."[25] Bimala says: "The ashes of lifeless Bengal suddenly spoke up: 'Here am I.' . . . This moment of our history . . . had no resemblance to our past; and so we were led to hope that all our wants and miseries would disappear by the spell of some magic charm, that for us there was no longer any boundary line between the possible and the impossible" (90–91). For Bimala, a sexual and political awakening are one and the same: "the thing that was agitating me within was merely a variation of the stormy passion outside, which swept the country from one end to the other" (93). Nationalism carried the potential for revolutionary change: Tagore recognizes that transformative capacity – of making fantasy real – but warns of the risks of such euphoria.

Tagore's powerful critique of nationalism's need for romance serves as a kind of check on Du Bois' enthusiasms. Sandip, the revolutionary, notes that "the geography of a country is not the whole truth. No one can give his life up for a map" (73). On hearing his speeches, Bimala, the "caged bird" who is being coaxed by her husband to come outside of domesticity, realizes that "I was no longer the lady of the Rajah's house, but the sole representative of Bengal's womanhood" (31). She says, "I would make my country a Person, and call her Mother, Goddess, Durga – for whom I would redden the earth with sacrificial offerings" (38). The novel critiques the process of such symbolization, as the Mother India of the nationalists becomes a cult of the goddess Kali, simultaneous symbol of destruction and creation. As Nikhil puts it, "I am willing to serve my country; but my worship I reserve for Right" (29).

Du Bois takes up the same trope, transforming it not into Mother Bengal or Mother India but what he terms the "primal black All-Mother of men down through the ghostly throng of mighty womanhood, who walked in the mysterious dawn of Asia and Africa." The princess tells Matthew, "your Mother is Kali, the Black One; wife of Siva, Mother of the World!" (220). When the two pray together, "the sacrifice of flame and blood" becomes at once the ceremony of the princess's fathers and that which came down to the mother from Shango of West Africa (221). The future at the end of the novel, then, is a revival of an Afro-Asian primal past, as the princess claims that "Out of black India the world was born. Into the black womb of India the world shall creep to die" (227). The novel thus speaks to the Afrocentric mythologies Du Bois constructs in such works as *The Negro* (1915) rather than to a socialist internationalism alone and is vulnerable to the same critiques as those launched against nationalism by feminist and subaltern scholars. Such tension runs throughout Du Bois' vast career, evident even in the late historiographical text *The World and Africa* (1947), in which Du Bois at once admits that "they had no name for race" and then goes on to locate the "Negroid" origins of Egyptians, who "by tradition believed themselves descended not from the whites or the yellows but from the black peoples of the south" and gradually became "a separate inbred people."[26]

It is important to counterpoise Tagore's critique of the cult of Kali to Du Bois' recuperation of it as the inspiration for his vision of transnational solidarity, because Tagore shows how what stands as an alternative in the U.S. mind – a symbol of precolonial contact in the Global South – has a dangerous hegemonic value within the politics of Indian anticolonialism, as Hindu revivalism threatens internal minorities such as Muslims and Dalits. Minority–minority dialogue should ideally lead to a redefined universal, but such aporias of transnational communication linger. Tagore's novel critiques extremist nationalism, the fetish of the nation, and the subordination of morality or ethics to worship in order to warn Indians away from such politics, which involve aestheticizing a Hindu vision of the past.

In *The Home and the World*, Bimala is both symbol and flesh to both men. Nikhil acknowledges that his plans for Bimala had been wrong: "We, men, are knights whose quest is that freedom to which our ideals call us. She who makes for us the banner under which we fare forth is the true Woman for us. We must tear away her disguise of her who weaves our net of enchantment at home, and know her for what she is. We must beware of clothing her in the witchery of our own longings and imaginings" (110). He learns to not make her an abstraction that reflects his own desires, realizing that "there was a despotism in my desire to mould my relations with Bimala in a hard, clear-cut, perfect form" (197). Meanwhile, Sandip claims that women "are creatures of this world of reality and do not roam about in cloud-land, as men do, in idea-filled balloons" (47). He tells Bimala, "You women, you have desired to conceive reality with body and soul. You have given birth to reality. You have suckled reality at your breasts" (57). But at the same time, in order to manage his attraction to Bimala, and to seduce her, he very calculatingly uses the idea of the modern as a weapon, wanting her to come to the conclusion that to accept passion is "to be modern": "if she finds shelter in some such word as 'modern', she will find strength" (62).

Tagore thus exposes the fetish of the modern as a fetish – not real, but as made up as anything else – unveiling the process of the nationalist invention of tradition and modernity. Sandip consciously decides to fuse his ambition as a leader with his romance for Bimala: "I shall simply make Bimala one with my country. The turbulent west wind which has swept away the country's veil of conscience, will sweep away the veil of the wife from Bimala's face, and in that uncovering there will be no shame" (84). He deliberately revives the cult of Kali, remade as Mother India, as women freed from the artifice of custom become "on earth the living image of Kali, the shameless, pitiless goddess" (84). One of the central beliefs of Hindu nationalism was the notion that if the unlettered masses could construct the nation as the object of religious devotion, they would then generate a collective subjectivity that could recover the lost glory of Hindu culture. For Sandip, "True patriotism will never be roused in our countrymen unless they can visualize the motherland. We must make a goddess of her" (120). He argues that Bengal created Durga as a "political goddess ... the image of the Shakti of patriotism" in response to Muslim incursion, and wants to expand the same process: "Bengal must now create a new image to enchant and conquer the world. *Bande Mataram!*" (125).

As the historian Tanika Sarkar notes, it was difficult for Indian nationalism to think outside "the mould of Mother-worship" (35).[27] Sarkar shows how nationalist discourse embodied women as at once the repository of traditional values and the symbol of revolutionary hope for the future. Bimala fully inhabits this complexity. Tagore underscores precisely these questions as the novel foregrounds Bimala's voice in dialogue with the two men who view her as flesh *and* symbol. Sarkar notes that "the self-representing woman is not only a newcomer in Rabindranath's writing, she is a startling new character on the Bengali literary and social landscape" (29). Nationalism wanted to convert the effeminate Indians of colonial imaginings into virile men worshiping and sacrificing for Mother India. This often meant exalting women as symbols and subordinating them as people. Bimala stages this contradiction in her vision: "In the future I saw my country, a woman like myself, standing expectant. . . . She is no mother. . . . She has left home, forgotten domestic duties; she has nothing but an unfathomable yearning which hurries her on" (93–94). This combination of eroticism in the image of Mother India, as well as a confusion over what this means for the domestic duties of actual women, proves to be incoherent, and Sandip has to change his watchword: "It is no longer Bande Mataram (Hail Mother), but Hail Beloved, Hail Enchantress. The mother protects, the mistress leads to destruction – but sweet is that destruction" (177).

While it may seem logical to juxtapose Kautilya and Bimala as women emerging out of domestic roles into political ones, it turns out that it is Matthew who follows a parallel trajectory to Bimala, as both are coaxed out of purdah or come out from behind the veil into the world. The purdah in Tagore and the veil in Du Bois serve as similar metaphors for obscured vision, a result of tradition, racial and colonial oppression, and the internalization of hierarchies. Both Matthew and Bimala must step out from behind the veil and be tempted and tested in the world. In each case, the romantic relationship is mediated through the exchange of objects. In *Dark Princess*, a Turkish vase and a Chinese carpet symbolize the exotic beauty and aesthetic freedom Matthew associates with Kautilya. But these objects appear as Oriental objects that somehow exist outside the marketplace of U.S. machine politics. This is why they signal a utopian beyond, a withdrawal from the world, and a private space of aesthetics, beauty, and meditation. But this utopia can only exist because these objects are rendered timeless, shorn from a history of exchange or circulation. In Tagore's novel, the question of foreign cloth is what propels the plot of national resistance as well as the definition of community, as the three central characters debate the value of using Indian or British cloth, soap, and pens.

Reading the two novels together thus enables a different kind of comparison – not literal or about physical travel, but rather a shared understanding of a mediated relationship to modernity – one that is desired, yet withheld. As Simon Gikandi has noted, the fruits of modernity are denied, yet promised under the sign of colonial values as universal.[28] At the same time, colonial subjects are told that they will always be belated, what Homi Bhabha memorably termed "almost total but not quite," almost but "not quite/not white."[29] So far, scholars have treated these narratives of African American and colonial modernity as following different trajectories, which may seem compatible but only truly converge in the 1950s and 1960s, in the era of Bandung, Civil Rights, Decolonization, and Black Power. But a prehistory of Bandung is already visible if we compare diverse modernisms around the world, Du Bois and Tagore are clearly commensurable in their efforts to represent the souls of a subjugated people. What Amit Chaudhuri terms "Tagore's complex and difficult position as a modern Indian, a colonial subject, an elite cosmopolitan, an inheritor and inventor of Eastern civilizational values, and a progeny of the Enlightenment" (xxiii) affords him a unique position both inside and outside dominant conceptions of modernity, similar to what Gilroy calls a "counterculture to modernity," evident in Du Bois.[30]

The two monumental thinkers were themselves attuned to such similarities, as is clear from Du Bois' numerous efforts to see Indian colonization by Britain as analogous to African American experiences of subordination. Both thinkers imagine a poetics of internationalism, as their fiction weighs the potential of anticolonialism against the lure of the universal, conducting a vibrant dialogue about the contingent conditions that attend any comparative endeavor. Each thinker is provincialized, in a sense, when juxtaposed, and placed in an alien intellectual history, thus revealing the difficulties of elaborating abstractions such as the Global South, Afro-Asia, or the Third World, each of which depend (as a condition of their existence) on the possibility and necessity of comparison.[31] Untangling the uses of Orientalism and Africanism in Du Bois and Tagore (their use of an Indian princess, an Arab dancer, a black eunuch) would help reveal the logic of their search for a third figure beyond the binary of black and white, colonizer and colonized.

The two writers were also remarkably similar in their formulation of a modernism that would remain fascinated by mysticism, registering the appeal of early twentieth-century movements such as theosophy, the occult sciences, new psychology, and the gothic. Both make extensive use of Orientalism as well and dabble in genres such as science fiction and fantasy, even though they are often seen as attached to Victorian social mores. In quest of truth and beauty, Tagore imagined India, China, and Japan as sharing an "Eastern" body of cultural values, with Buddhism as a common link, which could save the world as a whole from materialism. Pan-Asia would thus spiritually regenerate world civilization. Similarly, Du Bois theorized Pan-Africanism as a victory of the soul and imagined a global alliance of the darker races that would end white supremacy. What Partha

Chatterjee influentially analyzed as a split in nationalist thought – between spirit and matter, home and world, East and West – can thus be usefully compared to Du Bois' theorization of the souls of black folk as "the sole oasis of simple faith and reverence in a dusty desert of dollars and smartness."[32] Exploring their negotiation of racial and colonial power inside and outside binaries of provincialism and universalism reveals not a simple formula for comparing African American and anticolonial thought, but rather a productive noncoincidence between such terms as postcolonial, transnational, and global. What such a comparison also reveals is that no simple polarity between the national and the transnational may be assumed, as each of these writers moves in, out, and across local and global circuits to show how place helps fashion the very meaning of modernity itself. Neither Hopkins nor Du Bois can take the modern for granted and must turn to faraway places such as Africa and India to seek alternatives that are themselves shaped by different kinds of historical contingencies. Reading American modernists alongside such global ones as Tagore helps not only highlight the fault lines and inconsistencies that make such utopian visions possible, but also suggests a way forward to a more supple method of transnational analysis.

NOTES

1. Douglas Mao and Rebecca Walkowitz, "The New Modernist Studies," *PMLA* 123, no. 3 (2008): 737–748.
2. See Susan Stanford Friedman, "Periodizing Modernism: Postcolonial Modernities and the Space/Time Borders of Modernist Studies," *Modernism/modernity* 13, no. 3 (2006): 493–513, and David James and Urmila Seshagiri, "Metamodernism: Narratives of Continuity and Revolution," *PMLA* 129, no. 1 (2014): 87–100.
3. Edward Said, *Culture and Imperialism* (New York: Vintage, 1993); Fredric Jameson, "Modernism and Imperialism," in *Nationalism, Colonialism and Literature*, eds. Terry Eagleton, Fredric Jameson, and Edward W. Said (Minneapolis: University of Minnesota Press, 1990), 43–66; Paul Gilroy, *The Black Atlantic: Modernity and Double Consciousness* (Cambridge: Harvard University Press, 1993); and Amy Kaplan, *The Anarchy of Empire in the Making of U.S. Culture* (Cambridge: Harvard University Press, 2002).
4. Laura Doyle and Laura Winkiel, eds., *Geomodernisms: Race, Modernism, Modernity* (Bloomington: Indiana University Press, 2005), 3.
5. Édouard Glissant, *Caribbean Discourse: Selected Essays*, trans. Michael Dash (Charlottesville: University Press of Virginia, 1989).
6. Wai Chee Dimock, *Through Other Continents: American Literature across Deep Time* (Princeton, NJ: Princeton University Press, 2008).
7. Michael Levenson, *Modernism* (New Haven, CT: Yale University Press, 2011).
8. Andreas Huyssen, *After the Great Divide: Modernism, Mass Culture, Postmodernism* (Bloomington: University of Indiana Press, 1986).

9. Rita Felski, *The Gender of Modernity* (Cambridge: Harvard University Press, 1995), 18.

10. See Susan Gillman, *Blood Talk: American Race Melodrama and the Culture of the Occult* (Chicago: University of Chicago Press, 2003).

11. Partha Chatterjee, *The Nation and Its Fragments: Colonial and Postcolonial Histories* (Delhi: Oxford University Press, 1995).

12. Julia Kristeva, "Women's Time," trans. Alice Jardine and Harry Blake, in *The Kristeva Reader*, ed. Toril Moi (New York: Columbia University Press, 1986), 187–213; Margaret Ferguson, "Feminism in Time," *MLQ* 65, no. 1 (March 2004): 7–27.

13. Gayatri Chakravorty Spivak, "Three Women's Text and a Critique of Imperialism," *Critical Inquiry* 12, no. 1 (1985): 243–261; Chandra Talpade Mohanty, *Feminism without Borders: Decolonizing Theory, Practicing Solidarity* (Durham: Duke University Press, 2003).

14. Kaplan, *Anarchy of Empire*, 12.

15. Claudia Tate, *Domestic Allegories of Political Desire: The Black Heroine's Text at the Turn of the Century* (New York: Oxford University Press, 1992); Hazel Carby, *Reconstructing Womanhood: The Emergence of the Afro-American Woman Novelist* (New York: Oxford University Press, 1988).

16. I make this point in extended fashion in *Romance, Diaspora, and Black Atlantic Literature* (Cambridge: Cambridge University Press, 2010): 25–58.

17. Pauline Hopkins, *Of One Blood, or the Hidden Self*, in *The Magazine Novels of Pauline Hopkins*, introd. Hazel Carby (1902–1903; New York: Oxford University Press, 1988), 556; hereafter cited parenthetically.

18. Freud labeled women as the "dark continent," echoing Henry Morton Stanley's description of Africa. See Ranjana Khanna, *Dark Continents: Psychoanalysis and Colonialism* (Durham: Duke University Press, 2003).

19. W.E.B. Du Bois, *The Souls of Black Folk* (New York: Penguin, 1989).

20. See Dipesh Chakrabarty, *Provincializing Europe: Postcolonial Thought and Historical Difference* (Princeton, NJ: Princeton University Press, 2000); Bill Mullen, *Afro-Orientalism* (Minneapolis: University of Minnesota Press, 2004).

21. Gilroy, *Black Atlantic*, 1–40.

22. Doris Sommer, *Foundational Fictions: The National Romances of Latin America* (Berkeley: University of California Press, 1993).

23. Gilroy, *Black Atlantic*, 144.

24. W.E.B. Du Bois, *Dark Princess: A Romance* (Jackson: University Press of Mississippi, 1995), 311.

25. Rabindranath Tagore, *The Home and the World*, trans. Surendranath Tagore (London: Penguin, 2005), 26.

26. W.E.B. Du Bois, *The World and Africa* (New York: Oxford University Press, 2007), 68.

27. Tanika Sarkar, "Many Faces of Love: Country, Woman, and God in *The Home and the World*," in *Rabindranath Tagore's The Home and the World: A Critical Companion*, ed. Pradip Kumar Datta (London: Anthem Press, 2005), 27–44.

28. Simon Gikandi, "Reason, Modernity and the African Crisis," in *African Modernities: Entangled Meanings in Current Debate*, eds. Jan-Georg Deutsch, Peter Probst, and Heike Schmidt (Oxford: James Currey, 2002), 135–157.

29. Homi Bhabha, *The Location of Culture* (New York: Routledge 1994), 91–92.

30. Amit Chaudhuri, "Foreword: Poetry as Polemic," in *The Essential Tagore: Rabindranath Tagore*," eds. Fakrul Alam and Radha Chakravarty (Cambridge: Harvard University Press, 2011), xv–xxxiv.
31. On comparison, see Susan Stanford Friedman, "Towards a Transnational Turn in Narrative Theory: Literary Narratives, Traveling Tropes and the Case of Virginia Woolf and the Tagores," *Narrative* 19, no. 1 (2011): 1–32.
32. Du Bois, *Souls of Black Folk*, 11.

7

MARY PAT BRADY

Borderlands Modernism

The center of modernism was El Paso, Texas, and Virginia Woolf must have known this when she remarked, "on or about December 1910 human character changed."[1] Surely she remembered that El Paso was the locale where Mariano Azuela's world-changing novel, *Los de abajo*, was first published; or maybe she recalled that El Paso was the departure point for many of the various participants in the Mexican Revolution; or perhaps she had heard that El Paso was the home of the Mexican War Photo Postcard Company. *Los de abajo*, published first in serial form and immediately after as a book, illuminates the intersections of then forty-year-old *modernismo* and the still congealing and nascent American modernism, even though it must be said that both *movimientos* had already been ambivalently engaged or predicted for more than a decade by writers such as José Martí and Arturo Schomburg.[2] Certainly the waning modernismo would inspire figures as profoundly distant from it as Olga Beatriz Torres, Jovita González, and Américo Paredes.

Breaking Modernism/ismo

Borderlands modernism is a decidedly dis-urban modernism, contrapuntal in its relationship to modernism as envisaged by London-centered writers and adrift from a modernismo that captivated Francophilic Latin American poets. Both modernismo and modernism would ultimately fetishize 'the break,' would depend upon an ambivalent theatricality that would adore centered figures and centralized spaces and toward that end, the modernism of the borderlands would offer an obscure and disdainful disinterest. José David Saldívar describes writers of the *frontera* as working out "an uneven and contradictory frontier modernism" emerging out of "the *fin de siglo* quests for empire, politics, and subaltern difference."[3]

Latin American modernismo has a different temporal landscape than the hemispheric modernism attended to by literary critics focused on the United

States and Britain.[4] A multinational literary movement, modernismo thrived between 1870 and 1920 as a reaction against the perceived rigidities of Spanish literature and in an enchanted dance with the allegorical and symbolic architecture provided by French symbolists. It sought aesthetic planes that contrasted with the pronouncements of positivist technocratic managers. Modernismo played with poetic pyrotechnics and flights of fantasy that blended romanticism and symbolism and introduced new forms such as the prose *crónica*.[5] Its presence was felt everywhere that Spanish mattered, and the crónica effectively leveraged the flourishing format of newspapers and magazines. Spanish-language newspapers in the United States encouraged this form. Their readers would have been as familiar with it as audiences in Guadalajara or Bogotá.[6]

Borderlands modernism cannot be described as a movement in the manner of these other modernisms, although the texts discussed here share a set of formal techniques. They engage, for example, with photography and its claims to authoritative ascendancy; they push and pull against an emerging documentary realism; they fold ethnography into their fictional worlds and draw together multiple languages into ingenious configurations. These are texts with complicated, overlapping, and belated temporalities. They appear in print and disappear from memory; they appear later in archives and only find their typeset cognates many decades after their composition. Yet tying these texts together is their interest in the effects of many languages sutured together, creating a layered prose. And each struggles with perspective, with points of departure where visual optics matter profoundly. Discarded, rescued, and revived, these texts suggest a much richer borderlands modernism yet to be discovered and analyzed.

Circular Modernisms

Among the most celebrated works of this moment, celebrated but hardly well known outside circles of Hispanists, *Los de abajo* is an early novel by a prolific medical doctor, Mariano Azuela, who also fought in the revolution.[7] Midway through the insurrection, he left the fighting to live in El Paso, Texas, where he wrote the novel before moving to Mexico City, continuing his medical practice, and writing for the next thirty years. Originally published in serial form in the newspaper *El Paso del Norte* in 1915, an arm of the Carranza political machine, Azuela revised the novel and republished it, at his own expense, in 1920.[8] In 1924, after a series of debates among Mexican intellectuals about whether they had developed an adequate literature of the revolution (surely they had the weight of José Martí's legacy in mind), *Los de abajo* was championed, celebrated, and translated into German, French, and English. Its influence on other modernist writers, such as Ernest Hemingway, suggests that its importance extends beyond the Latin American literary canon.[9] Given the transnational *modernista* imaginary, the novel should also be read as one whose contrapuntal energies would have been resonant for writers across the frontera.

Los de abajo engages many of the formal mechanisms, particularly the crónica, which would render it a late modernista novel. But the novel itself appears entirely disinterested in such generic engagements. Instead, in tracking with a kind of profound ambivalence the story of Demetrio Macías' circular journey through Jalisco in support of Pancho Villa's forces during the revolution, the novel alternately engages with the discursive authority of anthropological reporting in its depictions of the poor, rural men and women who participated in a distended revolutionary struggle even as it slides away from a nascent documentary mode and back toward modernismo's effort to find succor in the romance of nature. Written in what the title announces as "cuadros y escenas" – that is, brief chapters or what one scholar describes as "installments" – and composed of narrative images bristling with austere prose telegraphed in short, elliptical paragraphs, the text repeatedly engages with a kind of doubling back on itself, a movement similar to Macías' own circumnavigation of northern Mexico.

The novel's title, *Los de abajo*, literally "those from below," straightforwardly describes the dispossessed people who struggle first against powerful caciques and later against the nascent troops of a new national army and finally against the colliding forces of greed and disarray. And certainly this understanding confirms the English translation of the title, *The Underdogs*. But early in the text when Macías cries out, "A los de abajo ... A los de abajo," it is the *federales*, the government troops, his enemy, to whom he refers, not his own impoverished companions. It is the movement of the enemy climbing the sierra to which the title directly refers, and it is this enemy that will give Macías a nearly fatal wound at the opening of the novel and kill him at its end. The title, and its translation, and its use in the text suggest the novel's own register of what would come to be a modernist principle – that the slippery relationship between signifier and signified should be highlighted so that realism's authority (an authority the reportorial-like descriptions of camp life seizes) is disentangled and documentary's apparently cozy relationship with the transparency of language exposed as no more "real" than the shadows covering the moon.

Similarly, the novel's subtitle translates easily as images and scenes, indicating a visual register. In this sense the novel anticipates a much later modernist turn toward the documentary, and toward a tendency to emphasize the evidential force of the visual as the final arbiter of the real and the truthful. The terms are also theatrical ones: a *cuadro* is a subsection of an *escena*, a scene in the "act" of a play – or, in this case, a novel divided into three parts. Further, the novel's subtitle in its first serialized publication is the "revolucíon actual" (the real revolution or the current revolution), but in subsequent editions it is the "revolucíon mexicana." In other words, the novel itself puts into juxtaposition the figural or performative alongside the claim to a documentary authority.

The text's doubling suggests not a range of allegorical relationships or a receding line of symbols, one as surrogate for another, but in its excess denies an authoritative center; what may be a collection of reportorial or ethnographic scenes could well be also a performance, a fantasy of the "revolucíon actual." A novel purporting to describe the experiences of a band of revolutionaries could well be also the story of the entrenched elite's power to come from behind and reestablish themselves. Thus, the text's gesture toward the report – mimicking the intensive photographing of the war through a set of subtly disconnected episodes and reminding us of news accounts produced by the swarm of journalists from around the world who joined pen to rifle – could also be a deeply cynical critique of any representative claim to authority over the "real."

Put differently, the novel is alive to the shadows haunting and making meaning elusive, akin to the light in the sierras after federales threaten Macías and his wife and force them to flee their home:

> Salieron juntos; ella con el niño en los brazos.
> Ya a la puerta se apartaron en opuesta dirección.
> La luna poblaba de sombras vagas la montaña.
> En cada risco y en cada chaparro, Demetrio seguía
>   mirando la silueta dolorida de una mujer con su niño
>   en los brazos.
> Cuando después de muchas horas de ascenso volvió los
>   ojos, en el fondo del cañón, cerca del río, se levan-
>   taban grandes llamaradas.
> !Su casa ardía! . . .   (*Los de abajo*, 12)

> They went out together, she holding the child in her
>   arms. At the door they went in opposite directions.
> The moon peopled the mountain with vague shadows.
> At every ridge and every bush, Demetrio still saw the
>   sad silhouette of a woman with a child in her arms.
> After many hours of climbing when he turned to look, at the bottom of
>   the canyon near the river, huge flames rose. His house was burning.
>   (*The Underdogs*, 3)

Of course, these "sombras vagas" refer to hazy, wandering shadows, but *vaga* can also mean crazy, even insane, and so the shadows may cover the moon or they may dance before Demetrio in an otherworldly fashion, one that does not comport with the rational. The shadows on the canyon walls repeatedly shift into images of his loss and departure. This loss is sealed at the close of the scene by the flames swallowing his home. From this dramatic opening, the novel moves to its focus on the revolutionary battles.

Azuela deploys what Joshua L. Miller has identified as an important attribute of modernist writing: linguistic defamiliarization.[10] While the dialogue of the novel is largely colloquial Spanish, it is filled with words that have their roots not in Castilian but in the many indigenous languages still in vibrant use in Mexico at the time of the text's production. The texture of the novel is thus densely interwoven with poetic language and colloquial phrases interspersed with the words of more than one indigenous tongue. Azuela creates a textual fabric out of these linguistic abutments. The rhythms of one language engage with others, calling attention to the sonic dimension of words in a manner more typically expected in poetry than prose.

As a novel of the frontera, *Los de abajo* can also be effectively read within the rubric of Latino and Chicano literature.[11] It engages questions that would be taken up again by post–World War II writers who, as José David Saldívar notes, developed a sense of postmodernism, which "thinks of itself as an alternative and a renewal – disrupting and displacing years of long cultural ossification."[12] Part of the cultural ossification entailed tangling with the Mexican elites' determined and "protonationalist" characterization of U.S. mexicanos as "inauthentic" and "pathological" – a narrative celebrated and made famous by Octavio Paz in his cynical portrayal of Chicanos.[13] Paz, of course, was not the first to offer such a characterization; rather, we can see this accounting of difference embedded into borderlands modernism at least as early as 1918, where the inauthentic is at once the estranged and the stage for alienation.

The Light That Breaks

Originally published in the same newspaper as *Los de abajo* and appearing as a book in 1918, Olga Beatriz Torres' text, *Memorias de mi viaje*, is constructed as a series of letters by the thirteen-year-old daughter of a wealthy Mexican family fleeing the revolution.[14] In a text providing an extraordinary counterpart to Azuela's novel, the family travels from Mexico City to Veracruz, boards a ship bound for a Texas port, and travels to Houston and eventually to a five-bedroom rental in El Paso. The political and violent rupture caused by the revolution is registered in these pages less than the author's fascination with various conveyances – trains, streetcars, wagons, carriages, ships, and automobiles – and architecture including court houses, train stations, mansions, stores, and shacks.[15]

Torres would likely have been aware of Azuela's novel. More particularly, she knew the way photography was already producing a story of the war that demanded a new narrative style. Reading *Memorias* at this moment and alongside *Los de abajo* provides us with the opportunity to see some of the groundwork being laid for the documentary form that would emerge fully in the next decade. In several of Torres' reportorial and largely unsentimental letters to her aunt, she mentions that she likes to purchase postcards and maps because they provide her with an authoritative overview of the city she is visiting (*Memorias*, 16). Titling her penultimate letter "A Vuela Pájaro," translated as "A Birds-Eye View," she links together techniques of narrative brevity and photography's claim to authority.

Given this investment in photography, it might not be surprising that the text is also focused on the effects of light and begins lyrically, "Amanecía en Mixcoac" (*Memorias*, 85). Here light is indicated multiply – first by the reference to dawn (amanecía) and second by her region's name, Mixcoac, which translates from the Nahuatl as the cloud serpent, Mixcóatl, the god of storms. The dawning light, suffusing a departure from the storm of revolution, shifts across the letters, transporting the author, who continues her meditations, noting first how overwhelmed she is by the beauty of the ocean:

> Y de mí sé decir, que sentí admiración y miedo. Admiración porque el paisaje es grandioso y bello, la luz al quebrarse sobre las olas produce arabescos de colores tan variados, que los que hablan del "mar azul" del "mar verde" están en un error. La luz le dá a la superficie movediza del mar tantos colores, que ni es verde ni es azul, es una infinita variedad de colores, es una policromía admirable. (*Memorias*, 95)

> [As for me, I must say that I felt admiration and fear: admiration because the landscape is grandiose and beautiful – the sunlight as it broke over the waves produced an arabesque of different colors so varied so those who speak of the "blue sea" of the "green sea" are mistaken. The sunlight projects so many colors on the moving surface of the sea that it is neither green nor blue; it is an infinite variety of colors. It is an admirable polychrome.] (*Memorias*, 38)

When the light shatters the waves of the Gulf of Mexico, Torres suggests the imprecision of standard representative narratives. The release into the infinity of colors provides a contrast to the damage to Veracruz wrought by the U.S. invasion and which she has just described in disdainful terms and almost shelters the reader from the descriptions to follow, which include the ship's sulfuric bath and its passengers' mandatory vaccinations. Light continues to

suture together the letters as we follow Torres' travels across Texas, including her encounters with Jim Crow segregation and her racist descriptions of
African Americans.

Torres' vocal disdain for African Americans dovetails with her descriptions of the revolutionary insurrection attempting to dislodge a Mexican elite
from entrenched power and ultimately merges with her dismissive and
patronizing account of a woman her family hires to provide domestic
labor. In the closing letter of the *Memorias*, Torres gleefully describes her
servant's multilingual account of a trip involving a search for matches. The
letter is astounding given that it follows many, many dry descriptions of
buildings and trains. In this final account, the prose comes alive, though the
playfulness lies in the interplay between narrative form, class relations, and
translation. The servant, Carlota, also offers a travel narrative of a sort, one
that simultaneously maps her own movements across what William Gleason
has astutely identified as the broad segregation of El Paso between poor
barrios and a wealthy enclave of exiles, while also producing a poetics of
multilingual transformation.[16] Torres reports the story and then provides a
series of translations of the Spanglish, such as "*Babis* is an absurdity for the
English word babies." Torres evinces pride in her newly acquired translational skills, suggesting a sense of accommodation to her experience in the
broadly outernational milieu that is the frontera. But the closing sentences of
Memorias also suggest a complex alienation from border modernism's
hybrid and shifting cultures:

> Ya con estas explicaciones podrás traducir el incomprensible castellano de
> Carlota, (que así se llama la criada,) que es el mismo que usan la mayor parte
> de los trabajadores y servidumbre mexicano. Americanos y compatriotas,
> necesitan intérprete para entenderles!"   (*Memorias*, 140)

> [Now with these explanations, you should be able to translate the incompre-
> hensible Spanish of Carlota (which is the name of the maid), the same one that
> the majority of Mexican workers use. Americans and compatriots need inter-
> preters to understand them!]   (*Memorias*, 84)

The passage suggests that Torres now understands herself to have a role in
her newly configured home. She stations herself here as translator, just as at
the start of this final letter she describes herself as playing Mexico's national
anthem on the brand-new piano right after entering their home for the first
time. She even goes so far as to figure herself as planting a flag. But that flag
planting and her role as guarantor of cultural purity are partially and almost
immediately undercut by Torres' breathless accounting of a new linguistic
poetics that clearly enchants her. So enamored is she with Carlota's language

that she brushes past the humor-laced critique of elite Mexican presumptuousness. For a domestic worker to refer to herself as "Carlota" pokes fun at the elite's admiration for all things French during Porfirio Díaz's regime and recalls Mexico's last empresses. Torres may miss the maid's irony, but her critique of Chicano culture in El Paso predicts the snide remarks her more famous compatriot Octavio Paz would make thirty years later after visiting Los Angeles. In a strange twist, Paz was also born in Mixcoac shortly before Torres' family fled from the revolution.

Local Relics

If photography, postcards, and the reportorial but brief letter were technologies of authority for Torres, these would all merge together in documentary and ethnography a decade later and become immensely important for two innovative ethnographers and novelists. One of these, Jovita González, would write groundbreaking ethnographies of *tejano* communities. Born in south Texas, González worked as a folklorist for many years before turning to political activism and education. Most of her fiction would remain unpublished for decades after their composition. Her novel, *Caballero*, written in collaboration with Eve Raleigh in the late 1930s and '40s, offers us an exceptional account of a borderlands modernism that exploited these techniques to reset a historical narrative.[17] The novel also deploys a technique Sonnet Retman describes as typical of 1930s documentary "voice-of-God narration, the booming male voiceover," that found its fictional referent in the "omnipotent narratorial device invented in the era [which] self-consciously projects a sense of its story's importance for posterity, in part, by imposing coherence on its subject."[18] Set during the 1846–1848 Mexican-American War and following a wealthy landowning family as it negotiates the transformation of Texas and the arrival of Anglo soldiers and entrepreneurs, the novel begins with a drawing of the hacienda at the center of its plot and includes the sort of details that one might find in an ethnography, such as what herbs should be used for a particular ailment.

Caballero offers argument after argument about the importance of cultural cross-fertilization. Its meditation on the profound injustices of the land-grant ranching system, which secured hidalgos their wealth and peons their servitude, must be read through its ongoing examination of eugenics as the stance structuring cultural analysis and change. That is to say, the ranching-peonage system, which the novel vociferously critiques for its patriarchal racism, its dependence on a dehumanized working class, fails to adapt to a transformed world economy and changing sociocultural milieu; it is too narrowly rigid in its dedication to a Spanish colonialist model and ultimately too dependent on a philistinism that prohibits competing perspectives and an imaginative engagement with new possibilities. In this sense we must read the novel as yet another contrapuntal response to the "revolución actual," to the extent that *Caballero* extends Azuela's critique of the misery created by the hacienda/ranching system.

It is possible to trace this theme through a number of the novel's concurrent plots, but the theme is most clearly apparent in the portrayal of the Don's battle with his son, Luis, who wishes to become an artist. At the climax of their clash, Luis informs his father that he will leave for Baltimore to begin a formal study of art, and his father reacts with fury:

> Frustration wrenched him to agony that he, a Mendoza, the family that fathered *men*, had a son who painted pictures – a thing for the nuns in the convents to do. He looked at the land about him as he rode down draws white with short-stemmed daisies, past hollows rich with the velvet of winecups, between low hills purple with verbenas. Ah, *Cristo*, but it was beautiful! That anyone could say he did not like it was as great a crime as blaspheming the Creator. He had meant to temper his command to his son, but now all his restlessness and dissatisfaction came to culmination and he struck out sternly. He told Luis: "I, your father, command you to learn the things you must. I command you to be a *ranchero* as I am, as was your grandfather and his father before him. Your task begins today. As soon as you get home you will destroy those childlike things with which you amuse yourself, you will burn all your paints and crayons. This is my final command."   (*Caballero*, 196–197)

Don Mendoza rejects the possibility of artistry as unmanly and immature. Yet the narrative adds an interesting intervention: the Don himself looks out at the beauty of his rancho and appreciates it, as the narrative asks its readers to imagine the multicolored landscape of flowers and herbs. But the unsympathetic portrayal of the Don makes it clear that if he can appreciate his ranch's beauty, he cannot understand that his appreciation is as much a mediated, romanticized form of aesthetic representation as is his son's efforts to paint, and by extension, the novel's engagement with the imagination. And if the Don fails to appreciate the creative arts, he also fails to understand the social-cultural transformation looming before the wealthy and insular tejano elite. His rejection of his son's wishes ultimately predicts the end of his own desires as well: he dies gripping the very earth he fruitlessly commanded his son to tend.

It is useful here to point out that borderlands modernism has a temporal multivalency caused by the still-swirling and unresolved tensions created by the wars and treaties of 1848 and 1898 and the discursive structures that enabled them. This sense of the presence of the past also informs one of

González's most curious narratives.[19] "Shades of the Tenth Muses" opens with a description of a borderlands room of one's own:

> The air in the room is close and smoky; I can still smell the rosemary and lavender leaves I have just burnt in an incense burned to drive out the mosquitoes that have driven me insane with their monotonous, droning music. For, in spite of the family's efforts to have me work in the house I prefer my garage room with its screenless windows and door, its dizzy floor, the plants of which act like the keys of an old piano, and walls, hung with relics which I like to gather as I go from ranch to ranch in my quest for stories of the ranch folk. A faded Saint Teresa, in a more faded niche smiles her welcome every morning and a Virgin of Guadalupe reminds me daily that I am a descendant of a proud stoic race. Back of the desk, a collection of ranch spits is witness of my ranch heritage, an old, crude treasure chest holds my only possession, a manuscript which will sometime be sold, if I am among the fortunate. (108)

The ritual of warding off mosquitoes that must be driven out because they drive the narrator crazy folds into the sly point that the presumably female narrator has also been driven out of the house. The passage offers a slippery picture of determination: the narrator retreats to the garage "in spite of the family's efforts to have me work in the house."[20] We don't know what kind of work she would do in the house, but it would not be too difficult to conclude that it would not be writing. The writer's retreat is guarded by signs of faith in two registers: a Catholic faith represented by powerful iconic figures and an ethnographic faith in local knowledge or "local relics." The opening also signals a third form of faith – that of artistic production and the uncharacterized and unpublished manuscript held in a treasure chest awaiting its fortune.

This beguiling introduction in no way prepares us, however, for the narrative to follow: a fantastical dream sequence in which two women converse. Sor Juana Inez de la Cruz and Anne Bradstreet, near contemporaries to one another, sharing the accolade "the tenth muse," enter the writer's garage-office and immediately begin a debate over the status of a prayer the writer has framed and hung above her desk. Their clash over its artistry and humor characterizes their conversations throughout the cuento. Or, as Sor Juana notes, "I do not like to contradict. Pirate or patriot, it is the same. It merely is a matter of point of view" (112). This encounter between the two muses emphasizes the struggle over interpretation – Anne Bradstreet repeatedly responds with dismay to Sor Juana's provocations and comments, such as the following: "Pooh, pooh! My dear Anne, you talk like an old woman! I've never been ashamed or afraid to express anything I wish. I discuss earthly love with the same freedom as I do love divine. Love is the spark that keeps us happy" (115).

González's emphasis here on the importance of point of view echoes what Vicki Mahaffey describes as a crucial feature of modernism, because modernist writers were "deeply engaged with questions of how we categorize, define, identify, and interpret the multiplicity of the world around us."[21] In this sense, the contrasting attitudes of Sor Juana and Anne Bradstreet outline a structure of approach to knowledge and to the delineation of experience. Sor Juana advocates an openness to experience and humor; Bradstreet remains committed to an authoritarian rigidity and idealism. This amusing staged conversation creates an aperture into the sort of borderlands modernism that González evidently desired – that is, the opportunity for two cultures that had functioned largely in ignorance of each other's artistic production to begin engaging with one another more meaningfully. For Jovita González, the contemporary moment provided the opportunity to move past a fetishization of cultural purity and toward a multifaceted engagement with multiple cultures and affective stances. One might understand her approach visually – giving us an image produced not by a single artist, but rather a collage akin to the work of Romare Beardon, in which beauty *and* humor emerge from juxtaposition, engagement, and acknowledgment of multiple histories, multiple intellectual and linguistic traditions.

But the story also sets the readers into a queer outer zone when, at its conclusion, Sor Juana seems to flirt with a mystified Anne Bradstreet:

> "It has been a great honor and a pleasure to know another Tenth Muse. I thought I had the monopoly on the title. Come up and see me again."
>
> "'Come up and see me.' Where have I heard that before?"
>
> "Never mind, you wouldn't even recognize her name if I told it to you; but do come again."
>
> "That I will my dear Juana," answered the New England Tenth Muse, kissing the nun on the forehead, "but please put the sinful prayer away, I shudder at the levity of it!"
>
> "The one written by your countryman? I really must meet that man; he may not be a poet, but I bet he has a sense of humor and is clever."
>
> Anne faded away. Sor Juana stood up, yawned, looked at me with what I thought was a wink, and following her companion she also disappeared in the dimness of space." (115)

Perhaps it shouldn't be surprising that in a story pairing Sor Juana and Anne Bradstreet, the fabled nun would quote Mae West so impishly. Bradstreet seems entirely befuddled, and Sor Juana takes pleasure in both the utility of the double entendre and the unidentified narrator's appreciation of the moment. Why else would she wink as she "disappeared into the dimness of space"? The implication of a subtle erotics not only recalls Sapho, who first held the moniker of Tenth Muse, but also reinforces the playful sensuality that Sor Juana advocates embracing and thus underscores the earlier moment in the dialogue when she rails against the hypocrisy of patriarchal control of women's sexuality.

Sor Juana's exuberance stands as a contrast to the duty-bound rigidity of Anne Bradstreet, but what is more important is not that these two serve as iconic or allegorical figures for the cultures they represent, but rather that in bringing them together González positions herself, the narrator, and the reader within a swirling interstitiality in which we can negotiate competing approaches to artistry and the imagination. González seems to be schooling us on what possibilities can be opened when the cultures of New England and New Spain, or instead some of the legacies of those long-gone cultures, are entertained together.

Like *Caballero*, Américo Paredes' novel *George Washington Gómez* remained unpublished for decades after its original composition in the late thirties and thus also arrived to borderlands modernism belatedly.[22] More especially, the slow emergence of both of these novels indicates the rugged print terrain for novels so conceptually and aggressively disaggregating various aspects of a dominant U.S. modernity.[23] At the same time, both novels draw from many of the very themes that were popular in writing of the 1930s more broadly. As Retman has noted, "Four out of the five best selling novels of the thirties explored the search for security in history or on the land, with repressive gender and racial hierarchies firmly in place," so it is not surprising that *Caballero* and *George Washington Gómez* are urgently interested in examining the relationship between security, history, and land.[24] Furthermore, as a number of scholars have shown, Paredes' novel vividly engages with the terms of late modernism. Born in Brownsville, Texas, Paredes completed a PhD at the University of Texas at Austin after serving in World War II. His scholarship on the corrido helped lay the foundations for contemporary Chicano studies. Late in life he published fiction and poetry, much of which was written during the 1930s.

George Washington Gómez tracks the development of a young boy born into the hostile and violent Texas borderlands. As he grows up he learns to navigate a racialized school system, the deprivations of the Depression, the hostility of an Anglo power structure, and the intensified militarization of a border he ultimately helps enforce as an undercover army officer. Crucial to his seemingly straightforward narrative is Paredes' deployment of the corrido form – a musical ballad with a rich legacy of chronicling tejano resistance to racial violence. But the corrido, the novel suggests, does not adequately serve the new era in which the sporadic or chaotic violence of vigilantes has been replaced by the institutional and more systematic violence of school systems, segregation, and political demonization.

Joshua L. Miller argues that in addition to its formal innovations – for the novel also finds the bildungsroman limiting as well – the text's interplay with a multilingual narrative voice makes it "daringly experimental" and intensifies or underscores its innovative turn on genre.[25] He suggests that Paredes' linguistic interplay makes for a different kind of modernist difficulty, creating a potential opacity that signals another register of epistemology and removing what Mahaffey calls a textual crutch.[26] Although Mahaffey is referring to the "omniscient and trustworthy narrator," the term can also be applied to the work that English as the dominant language does.

Paredes playfully directs our attention to the force of English dominance when a young Guálinto (George) is introduced to the schoolroom. In a scene with a remarkable movement across languages – vernacular Spanish, the cultural play of nicknaming, the interplay with English – Guálinto's soon-to-be fast friend Orestes describes their soon-to-be enemy, their teacher, Miss Cornelia: "And if she doesn't like your name she'll give you a silly nickname.... She said Oresets wasn't a name so she started calling me 'Arrestas'. That's what the *palomilla* call me now, Arrestas. And they kid me that I'm going to grow up and be a cop" (114). The text makes a clever point about the relationship between racialization (naming practices as such a process) and the intrinsic link between racialization and policing. Yet further imbedded in the passage is the untranslated *palomilla* – a playful and colloquial term (literally "moth") describing Oreste's gang of friends. This continual shift into the untranslated vernacular provides a textual density across the novel and opens its trenchant reach into a critical and contestatory relationship with a modernization that continues an uneven and violently enforced racial hierarchization.

Américo Paredes, Jovita González, Olga Beatriz Torres, and Mariano Azuela each engage with the machinery of empire building by disengaging from a narrative of progress and triumph. Their contrapuntal modernisms are not laconic treatises against the rise of a consumer-oriented commercial culture; instead, they are interested in a modernism that engages with the dynamics of living together within a hostile field of death and loss, with examining the dynamics that produce vulnerability and rage. They do not here produce "hard" texts whose opacity serves to ward off facile commercialism. Rather, they focus on creating an imaginary that helps us envisage a "general antagonism" to the violent dynamics of empire; their textual movements, interstitial and fugitive, braid together a new language and perspective in which their border is also their center.[27]

NOTES

1. Virginia Woolf, *Mr Bennett and Mrs Brown* (London: Hogarth Press, 1924), 4.
2. José Martí was a central figure in the international *modernista* movement. His poetry helped inspire the Cuban exile community and was central to their revolutionary struggle against Spain. His prose, particularly his *crónicas* and journalism, circulated across the Americas, helping to shape a new literary genre and develop a new decolonial imaginary. See Susana Rotker, *The American Chronicles of José Martí: Journalism and Modernity in Spanish America*, trans. Jennifer French and Katherine Semler (Habana, Cuba: Casa de las Américas, 1992). Arturo Alfonso Schomburg was a Puerto Rican activist and historian whose archives have helped solidify our understanding of the hemispheric modernist/modernista imaginary. For a helpful discussion of his relationship to American modernism more generally, see Lisa Sánchez González, *Boricua Literature: A Literary History of the Puerto Rican Diaspora* (New York: New York University Press, 2001).
3. José David Saldívar, *Border Matters: Remapping American Cultural Studies* (Berkeley: University of California Press, 1998), 159.
4. The literature on *modernismo* is vast. Among the most useful introductions are those by Cathy Jrade, "Modernist Poetry," and Aníbal González, "Modernist Prose," both in Roberto González Echevarría, in *The Cambridge History of Latin American Literature Volume 2: The Twentieth Century* (Cambridge: Cambridge University Press, 1996). But see also Julio Ramos, *Divergent Modernities: Culture and Politics in Nineteenth Century Latin America*, trans. John D. Blanco (Durham: Duke University Press, 2001).
5. The crónica was a central innovation of modernista writers such as Rubén Darío and José Martí. These short portraits, travel accounts, and fantastical material histories were frequently published nearly simultaneously in multiple newspapers across the hemisphere. See Andrew Reynolds, *The Spanish American Crónica Modernista, Temporality and Material Culture: Modernismo's Unstoppable Presses* (Lewisburg: Bucknell University Press, 2012).
6. The vibrant U.S.-Spanish language press deserves additional study, although a number of wonderful monographs already provide important analyses. See, for example, A. Gabriel Meléndez, *So All Is Not Lost: The Poetics of Print in Nuevomexicano Communities, 1834–1958* (Albuquerque: University of New Mexico Press, 1997); Raúl Coronado, *A World Not to Come: A History of Latino Writing and Print Culture* (Cambridge: Harvard University Press, 2013).
7. Gustavo Pellón provides a helpful publication history, and I use his translation of the novel here; Mariano Azuela, *The Underdogs with Related Texts* (Indianapolis, IN: Hacke Publishing Company, 2006). Spanish quotations are taken from Mariano Azuela, *Los de abajo: Novela de la revolución mejicana* (Bilbao: Espasa-Calpe, 1930). The essays that accompany Frederick Fornoff's translation of the novel are helpful. See Frederick Fornoff, *The Underdogs: Critical Edition* (Pittsburgh: University of Pittsburgh Press, 1992). Stanley Robe located and translated the original serialized version of the novel. His translation also includes careful historical discussion of Pancho Villa's movements, the major battles in the north, and a useful discussion of Azuela's composition process. Stanley Robe, *Azuela and the Mexican Underdogs* (Berkeley: University of California Press,

1979). See also John Englekirk, "The 'Discovery' of *Los de abajo*," *Hispania* 18 (February 1935): 53–62.

8. Venustiano Carranza led one faction of the Mexican Revolution; he eventually succeeded in becoming president of the republic and drafted the constitution that governs the nation to this day.

9. See, for example, Sherry Lutz Zivley, "The Conclusions of Azuela's *The Underdogs* and Hemingway's *For Whom the Bell Tolls*," *Hemingway Review* 17, no. 2 (Spring 1998): 118–123. Maryse Bertrand de Muñoz, "*Los de abajo* de Mariano Azuela y *For Whom the Bell Tolls* de Ernest Hemingway," *La Torre Revista General de la Universidad de Puerto Rico* 73–74 (1971): 237–246.

10. Joshua L. Miller, "The 'Gorgeous Laughter' of Filipino Modernity: Carlos Bulosan's *The Laughter of My Father*," in *Bad Modernisms*, eds. Douglas Mao and Rebecca Walkowitz (Durham: Duke University Press, 2006), 238–268.

11. For an expanded and wonderful discussion of this novel's resonance for Chicana writers, see Yolanda Padilla's forthcoming monograph, *Revolutionary Subjects: The Mexican Revolution and the Transnational Emergence of Mexican American Literature and Culture, 1910–1959*.

12. Saldívar, *Border Matters*, 32.

13. Octavio Paz, *El laberinto de la soledad* (1959; Mexico: Fondo de Cultura Económica, 1972).

14. Very little seems to be known about the author. Juanita Luna-Lawhn provides a remarkably useful analysis of the memoir and a beautiful translation. See Olga Beatriz Torres, *Memorias de mi viaje/Recollections of My Trip*, trans. Juanita Luna-Lawhn (Albuquerque: University of New Mexico Press, 1994).

15. See William Gleason for an insightful discussion of the text *Sites Unseen: Architecture, Race, and American Literature* (New York: New York University Press, 2011), 105–148.

16. Gleason, *Sites Unseen*, 143–144.

17. Jovita González and Eve Raleigh, *Caballero: A Historical Novel* (College Station: Texas A&M University Press, 1996). See María Cotera, *Native Speakers: Ella Deloria, Zora Neale Hurston, Jovita González, and the Poetics of Culture* (Austin: University of Texas Press, 2008); Louis Mendoza, *Historia: The Literary Making of Chicana and Chicano History* (College Station: Texas A&M University Press, 2001); Leticia Garza-Falcón, *Gente Decente: A Borderlands Response to the Rhetoric of Dominance* (Austin: University of Texas Press, 1998); Pablo Ramirez, "Resignifying Preservation: A Borderlands Response to American Eugenics in Jovita González and Eve Raleigh's *Caballero*," *Canadian Review of American Studies* 39, no. 1 (2009): 21–39; and Marci MacMahon, "Politicizing Spanish-Mexican Domesticity, Redefining Fronteras: Jovita González's *Caballero* and Cleofilas Jaramillo's *Romance of a Little Village Girl*," *Frontiers: A Journal of Women Studies* 28, nos. 1–2 (2007): 232–259.

18. Sonnet Retman, *Real Folks: Race and Genre in the Great Depression* (Durham: Duke University Press, 2011), 7.

19. Jovita González, "Shades of the Tenth Muses," in *The Woman Who Lost Her Soul and Other Stories*, ed. Sergio Reyna (Houston, TX: Arte Públio Press, 2000), 108–115.

20. For alternative interpretations, see Melina Vizcaíno-Alemán, "Rethinking Jovita González's Work: Bio-ethnography and Her South Texas Regionalism," *Southwestern American Literature* 37, no. 2 (2012): 38–47, and María Cotera, "Engendering a 'Dialectics of Our America': Jovita González's Pluralist Dialogue as Feminist Testimonio," in *Las Obreras: Chicana Politics of Work and Family*, ed. Vicki L. Ruiz (Los Angeles: UCLA Chicano Studies Research Center, 2000), 237–256.

21. Vicki Mahaffey, *Modernist Literature: Challenging Fictions* (Malden, MA: Blackwell, 2007), 3.

22. Américo Paredes, *George Washington Gómez* (Houston, TX: Arte Público Press, 1990).

23. Américo Paredes' oeuvre is perhaps the most studied in Chicano literature. Among the most prominent texts are Ramón Saldívar, *The Borderlands of Culture: Américo Paredes and the Transnational Imaginary* (Durham: Duke University Press, 2006), and Héctor Calderón, *Narratives of Greater Mexico* (Austin: University of Texas Press, 2004). Also relevant is Christopher Schedler, "Inscribing Mexican-American Modernism in Américo Paredes' *George Washington Gómez*," *Texas Studies in Literature and Language* 42.2 (2000): 154–176.

24. Retman, *Real Folks*, 14.

25. Joshua L. Miller, *Accented America: The Cultural Politics of Multilingual Modernism* (New York: Oxford University Press, 2011), 278.

26. Mahaffey, *Modernist Literature*, vii.

27. See Stefano Harney and Fred Moten, *The Undercommons: Fugitive Planning and Black Study* (Brooklyn: Autonomedia, 2013), for a discussion of "general antagonism." See José David Saldívar, *Trans-Americanity: Subaltern Modernities, Global Coloniality, and the Cultures of Greater Mexico* (Durham: Duke University Press, 2012), for a detailed discussion of his concept of braided languages.

8

SCOTT HERRING

Queering Modernism

Beginning in the 1980s, scholarly forays into the queerness of the American modernist novel heavily documented the genre's sexual thematics. Whether discussing lesbian longing in notoriously difficult works such as Djuna Barnes' 1936 *Nightwood*, tracing hidden same-sex passion in Willa Cather's 1918 *My Ántonia*, or studying "sapphic primitivism" undergirding Gertrude Stein's 1903 *Q.E.D.*, literary critics mined this genre as a rich archive for nonheteronormative eroticism across gender, and, increasingly, race and ethnicity.[1] In this latter regard, it is important to remind ourselves that, alongside its more elite Anglo counterparts, Afro-modernist experiments of the Harlem (New Negro) Renaissance produced a slate of novels brimming with queer content – such as Wallace Thurman's 1932 satire *Infants of the Spring*, Claude McKay's 1928 picaresque *Home to Harlem*, and Nella Larsen's 1929 melodrama *Passing*. Observes Henry Louis Gates Jr. in an epigrammatic line published near the onset of what is now called queer theory: the Renaissance "was surely as gay as it was black, not that it was exclusively either of these."[2]

At the same time that many of these literary investigations were underfoot, social historians and American studies scholars also alerted readers to queer personages haunting modern U.S. literatures. George Chauncey's seminal 1994 study *Gay New York*, for one, archived the city's intricate urban subcultures of immigrant sex publics, male inverts (men, often bourgeois, who felt themselves women "confined" in the bodies of the male sex), fairies (working-class men who had sexual relations with other males), and other queer personages captured in works such as Ralph Werther's modernist 1918 memoir *Autobiography of an Androgyne*.[3] Lisa Duggan's 2000 *Sapphic Slashers* likewise revealed how the 1892 insanity hearings of Alice Mitchell for slaying her lover Freda Ward provided fodder for texts such as British author Radclyffe Hall's 1928 lesbian classic *The Well of Loneliness* (itself the centerpiece of a U.S. obscenity trial in 1929 and an influence for *Nightwood*).[4] Published the same year as Duggan's history, Siobhan

B. Somerville's *Queering the Color Line* plumbed novels such as James Weldon Johnson's *The Autobiography of an Ex-Colored Man* (1912) for interracial desire and the "scientific racism" of sexology, an international medical script that facilitated modern understandings of same-sex desire across gender since the later nineteenth century.[5]

These contributions remain crucial to scholarship, because they individually and collectively excavated historical constructions of sexual and racial identity formations. Of late, new strains in queer studies and modernist studies extend their findings to broaden not only definitions of modernism and modernity but of queerness itself. One of the strongest advocates for modernism's dilation has been feminist studies scholar Susan Stanford Friedman, who breaks with conventional chronological wisdom to redefine modernity – and aesthetic reactions to it – as "the condition or sensibility of radical disruption and accelerating change wherever and whenever such a phenomenon appears."[6] Making good on this magnification, subsequent scholars inside and outside queer studies – such as Benjamin Kahan, Heather Love, Kathryn Bond Stockton, Brian Glavey, and Fiona I.B. Ngô – trace what Kahan usefully terms the field's "profound capaciousness – open to aesthetics, subject matters, politics, and sexual cultures that fall outside mainstream semiotic systems."[7] Part of this spaciousness, it should also be said, has included a deeper attention to modern sexuality's geographic dynamics as critics such as Martin Joseph Ponce, Monica Miller, and Denise Cruz have turned to the transnational erotics played out across the circulation of modernist literatures.[8]

Simpatico with Friedman's widened scope, these scholars and their compeers often utilize American modernist novels to substantiate under-studied forms of queerness as they address matters of affect, region, nation, globality, and childhood subjectivity, to name but five avenues of thought. Love's *Feeling Backward*, for instance, embraces Cather's melancholy *The Professor's House* (1925) to remind contemporary LGBTQ activists about the importance of negative feeling in the wake of affirmative Gay Pride ideologies launched after the 1969 Stonewall riots in downtown New York City – an event, however erroneously, often considered to be the historical takeoff of radical homosexual organizing in America.[9] Judith (Jack) Halberstam makes mention of a global assortment of modernist writers to confirm his theory of *metronormativity*, the uncritical assumption that queers past and present should inhabit urban dwellings.[10] Taking up Barnes and Henry James in meticulous deconstructionist readings of child-hood perversion, Bond Stockton interprets deviant youth as an ongoing problematic from the later nineteenth century to the twenty-first.[11]

Given these evolving intimacies between queer studies and inquiries into the modernist American novel, we can say with confidence that the two will remain close confidants. Just as contemporary strains of queer studies defy normativity with moments from the modernist novel, so too did modernist authors offset their own emergent normalizations with multifarious depictions of queerness at large. Historians and cultural critics have long stressed that the standardization and rationalization inaugurated by modernization fundamentally reformatted modern subjectivities. As queer historian Nayan Shah notes, "standardization moved from governing the technological developments in the workplace and marketplace to shaping social life and the political order."[12] He also, tellingly, finds that normalization did so as well. "New concepts of the citizen and the human subject," he observes, "became the frame by which the process of normalization was organized on the individual, local, and national levels" – a process he dates from the "1870s to [the] 1930s."[13] Overlapping with a traditional periodization of American modernism, such normalization spilled over into personhood, citizenship, material culture, affective life, desire, and, unsurprisingly, narrative form. While reactionary in essence, normalization was an especially acute example of the "radical disruption and accelerating change" with which queer modernist novels grappled.

My position from the outset is that this struggling is not altogether unexpected given U.S. modernism's general self-understanding and its customary critical reception. As a literary movement that shifted across and within national borders, modernism has often been conceived as a formal disruption of earlier genres, one that attempted to work through various epistemological crises introduced by Einsteinian physics, unruly psyches dictated by the Freudian unconscious, and the global atrocities of World War I. Such "radical disruption" across historical, psychic, and aesthetic levels was complemented by other cultural disturbances, including the gradual dominance of a hetero-/homosexual binary tracked by many of the historians and cultural critics earlier mentioned. These various instances of "accelerating change" – and their ripple effects across the lives of novelists and the characters they conjured – were sometimes celebrated with narrative innovations such as stream of consciousness. At other times, scholars observe, they were rebelled against at levels of both content and form.

How might we further extend these far-reaching evaluations of queer modernist traditions? Tracing a few instances of experimentalist prose fiction from the late nineteenth century to the 1930s, this chapter charts how the genre further resisted inchoate forms of normalization not just for individuals but for the spaces they inhabited and the new objects they used – what Kahan deems "modernism's desire to thwart normative aesthetics, knowledges, geographies, and temporalities."[14] To do so, my essay first addresses the figure of the queer child as this typology troubled modern plots of standard maturation. It then turns to the queer role that regions played in a moment of fervent Americanization and global migration. Finally, it examines how the novel recorded the perversions of unorthodox goods amidst an increasing uniformity of modern consumer cultures. As we will see, such persons, places, and properties confirm how peculiar the queer modernist novel continues to be – and thus how useful it remains for undermining normativities of all persuasions then and now.

Queer Children

The historical invention of childhood, as thinkers such as Philippe Ariès have discussed at great length, emerged much earlier than the twentieth century, but this novel swath of an individual's lifespan became an especially acute subject of interest for psychologists, psychiatrists, and even presidents during the quickening of American modernism.[15] In 1904, G. Stanley Hall published *Adolescence*, a two-volume tome that advocated for spirited youth and their normal development.[16] In 1900, Theodore Roosevelt delivered his talk "Character and Success," which found budding young men to be the future cornerstones of civic heteronormativity – harbingers of "national greatness" who must avoid "moral corruption."[17] Young girls were by no means exempt from these ideologies as children became the focus of intense concern: they embodied both national promise and potential developmental failure that could sully the normalization efforts identified by Shah.

The queer novel probed these narratives of development, none more so than Henry James' protomodernist 1897 *What Maisie Knew*. Told in what would become a hallmark of modernist technique – unreliable narration – and a forerunner to James' later experimentalist works such as *The Golden Bowl* (1904) and *The Ambassadors* (1903), the novel makes hash of proper child rearing. It traces the redemptive tale of Maisie Farange, a young white girl thrown between divorced parents and stepparents who lands comfortably into the loving arms of her working-class governess, Mrs. Wix, at the novel's close. *Maisie*'s narrator repeatedly comments on the "impropriety" of the adults who neglect the child and confirms deviant heterosexuality as one of its central themes.[18] The child's promiscuous mother, for instance, engages in cross-generational affairs (84). Her equally promiscuous biological father, Beale Farange, is seen in public with Mrs. Coudon, an African American woman of whom Maisie is immediately wary. She registers the social inappropriateness of this interracial relation upon first sight of the two: "all in a moment she had had to accept her father as liking someone whom she was sure neither her mother, nor Mrs Beale, nor Mrs Wix, nor Sir Claude, nor the Captain, nor even Mr Perriam and Lord Eric could possibly have liked" (158–159).

This intricate "domestic labyrinth" produces, in the words of philosopher Michel Foucault, an instance of "children wise beyond their years," and these perverse adult dalliances nevertheless queer – as in "spoil" – her childhood (90).[19] James himself says as much in his 1909 preface, which finds that the novel traces "the death of her childhood" thanks in part to "a perversity in the step-parents" (28, 25). His observation is not inaccurate, given that Maisie's growing awareness of the sexual and racial deviance swirling about her contributes to an aberrant maturation even as her character retains its success. "'One would think you were about sixty,'" her stepfather Sir Claude observes, "'and that I – I don't know what anyone would think *I* am'" (247). Maisie ages too suddenly into adulthood, her lost childhood confirming a deviant developmental narrative.

Although the novel denounces decadent high society for this ruination, at the same time it paradoxically assaults any idealization of a normative nuclear family. The novel ends with Maisie and Mrs. Wix heading off on a journey outside the child's damaging parental units: they "found themselves on the [ship] deck so breathless and so scared that they gave up half the voyage to letting their emotion sink" (266). The novel earlier codes this queer bond between a young girl and an older woman as "the beginning of better things" (209), but it also characterizes their close friendship as a same-sex passion: "they were hand in hand; they had melted together" (249). In so doing, *What Maisie Knew* imagines a cross-class romance between Maisie and her "poor and queer" Mrs. Wix that is not lesbian but certainly is peculiar (50).

If children were not perverted – for good or for ill – by family in the modernist novel, then there was always the Great War (1914–1918). That, at least, is one thesis of Ernest Hemingway's 1924 *In Our Time*, a menagerie of interlocking and international experimental tales that inverts Roosevelt's "Character and Success" by transforming young men into infantilized boys traumatized as much by conventional family dynamics as by the trenches. Discounting his gender-bending *The Garden of Eden* (posthumously published in 1986), Hemingway, unlike James, is not usually cast as a queer writer. With its fractured, truncated narratives and sparse prose beholden as much to Ezra Pound's Imagist movement as to Hemingway's spell as a *Kansas City Star* journalist, *In Our Time* is, however, rife with deviant and traumatized children. Think of a young Nick Adams witnessing the suicide of a "squaw" in "Indian Camp" or a spine-injured Nick recuperating from war injury (and disappointing female relationships) in the two stories that constitute "Big Two-Hearted River."[20]

This queerness is equally apparent in "Soldier's Home," the tale of Harold Krebs, returning from the war to his "home town in Oklahoma" to the celebration of absolutely no one (69). Instead, Krebs' parents ceaselessly hound Harold for his failure to mimic a local heteronormative ideal, Charley Simmons. "'Your father is worried, too,' his mother went on. 'He thinks you have lost your ambition, that you haven't got a definite aim in life. Charley Simmons, who is just your age, has a good job and is going to be married. The boys are all settling down; they're all determined to get somewhere'" (75). It is clear from this passage that Charley's success is not simply financial ("a good job"); it is also sexual given Simmons' engagement and his conventional "married" life to come. Charley is, in brief, a standardized "aim in life" that Krebs fails to mirror.

Unlike Charley or the other "boys," Krebs remains single, frozen at home, and transformed into a queer child by his parents, despite their wish for him to leave the nest. He provides another example of an off-kilter maturational narrative as his parents constantly infantilize him: "His mother would have given him breakfast in bed if he had wanted it" (70). Though "Papa" Hemingway is often stereotyped in popular lore as the manliest of modernist authors, it is unclear from "Soldier's Home" if his failed male characters are haunted more by "machine-gun fire" than by the constraints of hetero-domesticity (63).

Queer Regions

As much as the modernist U.S. novel tracked the normative pressures of standardizing life narratives for queer children of all ages, so too did it negotiate the normalizations of spatial relations. The traditional moment of American modernism, as numerous historians and cultural critics have observed, was also one of aggressive nativism intent on regulating supposedly deviant foreigners via Americanization as jingoistic faith in the idea of "America" took stronger root.[21] Whereas the nation's regions were often used to confirm these nationalist ideologies – much as they were in late nineteenth-century local color writings – alternate spaces of queerness persisted within the modernist novel.[22] Indeed, the genre's aestheticized locales recorded counterdiscourses in geographies as dissimilar as the sparsely populated Great Plains and the dense neighborhoods of global Manhattan.

Willa Cather's 1918 *My Ántonia* testifies to this dynamic tension between nativism and queer georesistance. Set largely in 1880s rural Nebraska (and patterned off of Cather's childhood upbringing in the tiny town of Red Cloud, Nebraska), the novel traces social exchanges between the Bohemian-born Shimerdas and the American-born Burdens as the two families navigate the difficulties of Plains living. Structured via a frame narrative – we read Jim Burden's memoir entitled "My Ántonia" – this impressionistic retelling at times confirms the supposed deviance of transnational immigrants. After Jim's grandmother receives a gift of mushrooms from Mrs. Shimerda, for example, she discards them and tells her grandson: "They might be dried meat from some queer beast, Jim. They ain't dried fish, and they never grew on stalk or vine. I'm afraid of 'em. Anyhow, I shouldn't want to eat anything that had been shut up for months with old clothes and goose pillows."[23] Such a moment epitomizes the paranoid anti-immigrant sentiment of Cather's time as well as its attendant racial and material normalizations.

Despite Mrs. Burden's dismissal of the Shimerdas' expressive culture, however, queer theorists such as Judith Butler, Eve Kosofsky Sedgwick, and Jonathan Goldberg have justifiably focused on what Butler terms the "passion" between Jim and Ántonia.[24] As they become closer friends in the first third of the novel, the portrayal of the two has been read by these critics as but one way in which Cather announces her desire for women into modernist narrative – how this author, using a keyword from Sedgwick, stages a "cross-identification" with Jim in order to better appreciate Ántonia's body.[25] Butler's and Sedgwick's readings of Cather are forceful and accurate ones since we find at the novel's start that the spouse of a middle-aged Jim "has her own fortune and lives her own life" (n.p.). His most dear memories (and perhaps some of Cather's) are those of the regional spaces shared with Ántonia during his youth, and others have noted as much.[26]

Given Cather's love for women such as Louise Pound and Edith Lewis, a reading such as Sedgwick's or Butler's seems indisputable, but I also note, following Goldberg, that My Ántonia's queerness relies not only on same-sex female eroticism but upon regionally based "cross-racial" and cross-ethnic desire.[27] Unlike the white women of the town, non-Americans such as Ántonia are cast as a foreign "menace to the social order" (201). As an Anglo-American born in Virginia, Jim's associations with Ántonia thus implicate him in the social non-normativity of these racialized and ethnicized bodies, and Cather's rural Midwest at times appears to be a "borderlands zone" that "rivaled the depths of biological kinship relationships."[28] That the novel insists on the pleasures afforded by the queer contacts that spaces such as Black Hawk (the central town of the novel) offered in the midst of U.S. nativism is courageous. At the novel's end, Jim romantically recalls himself and the novel's title character "bedded down in the straw" on their initial trip to hinterlands that would become their respective home (371). For Jim, this culturally unsanctioned intimacy between a native and a foreigner is "precious" (372). For others at this time of queer transnationalism, this alliance would be anathema, and to some criminal.

A much more contemptuous novel – yet one as pointed in its critique of normative American spatiality – is Nathanael West's 1934 Great Depression–era sendup, *A Cool Million, or, the Dismantling of Lemuel Pitkin*. A merciless takedown of American normativity that implodes the narratological ploys of quick-success stories, the novel relentlessly parodies American hetero-nationalism via outrageous representations of sexual and racial queerness. To do so, it turns the idealized wholesomeness of regional Americana on its head. With what Rita Barnard terms "writing that is both in and against the American grain,"[29] *A Cool Million* traces the literal dismantling of "the American boy" Lemuel Pitkin, a northeastern Yankee born "near the town of Ottsville in the state of Vermont."[30] The portrayed bodily disfiguration – Lemuel loses his eye, his teeth, his leg, his scalp, and finally his life, over the novel's plot – is as much the disfiguration of the growing norm of American heterosexuality given that Pitkin stands in for a prototypically straight white citizen. His regional New England body, I mean to say, is at once a nationalized one, and the novel tears apart the country's 1930s domestic bromides.

As it does so, *A Cool Million* derides an intensifying American hetero-normativity in the midst of the Depression. Early in the novel, one of Lemuel's neighbors, Betty Prail, is captured by a white slaver, Wu Fong, and prostituted in his New York City–based "House of All Nations" (93). A parody of moral panics surrounding Chinatown dens, this House ridiculously becomes "an hundred per centum American place" after "the [William Randolph] Hearst papers began their 'Buy American' campaign" (126). Wu Fong, we find, "engaged Mr. Asa Goldstein to redecorate the house and that worthy designed a Pennsylvania Dutch, Old South, Log Cabin Pioneer, Victorian New York, Western Cattle Days, California Monterey, Indian, and Modern Girl series of interiors" (126). Teasing out West's debt to surrealism here, Barnard cites this makeover and incisively reads it as an attempt on West's part to craft "a parodic museum of American regional cultures and artifacts."[31] A complementary irony, I add, lies in West's dismantling of frontier tropes, of Old New York, and of other U.S. regions used to substantiate an insipid imaginary of heteronormative America. In *A Cool Million*, a culturally treasured regional stereotype such as the "Log Cabin Pioneer" becomes a female sex worker, and this topsy-turvy world applies to men as well. Lemuel finds himself imprisoned in Wu Fong's brothel, and "the poor lad was taken to a room that had been fitted out like a ship's cabin. The walls were paneled in teak, and there were sextants, compasses and other such gear in profusion. His captors then forced him to don a tight-fitting sailor suit" (130). Given that Lemuel becomes the object of affection from "the Maharajah of Kanurani, whose tastes were notorious," West uses queer regionalism (and a queasy queer

Orientalism) to figuratively disassemble the national body of "nice-looking American boys" who, for a few days at least, are treated as gigolos (130).

Queer Goods

Though less discussed by scholars in queer studies and modernist studies, attendant normalizations not only of persons or places but also of things emerged in the first decades of the twentieth century thanks to swift advances in consumer cultures. The queer modernist novel responded accordingly, if not approvingly. The scale of new goods introduced to U.S.-based citizens from the least populated towns of the Deep South to the megalopolis of New York City was, frankly, bewildering: automobiles, mass-produced accessories, and increased electric wiring for houses, to cite a select few examples. Alongside these novel material developments were innovations in the delivery of merchandise, their storage, and their promotion – marketing that sold the promise of a rich material life for individuals (now conceived as avid consumers) across socioeconomic and, increasingly, racial divides.[32] Scholars have long observed that modernist productions picked up on this fascination with new objects.[33] Yet in keeping with Shah's assessment of normalization's spread throughout the twentieth century, I stress that this ever-expanding consumer culture produced its own normative relations to material interactions: what to purchase, when to buy it, where to put it. As much as they did for children such as Maisie or places such as Black Hawk, modernist novels archived deviations from these developing imperatives.

Although an unlikely candidate for sexualized queerness, given its emphasis on heterosexual relations, Zora Neale Hurston's *Their Eyes Were Watching God* (1937) is nonetheless highly resistant to modern goods as its main character, Janie Crawford, finds herself refusing inchoate dictates of consumption. In many ways the novel follows the historical trajectory of a burgeoning U.S. consumer culture. After Janie leaves her first husband, Logan Killicks, for Joe (Jody) Starks, the two settle into a life of seemingly productive consumerism in the small town of Eatonville, Florida. This new town is soon incorporated into this life, and Starks opens up "uh store": "it all looked too big and rushing for her to keep track of. Before the store had a complete roof, Jody had canned goods piled on the floor and was selling so much he didn't have time to go off on his talking tours."[34]

Jody also treats Janie as a prized commodity to be consumed at this store (but for himself alone): "she was there in the store for *him* to look at, not those others" (55). This circumstance is, depressingly, nothing new – as anthropologist Gayle Rubin has remarked, the "traffic in women" has structured civilizations for centuries – but Hurston highlights how her entrepreneur-husband Jody transforms Janie into a priceless keepsake and how her subsequent relationship with her next partner, Tea Cake, enables her to step outside these sexualized rhythms of things.[35] After Starks' death, "she had found a jewel down inside herself and she had wanted to walk where people could see her and gleam it around. But she had been set in the market-place to sell" (90). With Tea Cake, however, Janie frees herself from these interlocking forms of consumption. This is not to imply that "the market-place" is ever entirely absent in this worldly novel – Hurston writes that "Tea Cake and Janie had friended with the Bahaman workers in the 'Glades" – but that her relation with Tea Cake is an engine for a different way of approaching objects (including her gendered self) outside the gendered market of commodity goods (154).[36] As she tells her friend Pheoby at the novel's beginning, "Ah ain't brought home a thing but mahself" (4).

Janie's self-extraction from modern materialism makes the townspeople of Eatonville both nervous and jealous at the same time as it queers Hurston's main character: "seeing the woman as she was made them remember the envy they had stored up from other times. So they chewed up the back parts of their minds and swallowed with relish. They made burning statements with questions, and killing tools out of laughs. It was mass cruelty" (2). These four sentences make sense when placed into their historical context. According to Kathy Peiss, the novel coincides with a "new beauty culture that spread throughout black communities in the early twentieth century."[37] When Janie returns to Eatonville as an aging ("ole forty year ole"), striking, single woman content to live with memory, she represents an alternative way to relate to things other than those promoted in advertisements for modern goods in "nascent black consumer culture" (2).[38] There is a punitive social cost for this as Janie turns into a pariah, but *Their Eyes'* narrator advocates her non-normative ethos of anticonsumption: "Sometimes Janie would think of the old days in the big white house and the store and laugh to herself. What if Eatonville could see her now in her blue denim overalls and heavy shoes?" (134).

Similar instances of queer things occur in other modernist novels of the decade such as Faulkner's *As I Lay Dying* and Michael Gold's *Jews without Money* – both published in 1930. The former concentrates on the queerness of an off-white (or, to use a harsh vernacular, "white trash") family in nonmetropolitan Mississippi. According to critics such as Matt Wray and historians such as Anthony Harkins, Faulkner's characters would have been cast as sexual deviants according to the unforgiving representations of rural southerners at this time, and the author certainly toys with this stereotype by having one of the novel's female characters – Dewey Dell – impregnated outside of monogamous marriage.³⁹ Yet in aestheticizing the tragicomic tale of the "white trash" Bundrens, the novel also uses a queer strategy of *defamiliarization* described by Russian literary theorist Viktor Shklovsky in his 1917 essay, "Art as Technique."⁴⁰ In essence, defamiliarization's promise is "to make objects 'unfamiliar,' to make forms difficult, to increase the difficulty and length of perception because the process of perception is an aesthetic end to itself and must be prolonged."⁴¹ As such, we might say that defamiliarization is one form of queer reading in that it renders odd – another omnipresent definition of the word *queer* – the things that make up modern everyday life. *As I Lay Dying* does this especially well as the narrative *formally* queers the *socially* queered characters that inhabit Faulkner's fictional world as well as the burgeoning consumer culture that encroaches upon them.

The novel's defamiliarizing transformation of humans into peculiar things is, in fact, apparent from one of its most famous lines. Pondering his dead mother, Addie, boxed into a homemade coffin made by his brother, a young Vardaman Bundren thinks to himself in a one-line chapter that "my mother is a fish."⁴² What's fascinating is how the novel queerly defamiliarizes modern material conditions as well. Later in the novel, after the family has made their way toward the town of Jefferson, Mississippi, he observes that "the stores are dark, but the lights pass on the windows when we pass. The lights are in the trees around the courthouse" (249). Naively, Vardaman transfigures inanimate electricity poles and their light bulbs into a glowing natural forest. This makes him an autodidactic modernist of sorts as he queers modernization, but it also testifies to both his backwardness and his speedy entry into an emergent world of goods as the family encounters "the [advertising] signs for sometime now: the drug stores, the clothing stores, the patent medicine and the garages and cafés" (226).

Removed from Faulkner's formal stylization yet similarly invested in tracking the queerness of modern goods is Gold's proletariat novel *Jews without Money*, a mournful and enraged autobiographical paean to Lower East Side immigrant cultures. Though not traditionally modernist in form, it nevertheless responds to the normalization of things and the standardization of commodities as it celebrates the supposed aberration of ethnic material cultures. In an apostrophic elegy to his neighborhood, Gold writes:

> O home of all the twisted junk, rusty baby carriages, lumber, bottles, boxes, moldy pants and dead cats of the neighborhood – every one spat and held the nostrils when passing you. But in my mind you still blaze in a halo of childish romance. No place will ever seem as wonderful again.⁴³

Refusing to devalue working-class Jewish immigrant things in a moment of material uniformity, Gold champions their "excitement, dirt, fighting, chaos!" (14). Explicitly alluding to the "unreal city" that T.S. Eliot captured in his high Anglophone opus *The Waste Land* (1922), Gold refuses to normalize the literal and figurative "dirt" of Lower Manhattan tenements, and this applies to supposedly morally dirty persons as well (126). One of the novel's more memorable minor characters is, after all, "a fat, haughty prostitute [who] sat on a chair two tenements away. She wore a red kimono decorated with Japanese cherry trees, mountains, waterfalls and old philosophers. Her black hair was fastened by a diamond brooch" (17).

How is this unnamed sex worker – another instance of a perverse transnationalism given her immigrant status – not an exquisite emblem of queer modernity amidst modern U.S. literatures? Draped in the mass-produced fabric of an outdated Japonisme craze, sitting triumphant on the stoop of a cosmopolis that sheltered thousands of immigrants, Gold's obese harlot takes something ancient ("old philosophers") and makes them perversely new. In so doing, she bridges fictive modernist studies of sexual dissidence from the 1930s with our scholarly forays in the present. Her non-normativity stands comfortably alongside the degenerate youth of James' elite Western Europe, the man-children of Hemingway's war-torn Plains, the aging consumers of Hurston's Florida, the deviant Bohemians of Cather's striving Midwest, and the yokels marveling at the accelerating changes to Faulkner's rural Mississippi.

These individuals – Janie Crawford, Harold Krebs, Ántonia Shimerda, Vardaman Bundren, and Maisie Farange, to name but five that this chapter surveyed – are as queer as the fairies who cruised the streets of gay New York or those who clapped furiously after lesbian blues singer Gladys Bentley finished her set at Harlem's Clam House. They reconfirm the "profound capaciousness" of sexuality that scholars of modernist studies have often cast as one of the genre's most telling traits, and they point to the pluralities of queerness that marked their own era as much as they anticipate the range of eroticism that characterizes our age and those later to come.[44]

Like so many of us in the twenty-first century, these moderns negotiated wave after pounding wave of normalization across a variety of punishing social and material fields. They too rode them out as best they could. Although the disparate styles they occupied – elite protomodernism, proletariat realism, modernist regionalism, imagist-influenced war tales, surrealist parody, and lush folklore narratives – may no longer be in fashion, their queer engagements with novel forms of modernity still have much to teach us as we navigate our own ceaseless changes of sexual pace.

NOTES

1. On Barnes, see Joseph Allen Boone, *Libidinal Currents: Sexuality and the Shaping of Modernism* (Chicago: University of Chicago, 1998), 232–251; on Cather, see Jonathan Goldberg, *Willa Cather and Others* (Durham: Duke University Press, 2001), 22–32; on Stein, see Jaime Hovey, "Sapphic Primitivism in Gertrude Stein's *Q.E.D.*," *Modern Fiction Studies* 42, no. 3 (1996): 547–568.

2. Henry Louis Gates Jr., "The Black Man's Burden," in *Fear of a Queer Planet: Queer Politics and Social Theory*, ed. Michael Warner (Minneapolis: University of Minnesota Press, 1993), 233.

3. George Chauncey, *Gay New York: Gender, Urban Culture, and the Making of the Gay Male World, 1890–1940* (New York: Basic Books, 1994), outlines these taxonomies in great detail. For his extensive discussion of Werther, see, for example, 42–44, 59–60.

4. Lisa Duggan, *Sapphic Slashers: Sex, Violence, and American Modernity* (Durham: Duke University Press, 2000), discusses Hall at 188–191.

5. Siobhan B. Somerville, *Queering the Color Line: Race and the Invention of Sexuality in American Culture* (Durham: Duke University Press, 2000), addresses Johnson at 111–130 and scientific racism at 15–38.

6. Susan Stanford Friedman, "Definitional Excursions: The Meanings of Modern/Modernism/Modernity," *Modernism/modernity* 8, no. 3 (2001): 503.

7. Benjamin Kahan, *Celibacies: American Modernism and Sexual Life* (Durham: Duke University Press, 2013), 6. See also Brian Glavey, *Queer Ekphrasis: Modernism, Form, and the Descriptive Turn* (New York: Oxford University Press, 2015), and Fiona I.B. Ngô, *Imperial Blues: Geographies of Race and Sex in Jazz Age New York* (Durham: Duke University Press, 2014).

8. See Martin Joseph Ponce, *Beyond the Nation: Diasporic Filipino Literature and Queer Reading* (New York: New York University Press, 2012), 58–88; Monica L. Miller, *Slaves to Fashion: Black Dandyism and the Styling of Black Diasporic Identity* (Durham: Duke University Press, 2009); and Denise Cruz, "José García Villa's Collection of 'Others': Irreconcilabilities of a Queer Transpacific Modernism," *Modern Fiction Studies* 55, no. 1 (2009): 11–41.

9. Heather Love, *Feeling Backward: Loss and the Politics of Queer History* (Cambridge: Harvard University Press, 2007), 81–87.

10. Judith Halberstam, *In a Queer Time and Place: Transgender Bodies, Subcultural Lives* (New York: New York University Press, 2005), 36–37, 41–42.

11. Kathryn Bond Stockton, *The Queer Child, or Growing Sideways in the Twentieth Century* (Durham: Duke University Press, 2010), 61–88, 90–94.

12. Nayan Shah, *Contagious Divides: Epidemics and Race in San Francisco's Chinatown* (Berkeley: University of California Press, 2001), 253.

13. Ibid., 253. For a few scholarly instances that compare well with Shah, see Alan Trachtenberg on "the standardization of parts, measurements, and human effort" as well as "the process of continual refinement and rationalization" in *The Incorporation of America: Culture and Society in the Gilded Age* (1982; New York: Hill and Wang, 2007), 56; Julian B. Carter, *The Heart of Whiteness: Normal Sexuality and Race in America, 1880–1940* (Durham: Duke University Press, 2007); and Michael Warner, *The Trouble with Normal: Sex, Politics, and the Ethics of Queer Life* (New York: Free Press, 1999), 56–59.

14. Benjamin Kahan, "Queer Modernism," in *A Handbook of Modernism Studies*, ed. Jean-Michel Rabaté (Malden, MA: Blackwell, 2013), 348.

15. Philippe Ariès, *Centuries of Childhood: A Social History of Family Life* (New York: Knopf, 1962).

16. G. Stanley Hall, *Adolescence*, 2 vols. (New York: Appleton, 1904).

17. Theodore Roosevelt, "Character and Success," in *The Strenuous Life and Other Essays* (1900; New York: Century, 1903), 116, 121.

18. Henry James, *What Maisie Knew* (1897; London: Penguin Classics, 1985), 153; hereafter cited in text. See Kevin Ohi, "Narrating the Child's Queerness in *What Maisie Knew*," in *Curiouser: On the Queerness of Children*, eds. Steven Bruhm and Natasha Hurley (Minneapolis: University of Minnesota Press, 2004), 81–106, for the definitive reading of queerness in this text.

19. Michel Foucault, *The History of Sexuality, Vol. 1: An Introduction*, trans. Robert Hurley (New York: Vintage, 1990), 40.

20. Ernest Hemingway, *In Our Time* (1924; New York: Scribner, 2003), 17; hereafter cited in text.

21. For more on this matter, see Marcus Klein, *Foreigners: The Making of American Literature, 1900–1940* (Chicago: University of Chicago Press, 1981); Walter Benn Michaels, *Our America: Nativism, Modernism, and Pluralism* (Durham: Duke University Press, 1997); and Mae M. Ngai, *Impossible Subjects: Illegal Aliens and the Making of Modern America* (Princeton, NJ: Princeton University Press, 2005).

22. For an in-depth account of late nineteenth- and early twentieth-century U.S. regionalism that considers the movement's formalist desires for national unification, see Stephanie Foote, *Regional Fictions: Culture and Identity in Nineteenth-Century American Literature* (Madison: University of Wisconsin Press, 2001).

23. Willa Cather, *My Ántonia* (1918; Boston: Houghton Mifflin, 1954), 79; hereafter cited in text.

24. Judith Butler, *Bodies That Matter: On the Discursive Limits of "Sex"* (New York: Routledge, 1993), 147.

25. Eve Kosofsky Sedgwick, *Tendencies* (Durham: Duke University Press, 1993), 14.

26. See, for example, Marilee Lindemann, *Willa Cather: Queering America* (New York: Columbia University Press, 1999).

27. Goldberg, *Willa Cather*, 70. Goldberg provides an extensive close reading of this relation's eroticism and finds that "across time and distance, [Jim and Ántonia] are coupled (but not married to each other). The pair derives its figurative force ... from the ways in which it variously minoritized difference – male homosexual, lesbian, immigrant, Native American – to glimpse a future that does not efface difference" (32).

28. Nayan Shah, *Stranger Intimacy: Contesting Race, Sexuality, and the Law in the North American West* (Berkeley: University of California Press, 2011), 31, 102.

29. Rita Barnard, *The Great Depression and the Culture of Abundance: Kenneth Fearing, Nathanael West, and Mass Culture in the 1930s* (Cambridge: Cambridge University Press, 1995), 147.

30. Nathanael West, *A Cool Million, or, the Dismantling of Lemuel Pitkin*, in *A Cool Million and The Dream Life of Balso Snell* (1934; New York: Noonday, 1996), 179, 67; hereafter cited in text.

31. Barnard, *Great Depression*, 146.

32. See, for instance, Jackson Lears, *Fables of Abundance: A Cultural History of Advertising in America* (New York: Basic Books, 1994); Roland Marchand, *Advertising the American Dream: Making Way for Modernity, 1920–1940* (Berkeley: University of California Press, 1985); and Marina Moskowitz, *Standard of Living: The Measure of the Middle Class in Modern America* (Baltimore: Johns Hopkins University Press, 2004).

33. For discussions of links between the objects of modern material cultures and U.S. modernisms, see Bill Brown, *A Sense of Things: The Object Matter of American Literature* (Chicago: University of Chicago Press, 2004), 177–188; and Douglas Mao, *Solid Objects: Modernism and the Test of Production* (Princeton, NJ: Princeton University Press, 1998).

34. Zora Neale Hurston, *Their Eyes Were Watching God* (1937; New York: Harper Perennial Modern Classics, 2006), 40, 41; hereafter cited in text.

35. See Gayle Rubin, "The Traffic in Women: Notes on the 'Political Economy' of Sex," in *Toward an Anthropology of Woman*, ed. Rayna Reiter (New York: Monthly Review Press, 1975), 157–185.

36. A fine reading of this aspect in Hurston's novel is Martyn Richard Bone, "The (Extended) South of Black Folk: Intraregional and Transnational Migrant Labor in *Jonah's Gourd Vine* and *Their Eyes Were Watching God*," *American Literature* 79, no. 4 (2007): 753–779.

37. Kathy Peiss, *Hope in a Jar: The Making of America's Beauty Culture* (New York: Henry Holt, 1998), 206.

38. Ibid., 202. See also Patricia Yaeger, *Dirt and Desire: Reconstructing Southern Women's Writing, 1930–1990* (Chicago: University of Chicago Press, 2000), on the novel's "need to generate a set of objects that have not been marked or soiled by whiteness" (202).

39. See Matt Wray, *Not Quite White: White Trash and the Boundaries of Whiteness* (Durham: Duke University Press, 2006), and Anthony Harkins, *Hillbilly: A Cultural History of an American Icon* (New York: Oxford University Press, 2005).

40. Viktor Shklovsky, "Art as Technique," in *Russian Formalist Criticism: Four Essays*, eds. and trans. Lee T. Lemon and Marion J. Reis (1917; Lincoln: University of Nebraska Press, 1965), 13.

41. Ibid., 12.

42. William Faulkner, *As I Lay Dying* (1930; New York: Vintage International, 1995), 84; hereafter cited in text.

43. Michael Gold, *Jews without Money* (1930; New York: Carroll and Graf, 1994), 46; hereafter cited in text. See also Jani Scandura, *Down in the Dumps: Place, Modernity, American Depression* (Durham: Duke University Press, 2008), for a detailed reading of urban geographies such as New York City – particularly Harlem – and their relationship to modern waste.

44. Kahan, *Celibacies*, 6.

9

STEVEN MEYER

The Scientific Imagination of U.S. Modernist Fiction

> Now in attempting to write literary history, one must guard against giving
> the impression that these movements and counter-movements necessarily
> follow one another in a punctual and well-generalled fashion.[1]
> – Edmund Wilson

Rigid and Robust Empiricisms

One might be excused for supposing that a reasonable way to proceed in investigating the U.S. modernist novel of science would be to treat the "of" as what is commonly called an objective genitive and go looking for novels *about* science. When one does this, the following problem arises: despite the United States in the twentieth century having been profoundly marked by science, and with this heroic period already well under way at the start of the century – just think of *The Principles of Psychology*, William James' masterful 1890 consolidation of psychology as a science, or indeed of Edison in Menlo Park – little effort was made in modernist fiction to represent all this activity. True, the central protagonist of Fitzgerald's *Tender Is the Night* (1934) is a psychiatrist; and, yes, Dos Passos included carefully wrought vignettes of scientists and engineers in his *U.S.A.* trilogy (1938). The 1926 Pulitzer Prize was awarded to Sinclair Lewis' *Arrowsmith*, whose eponymous protagonist cycles through every conceivable identity available to someone trained in biology and medicine in the early years of the century – unfortunately, there is nothing the least bit modernist about the novel!

In the pages that follow, I propose that the emergence in the United States of modernist fiction capable of exploiting science as legitimate subject matter was blocked by the strength of the engagement with science of an immediately preceding (and to some extent, contemporaneous) mode of U.S. fiction: that of literary naturalism. Insofar as the American modernist novel resists the naturalist portrayal of brute mechanical force – by no means always – and identifies such force with the object of science generally, representations of science may be the first thing to go. An alternate understanding of the phrase *novel of science* is called for – one that treats

137

the "of" as a subjective genitive and refers to novels *informed* by science rather than expressly being *about* it.

Certainly, many works of naturalist fiction fit this category, as do several works that possess seminaturalist, semimodernist hybrid status: Mark Twain's conjoined tales of 1894, *Pudd'nhead Wilson* and *Those Extraordinary Twins*, and Gertrude Stein's innovative novelistic fictions, *Three Lives* (1909) and *The Making of Americans* (1925). It is in the context of Stein's writing, and the many American modernist novelists who followed her (in agreement, disagreement, or some combination of these), that I will distinguish traditional empiricism – "rigid empiricism," Alfred North Whitehead called it – from the more robust empiricisms exhibited in much twentieth-century science and in U.S. modernist fictions of science, albeit often without being recognized as such. Among the writers building on Stein's earlier work was Stein herself in the novel *Lucy Church Amiably* (1930), addressed in the concluding section of this essay.

Literary Naturalism and the U.S. Modernist Novel of Science

For the U.S. novel, 1925 was an annus mirabilis. Works that appeared that year, in addition to *Arrowsmith* and *The Making of Americans*, included Theodore Dreiser's *An American Tragedy*, Edith Wharton's *The Mother's Recompense*, John Dos Passos' *Manhattan Transfer*, Sherwood Anderson's *Dark Laughter*, Carl Van Vechten's *Firecrackers*, F. Scott Fitzgerald's *The Great Gatsby*, and Willa Cather's *The Professor's House*. Alain Locke's revelatory anthology, *The New Negro*, with fiction by Jean Toomer and Zora Neale Hurston among others, also dates from 1925, as does Ernest Hemingway's breakthrough collection of stories, *In Our Time*. This list mixes naturalists (Dreiser, Wharton) and modernists (everyone else except for Lewis) and includes among the modernists some whose writing was expressly and variously associated with science (Dos Passos, Stein, Cather, Hurston). The remaining figures, aside from Toomer, all possessed strong ties to Stein, whose 925-page novel is, chronologically speaking, the outlier in the group – composed between 1906 and 1911, in the decade before the War, yet, despite a great deal of effort having been expended to place it, unpublished till the mid-twenties.

Edmund Wilson, in his 1931 "study in the imaginative literature of 1870–1930," *Axel's Castle*, nicely summed up literary naturalism as holding that "humanity was the accidental product of heredity and environment, and capable of being explained in terms of these."[2] Unlike the naturalism of Émile Zola, modeled on experimental physiology, most American naturalism derived from social Darwinist doctrines. Perhaps the purest of the

American naturalists, Dreiser recalled his discovery in the late 1890s of Herbert Spencer, who "quite blew me, intellectually, to bits": "Man was a mechanism, undevised and uncreated, and a badly and carelessly driven one at that ... drawn or blown here and there by larger forces in which he moved quite unconsciously as an atom."[3]

Into this still-inchoate naturalist literary environment Twain ventured with *The Tragedy of Pudd'nhead Wilson and the Comedy Those Extraordinary Twins*. Where the argument in *Pudd'nhead Wilson* concerns "the power of environment in shaping character," the attached farce investigates the complications that might arise when two persons – "conglomerate twins," as it were – share a body, "a combination consisting of two heads and four arms joined to a single body and a single pair of legs."[4] The figure of conjoined twins resonates unmistakably with the dual structure of Twain's notoriously ungainly work. Yet despite such formal play, the trouble with characterizing Twain as a modernist is that no self-respecting author of modernist fiction would label himself or herself an incompetent, and Twain seems to do just that in the opening pages of the farce, which serve as connective tissue between the two halves of the work. The sharp critique of "the coherent, autonomous self" that George Marcus locates at the core of *Pudd'nhead Wilson* extends not just to the author but to the reader as well.[5]

Like Twain in his tragicomedy, Stein in her novella "Melanctha" – composed in 1905–1906 and the centerpiece of the 1909 collection *Three Lives* – combines features associated with literary naturalism and with the literary modernism that followed it. Each work is a fiction of science, exhibiting the objective as well as the subjective senses of the genitive. Marcus rightly identifies the vehicle for Twain's criticism in the various ways in which the author handles the characters and their interactions in *Pudd'nhead Wilson*, in the process exemplifying "the burgeoning interest in the psychopathology of dual personality during the later nineteenth century" even as less speculative aspects of science, such as late nineteenth-century advances in fingerprinting, also comprise a significant part of the work's subject matter (194).

Although Twain's conglomerate tale time and again approaches the requisite degree of compositional and psychological innovation, dual hallmarks of modernist fiction, it never quite crosses the bar. Still, the protomodernist work demonstrates that writing such as Stein's – at once informed by and about multiple aspects of science, formally innovative, and critical of unrestricted modernization – was not something she invented out of thin air. The first of Stein's "three histories" actually started as a translation of one of Gustave Flaubert's *Three Tales* (1877), and Lyn Hejinian has argued that, beginning with *Three Lives* and continuing through decades of "subsequent writings," Stein "accomplished the work that Flaubert dreamed of" – "psychological analysis," as he had put it, written from a "standpoint" in which "there are no noble subjects or ignoble subjects" and in prose "that would be rhythmic as verse, precise as the language of the sciences."[6]

For Stein, Hejinian observes somewhat cryptically, "to have a psyche is to be in composition" (269). "Nothing extraordinary happens," yet each of the "central figures [in *Three Lives*] dies as if exhausted by a surfeit of experience" (270). "It is not socially imposed conventions," as one would expect in accord with naturalist norms, "but internally composed ones that defeat them" (281). Herein lies the basis for an account such as Stein's of any manner of inner experience (including but not limited, as we shall see, to psychological experience) as a form of composition. The person is not, as Dreiser would have it, "blown here and there by larger forces in which [she moves] quite unconsciously as an atom." We are no longer dealing with Dreiser's naturalism, yet at least in the aggregate the perspective remains naturalist inasmuch as it emphasizes the inevitability of any single life's defeat – only now *at its own hands*.

There is more to Stein's "character studies" than that, especially with regard to the central figure in the triptych, Melanctha Herbert (270).[7] The obverse of the "clinical ... impulse" (that "nothing ... can be considered unworthy of attention") is that everything, every occasion, is held equally to be worthy of attention (286). Stein's nonhierarchical stance had many likely sources, but what Hejinian calls her "radical force of attention" derived from the exemplary scientific training she received at Radcliffe and Johns Hopkins and, most decisively in this context, from the innovative analysis of attention furnished by her mentor, Harvard psychologist and philosopher William James (96).

William James and the U.S. Modernist Novel of Science

"Gertrude Stein, born in Allegheny, Pennsylvania, a student of psychology and medicine who is said to have been considered by William James the most brilliant woman pupil he had ever had, published in 1909 a book of fiction called 'Three Lives.'"[8] So begins Edmund Wilson's account of Stein, one of six writers who, "hav[ing] largely dominated the literary world of the decade 1920–30," together comprise the main focus of *Axel's Castle* (841). Just how is it, then, that Stein was able to complicate the naturalism in a work such as "Melanctha" with what would subsequently come to be regarded as modernist procedures, so as to produce a U.S. modernist fiction informed by science rather than a protomodernist one, as Twain had already done?

Basically, in a work such as "Melanctha," the deterministic naturalist framework (in this case the narrator's classificatory color scheme) exists in irreconcilable tension with the experience portrayed within that framework – more various and more complex than the framework can accommodate. When Stein writes of "intelligent, attractive, half white" Melanctha as being (in the narrator's words) "full with mystery and subtle movements and denials and vague distrusts and complicated disillusions," we recognize the characteristic richness of modernist portraiture.[9] We also find in the phrasing unmistakable echoes of William James' multifaceted rendering of human experience.[10]

Where the present essay is concerned, the key feature that distinguishes Jamesian physiological psychology (and the pluralistic philosophy he developed to make sense of the psychology in relation to nonpsychological factors) from more traditional empiricist and associationist accounts may be summarized as follows: Instead of positing, at any level of analysis, *unconscious atoms* (to use Dreiser's figure) that are then set in motion, or *associated*, by external forces, James turned the model inside out.[11] He supposed that the various states of overlap, ordinarily accounted for in terms of interactions or connectivity between preexisting atoms (sense data, for instance), actually existed more concretely than the atoms did. However counterintuitively, the atoms in James' robust empiricist account are held to be abstractions derived for explanatory or interpretive purposes from the much more confused or interfused phenomena of "real experience," overlapping pluralistically *all the way down*.[12]

"Melanctha all her life was very keen in her sense for real experience," Stein's narrator observes, and it is owing to Melanctha's keenness in this regard that she escapes the grasp not just of the narrator but also of her lover (133). "Sometimes you seem like one kind of a girl to me," Jeff Campbell says, "and sometimes you are like a girl that is all different to me, and the two kinds of girls is certainly very different to each other, and I can't see any way they seem to have much to do, to be together in you" (164). Reasonably, Brenda Wineapple reads this as an expression of Jeff's "divided feelings ... project[ed] onto Melanctha" as well as of Stein's own "conflict-ridden adherence to 'just living regularly.'"[13] Yet the hypostasization of "two kinds of girls" existing in one individual also suggests, in their unlikely overlap, Melanctha's truly complex nature – containing multitudes, as Whitman said of himself.[14]

Here is the promised sketch of Stein's naturalism-modernism hybrid. To start with, the narrator's rigid color scheme operates deterministically and naturalistically, much as fingerprinting does in *Pudd'nhead Wilson*. Also, like Twain, Stein refuses to exempt herself as author, or the reader as reader, from vertiginous critique, although in her case the ensuing ironies hinge on the reader's confusion of author and narrator rather than on Twain's devilish play with his own self-representation as author. Yet Stein possesses the modernist capacity, as her narrator decidedly does not, of writing something (and about someone) capable for a time of escaping the naturalist frame. It is with regard to this feature that her Flaubertian "psychological analysis" acquires its Jamesian robustness by contrast with Twain's cruder investigation of dual personality.

The Making of Americans as U.S. Modernist Novel of Science

In *Three Lives* Stein assembled several preliminary studies for what eventually materialized as *The Making of Americans*, itself a prototypical U.S. modernist novel of science, incorporating the subjective and objective genitives in a manner consistent with the earlier collection. The first thing to note is that the title itself riffs on the genitive ambiguity – referring at once to how one makes Americans (objective genitive) and how Americans make whatever they exhibit a tendency, as Americans, to make, as exemplified in works such as *Three Lives* and *The Making of Americans* (subjective genitive).

The unnamed narrator of *The Making of Americans* shares several features with Stein – most obviously a fascination with psychological classification and a developing role as the writer of the volume – but otherwise lacks clear personal attributes. No mere stand-in for the author, the narrator instead serves a carefully calibrated double function, enabling Stein to investigate a deterministic psychological scheme along with a correspondingly robust sense of the modes of attention and knowledge that writing involves, which it may, under suitable conditions, render accessible to inquiry such as that pursued in the novel.

Much as Twain's figure of the author had, the narrator of *The Making of Americans* serves as a vehicle for investigation rather than as a direct rendering of the investigator. Stein pits the narrator's increasingly nuanced appreciation for the compositional practices involved in writing a work such as *The Making of Americans*, an appreciation strongly informed by James' physiological-introspective construction of the stream of thought, against an alternate model of escape from the constraints of determinism, figured in the slow, deliberate death of the protagonist, who brings the ironically labeled "family's progress" to a close.

Similar to the account of Melanctha Herbert, that of David Hersland is, as the narrator tells it, coterminous with "the history of the ending of his living."[15] Yet where Melanctha dies having exhausted her options, her counterpart in *The Making of Americans* displays a very different response within the naturalist framework carried over from *Three Lives* – what I have described as the inevitability of any life's defeat at its own hands. In both works, an individual life is portrayed in the process of experiencing its inevitable defeat, yet the striking thing is that Hersland does not experience it as a defeat – that is to say, as *his own* defeat (which would require still feeling the need to "be one going on being living," as he manifestly does not [900]).

Hersland and the narrator represent different variants of what in a conversation recounted in *The Autobiography of Alice B. Toklas* (1933) – it originally occurred two decades earlier at the country house of Alfred North Whitehead – Stein referred to as "the disembodied abstract quality of the american character."[16] Increasingly disembodied in a quite literal sense – his death comes about in conjunction with ever greater limitations he sets on his own eating practices – Hersland successfully abstracts himself from any concrete need to "go on being living" and thereby illustrates one possible interpretation of "american character." In direct contrast, the narrator of Stein's novel exhibits a form of disembodiment that has nothing to do with death but instead with a loosening of one's attachments to the fixed anatomical body. We have no idea what the narrator looks like, no external perspective on this person, yet we know a good deal regarding the experience of writing the work. Stein provided herself, and us, with an internal perspective that in the Jamesian manner is at once physiological and introspective, yet abstracted from any given anatomical instantiation. Disembodiment of this variety is no longer identified with loss, whether of life, as with David Hersland, or of one's way, as with Melanctha Herbert, at the close of her "Life."

"Melanctha was lost, and all the world went whirling in a mad weary dance around her" – so concludes a paragraph near the tale's end.[17] With these words Melanctha, as we and she have come to know her, ceases to exist; all that remains is an atom at the mercy of external forces, entrained, as it were, within Dreiser's naturalist vision. The wandering that defined her from early on, introducing the young "child" to "a wonder world of mystery and movement," a world superseding anatomical determinism, all that was now lost – although not to Stein and her proxy in the novel completed just two years after the publication of *Three Lives* (134).

Romance and the U.S. Modernist Novel of Science

As a novel of science *The Making of Americans* follows "Melanctha" in combining a naturalist or deterministic objective genitive and the characteristically modernist subjective genitive involving the investigation of aspects that permit an individual to escape such determinism. Stein learned from James how to conduct investigations such as these, but the exceptionally robust empiricism he elaborated did not come from nowhere. Consequently, when Stein turned from science to literature, she did not have to adapt a recalcitrant medium in a direction to which it was unsuited. On the contrary, she was returning James to one of his sources – as the late fictions of his younger brother suffice to confirm. (Already in the 1903 novella *Quod Erat Demonstrandum*, Stein had a character allude to Henry James' *The Wings of the Dove*, published the year before.)

Modernist fiction is often said to have quite deliberately moved beyond, in reacting against, romanticism; yet actually many U.S. modernist novels of science are deeply imbricated in romance thought and practice.[18] Naturalist tendencies typically serve as the object of sometimes more, sometimes less successful critique, and contrary romance tendencies provide tools for such critique as well as corresponding speculative resources for investigating nondeterministic aspects of human and nonhuman experience. A prevailing reluctance to acknowledge the intimate connection between modernist fiction and romance has resulted in the conundrum with which we began – namely, *the apparent scarcity of U.S. modernist novels of science*. It now becomes possible to see how this impression might arise. Insofar as the romance element in U.S. modernist fiction has typically either been overlooked or regarded as evidence of atavistic retreat in the face of modernity – and it is this very element that often indicates the scientific interest of such works – it follows that relatively few U.S. modernist novels would seem to have anything particular to do with twentieth-century science.[19]

Stein's fiction, and especially the quest romance occupying the extended middle of *Three Lives'* centerpiece – when Melanctha wanders around the city of Bridgepoint (Baltimore) in search of knowledge at once sexual, social, affective, and intellectual – stood out for many of the writers who went on to produce core instances of the U.S. modernist novel of science. As Wilson noted in 1931, referring to Stein's accomplishment a quarter century earlier, "we are still always aware of her presence in the background of contemporary literature – and we picture her as the great pyramidal Buddha of Jo Davidson's statue of her, eternally and placidly ruminating the gradual developments of the processes of being, registering the vibrations of a psychological country like some august human seismograph whose charts [especially in more recent works such as *Tender Buttons* and *Geography and Plays*] we haven't the training to read."[20]

Already in the lead of a famous 1924 review, Wilson linked Ernest Hemingway directly with Stein: "He must be counted as the only American writer but one – Mr. Sherwood Anderson – who has felt the genius of Gertrude Stein's *Three Lives* and has been evidently influenced by it. Indeed, Miss Stein, Mr. Anderson, and Mr. Hemingway may now be said to form a school by themselves" (105). "You would have felt the book more remarkable," F. Scott Fitzgerald wrote in 1935 to H.L. Mencken, to whom he had recently sent a copy of *Three Lives*, "had you read it in 1922 as Wilson and I did. She has been so imitated and through Ernest her very rhythm has gone into the styles of so many people. I still believe [she] is some sort of punctuation mark in literary history."[21] As both Wilson and Fitzgerald stressed, it was the careful investigation in *Three Lives* of psychological states that Stein's protagonists find exceedingly difficult to name as such that appealed so strongly to U.S. writers of modernist fiction. Other leading modernists who credited *Three Lives* with a decisive role in their literary development included Richard Wright and Nella Larsen, who wrote to Stein of "hav[ing] often talked with our friend Carl Van Vechten about you. Particularly about you and Melanctha. . . . I never cease to wonder how you came to write it and just why you and not some one of us should so accurately have caught the spirit of this race of mine."[22]

The point in enumerating links such as these is not to insist on Stein's place at some hypothetical center of U.S. modernism, but to suggest that with *Three Lives* U.S. modernist fiction of science came into its own and that the distinctive features of Stein's collection also hold for subsequent works by other writers, regardless of whether they made overt references to science. Foremost among such features were the continuing challenge posed by naturalist fictions together with the manifest challenges that the presence of a servant class, a diverse African American population, and increasingly independent women posed to the democratic ethos of the United States. There was also the challenge confronting writers of fiction in the emergence of the full-fledged, deeply riven science of psychology recorded and exemplified by James.

Like it or not, Stein was "always" there "in the background," and not just for those who, like the novelists I have enumerated, found much to admire in her.[23] The relation may be one of literary triangulation – for instance, Faulkner, by way of Anderson – or of differing emphasis, as when Dos Passos replaces Stein's focus on familial ties in *The Making of Americans* with nonfamilial social ties in the equally huge *U.S.A.*; or a greater concern with the deleterious effects of modernization, such as that displayed by Willa Cather in *The Professor's House*; or a related academic training, as in the case of Zora Neale Hurston's study of folklore and cultural anthropology; or even the relation of caricaturist to subject, as with Djuna Barnes, whose 1937 novel *Nightwood* transposed "Melanctha" to 1920s Paris and who in 1923 had published a famous caricature of Stein, labeled "spiritual mother of all the modernists," in the *New York Tribune*.[24]

A.N. Whitehead and the U.S. Modernist Novel of Science

In Wilson's account of international modernism, he relied on the perspectives of several of his college teachers, including the Scottish philosopher Norman Kemp Smith. A 1927 essay of Wilson's summarized Kemp Smith's "exposition" of "earlier books" by Whitehead that provided the "foundations" upon which more recent work, such as *Science and the Modern World* (1925), was constructed.[25] Already in 1925, Wilson had enthusiastically endorsed Whitehead's proposal that "the discoveries of modern science supply the basis of a regenerative philosophy," and this was followed a year later in The *New Republic* (where Wilson was an editor) by an early draft of what would become the opening pages of *Axel's Castle*, starting: "Doctor Whitehead, in his *Science and the Modern World*, has suggested that the romantic movement of the early nineteenth century was, not merely a literary phenomenon, but really a philosophical reaction against the ideas of contemporary science" (47, 50). Wilson also adapted Whitehead's cyclical model of interactions among literature and science to the late nineteenth century: hence, with "French 'symbolism'" – in which "almost all that we consider characteristically 'modern' has its roots" – "the pendulum [swung] back again to an equivalent of romanticism" (52–54).

Wilson was clearly confident that the readers of The *New Republic* were every bit as interested as he was in acquiring a better grasp of the surprising argument of James' successor at Harvard. In particular he wished to see how Whitehead might square "the function of symbolism" – "to make things unscientific and mysterious again" – with a philosophy based on the findings of modern science and capable both of "preserv[ing] the theories of science" and "supply[ing] a new and necessary significance to a world of which the old accepted meanings have so disastrously come to be discredited" (53, 70).

Some two decades later when Stein herself sharply criticized science in *Wars I Have Seen* (1945), it was not science per se but the nineteenth-century science of literary naturalism that she rejected – and Whitehead would have been entirely in agreement.[26] Between "Melanctha" and at least through *The Geographical History of America* (1937), *The World Is Round* (1939), and *What Are Masterpieces* (1940), Stein's modernist project took the form of an extended critique of the scientifically inflected determinism presumed by literary naturalism. The extent to which Stein remained engaged with the discourse of naturalism is made apparent when one compares the titles of the works just listed with Wilson's observation concerning naturalist "historians and critics like [Hippolyte] Taine," who "attempted to account for master-pieces by studying the geographical and climatic conditions of the countries in which they had been produced."[27]

Supplementing the ongoing critique of naturalism, Stein proceeded more positively to investigate romance aspects that enabled her and Melanctha, and the adventurous Rose in *The World Is Round*, to operate in ways that at least for a time ran counter to the deterministic mechanisms of literary naturalism. Stein was well aware that many conclusions James arrived at in his *Principles of Psychology*, and in particular his famous instruction to "re-instat[e] the vague to its proper place in our mental life," were inconsistent with the dominant determinism of nineteenth-century science; like James and his novelist brother, her concern was not with generic vagueness of the sort rigid empiricisms sought to discredit but instead involved distinguishing specific varieties of vagueness through robust empiricist means.[28]

In their own "Romantic reaction" to much Victorian science (and its spillover into the twentieth century), Stein and other U.S. modernist novelists made similar assumptions to those Whitehead attributed, in the chapter of that name in *Science and the Modern World*, to Wordsworth and Shelley. Chief among the shared romance assumptions was the recognition, in line with James' attribution of greater concreteness to states of overlap by contrast with the structures abstracted from them, that an overemphasis on the clarity and distinctness of objects produces an increasingly inexact rendering of the world and the processes of which it consists. Stein's dissociation of her work from the science presumed by literary naturalism was therefore a necessary first step in the direction of modernist fiction such as her own. Typically, Stein's fellow U.S. modernist novelists of science were much less directly engaged with contemporary science than she had been; even so, their work continued to be informed by science through their engagement with her writing.

Realism in the U.S. Modernist Novel of Science, 1902–1946

The aesthetic innovations in "Melanctha," together with the investigation by both author and protagonist of forms of knowledge and consciousness grasped for whatever reason only in the vaguest manner, distinguish the work as modernist and at the same time as exhibiting romance features. Yet the novella's naturalist frame suggests that Stein's ambitions were in some degree realist as well – "realism of rather a novel kind," Wilson called it.[29] "A fine new kind of realism," James observed in a letter to Stein.[30] Among the many varieties of literary realism, Lyn Hejinian has noted, naturalism is "stark realism."[31]

So here we have a fourth literary historical category, *realism*, supplementing the other variously contrastive categories of *naturalism, modernism,* and *romance.* Like romance and modernism, realism and romance are often viewed as opposing categories, although that is by no means the case where the U.S. modernist novel of science is concerned.[32] If one "grand tradition" of fiction may "loosely and not incorrectly be characterized as 'realist' in its desire to do justice to the hard edges of life," the decidedly different realism embraced by Stein aimed instead to do justice to life's soft edges.[33] To this end, she adapted the compositional realism of the painter Paul Cézanne – "Cézanne's new mode of realism," Jayne Walker has termed it, echoing James and following Stein's own account.[34]

In an interview conducted shortly before her death in 1946, Stein explained Cézanne's effect on her: "Up to that time composition had consisted of a central idea to which everything else was an accompaniment and separate but was not an end in itself, and Cézanne conceived the idea that in composition one thing was as important as another thing. Each part is as important as the whole, and that impressed me enormously."[35] Onto these dichotomous modes of composition Stein mapped alternate ways of treating fictional characters, thereby distinguishing the realism of the twentieth-century novel from its nineteenth-century counterpart. Just as painters prior to Cézanne failed to conceive of composition in the manner he made his own – whereby "a blade of grass has the same value as a tree" and "one cannot live without the other" – so something comparable could be said of the great nineteenth-century realist novelists (16). In their case, the asymmetry involved setting up one character as "an end in itself" while another was relegated to the background, among the work's subordinate features.

In typical modernist fiction, however – certainly in U.S. modernist fiction of science – "the individual does not stick out enough for the people reading about him" (21). When in "Melanctha" Stein attempted "to convey the idea of each part of a composition being as important as the whole," it was, she believed, "the first time . . . anyone had used that idea of composition in literature" – even if "Henry James had a slight inkling of it" (15, 21). "The ensemble lives, but nobody gets excited about the [individual] characters" (21). Just as "to me," she insisted, "one human being is as important as another," so within a modernist ensemble – the 1902 *Wings of the Dove,* the 1905–1906 "Melanctha" – each human being possesses equal value, and each aspect of any human being possesses "the same value" as every other aspect (16). It is the nonhierarchical quality, the absence of subordination whether in ensemble, character or work, that is exciting and part and parcel of the ensuing interconnectedness: lack of subordination without loss of coordination.

To understand character compositionally in the Cézannesque sense (hence as possessing the specific liveliness of a Jamesian ensemble) is therefore to write in terms of what, in a classic study *The Cosmic Web: Scientific Field Models and Literary Strategies in the Twentieth Century* (1984), Katherine Hayles speaks of as "the field concept."[36] Here is the surprising thing: as Stein excised the scientific ambitions she brought to writing, gradually "abandon[ing the] goal of systematized [and totalizing] understanding" and instead increasingly followed Cézanne's lead in her compositional practices and cognitive aims – to the point of being prepared to assert, as she did in one journal entry, that "aesthetic has become the whole of me" – her practices and objectives converged more and more closely with the new directions science was already moving in, and which James and Whitehead not only contributed so much to but also sought to understand philosophically.[37]

Stein's first mature fictions, *Three Lives* and *The Making of Americans*, initiated a rapprochement between science and literature in U.S. modernist fiction that was by no means limited to Stein. Nevertheless, much of her own writing has proven an especially hard nut to crack, and it is to Wilson's credit that he knew he often did not know how to read her – as he acknowledged in *Axel's Castle* when he characterized her as "registering the vibrations of a psychological country like some august human seismograph whose charts *we haven't the training to read.*" Stein's own training, enabling her to operate as well as read the seismograph in question, came about partly from building on the foundation of largely rigid empiricist observational practices she had been exposed to at Radcliffe and Johns Hopkins, and partly from utilizing robust physiological-introspective constructions of the sort she introduced in her early fictions of science, and which she continued to investigate in the many and varied works that followed.

Further Directions Taken by the U.S. Modernist Novel of Science, 1924–2006

For more than a dozen years, these works included no novels. No doubt many factors contributed to Stein's return to the novel of science in the mid-1920s, chief among them the publication of *The Making of Americans* and her exposure to the new cadre of postwar U.S. writers, including Anderson, Fitzgerald, and especially Hemingway, whose encounters with *Three Lives* strongly informed how they understood their own objectives in writing fiction. I stress Hemingway's role not only because he was intimately involved in the 1925 publication but also because the first of the two episodes with which I will close concerns the highly competitive, mutually beneficial relations between him and Stein.

Substantial sections of *The Making of Americans* appeared serially in 1924 at Hemingway's instigation, and while he was proofreading this material for *the transatlantic review*, Hemingway began composing "Big Two-Hearted River," one of his signature works. Already in August 1924 he mentioned to Stein that he was "trying to do the country like Cézanne."[38] As is well known, Stein advised him to remove the concluding pages of the tale, which he did. These included additional ruminations on Cézanne, parroting what Stein had explained to him with regard to her earlier writing in the context no doubt of the "landscape plays" she composed the previous winter in Provence.[39] There, she resumed the practice of writing with a Cézanne before her – only now it was the original of Cézanne's Provence landscapes that suggested the "conception of landscape as a play" to her (864).[40] Hemingway's subsequent transposition of Stein's objective from plays to fiction seems to have motivated her to write *Lucy Church Amiably*, a novel that really did the country as Cézanne would have, had he written fiction.

Also in 1924, Stein and her partner, Alice Toklas, discovered the countryside around Belley, in southeastern France, where they lived on and off for the next twenty years and where "the following summer," Toklas recalls in the *Autobiography*, they "correct[ed] proofs of The Making of Americans" and would "leave the hotel in the morning with camp chairs, lunch and proof. ... We used to change the scene of our labours and we found lovely spots but there were always to accompany us those endless pages of printers' errors" (879). One result of this summer of proofreading was that when, two years later, Stein went about composing her landscape novel in the same setting, she did so not just in the midst of a Cézannesque landscape but in a French landscape thoroughly informed by *The Making of Americans*!

To observe, then, of the landscape recreated in *Lucy Church Amiably* that it exhibits the "disembodied abstract quality of american character," is really no more than to say that Stein portrayed in the novel a landscape that, although located in a particular region in France, had ceased to be organized along hierarchical principles such as those Stein identified with Europe.[41] It is a landscape in which one is encouraged to wander much as Melanctha wandered about Baltimore – a world, as I put it earlier, that supersedes anatomical determinism. If "to have a psyche is to be in composition," it does not follow that being in composition requires having a psyche. All that is needed is the possession of internal relations of some sort – interconnections capable of being described as physiological in an expanded sense and which, despite corresponding as such to psychological activity, need not actually be psychological. Any manner of inner experience, including the movements *in* a landscape that constitute its internal reality, qualifies as "being in composition" so far as the Whiteheadian, Cézannesque world is concerned. Rather than escaping from the world, Stein, like Melanctha, was "escaping into" it.[42]

Science may seem to have all but disappeared in the embrace of Cézanne, yet it has not. Rather, Hemingway and Stein wrote U.S. modernist fictions of science in the mid-1920s where the genitive is principally to be understood – as it is in many of the works directly informed by "Melanctha" – in the subjective sense, and the conjunction of literature and science takes a decidedly aesthetic direction.[43] A work such as Thomas Pynchon's 2006 masterpiece, *Against the Day* (comprising the promised second episode in the century-long rapprochement of science and literature in U.S. modernist fiction), reverses the direction.[44] Like *Three Lives* and *The Making of Americans*, it expressly incorporates both genitive modes of U.S. modernist fiction of science, and the interaction of science and literature in it takes on a decidedly scientific flavor. Published three-quarters of a century after both *Axel's Castle* and *Lucy Church Amiably*, the novel's subject matter is highly atypical for a U.S. modernist novel of science. It does not just concern itself with science but portrays scientific controversy in the period between 1893 and the late 1920s – exactly the time frame, up to now, of the present essay.

Although the constant attention paid to such phenomena as "the nocturnal light," "somewhere else co-conscious with the day," and "a lateral world, set only infinitesimally to the side of the one we think we know," will be familiar to any reader of the works of fiction discussed so far, the factors of the modernizing world investigated in *Against the Day* are sufficiently different from Stein's concerns in *Lucy Church Amiably* (and before the War in *Three Lives* and *The Making of Americans*) as to seem worlds apart.[45] In addition, Pynchon focuses on an entirely different level of the scientific imagination than Stein did – namely, that of imaginary numbers and their massive contribution to the development of late nineteenth- and early twentieth-century science (and continuing ever since). "The Quaternion Wars" may not be everyone's idea of exciting, yet there is no better example of the indispensable role speculation plays in scientific and literary reconstructions of the actual world: "within the scalar term, within the daylit and obvious and taken-for-granted has always lain, as if in wait, the dark itinerary" (815). Pynchon's is discernibly the same, barely perceptible, Jamesian and Whiteheadian world Stein was already investigating in 1905 – and, again, attending to different aspects of it, in 1927.

From a robust empiricist perspective, *Against the Day* is unmistakably a work of twenty-first-century modernism, to adapt a phrase Marjorie Perloff has used for poets such as Lyn Hejinian to the quite different, albeit overlapping, ecosystem of the U.S. modernist novel of science. The nearly "ubiquitous" application of "a theory of literary postmodernism" to Pynchon's fiction appears necessary only against a rigid empiricist backdrop such as that assumed at the outset of the present essay, in which the phrases *novel of science* and *U.S. modernist fiction* seem mutually exclusive.[46] A richer, more historically accurate account leaves plenty of room for inquiries of the sort Pynchon undertakes in *Against the Day* regarding the "disembodied abstract quality of american character," complementing Stein's early twentieth-century investigations and the many others to be found in the strange congeries of works that together comprise the U.S. modernist novel of science.

NOTES

1. Edmund Wilson, *Literary Essays and Reviews of the 1920s & 30s*, ed. Lewis M. Dabney (New York: Library of America, 2007), 651.
2. Wilson, *Literary Essays and Reviews*, 641.
3. Theodore Dreiser, *A Book about Myself* (New York: Boni and Liveright, 1922), 457–458.
4. Sherley Anne Williams, "In Time: *The Tragedy of Pudd'nhead Wilson*," in *The Tragedy of Pudd'nhead Wilson and the Comedy Those Extraordinary Twins*, by Mark Twain (New York: Oxford University Press, 1996), xli; Mark Twain, *Pudd'nhead Wilson* and *Those Extraordinary Twins*, 2nd ed., ed. Sidney E. Berger (New York: W.W. Norton, 2005), 129, 126.
5. George E. Marcus, "*What did he reckon would become of the other half if he killed his half?* Doubled, Divided, and Crossed Selves in *Pudd'nhead Wilson*; or, Mark Twain as Cultural Critic in His Own Times and Ours," in *Mark Twain's* Pudd'nhead Wilson: *Race, Conflict, and Culture*, eds. Susan Gillman and Forrest G. Robinson (Durham: Duke University Press, 1990), 193. A long line of readers neglected to notice Twain's duplicity in crediting his characters with having taken the management of the tale out of his hands. And, in their failure to do so, the joke proved to be on their inadequacy as readers no less than on Twain's own profoundly felt limitations as an author "driven ... by larger forces."
6. Lyn Hejinian, *The Language of Inquiry* (Berkeley: University of California Press, 2000), 287–288. Flaubert cited from *The Letters of Gustave Flaubert, 1830–1857*, ed. and trans. Francis Steegmuller (Cambridge MA: Harvard University Press, 1980).
7. Daylanne K. English offers helpful contextualization in light of Stein's "clinical rotation at Johns Hopkins" (Daylanne K. English, *Unnatural Selections: Eugenics in American Modernism and the Harlem Renaissance* [Chapel Hill: University of North Carolina Press, 2004], 99). As Joan Richardson demonstrates, however, in the broader context of the rediscovery of Mendelian genetics and of Stein's engagement with William James, this comes at the expense of failing to register Stein's actual "critiqu[e of] the limited eugenicist view" English too hastily attributes to her (Joan Richardson, *A Natural History of Pragmatism: The Fact of Feeling from Jonathan Edwards to Gertrude Stein* [Cambridge: Cambridge University Press, 2007], 242).

8. Wilson, *Literary Essays and Reviews*, 805.
9. Gertrude Stein, *Writings 1903–1932*, eds. Catharine R. Stimpson and Harriet Chessman (New York: Library of America, 1998), 125, 127.
10. The French psychological terminology that James introduced in the United States had developed in symbiosis with the symbolist attention to vagueness and suggestiveness emphasized by Wilson. For an excellent account of James' alignment with late nineteenth-century French symbolism, see Richard Cándida-Smith, *Mallarmé's Children: Symbolism and the Renewal of Experience* (Berkeley: University of California Press, 1999); also see Marilyn M. Sachs, *Marcel Proust in the Light of William James: In Search of a Lost Source* (Lexington, KY: Lexington Books, 2013), for a thoughtful study of the many parallels exhibited by James and Proust.
11. Uniquely among late nineteenth-century psychologists, James was in regular and ongoing conversation with representatives of all the major national traditions in Europe as well as the most innovative American practitioners; for an excellent account of his interactions with, among others, British psychical researchers, French experimental psychologists of the subconscious, and German laboratory experimentalists, see Eugene Taylor, *William James on Consciousness beyond the Margin* (Princeton, NJ: Princeton University Press, 1996). Edward S. Reed provides a superb summary of the flip side of all this activity – namely, James' "critique of the new [positivist] psychology" (Reed, *From Soul to Mind: The Emergence of Psychology, from Erasmus Darwin to William James* [New Haven, CT: Yale University Press, 1997], 202).
12. See William James, "The Place of Affectional Facts in a World of Pure Experience" and *A Pluralistic Universe* in *Writings 1902–1910*, ed. Bruce Kuklick (New York: Library of America, 1987), 1206–1214, 625–819.
13. Brenda Wineapple, *Sister Brother: Gertrude and Leo Stein* (New York: Putnam, 1996), 238.
14. Stein is likely to have been familiar with W.E.B. Du Bois' general attribution of "double consciousness" to African Americans in *The Souls of Black Folk* (1903), as she made sure to send him a copy of *Three Lives* after it was published. Du Bois, like Stein, had studied with James. The year 1903 also saw the serial publication in the *Colored American Magazine* of Pauline Hopkins' novel *Of One Blood*, which "begins by quoting" a passage ostensibly by the French psychologist Alfred Binet (Thomas Otten, "Pauline Hopkins and the Hidden Self of Race," *ELH* 59 [1992]: 227). "In fact," Thomas Otten notes, it is "drawn from … a review essay" that James had published on Binet and Pierre Janet (228). The title of James' essay, "The Hidden Self," is the subtitle of Hopkins' novel.
15. Gertrude Stein, *The Making of Americans* (Normal: Dalkey Archive, 1995), 724.
16. Stein, *Writings*, 811.
17. Stein, *Writings*, 237.
18. I prefer to speak of romance rather than romanticism to emphasize that the mode of thought in question has regularly recurred in English-language writing since at least the quest romances of the late Middle Ages. British romanticism presents one such iteration; the U.S. modernist novel of science is another. In the 1920s the phrase *Romantic revival* was used by the Anglo-American philosopher Alfred North Whitehead and the British literary critic and poet

William Empson, among others, as a synonym for British romanticism that permitted them to stress the cyclical nature of romance inquiry. Unfortunately, it soon fell out of fashion.

19. For a particularly clear instance of this stance regarding a seemingly atavistic neoromanticism, see Cecelia Tichi on Cather's *Alexander's Bridge* (1912) and Anderson's *Poor White* (1920) in *Shifting Gears: Technology, Literature, Culture in Modernist America* (Chapel Hill: University of North Carolina Press, 1987).

20. Wilson, *Literary Essays and Reviews*, 815.

21. Matthew J. Bruccoli and Margaret M. Duggan, eds., *Correspondence of F. Scott Fitzgerald* (New York: Random House, 1980), 412.

22. Donald Gallup, ed., *The Flowers of Friendship: Letters Written to Gertrude Stein* (New York: Octagon Books, 1979), 216.

23. See Paula Rabinowitz, "The Future of the Novel and Public Criticism in Mid-Century America," in *The American Novel 1870–1940*, eds. Priscilla Wald and Michael A. Elliott (Oxford: Oxford University Press, 2014), 566–582, for a fascinating account of Stein's place in U.S. critical discourse in the 1930s.

24. Djuna Barnes, "Three American Literary Expatriates in Paris," *New York Tribune* 83, November 4, 1923, 17. For examples of essays that highlight areas of overlap of these authors with Stein, see Merrill Maguire Skaggs, "Willa Cather: Flaubert's Parrot?" in *A Writer's Worlds*, eds. John J. Murphy, Francoise Palleau-Papin, and Robert Thacher (Lincoln: University of Nebraska Press, 2010), 164–175, and Dana Seitler, "'Wolf-wolf!': Narrating the Science of Desire," in *Atavistic Tendencies: The Culture of Science in American Modernity* (Minneapolis: University of Minnesota Press, 2008), 94–128. Also see Judith Brown's excellent article, "A Certain Laughter: Sherwood Anderson's Experiment in Form," *Modernist Cultures* 2 (Oct. 2006): 138–152, concerning Anderson's controversial "novel of '25," *Dark Laughter*.

25. Edmund Wilson, *From the Uncollected Edmund Wilson*, eds. and intro. Janet Groth and David Castronovo (Athens: Ohio University Press, 1995), 62.

26. See Gertrude Stein, *Wars I Have Seen* (New York: Random House, 1945), 61.

27. Wilson, *Literary Essays and Reviews*, 648.

28. William James, *The Principles of Psychology* (Cambridge: Harvard University Press, 1983), 246.

29. Wilson, *Literary Essays and Reviews*, 874.

30. Gallup, *The Flowers of Friendship*, 50.

31. Hejinian, *The Language of Inquiry*, 86.

32. Nor, as Eric Sundquist has demonstrated, is it the case where much post–Civil War U.S. fiction is concerned either; see "Introduction: The Country of the Blue," *American Realism: New Essays*, ed. Eric J. Sundquist (Baltimore: Johns Hopkins University Press, 1982): 3–24.

33. Peter Brooks, "What Flaubert Knew," *The New York Times Book Review* (August 2, 1998): 20.

34. Jayne L. Walker, *The Making of a Modernist: Gertrude Stein from* Three Lives *to* Tender Buttons (Amherst: University of Massachusetts Press, 1984), xviii.

35. Gertrude Stein, "A Transatlantic Interview 1946," in *A Primer for the Gradual Understanding of Gertrude Stein*, ed. Robert Bartlett Haas (Los Angeles: Black Sparrow Press, 1971), 15.

36. "In marked contrast to the atomistic Newtonian idea of reality," Hayles explains, "in which physical objects are discrete and events are capable of occurring independently of one another and the observer, a field view of reality pictures objects, events, and observer as belonging inextricably to the same field" (N. Katherine Hayles, *The Cosmic Web: Scientific Field Models and Literary Strategies in the Twentieth Century* [Ithaca, NY: Cornell University Press, 1984], 15–16). The resemblance of the field view to the stances of Whitehead, Cézanne, and Stein should be as obvious as it is to the following statement by William James in "The Place of Affectional Facts in a World of Pure Experience" (1904), serving as an epigraph to Marcus' essay on Twain: "Subjectivity and objectivity are affairs not of what an experience is aboriginally made of but of its classification" (George E. Marcus, "What did he reckon," 190). Hayles focuses on twentieth-century advances in the physical sciences and on works by Lawrence, Borges, Nabokov, and Pynchon, "arranged in ascending order of the complexity of the authors' resistances to the field concept"; unsurprisingly, in light of the considerations raised at the beginning of this essay, the U.S. modernist novel as traditionally construed remains largely absent from her study (Hayles 1984, 11).

37. Walker, *The Making of a Modernist*, 101; Wineapple, *Sister Brother*, 294.

38. Gallup, *The Flowers of Friendship*, 164.

39. Stein, *Writings*, 864.

40. See Linda Voris, "Interpreting Cézanne: Immanence in Gertrude Stein's First Landscape Play, *Lend a Hand or Four Religions*," *Modernism/modernity* 19, no. 1 (January 2012): 73–93. Also see Monika Gehlawat's excellent "Painterly Ambitions: Hemingway, Cézanne, and the Short Story," *Journal of the Short Story in English* 49 (Autumn 2007): 189–205.

41. Donald Sutherland, in his always-insightful *Gertrude Stein: A Biography of Her Work* (New Haven, CT: Yale University Press, 1951), correctly identifies *Lucy Church Amiably* as a pastoral romance. A more thorough account of the U.S. modernist novel of science would require careful consideration of a *fifth* literary historical category: a distinctly American "version of pastoral" supplementing the English versions explored so brilliantly by William Empson in his groundbreaking *Some Versions of Pastoral* (London: Chatto & Windus, 1935).

42. Stein, *Writings*, 132. As noted at the end of the previous section, Stein's "seismographical" training, permitting her to compose a work such as *Lucy Church Amiably*, typically involved some combination of observational and physiological-introspective practices. Leon Katz's reconstruction of the "seriousness" and "intensity" of her mode of observation at the time she was writing *The Making of Americans* suggests the extent to which Stein carried over her prior empiricist training into daily life and the Paris art world. It is fairly easy to extrapolate a similar approach in subsequent writing, despite the fact that the locales vary enormously, and after 1911 Stein ceased to organize the results in the same sort of "formal schemes" (Katz, "Matisse, Picasso and Gertrude Stein," in *Four Americans in Paris: The Collections of Gertrude Stein and Her Family* [New York: The Museum of Modern Art, 1970], 51–52).

43. *Lucy Church Amiably* and "Big Two-Hearted River" also involve naturalist practices – not, however, in the sense of literary naturalism but of natural history. See Susan F. Beegel, "Eye and Heart: Hemingway as a Naturalist," in *A*

Historical Guide to Ernest Hemingway, ed. Linda Wagner-Martin (Oxford: Oxford University Press, 2000): 53–92.

44. When, on the last page of *Axel's Castle*, Edmund Wilson contemplates the prospect of "arriv[ing] at a way of thinking, a technique for dealing with our perceptions, which will make art and science one," he leaves unspecified whether the unification is to be understood reductively or, as the examples of Stein and Pynchon require, pluralistically (845). The former interpretation corresponds to the brief for "consilience" made in recent decades by the sociobiologist E.O. Wilson, the latter to Stephen Jay Gould's correction of his Harvard colleague as well as the "cosmopolitical proposal" associated with the philosopher of science Isabelle Stengers and the sociologist of science Bruno Latour.

45. Thomas Pynchon, *Against the Day* (New York: Penguin, 2006), 563, 815, 461.

46. Brian McHale, "Pynchon's Postmodernism," in *The Cambridge Companion to Thomas Pynchon*, eds. Inger H. Dalsgaard, Luc Herman, and Brian McHale (Cambridge: Cambridge University Press, 2012), 97.

PART III

Textualities

10

JEFF ALLRED

Visual Cultures of American Modernism

Introduction

Over the past two decades or so, the rise of visual culture studies and the "new modernisms" in literature have exploded inherited canons of art historical artifacts and literary texts. The "visual turn" of the 1990s ushered in a breathtaking expansion of the scope of art history, expanding its archive to include all manner of objects, from natural to mass cultural to virtual, and widening its theoretical scope to rethink the cognitive, technological, and ideological structures of vision itself.[1] In parallel fashion, modernist studies has superseded a restrictive canon of texts bound by a "high" sensibility and commitment to "difficulty" to encompass an enormous range of heterogeneous material – a shift expressed most succinctly in the pluralization of "modernism" and the proliferation of modifiers attached to the term. The new modernisms are old modernism gone viral: modernisms *queer* and *cruising, ethnic* and *sensational, pop* and *virtual, cosmopolitan* and just plain *bad.*[2] Thus critics examining "visual cultures of modernism" stand at a fast-moving, densely populated crossroads: in a recapitulation of the "urban shock" felt by modernist-era subjects in the face of the modern metropolis, those working in this field may feel an analogous mixture of pleasure and vertigo in the face of such complexity and scale.[3] A number of recent critics have succeeded in broadly articulating the relationship between the two fields and theorizing the distinctive "way of seeing" that emerged in the early twentieth century.[4] Given the focus of this volume on the novel genre, I will work within a narrower (though still considerable) scope, analyzing the interplay between visual and verbal forms in the first half of the twentieth century, revealing ways in which the landscape of an emergent modernity left its impress on literary forms, and describing how literature attempted to analyze and revise the process of looking.

To get at the complexity of this two-way flow of influence between visual phenomena and verbal forms, it seems best to work inductively, starting with a text that argues, both in form and theme, that the turn of the nineteenth century ushers in new visual modes and, especially in cities, new kinds of people, places, and things to look at. Henry James' travelogue, *The American Scene* (1907), was composed during James' first return to the United States after two decades of expatriate life. It was written in the first years of the twentieth century at the dawn of what we now call "modernism" in the United States, it registers the disruptive force of modernity upon a subject formed by Victorian-era norms and accustomed to expatriate life, and it renders with extreme subtlety the problems and possibilities of translating the teeming visual field of modernity into words into prose narrative. I will focus on James' impressions of New York City in the text (chapters 2–5), for it is there that James explores what is new about modernity in the greatest detail. Above all, New York confronts James with its too-muchness, a superfluity that James renders in overwhelmingly visual terms. As James circumnavigates Manhattan on the Circle Line, skitters through traffic to enter the Waldorf-Astoria, and wades through the density of downtown ethnic life, he notes that New York is "all formidable foreground," a landscape that squares too-muchness with too-closeness and eludes the realist gaze's masterful ordering of visual data.[5] The scale and velocity with which capital continually transforms the landscape strikes James with bluntest force in the financial district, where he observes the way the "monstrous phenomena" of the new skyscrapers escape "any possibility of poetic ... capture" even as they visually pummel Trinity Church into submission in a declaration of a new (dis)order (65). James' shock here is close kin to the broken "historical neck" Henry Adams sustained around the same time in contemplating the meaning of the dynamo in modern life, but James uses the shock of the new to different ends.[6] When he visits the site of his boyhood home near Washington Square and hardly recognizes it amid the creative destruction of the New York real estate industry, he feels "amputated of half [his] history" (71). In condensing modernity, looking, and bodily disability, the figure neatly captures the way modernist textuality revises the Cartesian model of disembodied subjectivity, of looking as a purely mental process that is deeply enmeshed with the act of thinking itself. In the prior model, vision supplies a pure knowledge, expresses an abstract, disembodied authority, and shores up the viewer's identity. Here, however, in a performance of what Martin Jay calls the "crisis of ocularcentrism" that arises at the turn of the century, James' looking issues from a hyperembodied subject whose identity is open to question.[7] What has broken for James is, above all, the literary realism of the prior century: New York's "formidable foreground" erodes the underpinnings of, for example, omniscient narration, orderly plotting, stable representations of space, and constellations of recognizable social types, and demands the invention of new forms that are looser and more contingent.

The foreground that so presses in on James teems with heterogeneous elements: there are tall buildings with short setbacks, rapidly moving street-cars and carriages, an endless procession of signs and words to decode, but it is the presence of ethnic others that most emphatically underscores the fracturing of the realist gaze in James' text. In a long passage rendering James' tour of the Lower East Side, the Jews he sees on sidewalks, stoops, and fire escapes compose a "phantasmagoria" that renews itself through their "multiplication" and "overflow" before James' eyes (100). James' use of animal metaphors has often been read as a mirror of his partaking of the racism and anti-Semitism endemic among WASPs in the period: notoriously, he imagines Jews as "human squirrels and monkeys" at play in "a vast zoological garden" (102) or as the kind of "snakes or worms" who, "when cut into pieces, wriggle away contentedly and live in the snippet as completely as in the whole" (100). This reading, however, misses the weight that lands on the questions of identity and origin throughout this section of the text. James notes, for example, that the denizens of the Lower East Side are "at home" there (96), perhaps more than he, who is a "restored absentee" and stems from "migrations" that are "extremely recent," if one takes the long view (95). Crucially, James notes that the city's Jews are participating in the recomposition of the very language he speaks: if it sounds to him like the "torture-room of the living idiom," he acknowledges nonetheless that it is the "Accent of the future" and hence destined to infiltrate his very mode of expression and sense of self (106). To sum up, James' intimacy with American modernity impresses upon him a recognition of the way the "other" in such spaces also bears a look, contributes to the subsuming sociocultural constructs, is both "alien" and "at home."[8] Thus the pun in the title becomes audible: the American scene conveys to its seer the uncanny sense of being an American *seen*. And James, as self-styled "amputee," thus resembles the worm that regenerates itself from the severed part, sharing with his Jewish counterparts the "equality of condition that, from side to side, made the whole medium so strange" (96). James' linkage of vision to questions of identity and otherness resonates deeply with a text published a year prior to the trip to New York, W.E.B. Du Bois' *Souls of Black Folk* (1903). Like James, Du Bois insists that modernity is grounded in the problem of consolidating an identity in a world that refracts one's vision of both self and other. If, as Du Bois famously argues, the "color line" is the "problem of the twentieth century," confronting this problem requires a recalibration of vision.[9] Du Bois' narrating voice issues from behind a "Veil," such that neither (black) narrator nor (white) reader can see/know one another without an agonized process of reckoning with a set of vexing historical and social antagonisms. Thus a central problem of visual culture in U.S. modernism is how to see and be seen in a visual field in which determinations of self and other are mediated by various kinds of ideological screens and filters.[10]

If one aspect of modernity in the United States is its centrifugal force that lops off members, shoots bodies across town at breakneck speed, and mixes social groups promiscuously, James also introduces a second, centripetal aspect in the "hotel-world" that he finds in the meticulously administered space of the Waldorf-Astoria (78). The Waldorf is also a site of excess, but it is an excess that manifests as spectacle and subjects its viewers such that they *feel* free but are in fact integrated into "a social order in positively stable equilibrium" (80). In an arresting figure, James imagines the Waldorf as an "orchestral leader" who pulls the strings of an "army of puppets" who nevertheless "think of themselves as delightfully free and easy" (82). James' interpretation of the "American spirit" as the "hotel-spirit" (79) anticipates by some thirty years Adorno and Horkheimer's analysis of the "culture industries" that employ image-driven mass media to produce new, submissive modes of subjectivity in a vision of the "administered life."[11] As in the Frankfurt School mode of analysis, James posits aesthetic form as the central mode of resistance to this "hotel spirit" and its spurious unity. Throughout the text, James' narrating "I" is called the "restless analyst," a peripatetic figure who circulates relentlessly amid other restless objects and agents, collecting impressions and collaging them in ways that are intimately linked to the arts of photography and layout. If the "hotel-spirit" anticipates the "continuity style" that coalesced in Hollywood film in the 1920s and became the template by midcentury for all manner of mass media from photo magazines to television, James' restless analysis equally anticipates modernist form across a wide range of genres and media as issuing from an "aesthetics of interruption."[12] James' narrative reflects a mind in constant, self-reflexive motion, doubling back on itself, digressing constantly, and folding spaces and times from past and future into the present of narration. Like many subsequent modernist texts, it hails its readers as active participants who eschew the "hotel-spirit" in the struggle to generate coherence from an often maddeningly labile text. To return to the problems of definition from the beginning of the essay, if there is a viable criterion of what qualifies as modernist within visual culture, it is precisely this use of aesthetic form to represent the sublimity of mobile, urban modernity and interrupt the "administered" continuities of fabricated visual spectacles. Modernist textuality denatures vision, in other words, just as modern spectacles and technologies of vision derange the various literary genres associated with nineteenth-century realism. What the texts that occupy this intersection have to teach, first and foremost, is that vision is not mimetic but productive: looking is a form of labor that constructs knowledge and identity rather than mirroring them.

"Who Came First?": Stein, Williams, and Visual Art

The relationship between modernism and modernity in the United States is distinctive for its cultural lag. Many observers from the period noted the gap between American technological and economic advances and a relatively staid culture: hence Gertrude Stein's rather defensive claim that the United States was "the oldest country in the world" because "she was the first country to enter into the twentieth century," though in the form of mass production rather than advanced art, and Marcel Duchamp's pithier statement that "the only works of art America has given are her plumbing and her bridges."[13] The excitement surrounding New York's 1913 Armory Show is a useful symptom of this phenomenon, as it confronted a mass of American viewers with a body of painting dominated by Spanish and French work from the first two decades of the century that was scandalous in its novelty. As Marjorie Perloff has argued, to the extent that an American avant-garde even existed among visual artists in the interwar years, it relied heavily upon infusions of energy and ideas from Europeans such as Duchamp in the 1910s and surrealist exiles in the 1940s.[14]

A similar dynamic, though perhaps more strenuously contested, occurred between experimental writers of the period and their counterparts in visual art and especially painting, which enjoyed the highest cultural profile of the visual arts in the interwar years. Stein and William Carlos Williams are the most significant examples of the interplay between experimental writing and art: both had intimate ties to a wide range of contemporary artists, and both engaged modernist painting in a complex, two-way flow of influence, on the one hand attempting to translate visual experiments in representing fractured space and time to the written page, and, on the other, shaping the reception of artists' work and inspiring new artworks in turn. Stein's relationship with Pablo Picasso is one of the most sustained and compelling examples of this interplay in the history of modernism. When Picasso completed a portrait of Stein in 1906 and viewers complained that it failed to resemble Stein, Picasso turned the tables by promising that Stein would grow into her portrait: "She will," he replied (Figure 10.1).[15] The anecdote gestures to modernist art's claims to reveal aspects of experience that remain obscure in realist representation, but especially to its claims to occupy the future, as it were, and subordinate other objects in the cultural field to its slipstream. Stein's many verbal "portraits" of artists from the period, including two of Picasso, aggressively confront the relationship between avant-garde painting and the modernist writing that belatedly attempts to represent, revise, or recapitulate its novelty. Stein's broad strategy in these works is not to mirror the physical features of the subjects, nor does she translate their characteristic

FIGURE 10.1: Pablo Picasso, *Gertrude Stein*, 1905–1906.
Metropolitan Museum of Art, Bequest of Gertrude Stein, 1946.
© 2014 Estate of Pablo Picasso / Artists Rights Society (ARS), New York.

visual styles into corresponding verbal imagery. Rather, she most often works on a metalevel, ruminating on the way experimental art unfolds in a dialectic of, on the one hand, shocking novelty and singularity, and on the other, reception, in which social processes invest works with prestige and meaning.

In "Picasso" (1912), Stein's undulating prose vamps on Picasso as a "one" who is the subject of an always-original "working" that "something was coming out of," but also the object of a "following."[16] Although the poem primarily celebrates the singular genius of Picasso as inimitable, and hence implies that the poem itself is an act of belated "following," the concept of following haunts its object as well, raising the deflating possibility that the genius depends upon a possibly fickle "following" for his prestige or that his "followers" will themselves innovate and retroactively diminish the uniqueness of the precursor work of the "one." Stein's second portrait, "If I Told Him: A Completed Portrait of Picasso," boldly claims to bring the prior attempt to completion by folding the portraitist into the portrait and breaching the bounds between subject/object, original/copy, and pioneer/follower. Like the prior portrait, this text aggrandizes its subject, casting Picasso as a "Napoleon" who is the "first," a "king," a "father."[17] But here the speaker, who reverently flatters the "one" in the earlier poem, is ubiquitous and subverts claims to originality: Picasso is a copy of Napoleon I, after all, and his narcissism is vulnerable to what "I told him" from the very title onward. More subtly, the poem's reiterations and variations often reverse the poles of originality and belatedness, using subversive humor at several points to mock male pretensions to autonomy and singularity. For example, the repeated question "Who came first? Napoleon at first" smuggles into the patriarchal discourse of founding a line a feminist affirmation of the benefits of coming in second in some situations, an implication that is underscored a few lines below when the repetition of the masculine "he" devolves into laughter ("he he he he"): she who comes second, comes loudest. The broader point of this "completed" portrait is that the way forward for modernist aesthetics is not the pursuit of the plenary, autonomous work but the navigation of the crossroads where verbal and visual supplement one another in a pleasurable failure to finish.[18]

Williams shares with Stein an intense bond with a group of contemporary artists, though both the artists and the nature of the bond are quite different.[19] In thematic terms, Williams' work obsessively engages the sights and sounds of American modernity: for example, the neo-Whitmanic "crowd" that "are beautiful ... in detail" and the sensations and perspectival shifts that new modes of mobility bring.[20] In formal terms, his work diverges from Stein's in its commitment to precision and indexicality rather than iterativeness and intersubjective dialogue. Williams takes from his visual artist peers a desire to renovate perception of ordinary people, processes, and things via metonymy, in ways that link his work to photography, and especially the layout of photographs in series and montages. The poem "The Great Figure" (1921) is exemplary: it relates a spectacular scene – that of a fire truck tearing through the city, all "gong clangs" and "siren howls" – but it does so at a tangent, shifting the focus from the who/what/when/where of conventional dramatic narrative to the queerly arbitrary detail of the engine's "figure 5/in gold."[21] In contrast to the truck itself and the spectacle in which it participates, the "figure" is presented as "moving/tense/unheeded," part of a peripheral and private drama that reflects back on the poem's title. Williams performs a mode of perception that draws inspiration from Duchamp's "readymades"; here Williams finds rather than makes, creating what Kenneth Burke called a "triumph of anti-Culture" by transforming something ordinary and unaesthetic into art sheerly by the act of framing it.[22] Who, or what, cuts a great figure? the poem asks, and provides an implicit answer: that the poet or painter who vividly links "ideas" with "things" finds something numinous in the framing of quotidian detail in a transvaluation of values rich with cultural political significance. In a further bit of evidence of the two-way flow of influence between verbal and visual form in the era, Williams' poem inspired his friend, the precisionist painter Charles Demuth, to paint a portrait of sorts of Williams, *I Saw the Figure 5 in Gold* (1928), that recapitulates the poem's form by magnifying and repeating the gold "5" at the focal point of the image and constellating around it fragmented pieces of the urban fabric, including fragments of Williams' name, "Bill" and "Carlos" (Figure 10.2). The portrait perceptively encapsulates both the broadly distributed wish of modernist artists to put the artwork rather than the artist on center stage and the more idiosyncratic emphasis of Williams on expressing abstract "ideas" through material "things."

"Book or Film?": John Dos Passos' *U.S.A.*

If American modernity is "all formidable foreground," a site of teeming visual stimuli that disables traditional modes of perception and representation, how did these changes register in the novel genre? What kinds of experiments did novelists undertake to represent this new social content? How did the modernist novel attempt to feed back into this emergent modernity, shaping readers' understandings of its values and meanings? The Depression era saw the rise of a "late modernism" that incorporates the violence and incoherence of modern urban life, and especially its raucous mass cultural forms, in a deformation of high modernist formal mastery.[23] Examples of late modernism in the novel include Djuna Barnes' *Ryder* and *Ladies' Almanack* (both 1928), which explore non-normative gender and sexual roles via pastiches of archaic literary and visual forms; Lynd Ward's six wordless novels of the 1930s and '40s, which fashion long-form narratives out of sequences of woodcuts; and Nathanael West's *Miss Lonelyhearts* (1933), an experiment in creating a "novel in the form of a comic strip," jettisoning the novel's traditional painstaking development of character, setting, and plot in favor of a tabloid-inflected, violent mode of narration in which "you only have time to explode."[24]

FIGURE 10.2: Charles Demuth, *I Saw the Figure 5 in Gold*, 1928.
Metropolitan Museum of Art, Alfred Stieglitz Collection, 1949.

It is John Dos Passos' *U.S.A.* trilogy (1930–1936), however, that is the richest example of late modernist use of "low" and mass cultural forms to deform the novel. Like James, Dos Passos engages the mobile, overdetermined modernity of a rapidly changing society through an aesthetic of restless analysis. But the primary site of restlessness in the trilogy occurs at a metalevel, in the way Dos Passos structures the novels around four very different modes of writing: the cinematic impressionism of the "Camera Eye," narrated via stream-of-consciousness fragments from an unnamed but blatantly autobiographical protagonist; collations of collaged newspaper headlines, popular song, and other ephemera in the "Newsreels"; biographies of representative celebrities and "great men" rendered with acid irony;

and traditional realist fictions featuring twelve ordinary "types" of the era. The trilogy toggles among these modes abruptly, producing for the reader both a reflection of the disorienting shock of modernity and, through the many poetic linkages across the modes, an attempt at some kind of coherent metanarrative. Critics from Dos Passos' day to the present have noticed the intimate relationship between this interlaced, interruptive structure and cinema, particularly the 1920s Soviet cinema of Sergei Eisenstein and Dziga Vertov.[25] Dos Passos traveled to Russia in 1928, where he was deeply impressed by Eisenstein, director of *The Battleship Potemkin* (1925) and a pioneer in the theory and practice of montage, in which the narrative does not progress through the viewer's absorption in a realistic *mise-en-scène* but through the *interval* between shots, the "collision of two factors that gives rise to an idea."[26] The trilogy owes the largest formal debt to the work of Soviet filmmaker Dziga Vertov, from whose work Dos Passos borrows the "camera eye" label and who was also an innovator of the newsreel form in his *Kino-Pravda* series of the 1920s.[27] Vertov's masterpiece, *Man with a Movie Camera* (1929), shares with *U.S.A.* an orientation to revealing the staggering scale and complexity of modern metropolitan life coupled with a faith in self-reflexive modernist form to demystify that complexity for its audience. In ways that are reminiscent of James' narrator, the film's leitmotif features the presence of Vertov's brother and cinematographer Mikhail Kaufman in the frame, the eponymous "man with a movie camera" who runs tirelessly through the streets of Moscow and Leningrad, gathering impressions of the cities that will be edited into the film itself (Figure 10.3).[28]

In a parallel fashion, Dos Passos' "camera eye" sections are a kind of *kuenstlerroman* within a novel, featuring a narrator who will develop into the author of the trilogy and thereby injecting into the product a self-reflexive awareness of the process of researching and writing novels. "The Camera Eye (46)" underscores the ludic, Joycean stream of fragmentary impressions gathered by the narrator, along with his fascination with the visual detritus of the city:

> walk the streets and walk the streets inquiring of Coca-Cola signs Lucky Strike ads price tags in store windows scraps of overheard conversations stray tatters of newsprint yesterday's headlines sticking out of ashcans.[29]

Here the narrator performs much the same work as Dos Passos himself in the "Newsreel" sections, which also "inquire" of seemingly arbitrary materials what they might signify; moreover, the references to Lucky Strikes and ashcans summon up the artwork of left-wing contemporaries of Dos Passos, such as Stuart Davis and George Bellows.[30] In these "Newsreels," snippets of tabloids,

FIGURE 10.3: Still from Dziga Vertov, *Man with a Movie Camera*, 1929.
Personal collection of the author.

popular songs, celebrity gossip, and advertisements mix promiscuously in ways that mirror, on one level, the paralysis and confusion ascribed to consumers of mass media in the roughly contemporary cultural theory of Adorno and Horkheimer.[31] "Newsreel LXI," for example, braids together popular song, PR puffery, and news headlines:

> Giant airship breaks in two in midflight
> [...]
> *Shaking hands with the sky*
> It Is the Early Investor Who Will Share to the Fullest Extent in the Large and Rapid Enhancement of Values That Will Follow Such Characterful Development
> *Who's the big man with gold in his mouth?*
> *Where does he come from? He comes from the south*[32]

Here, as in many of the Newsreels, readers who "inquire" of the "signs" discover other layers of signification: the various snippets coalesce around the theme of the real estate bubble of 1920s Florida, enabled by gold-tongued southerners and "high" mental states and destined to crash abruptly. As is often the case, the montage works both within the section and between this section and other sections, as the plot of the Margo Dowling fictional narrative moves to Florida at just this point and engages themes of heady elevation and reckless speculation.

Here, however, a basic difference from the Soviet material emerges, one that points to distinctive features of U.S. modernism/modernity. Whereas Vertov (and, even more, Eisenstein) uses montage in an agitprop mode to construct epic narratives of the Revolution and celebrate (though not uncritically) its successful aftermath, Dos Passos' novel remains more circumspect about the present and the future. The novel has been read as an elegy for a "Lincoln Republic" that has fallen prey to what the trilogy's third volume calls "the big money," and it chronicles the way the culture industries, and the banks that underwrite their activities, undermine the republic's self-presence rooted in "the speech of the people" with lies that make words "slimy and foul."[33] The great aesthetic challenge Dos Passos confronts in the trilogy is how to present the full centrifugal force of monopoly capital's "creative destruction," especially via its culture industries, while preserving the genre's capacity to order experience and narrate historical change coherently. Dos Passos uses the martyrdom of Sacco and Vanzetti as a gesture of unity and closure: "Newsreel LXVI," "The Camera Eye (50)," and the last fictional narrative of Mary French, a radical journalist, all converge on this event, which inspires in the narrator of "The Camera Eye" the culminating epiphany, "all right we are two nations."[34] As it nears its end, the trilogy is an epic diverted into elegy by history: the epic's traditional equipoise between past and future, the singular hero and the nation's multitude, gives way to a fundamental asymmetry. The past of "old words" and republican virtue, the novel argues, is defeated by words and images broadcast to the masses by PR flacks, ad men, and monopolists of culture such as William Randolph Hearst, subject of the novel's penultimate biography.[35] This asymmetry appears in sharp relief in the trilogy's closing image, in which Vag, an unnamed vagrant, hitchhikes alone and looks up at an airplane. In the airplane sits an anonymous executive, who vomits his expensive New York lunch while thinking about the pleasures of L.A.[36] The vomit starkly captures Dos Passos' refusal of a modernist dialectic that would synthesize these two modernities with no remainder: that of speed, the godlike view of "flyover country," abstractions of value, and excess; and 30,000 feet below, that of slowness, blinkered perspectives, anxieties about the next meal, and, in the trilogy's closing words, "a hundred miles down the road."[37]

Books of Pictures as Books of Exercises: The Documentary Book

Dos Passos' s *U.S.A.* can be thought of as a "documentary novel," a hybrid form that includes "documents" (in the historian's sense) within a fictional frame. As such, it is part of a vast outpouring of "documentary expression" in the Depression era, ranging from ethnographic texts to murals to films to, especially, photographs and photo-texts.[38] Within this wide range, the documentary book, a hybrid form that combines photographs and text to document social conditions, represents one of the most significant areas of innovation, especially for its exploitation of the tensions that arise in the combination of verbal and visual forms in the same medium. A raft of documentary books appeared in the late 1930s and early '40s, featuring collaborations between prominent photographers (Dorothea Lange, Margaret Bourke-White, Walker Evans) and writers (Erskine Caldwell, Richard Wright, James Agee) and drawing from original fieldwork, existing photographs pulled from the growing Farm Security Administration archive then being produced by the New Deal's cultural wing, or both. The distinctiveness of these books is best appreciated by comparing them, on the one hand, to prior photo-documentary texts such as Jacob Riis' pioneering *How the Other Half Lives* (1890) and, on the other, the emergence of mass-cultural photo-essay forms in glossy magazines such as *Life* and *Look* in the late 1930s. Like Riis' work, Depression-era documentary books use photography to push a social reform agenda, but the later works often evince a much more skeptical, self-reflexive attitude toward the mimetic pretensions and ethical claims of doing documentary work. Riis' team famously illuminated spaces that were both literally and figuratively (in the minds of reformers such as Riis) dark with the new technology of flash powder. His "raiding party," in his arresting description, "carried terror wherever it went," and one senses always in Riis the fervor of his belief in such enlightenment and even terror in the service of progress, whatever the collateral damage.[39] One finds quite a different sensibility in James Agee and Walker Evans' *Let Us Now Praise Famous Men* (1940), in which Agee expends hundreds of pages doubting whether pictures or words can capture anything like the truth he witnesses among poor tenant farmers in Alabama. "If I could do it," he writes, "I'd do no writing at all here. It would be photographs; the rest would be fragments of cloth, bits of cotton, lumps of earth, records of speech, pieces of wood and iron, phials of odors, plates of food and excrement. ... A piece of the body torn out by the roots might be more to the point."[40] As in Riis, photographs have priority as bearers of truth (Agee writes, "handled cleanly and literally in its own terms ... [the camera] is ... incapable of recording anything but absolute, dry truth"), but the text constantly returns to the impossibility of any medium capturing the sublimity of human suffering and, especially, of a mass readership receiving from representations of such suffering their full impact.[41] T.V. Reed argues that Agee and Evans' text invents a mode of "cubist sociology," combining the referentiality and analysis of social science with a modernist aesthetic that shatters the masterful scientific gaze into a proliferating, bewildering combination of perspectives.[42] Thus the imperative for social reform, in this mode of modernist documentary, coexists uneasily with an imperative to examine one's own biases, limitations, and mixed motives.

The more pressing point of comparison for authors of documentary books was the competing mode of the "photographic essay" popularized at *Life* from 1936 onward. In *Life*, formal innovation was coupled not with social reform and self-reflexivity but with an exceptionalist view of the United States enabled by a seamless combination of images and text that gave readers a masterful perspective on the world. The "Prospectus" circulated to would-be investors in *Life* makes this claim through a soaring set of infinitives: "To see life; to see the world; to eyewitness great events; to watch the faces of the poor and the gestures of the proud ... to see and take pleasure in seeing; to see and be amazed; to see and be instructed."[43] The emphasis on precise representation of social reality aligns *Life*'s aims with those of Agee and Evans above, but Agee's angst modulates into a more cheerful key here, as *Life*'s readers are supposed to stop worrying and learn to love the photograph – and with it the status quo. The clearest counter-current to this increasingly dominant mode of verbal-visual media is Richard Wright's *12 Million Black Voices* (1941), a documentary book chronicling the formation of African American subjects from slavery to the present. The central conceit of the text is rooted in its eccentric use of the first-person plural. Whereas *Life* invites Americans to see themselves, in effect, occupying simultaneously the normative positions of masterful viewer and proper American as subject matter, *Black Voices* confronts its reader/viewers from the far side of a raced and classed divide, echoing Du Bois' prior work:

> Each day when you see us black folk upon the dusty land of the farms or upon the hard pavement of the city streets, you usually take us for granted and think you know us, but our history is far stranger than you suspect, and we are not what we seem.
>
> Our outward guise still carries the old familiar aspect which three hundred years of oppression in America have given us, but beneath [our] garb ... lies an uneasily tied knot of pain and hope whose snarled strands converge from many points of time and space.[44]

The text stages not so much a demand for recognition as an inquiry into the workings of recognition, especially in a society saturated with images and haunted with a traumatic racial history. The truth that lies beneath the surface photograph of the racial other is a "knot," a figure that conveys both the idea that black history might be "snarled" in that of a readership hailed as white and, smuggled in via the signifier, that the "knot" of race is a

FIGURE 10.4: Jack Delano, *Tony Thompson, born in slavery. Greene County, Georgia*, 1941. FSA-OWI Collection, Prints and Photographs Division, Library of Congress.

"not," a figure of radical contingency. The image that accompanies this passage is of an old blind sharecropper, and at first glance the image affirms the central enabling fantasy of naïve documentary work: that the camera can capture the "real thing," delivering an unmediated presence (Figure 10.4). But the text captions the image, so to speak, in ways that enable uncannier and more destabilizing readings: that it is the reader who is blind and that this blindness is bound up with the pathos of the very African American history that has formed this man.

In a discussion of August Sander, whose *Faces of the Age* attempted to map the heterogeneity of 1920s Germany in photographic portraits, Walter Benjamin proclaimed, "this is not a book of pictures; this is a book of exercises."[45] In like manner, Wright's book is a verbal/visual textbook teaching new, more humane ways of seeing and saying "we" in a society riven, like Sander's, with racial antagonisms and given to ignoring them in favor of facile and violent modes of visual sorting of bodies. Wright ends the text tentatively, with a complex figure of seeing/being seen that bookends the "knot" that opens the text:

> If America has forgotten her past, then let her look into the mirror of our consciousness and she will see the living past living in the present, for our memories go back ... to the time when none of us, black or white, lived in this fertile land.
>
> Look at us and know us and you will know yourselves, for we are you, looking back at you from the dark mirror of our lives![46]

In sharp contrast to the sunny coerciveness of *Life* and the violent flash that terrorizes the objects of Riis' reform, Wright leaves his readers with a lingering gaze into a dark space – one that contains a history implicating self and other, troubles easy identifications and disavowals, and demands a complex, ongoing process of working out and decoding.

Thinking about Wright's "book of exercises," along with the other texts engaged in this essay, as modernist pedagogical experiments in retraining one's vision sits uneasily with long-standing traditions in modernist studies. Above all, modernism has traditionally celebrated its "difficulties," its capacity to "shock the bourgeoisie," its "negative dialectic" that refuses resolution; thus aligning modernist visual practice with the orthographic spirit of the workbook might seem retrograde, if not downright schoolmarmish. The most important task for modernist studies at present may be to bind its restless energies to the kinds of constructivist pedagogical projects theorized recently as an ethos of "reparative reading" or a shift from "matters of fact" to "matters of concern."[47] In our cultural moment, the "hotel-spirit" thrives at the visual-verbal laboratories of Facebook and Google, where web users feel free as we pour ourselves as data into proprietary containers and networks. As all humanities increasingly becomes digital humanities, modernist studies has a crucial role to play in reminding readers of two things: first, the history of past engagements between readers, writings, and emergent media; second, the need to preserve an active, resistant, "writerly" disposition that collaborates in an ongoing revision of social codes rather than passively submitting to the inscriptions of inscrutable corporate others.

NOTES

I would like to thank Sophie Bell, Sarah Chinn, Joseph Entin, Hildegard Hoeller, and Amy Robbins for their helpful suggestions on this project.

1. For the classic argument in behalf of the rise of the "visual turn," see W.J.T. Mitchell, *Picture Theory: Essays on Verbal and Visual Representation* (Chicago: University of Chicago Press, 1994), 15.

2. See Rebecca L. Walkowitz, *Cosmopolitan Style: Modernism beyond the Nation* (New York: Columbia University Press, 2006); Joseph Entin, *Sensational Modernism: Experimental Fiction and Photography in Thirties America* (Chapel Hill: University of North Carolina Press, 2007); Douglas Mao and Rebecca L. Walkowitz, eds., *Bad Modernisms* (Durham: Duke University Press, 2006); Juan Antonio Suárez, *Pop Modernism: Noise and the Reinvention of the Everyday* (Urbana: University of Illinois Press, 2007); Werner Sollors, *Ethnic Modernism* (Cambridge: Harvard University Press, 2008); Michael Trask, *Cruising Modernism: Class and Sexuality in American Literature and Social Thought* (Ithaca, NY: Cornell University Press, 2003); Eric Haralson, *Henry James and Queer Modernity* (Cambridge: Cambridge University Press, 2008); Katherine Biers, *Virtual Modernism Writing and Technology in the Progressive Era* (Minneapolis: University of Minnesota Press, 2013).

3. On the shock experienced by modern subjects in metropolitan life, see Walter Benjamin, "On Some Motifs in Baudelaire," in *Illuminations*, ed. Hannah Arendt, trans. Harry Zohn (New York: Schocken, 1968), 160–165; Georg Simmel, "The Metropolis and Mental Life," in *On Individuality and Social Forms: Selected Writings of Georg Simmel*, ed. Donald Levine (Chicago: University of Chicago Press, 1971), 325–326.

4. See, for example, Sara Blair, "The Photograph's Last Word: Visual Culture Studies Now," *American Literary History* 22, no. 3 (2010): 673–697; Michael North, "Visual Culture," in *The Cambridge Companion to American Modernism*, ed. Walter B. Kalaidjian (Cambridge: Cambridge University Press, 2005), 177–194.

5. Henry James, *The American Scene*, ed. John F. Sears (New York: Penguin Books, 1994), 99; hereafter cited in text.

6. Henry Adams, *The Education of Henry Adams* (1918; New York: Modern Library, 1931), 382.

7. Martin Jay, "The Rise of Hermeneutics and the Crisis of Ocularcentrism," in *Force Fields: Between Intellectual History and Cultural Critique* (New York: Routledge, 1993), 105–106. I draw the broader argument regarding the disorienting shift from a disembodied to a hyperembodied subjectivity from Karen Jacobs, *The Eye's Mind: Literary Modernism and Visual Culture* (Ithaca, NY: Cornell University Press, 2001), 1–2.

8. See Ross Posnock, "Affirming the Alien: The Pragmatist Pluralism of the American Scene," in *The Cambridge Companion to Henry James*, ed. Jonathan Freedman (Cambridge: Cambridge University Press, 1998), 224–246.

9. W.E.B. Du Bois, *The Souls of Black Folk* (1903; New York: Penguin Books, 1996), v, 1.

10. For a reading of vision and culturally determined "screens," see Kaja Silverman, *The Threshold of the Visible World* (New York: Routledge, 1996), 131–137.

JEFF ALLRED

11. Theodor W. Adorno and Max Horkheimer, *Dialectic of Enlightenment* (1944; New York: Continuum, 1974), ix.
12. For a definition of literary modernism as a mode of "interruption" of normative public sphere discourse, see Astradur Eysteinsson, *The Concept of Modernism* (Ithaca, NY: Cornell University Press, 1990), 197–206.
13. Gertrude Stein, "The Coming of the Americans," in *Selected Writings of Gertrude Stein*, ed. Carl Van Vechten (New York: Random House, 1962), 704; William A. Camfield, *Marcel Duchamp, Fountain* (Houston, TX: Houston Fine Art Press, 1989), 38.
14. Marjorie Perloff, "The Avant-Garde Phase of American Modernism," in *The Cambridge Companion to American Modernism*, ed. Walter B. Kalaidjian (Cambridge: Cambridge University Press, 2005), 195–196.
15. Gertrude Stein, *The Autobiography of Alice B. Toklas* (New York: Penguin, 1996), 12.
16. Gertrude Stein, "Picasso," in *Writings, 1903–1932* (New York: Library of America, 1998), 282.
17. Gertrude Stein, "If I Told Him," in *Writings, 1903–1932*, 506.
18. See Ulla Haselstein, "Gertrude Stein's Portraits of Matisse and Picasso," *New Literary History* 34, no. 4 (2003): 723–743.
19. For a sketch of Williams' extensive connections to his artist contemporaries, see Peter Halter, *The Revolution in the Visual Arts and the Poetry of William Carlos Williams* (Cambridge: Cambridge University Press, 1994), 8–12.
20. William Carlos Williams, *The Collected Poems of William Carlos Williams, Vol. I, 1909–1939*, eds. A. Walton Litz and Christopher MacGowan (New York: New Directions, 1986), 233. Poems featuring transit include "The Young Housewife" and "The Right of Way," 205, 206.
21. Williams, *Collected Poems I*, 174.
22. *The Revolution in the Visual Arts and the Poetry of William Carlos Williams*, 98. Kenneth Burke, "Heaven's First Law," in *William Carlos Williams: The Critical Heritage*, ed. Charles Doyle (New York: Psychology Press, 1980), 73.
23. Tyrus Miller, *Late Modernism: Politics, Fiction, and the Arts between the World Wars* (Berkeley: University of California Press, 1999), 4–6.
24. Djuna Barnes, *Ryder* (1928; Normal: Dalkey Archive Press, 1990); Djuna Barnes, *Ladies Almanack* (1928; Normal: Dalkey Archive Press, 1992); Nathanael West, *Miss Lonelyhearts & The Day of the Locust* (1933 and 1939; New York: New Directions, 1969); Nathanael West, "Some Notes on Miss L," in *Novels and Other Writings* (New York: Library of America, 1997), 401; Lynd Ward, *Lynd Ward: Six Novels in Woodcuts* (New York: Library of America, 2010).
25. See, for example, Compton Mackenzie's 1932 review of *1919*, "Film or Book?" in *Dos Passos, The Critical Heritage*, ed. Barry Maine (London: Routledge, 1988), 109.
26. Sergei Eisenstein, "Beyond the Shot," in *Film Theory and Criticism: Introductory Readings*, eds. Leo Braudy and Marshall Cohen (New York: Oxford University Press, 1999), 21.
27. For Vertov's explanation of the origins of "Kino-Eye," see Dziga Vertov, "The Birth of Kino-Eye," in *Kino-Eye: The Writings of Dziga Vertov*, ed. Annette Michelson, trans. Kevin O'Brien (Berkeley: University of California Press, 1984), 40–41.

28. For a reading of Vertov's influence on Dos Passos, see Carol Shloss, *In Visible Light: Photography and the American Writer, 1840–1940* (New York: Oxford University Press, 1987), 149–163. Juan Suárez argues that Dos Passos wasn't influenced enough, in effect, by the newsreels of Vertov and other practitioners of leftist documentary in the 1920s and '30s; see Suárez, *Pop Modernism*, 104–108.

29. John Dos Passos, *The Big Money* (1936; New York: Mariner Books, 2000), 118.

30. See, for example, Bellows' *Disappointments of the Ash Can* (1915) and Stuart Davis' *Lucky Strike* (1922).

31. See especially "The Culture Industry: Enlightenment as Mass Deception," in Adorno and Horkheimer, *Dialectic of Enlightenment*.

32. Dos Passos, *The Big Money*, 272.

33. Michael Denning, *The Cultural Front: The Laboring of American Culture in the Twentieth Century* (New York: Verso, 1996), 163–199; John Dos Passos, *U.S.A.* (New York: Harcourt, Brace, and Company, 1938), vii.; Dos Passos, *The Big Money*, 371.

34. Dos Passos, *The Big Money*, 371.

35. Ibid.

36. Ibid., 448.

37. Ibid.

38. For a still-useful survey, see William Stott, *Documentary Expression and Thirties America* (Chicago: University of Chicago Press, 1986).

39. Jacob A. Riis, *The Making of an American* (New York: Macmillan, 1901), 174.

40. James Agee and Walker Evans, *Three Tenant Families: Let Us Now Praise Famous Men* (1941; Boston: Mariner Books, 2001), 13.

41. Ibid., 234.

42. T.V. Reed, "Unimagined Existence and the Fiction of the Real: Postmodernist Realism in *Let Us Now Praise Famous Men*," *Representations* 24 (1988): 162.

43. Qtd. in Robert T. Elson, *Time Inc.: The Intimate History of a Publishing Enterprise* (New York: Atheneum, 1968), 278.

44. Richard Wright, *12 Million Black Voices: A Folk History of the Negro in the United States* (New York: Viking Press, 1941), 11.

45. Walter Benjamin, "A Brief History of Photography," in *Classic Essays on Photography*, ed. Alan Trachtenberg (New Haven, CT: Leete's Island Books, 1980), 210.

46. Wright, *12 Million Black Voices*, 146.

47. Eve Kosofsky Sedgwick, "Paranoid Reading and Reparative Reading," in *Novel Gazing: Queer Readings in Fiction* (Durham: Duke University Press, 1997), 1–37; Bruno Latour, "Why Has Critique Run Out of Steam? From Matters of Fact to Matters of Concern," *Critical Inquiry* 30.2 (2004): 225–248.

11

EMILY J. LORDI

Jazz and Blues Modernisms

Why think music and literature together? With regard to U.S. modernism, social histories of the Harlem Renaissance can make the answer seem obvious. Several writers and performing artists now associated with the New Negro Movement were friends, collaborators, and allies who anthologized and wrote about each other's work. Langston Hughes hailed "the bellowing voice of Bessie Smith" in "The Negro Artist and the Racial Mountain" (1926) and recounted in his memoir, *The Big Sea* (1940), meeting Smith with Zora Neale Hurston.[1] In 1931, Duke Ellington couched his aspirations to compose works that represented African American life in literary terms: "What is being done by Countee Cullen and others in literature is overdue in our music."[2] Critics have sought to describe the expressive and historical correspondences between African American music and writing at least since James Weldon Johnson prefaced his 1922 *Book of American Negro Poetry* with a discussion of music and Alain Locke included essays on music along with poetry and prose in the 1925 *New Negro* anthology. Indeed, the practice of discussing black poetry in terms of music was already so prevalent by 1929 that Countee Cullen found it stifling: "May we not chant a hymn to the Sun God if we will, create a bit of phantasy in which not a spiritual or a blues appears ... in short do, write, create, what we will, our only concern being that we do it well and with all the power in us?"[3] This was a question that black writers and critics would ask many times over the following century.

Whereas modernist critics and writers frequently examined (or protested) the links between black music and writing, the scholarly practice of linking these mediums only coalesced as theorizations of the Black Aesthetic dovetailed with the institutionalization of African American literary studies at U.S. universities in the late 1960s. At this point, the notion that black writers engage with oral and musical forms helped scholars organize a distinctive cultural tradition and field of study. They generated that field's prehistory accordingly. Thus, for example, Black Arts poets inspired by Langston

Hughes' engagement with folk music helped canonize Hughes' blues poems, black feminist scholars such as Mary Helen Washington and Cheryl Wall recovered Zora Neale Hurston's writings on black performance, and scholars such as Robert O'Meally and Houston Baker helped establish Ralph Ellison as a key theorist of jazz and American culture.

All this is to say that as we examine U.S. literary and musical modernisms at this particular juncture, it is useful to treat the relationship between African American music and modernist literature not only as empirical fact (writers' and musicians' common milieu) but also as a critical orientation with its own history and methodologies. The story of thinking African American music and literature together is a story about the formation of a field. It is the story of the specific critical habits or hermeneutics these constellations have enabled, including the point at which critics begin to read not only poetry but also the novel through music. What follows, then, is a brief genealogy of critical approaches to this interplay, as well as several case studies that demonstrate methods for reading modernist novels through a jazz or blues lens. The opening section is meant to situate what scholars are doing when we read these forms together; the latter section hints at the range of methodological choices available to scholars now that critics have moved beyond classifying various poems or novels as jazz or blues texts. Insofar as ideas about the blues and jazz are often used to stand in for ideas about black formal culture as a whole, an overview of debates about music will also help illuminate recent scholarly claims that African American artists are quintessential modernists.

Black Writing and Song

Although literary representations of African American music are just that – historically situated representations that reveal as much about their authors' aims as they do about black music – there are tropes that appear with some consistency across time. For example, black writers have often represented African American song as the manifestation of a communal spirit or history that requires black translation to a white public. Frederick Douglass dismantles the notion that slaves' songs express contentment by insisting that their "every tone was a testimony against slavery."[4] Du Bois reads the "sorrow songs" as an index of black Americans' passage from "African" to "Negro." "The music of an unhappy people," these songs nonetheless express "a faith in the ultimate justice of things" and issue a challenge to white America: "Is such a hope justified? Do the Sorrow Songs ring true?"[5]

Pauline Hopkins' *Contending Forces* (1900), James Weldon Johnson's *Autobiography of an Ex-Colored Man* (1912), Nella Larsen's *Quicksand*

(1928), and Du Bois' *Dark Princess* (1928) all feature key scenes of performance in which the tones of African American music move black protagonists with a sense of racial kinship and longing. As Jim Crow policies dismantle the promises of Reconstruction, these authors all represent the lasting problem of national belonging that Wendell Phillips articulated in his preface to Douglass' 1845 *Narrative*: "In all the broad lands which the Constitution of the United States overshadows, there is no single spot ... where a fugitive slave can plant himself and say, 'I am safe'" (11). In this context, African diasporic music figures a would-be home for America's motherless children as well as a moral imperative, in Du Bois' terms, to help build it.

In these texts, music mediates between self and group by instigating a personal affective experience of racial belonging.[6] This dual sense of song as personally and collectively resonant has made black music fertile ground for debate throughout the twentieth century. In her essay "Spirituals and Neo-Spirituals" (1934), for example, Hurston contests Du Bois' representation of the spirituals through what we might call an energetic misreading: "The idea that the whole body of spirituals are 'sorrow songs' is ridiculous."[7] Instead, she asserts, the songs "cover a wide range of subjects from a peeve at gossipers to Death and Judgment" (870). Hurston's spirituals are part of the fabric of a complex everyday life that contains as much joy as sorrow – a claim that resonates with her refusal in "How It Feels to Be Colored Me" (1928) to be seen as "tragically colored."[8] By figuring the spirituals as dynamic, unrepeatable artistic events, rather than static objects, Hurston contests the reductive commodification of the spirituals and other forms of black performative culture through the concert performances of the Fisk Jubilee Singers of whom Du Bois writes so supportively in *Souls*. Hurston's sense of black song as fundamentally performative resonates with the dynamic narrative role that song plays in *Their Eyes Were Watching God* (1937), as I detail later.

Langston Hughes advances a similarly affirmative vision of black music by creating the genre of the blues poem in the 1920s, an innovation he explains in "The Negro Artist and the Racial Mountain." Here Hughes calls for an antibourgeois African American art that would embrace the romance of "the low-down folks" that he associates with blues and jazz (692–694). He explains that in his own poems he tries "to grasp and hold some of the meanings and rhythms of jazz" – "the tom-tom of revolt against weariness in a white world." And he deploys a trope that informs discussions of black music well into the twenty-first century: the "incongruous humor that so often, as in the Blues, becomes ironic laughter mixed with tears." Poet and scholar Sterling Brown soon worked to systematize such conceptions of black vernacular culture in the service of literary criticism. Brown's essays on the spirituals, blues, work songs, and jazz helped define a distinctive expressive culture and thus paved the way for theories of the Black Aesthetic promoted by artists such as LeRoi Jones (Amiri Baraka), who studied with Brown at Howard University.[9]

Among writers of this generation, Ralph Ellison wrote most eloquently and often about jazz – especially the big-band era music that Robert O'Meally describes as "danceably hard-swinging and steeped in the blues."[10] Ellison figures the (male) jazz musician as a prototype for U.S. democracy: the jazz artist models the need to improvise one's way through a changing modern landscape while working with and against an ensemble of other improvisers to "achieve his self-determined identity."[11] Jazz also gives Ellison a model for compositional practice: Ellison's ideal writer is an improviser and craftsman who, like the finest swing musicians of his day, strives for artistic excellence in the service of communal affirmation.[12] Finally, Ellison makes jazz the ground for an aesthetic system that valorizes techniques of intertextual quotation and collage. If scholars would eventually use this principle to codify a culturally black expressive tradition, Ellison also used it to claim an entire body of modernist literature for jazz. In a 1962 essay, he asks us to "consider that at least as early as T. S. Eliot's creation of a new aesthetic for poetry through the artful juxtapositioning of earlier styles, Louis Armstrong, way down the river in New Orleans, was working out a similar technique for jazz."[13]

For Ellison, black Americans, far from being alienated from the American cultural mainstream, had always created it. This position explains his argument with Jones/Baraka's *Blues People* (1963), the first full-length study of black American music written by a black critic. Against Ellison's notion of black citizens as quintessential Americans, Baraka offers this first chapter title: "The Negro as Non-American: Some Backgrounds."[14] While not specifically engaged with literary production, *Blues People* and Baraka's following study *Black Music* (1967) figure black music as the truest index or sign of black culture. This view of black music, partly indebted to Du Bois, Johnson, and perhaps most immediately to Black Arts writers' chosen elder, Richard Wright, informs theories of the Black Aesthetic developed in the early 1970s and, consequently, black critical theory today.[15]

Critical Approaches to Jazz and Blues

Efforts to codify the Black Aesthetic, however fraught, were meant to posit African American artistic production as a discrete cultural practice with its own values and aims. The codification of the Black Aesthetic enabled black writers to materially and rhetorically organize community and to assert that outsiders (for instance, white book reviewers) would need to obtain a degree of cultural literacy to reasonably evaluate many works by African American writers. They also helped with the process of canon formation. As I have suggested, the practice of invoking culturally black expressive forms as models and metaphors for literature was a key strategy through which critics organized the field of black literary studies. This strategy helped scholars construct a tradition by isolating "whatever was black about black American literature," in Henry Louis Gates' terms – beyond authors' shared "melanin and subject matter," as Toni Morrison put it.[16]

Early studies often focused on poetry. In a rigorous introduction to his 1973 anthology of "New Black Poetry," Stephen Henderson claims that "structurally speaking, ... , whenever Black poetry is most distinctly and effectively Black, it derives its form from two basic sources, Black speech and Black music" – a concept that Sherley Anne Williams particularizes by focusing on the blues in her 1979 essay "The Blues Roots of Contemporary Afro-American Poetry" (1979). While Henderson and Williams applied a musical paradigm to the study of African American poetics, other writers offered ways to read narrative in terms of black musical aesthetics. James Baldwin, Albert Murray, and Gayl Jones all relate their novels to black music in the 1960s and 1970s. Ellison's 1945 discussion of Wright's memoir *Black Boy* (1944) is an important precursor here: Ellison's classic definition of the blues – as "an autobiographical chronicle of personal catastrophe expressed lyrically"[17] – significantly arises from a reading not of poetry but of Richard Wright's prose narrative. But the work that most dramatically moved the field toward theorizing the vernacular aesthetics of the novel is Henry Louis Gates Jr.'s *The Signifying Monkey* (1988). This study, which popularized (not to say overdetermined) the critical practice of relating African American literary production to oral culture, proceeds through readings of narratives and novels (what Gates calls "talking books") by James Ukawsaw Gronniosaw, Wright, Hurston, Ellison, Ishmael Reed, and Alice Walker.

While augmenting the literary critical interest in black music, Hazel Carby also challenged scholars, in her important 1986 essay on blues women, to recognize key distinctions between the literary and the musical cultures of the 1920s and 1930s. Anticipating performance studies' interest in extraliterary expressive possibilities, Carby argues that classic blues singers of the '20s and '30s such as Ida Cox, Ma Rainey, and Bessie Smith carved out a cultural space that was unavailable to bourgeois black women novelists of the time – a space in which "black women ... constructed themselves as sexual subjects through song."[18] Angela Davis' indispensable book-length study of *Blues Legacies and Black Feminisms* (1998) elaborated the point to show how blues women's songs and performative choices helped create a working-class culture of black feminist resistance and pleasure.

Studies of black music and writing and critical approaches to this interplay have multiplied since the 1990s. Studies such as Davis' and George Chauncey's *Gay New York* (1995) enabled thematic connections between modernist performance cultures and literary representations of female and queer desire. Paul Anderson constructed a rich cultural history of literary and musical production during the Harlem Renaissance, as Farah Jasmine Griffin recently crafted a rich history of music, dance, and writing in the 1940s in New York.[19] Literary critics such as Steven Tracy and Craig Werner performed structural cross-media analyses using concepts such as "laughing to keep from crying" blues irony and call-and-response patterns.[20] Formal-theoretical studies by Kimberly Benston, Aldon Nielsen, and Nathaniel Mackey accented musical and literary techniques or poetics.[21] Fred Moten's performative account of a musical-literary "black radical tradition" (*In the Break*, 2003) innovated the form and practice of cultural theory. Daphne Brooks refashioned African American performance studies by highlighting black women's radical theatrical, musical, and literary performance in *Bodies in Dissent* (2006). Alexander Weheliye critiqued the scholarly tradition of treating black musical forms such as the blues as abstractions by examining specific sound-recording technologies in *Phonographies* (2005).[22] Geoffrey Jacques' and T. Graham Austin's recent studies of popular music and U.S. modernism combine Brooks' investment in popular culture with Weheliye's attention to media and format.[23]

These scholars have collectively embraced Hurston's view of a dynamic vernacular culture. They have sustained Ellison's emphasis on social resilience and Baraka's vision of unassimilated resistance. The dominant image of the blues in contemporary scholarship reconciles these views. As Adam Gussow expertly glosses it, "The blues are not sorrow songs (or not *only* sorrow songs), but *survivor* songs: the soundtrack of a spiritual warriorship that refuses to die – and, not coincidentally, wrests far more than its share of swaggering lyric joy out of an evil world, inscribing personhood and sustaining the tribe in the process."[24] The dominant image of jazz in the literary critical imagination is similar. Citing Albert Murray's description of swing music as "the velocity of celebration," Michael Borchuk captures this view: jazz "is exquisite art wrought from the vernacular, a socially complex form that observes the vicissitudes of racial inequity as it works to redress them. And it is the sound of American culture becoming modern . . . , confidently willing itself into secure existence."[25]

In her landmark study of American modernism, *Terrible Honesty* (1995), Ann Douglas associates this optimistic sensibility with African American literary modernists more than with their white peers: "Inured to but hardly acquiescent before extreme cultural displacement," black New Yorkers "did not strike the pose of disillusionment" but rather saw, in Langston Hughes' words, "tomorrow/ Bright before us/ Like a flame."[26] Douglas writes that African American modernists associated with the Harlem Renaissance "did not explore the quasi-Calvinist theological implications of being a 'lost' generation. ... Calvinism, with its emphasis on preordained sin, did not speak to black Americans as forcibly as it did to white ones; the sins of the nation did not lie at their door" (92).

Of course, the peril of this moment ran as deep as the promise. As Rita Barnard writes, "It is important to remember that the rapid pace of social change brought with it a hankering for tradition and that the revolution of modernity triggered its counterrevolutions."[27] George Kent enumerates these conditions in his 1972 literary critical study: "Few black workers were accepted into labor unions. The end of World War I saw extraordinary violence inflicted upon blacks, as whites became uneasy as to how blacks were going to adjust to post-World War 'normalcy.' Thus, in what is known as the red summer of 1919, race riots occurred in 25 cities. ... During the first year [after] World War I, whites lynched seventy blacks – ten of the group being soldiers still in uniform. Fourteen blacks were publicly burned – eleven while still alive."[28]

These conditions help explain why, as Geoffrey Jacques notes, "The oscillation between hope and despair is a commonplace in cultural products of this period."[29] As I have suggested, that affective dichotomy between laughter and tears, sorrow and protest, has characterized jazz and blues discourse for decades. Insofar as this dichotomy describes the particular contradictions and paradoxes of modernity, we can see why scholars have often figured black artists as the most modern of modernists. Rather than bracketing African American art as something apart from modernism, scholars increasingly extend the implications of Paul Gilroy's *The Black Atlantic* (1993) to theorize, in James Smethurst's terms, *The African American Roots of Modernism* (2011). In addition to Smethurst, Ann Douglas, Geoffrey Jacques, and Kevin Young (*The Grey Album*, 2012) all advance this argument in different ways. In so doing, they extend Du Bois' claim that African American artists who had been the victims of modernity were also the optimistic custodians of its future: laughing to keep from crying, keeping faith in the ultimate justice of things.

Reading Jazz and Blues Narratives

Studies of African American music and writing have necessarily responded, whether supportively or critically, to more general theoretical developments in in the U.S. academy – formalism, poststructuralism, feminism, queer theory, the transnational turn. However, given that musical-literary studies are motivated precisely by a cultural nationalist ambition to formalize "whatever is black about black American literature," they have consistently underscored the identitarian differences that theoretical modes such as poststructuralism can elide. For example, Stephen Henderson's broadly formalist study of "the New Black Poetry" marked a scholarly attempt to codify the Black Aesthetic. Insofar as the Black Aesthetic was a formal and philosophical matter, a text could be "in the tradition" whatever its subject – hence James Baldwin's 1956 novel *Giovanni's Room*, although it features no black characters, could theoretically be said to manifest a black aesthetic. Likewise, the codification of jazz and blues aesthetics meant that a text that was not about music could still be said to manifest "culturally black" expressive elements associated with these musical traditions. In the case of formal blues aesthetics, these generally include testimony, concreteness, economy, repetition, and understatement; formal jazz aesthetics often denote abstraction, citationality, hybridity, fragmentation, and parody.[30]

Henry Louis Gates Jr. offers perhaps the most abstract method of viewing literature through a jazz paradigm when he compares the practice of signifying or critically revising another writer's work to jazz musicians' quotations and revisions of standard songs. With regard to novels of the late modernist period, we might consider the way in which Richard Wright's *Native Son* (1940) signifies on William Faulkner's *Light in August* (1932). Bigger Thomas, like Joe Christmas, beheads and burns a northern liberal white woman who expresses a predilection for black men. The salient difference is that Joe is a black man who passes for white. In signifying on this narrative, Wright rejects the tragic mulatto narrative that Joe embodies and exposes the fear of black male sexuality at the heart of antimiscegenation laws. Both Joe and Bigger are hunted down after violent acts of preemptive self-negation. But rather than represent Bigger's death within the novel (a convention of the tragic mulatto narrative that Faulkner follows), Wright has Bigger insist that "what I killed for, I am!" and smile wryly at his "fate" from behind bars.[31] Critics such as Craig Werner have compared *Native Son*'s unadorned style (and the speeches of Bigger's lover, Bessie) to the spareness of the blues (about which more momentarily). My own reading suggests that we might also, following Cheryl Wall's 2005 study, relate Wright's intertextual troping to the blues practice of "worrying the line," or repeating a lyric or narrative with a telling difference. That we could just as readily associate this troping with a "*jazz* aesthetic," however, reveals the imprecision as well as the generative elasticity of these terms.

More detailed approaches to African American music and fiction highlight analogous expressive techniques. Although Nella Larsen's 1928 novel *Quicksand* is not about music, we can make a case for the novel's blues modernism by highlighting Larsen's use of understatement and narrative economy – both of which are common features in the blues. Consider how much narrative is encased and emotion contained in Bessie Smith's lyrics to "Backwater Blues" (1927): "Backwater Blues done caused me to pack my things and go, cause my house fell down and I can't live there no more." Hughes' blues poems, written in the form of twelve-bar blues, demonstrate this same compression: "When I was home de / Sunshine seemed like gold. / When I was home de / Sunshine seemed like gold. / Since I come up North de / Whole damn world's turned cold."[32]

Quicksand opens with realist attention to visual detail, as Larsen "frames" protagonist Helga Crane in a beautiful room.[33] However, Larsen quickly generates a sense of what is not seen or said. She does not render the thought process through which Helga decides to leave the southern black "uplift school" where she teaches. She does not represent Helga's sense of illegitimacy through direct speech even as Helga explains her mixed ancestry to another character (39). The novel moves quickly – one bad memory can catalyze a dramatic departure as Helga moves from the American South to Copenhagen to the tiny Alabama town where she sinks into marriage and motherhood. Larsen's narrative economy is partly a product of elision: Helga ultimately bears three children between chapters 22 and 23, and the lacuna between the last two sentences marks as unspeakable the sex that intervenes to impregnate Helga once again.

We can locate a similar blues-toned understatement and economy, as well as a blues-like repetition, in Ernest Hemingway's *The Sun Also Rises* (1926). Hemingway's streamlined prose effects chilling understatement when, for instance, narrator Jake realizes his beloved Brett has seduced a Spanish bull-fighter: "When I came back and looked in the café, twenty minutes later, Brett and Pedro Romero were gone. The coffee glasses and our three empty cognac-glasses were on the table. A waiter came with a cloth and picked up the glasses and mopped off the table."[34] Since all action is focalized through Jake, the reader doesn't see Robert Cohn's jilted lover, Frances, leave the story, and a supposedly significant trip Robert takes with Brett happens offstage. Finally, for a novel that is largely staged as a series of dialogues, a great deal goes unsaid or inadequately addressed: broken promises of marriage register simply as "rotten shame," "rotten luck" (54–55); journeys are "wonderful" (76, 80); World War I is an especially tired subject (24–25). Hemingway could be said to depart from Gertrude Stein's maximalist reiterative aesthetic in his use of linguistic repetition to foster understatement, to ironically hint at what goes unsaid.

If such a reading would, in Ellisonian terms, claim Hemingway for a blues-based American tradition, it would also need to reckon with the racial landscape this text creates. Hemingway's understated narrative represents but does not critique several moments of Jewish and black exclusion: the main characters constantly harass Robert Cohn about his Jewishness; a black drummer haunts the margins of a scene at a bar (69–71); and Bill recounts an energetically offensive story about a black boxer in Vienna (77–78). We can read critique into these moments, although like Kate Chopin's depictions of elusive characters of color in *The Awakening* (1899), *The Sun Also Rises* does not correct the problem it seems to expose. Hemingway does not offer a complex, centered portrayal of people of color that might dispute their abjection and marginalization in this text.

A similar issue confronts readers of *The Great Gatsby* (1925), a novel with a very different literary aesthetic but one more obviously affiliated with jazz due to scenes of musical performance and F. Scott Fitzgerald's writings on the Jazz Age. This text invites another interpretive method: critics such as Mitchell Breitwieser and T. Graham Austin read *Gatsby* through the songs Fitzgerald features in this work.[35] By examining Fitzgerald's allusion to W.C. Handy's "Beale Street Blues" (1916) in particular, we can see how Fitzgerald's representations of jazz suppress racial difference in favor of a romance of elusive nonwhite others; these others are destined to hover at the margins of his narrative. In this sense, the nostalgia that Graham associates with Fitzgerald's allusions to popular song is racialized.

In a party scene thought to parody Paul Whiteman's Aeolian Hall concert of 1924, in which the "King of Jazz" introduced jazz to an elite white audience, an orchestra performs a "Jazz History of the World." Breitwieser shows that in Fitzgerald's drafts of the novel, this performance proves resistant to Nick Carraway's efforts to narrativize it. The part of this challenging music that the white audience most enjoys is that which has "recognizable strains of famous jazz in it," such as "a recurrent hint of The Beale Street Blues."[36] While this description of jazz did not survive the final cuts, an allusion to the "Beale Street Blues" did. In a romantic evocation of Daisy's youth, Nick imagines, "All night the saxophones wailed the hopeless comment of the 'Beale Street Blues.'"[37]

This allusion is apt because the song's lyrics reflect the novel's events: the affairs of Tom and Daisy Buchanan ("If Beale Street could talk ... married men would have to take their beds and walk"); the dangers of Gatsby's romantic and financial enterprises ("You'll find that business never closes till someone gets killed"). Even the song's ultimate denial of Beale Street's appeal resonates with Nick's final retreat to the dock: "I'm goin to the river maybe by and by. ... Because the river's wet and Beale Street's gone dry." So whereas in the drafts Nick disparages the prospect of "[making] a story of" the "Jazz History,"[38] Fitzgerald translates song into story by making "Beale

Street" a soundtrack for the novel itself. We might say that by privileging the familiar tune, the novel suppresses the otherness of jazz as a marker of blackness. That jazz is not an immediate challenge but rather a sign of nostalgia illuminates *Gatsby*'s vision of American history: Fitzgerald may imply the gaps in the national history that Nick ultimately invokes – a population native to the "fresh green breast of the world," a people imported to work the "dark fields of the republic" – but the novel's melancholic nostalgia keeps that past and its legacies at bay (Fitzgerald, *Gatsby*, 189).

Gatsby's closest stylistic counterpart in the modernist period, although it is seldom recognized as such, is Hurston's *Their Eyes Were Watching God*. Both texts flaunt lush, romantic prose and feature narrators with a tendency toward the sagaciously matter of fact. From the Queensboro Bridge, Nick seems to see New York City "as if for the first time, in its first wild promise of all the mystery and beauty in the world" (73); Hurston describes Janie Crawford's sexual awakening to "the rose of the world breathing out smell" as she stands "waiting for the world to be made" (10). "Everyone suspects himself of at least one of the cardinal virtues, and this is mine: I am one of the few honest people that I have ever known," Nick muses (64). "She knew that marriage did not make love. Janie's first dream was dead, so she became a woman" (25), Hurston writes.

And yet to track musical allusions through *Their Eyes Were Watching God* is to glean a distinctive racial and musical politics in the Hurston treatment of song. By using song as a narrative engine to score the renewal of her protagonist's dreams, Hurston revises (or signifies on) Fitzgerald's use of song to figure loss. From the metaphorical song that signals Janie's sexual awakening to her courtship rituals with her guitar-playing lover, Tea Cake, to communal scenes of music-making in the Florida muck, Hurston uses song to score Janie's movement.[39] Janie voices a blues-phrased prophecy upon meeting Tea Cake – "Some of dese mornings and it won't be long, you guintuh wake up callin me and Ah'll be gone" – and she rides a train to meet him in the very next scene (114, 116). As in "Spirituals and Neo-Spirituals," Hurston depicts black music not as a sign of nostalgia but as an active force.

We can readily read *Their Eyes* through blues or jazz thematics – the struggle for self-determined identity that Ellison associates with jazz musicians, the "spiritual warriorship" that Gussow identifies with the blues. But a more historically grounded analysis would treat the blues as social history. Carol Batker, for example, reads *Their Eyes* through histories of women's blues by scholars such as Daphne Duval Harrison, as well as through histories of African American middle-class club women by Paula Giddings and Gerda Lerner. Situating Hurston's novel within both camps, she argues that

Their Eyes "refuses simple dichotomies between respectability and desire, and works with both blues and club discourse to legitimate sexual subjectivity."[40] In so doing, Batker not only situates Hurston in her own moment but also adds nuance to often-idealized portraits of women's blues culture that arose in the wake of Davis' and Harrison's crucial celebratory recoveries of these women's work.

In contrast to the practice of reading texts through established social and musical histories, scholars such as Nathaniel Mackey, Brent Edwards, and Anthony Reed analyze literary poetics to produce social and musical theory. As a literary critic (and poet) who deeply engaged musical cultures at a moment before interdisciplinary studies were in vogue, Mackey opened the door for rigorously imaginative and insistently associative readings of the musical-literary interplay. Specifically, Mackey innovated the field in the late 1980s by destabilizing hierarchical distinctions between musicology and creative writing and thus showing how literature might generate ideas about music rather than merely bearing them out.

Mackey's 1987 essay "Sound and Sentiment, Sound and Symbol" reads works by Wilson Harris, Jean Toomer, William Carlos Williams, and Ellison to develop several influential analytics, including the concept (following Harris) that music is a "phantom limb" that "reveals the illusory rule of the world it haunts" (236) and that literary citations of music express a "telling inarticulacy" that refuses permissible ways of making sense (252–253). In works such as Toomer's *Cane* (1922), which is "ventilated" with allusions to music, music is "a way of reaching toward an alternate reality" and of indicting the world that makes such reaching necessary (238, 236). So whereas we could follow Toomer himself in reading *Cane* as a "swan-song" for a folk culture whose imminent loss black music signifies – a view that might posit *Cane* as prefiguring the treatment of song I have critiqued in *Gatsby* – Mackey makes a different case. He extends the Du Boisian African American intellectual tradition of framing black music as an indictment of society. That this dissent takes shape beyond the bounds of nation is a point Mackey performs, in this essay alone, through engagements with the work of Wilson Harris, Kamau Brathwaite, and Yoruban and Papua New Guinean myths.

Brent Edwards extends this international focus in *The Practice of Diaspora* (2005). As in Mackey's criticism, literary representations of music are often the ground of theory in Edwards' work. His reading of Claude McKay's *Banjo: A Story without a Plot* (1929), for example, does not mobilize preexisting ideas about jazz so much as it uses McKay's depictions of jazz performance to illuminate the form of social organization the novel envisions, as well as its general plotlessness. As Edwards writes,

"Music is the only place the black boys stand – there is no other 'plot,' no other ground, or foundation, whether nation or narrative, that contains them" (240). This groundlessness likewise describes the novel's vision of sociality, what Edwards terms "vagabond internationalism": "If the dream to form an orchestra is the dream to institutionalize a vision of black internationalism, it is inherently an open and wandering, performative representation of the links between men of African descent" (220).

Banjo is unusual among the novels discussed here in that the black music it depicts is not coded as American. This is not only to say that the novel is set in Marseilles but that even though the novel centers around a black American who plays what is "preeminently the musical instrument of the American Negro," the music in Marseilles is not *based* on black American sound: "they played the 'beguin,' which was just a Martinique variant of the 'jelly-roll' or the Jamaican 'buru' or the Senegalese 'bombé.'"[41] Despite what the syntax of the sentence leads one to expect, the *beguin* is not a "variant" of a fundamentally American music ("the jelly-roll"), but is instead a form that bears some relationship to an evenly distributed field of national musics. In such moments, the novel anticipates and thwarts the image of jazz as America's national music and proudest "export" to the rest of the world – a myth that Alexandra Vazquez dismantles in her landmark study of Cuban music, *Listening in Detail* (2013).

That *Banjo*'s promising "vagabond internationalism," however, hinges upon the exclusion of women is a point that Edwards acknowledges and that Anthony Reed most recently elaborates by reading the novel's gendered politics of improvisation. Reed models rigorous engagement with the metaphor of improvisation so often used to link black music with writing.[42] He argues that *Banjo* sketches a potentially radical horizon of political possibility through improvisation, but shows how that possibility collapses as the novel reproduces a very conventional antipathy toward women and women's role in the revolutionary community.

Such critiques remain vital as studies of jazz and blues modernisms continue to exclude women. Despite the fact that Carby, Angela Davis, Deborah McDowell, Cheryl Wall, Farah Jasmine Griffin, Daphne Lamothe, Jayna Brown, and many other scholars have shown that black women artists play a significant role in any story about the modernist period, Michael Borshuk's 2006 monograph *Swinging the Vernacular: Jazz and African American Modernist Literature* focuses on male writers and musicians, and Jed Rasula's account of "Jazz and American Modernism" in the 2005 *Cambridge Companion to American Modernism* describes the members of Fitzgerald's literary and musical "generation" as a catalog of twenty-four men (161). As literary critics steadily broaden the definition of modernist artists to include women of color, they are also expanding definitions of black music to encompass many global "variants" and enhancing our sense of the recording technologies and industries that circulate this music. Expansion is not the only aim. We can also complicate totalizing systems through the critical practice of what Vazquez calls "listening in detail": carefully attending to the distinctive sounds, techniques, and poetics through which a musical-literary tradition continues to evade and invite.

NOTES

1. Langston Hughes, "The Negro Artist and the Racial Mountain," *Nation*, June 23, 1926, 694; Hughes, *The Big Sea* (1940; New York: Hill and Wang, 1963), 296.
2. Duke Ellington, "The Duke Steps Out," in *The Duke Ellington Reader*, ed. Mark Tucker (Oxford: Oxford University Press, 1993), 49, qtd. in Jed Rasula, "Jazz and American Modernism," *The Cambridge Companion to American Modernism*, ed. Walter Kalaidjian (Cambridge: Cambridge University Press, 2005),169.
3. Thanks to Imani Owens for highlighting James Weldon Johnson's preface. Countee Cullen, "Countee Cullen on Miscegenation" (1929), in *My Soul's High Song: The Collected Writings of Countee Cullen*, ed. Gerald Early (New York: Anchor, 1991), 568.
4. Frederick Douglass, *Narrative of the Life of Frederick Douglass, an American Slave*, eds. John W. Blassingame, John R. McKivigan, and Peter P. Hinks (1845; New Haven, CT: Yale University Press, 2001), 20.
5. W.E.B. Du Bois, *The Souls of Black Folk*, ed. Brent Hayes Edwards (1903; New York: Oxford University Press, 2008), 169, 175.
6. As Brent Edwards writes of Langston Hughes' "Jazz Band in a Parisian Cabaret" (1927), "The poem performs the intimacy, the erotics, of a sound that travels: what in the music takes you 'home,' and goes 'home' with you. . . . It attempt[s] to hold at least two things together in a fragile balance: on the one hand, an individual listener's affective connection to the music, and, on the other, the collectivity of listeners the music allows, the connections it fosters" (*The Practice of Diaspora: Literature, Translation, and the Rise of Black Internationalism* [Cambridge: Harvard University Press, 2003], 67).
7. Zora Neale Hurston, "Spirituals and Neo-Spirituals" (1934), in *Zora Neale Hurston: Folklore, Memoirs, and Other Writings*, ed. Cheryl A. Wall (New York: Library of America, 1995), 870.
8. Hurston, "How It Feels to Be Colored Me" (1928), *Folklore, Memoirs, and Other Writings*, 827.
9. See *A Son's Return: Selected Essays of Sterling A. Brown*, ed. Mark A. Sanders (Boston: Northeastern University Press, 1996).
10. Robert G. O'Meally, "Introduction: Jazz Shapes," in *Living with Music: Ralph Ellison's Jazz Writings*, ed. Robert O'Meally (New York: Modern Library, 2002), x.
11. Ralph Ellison, "The Golden Age, Time Past" (1959), in *Living with Music*, 61.
12. Several ethnomusicological and literary critical studies offer diverse methods for linking jazz improvisation to literary form and practice, including Ingrid Monson, *Saying Something: Jazz Improvisation and Interaction* (Chicago: University of Chicago Press, 1997); Rob Wallace, *Improvisation and the*

Making of American Literary Modernism (New York: Continuum, 2010); and Fred Moten, *In the Break: The Aesthetics of the Black Radical Tradition* (Minneapolis: University of Minnesota Press, 2003).

13. Ellison, "On Bird, Bird-Watching, and Jazz" (1962), in *Living with Music*, 69.

14. LeRoi Jones/Amiri Baraka, *Blues People: Negro Music in White America* (1963; New York: Perennial, 2002), 1.

15. See Richard Wright's "Blueprint for Negro Writing" (1937), as well as Wright's lecture "The Negro Literature of the United States" (*White Man, Listen!* 1957); the latter constitutes an early attempt to narrate the African American literary tradition through writers' relationships to vernacular expressive forms such as the spirituals and the blues. For more on Wright's engagement with black music and his relationship to Black Arts, see Emily J. Lordi, *Black Resonance: Iconic Women Singers and African American Literature* (New Brunswick: Rutgers University Press, 2013), 7, 27–65.

16. Henry Louis Gates Jr., *The Signifying Monkey: A Theory of African-American Literary Criticism* (New York: Oxford University Press, 1998), xxiv. Toni Morrison, "Unspeakable Things Unspoken: The Afro-American Presence in American Literature," *Michigan Quarterly Review* 28 (1989): 19.

17. Ellison, "Richard Wright's Blues" (1945), in *Living with Music*, 103.

18. Hazel Carby, "'It Jus Be's Dat Way Sometime': The Sexual Politics of Women's Blues" (1986), in *The Jazz Cadence of American Culture*, ed. Robert G. O'Meally (New York: Columbia University Press, 1998), 470.

19. Paul Allen Anderson, *Deep River: Music and Memory in Harlem Renaissance Thought* (Durham: Duke University Press, 2001). Farah Jasmine Griffin, *Harlem Nocturne: Women Artists and Progressive Politics during World War II* (New York: Basic Civitas, 2013).

20. Steven C. Tracy, *Langston Hughes and the Blues* (Urbana: University of Illinois Press, 1988). Craig Werner, *Playing the Changes: From Afro-Modernism to the Jazz Impulse* (Urbana: University of Illinois Press, 1994).

21. Kimberly Benston, *Performing Blackness: Enactments of African-American Modernism* (London: Routledge, 2000). Aldon Nielsen, *Black Chant: Languages of African-American Postmodernism* (Cambridge, UK: Cambridge University Press, 1997). Nathaniel Mackey, *Discrepant Engagement: Dissonance, Cross-Culturality, and Experimental Writing* (Tuscaloosa: University of Alabama Press, 1993).

22. Alexander Weheliye, *Phonographies: Grooves in Sonic Afro-Modernity* (Durham: Duke University Press, 2005), 6.

23. Geoffrey Jacques, *A Change in the Weather: Modernist Imagination, African American Imaginary* (Amherst: University of Massachusetts Press, 2009). T. Austin Graham, *The Great American Songbooks: Musical Texts, Modernism, and the Value of Popular Culture* (New York: Oxford University Press, 2013).

24. Adam Gussow, "'If Bessie Smith Had Killed Some White People': Racial Legacies, the Blues Revival, and the Black Arts Movement," in *New Thoughts on the Black Arts Movement*, ed. Lisa Gail Collins and Margo Natalie Crawford (New Brunswick: Rutgers University Press, 2008), 232.

25. Michael Borshuk, *Swinging the Vernacular: Jazz and African American Modernist Literature* (New York: Routledge, 2006), 2.

26. Ann Douglas, *Terrible Honesty: Mongrel Manhattan in the 1920s* (New York: Farrar, Straus, & Giroux, 1995), 88, 89.

27. Rita Barnard, "Modern American Fiction," in *The Cambridge Companion to American Modernism*, 44.
28. George E. Kent, *Blackness and the Adventure of Western Culture* (Chicago: Third World Press, 1972), 20.
29. Jacques, *A Change in the Weather*, 10.
30. In contrast with such formal approaches, Craig Werner and Kevin Young offer thematic and affective discussions of blues and jazz aesthetics in *Playing the Changes* (1994) and *The Grey Album: On the Blackness of Blackness* (Minneapolis, MN: Graywolf, 2012), respectively.
31. Richard Wright, *Native Son and "How 'Bigger' Was Born"* (1940; New York: Harper Perennial, 1993), 501, 502.
32. Langston Hughes, "Po' Boy Blues" (1927), in *The Collected Poems of Langston Hughes*, ed. Arnold Rampersad (New York: Vintage Classics, 1995), 83.
33. Nella Larsen, *Quicksand and Passing*, ed. Deborah McDowell (1928, 1929; New Brunswick: Rutgers University Press, 1986), 2.
34. Ernest Hemingway, *The Sun Also Rises* (1926; New York: Scribner, 1954), 191.
35. John Trombold also demonstrates this methodology in his reading of John Dos Passos' work in "Popular Songs as Revolutionary Culture in John Dos Passos' 'U.S.A.' and Other Early Works," *Journal of Modern Literature* 19, no. 2 (Fall 1995): 289–316.
36. Mitchell Breitwieser, *National Melancholy: Mourning and Opportunity in Classic American Literature* (Stanford, CA: Stanford University Press, 2007), 267. See *The Great Gatsby: A Facsimile of the Manuscript*, ed. Matthew J. Bruccoli (Washington, DC: Microcard Editions, 1973), 55–56.
37. F. Scott Fitzgerald, *The Great Gatsby* (1925; New York: Scribner, 1995), 158.
38. Breitwieser, *National Melancholy*, 267; *The Great Gatsby: A Facsimile*, 55–56.
39. Zora Neale Hurston, *Their Eyes Were Watching God* (1937; New York: Harper Perennial, 2006).
40. Carol Batker, "'Love Me Like I Like to Be': The Sexual Politics of Hurston's *Their Eyes Were Watching God*, the Classic Blues, and the Black Women's Club Movement," *African American Review* 32, no. 2 (Summer 1998): 200.
41. Claude McKay, *Banjo: A Story without a Plot* (1929; San Diego: Harvest, 1957), 49, 105.
42. Anthony Reed, "'A Woman Is a Conjunction': The Ends of Improvisation in Claude McKay's *Banjo: A Novel without a Plot*," *Callaloo* 36, no. 3 (Summer 2013): 758–772.

12

DANIEL KATZ

Translation and the American Modernist Novel

Recent scholarship has established beyond doubt the centrality of translation –
both as practice and site of theoretical inquiry – for American modernist
poetry. It would be difficult to make an analogous claim for American
modernist novels, despite such notable elements as John Dos Passos' translations of Blaise Cendrars or Gertrude Stein's reflections on translating.[1] At
the same time, however, no less than poets, American modernist prose
writers were caught up in debates around idiom, mode of expression, and
acrolect that implied the problems of translation for them as much as for
their colleagues in poetry. H.L. Mencken stated a common case succinctly,
if typically hyperbolically, when writing of hypothetical American college
students:

> What their professors try to teach is not their mother-tongue at all, but a dialect
> that stands quite outside their common experience, and into which they have to
> translate their thoughts, consciously and painfully. . . . Thus the study of the
> language he is supposed to use, to the average American, takes on a sort of
> bilingual character.[2]

Mencken here refers to the prestige of a presumably "foreign" linguistic
standard that apes the practice of southern England, and the task he proposes
is no less than the reclamation of the "mother-tongue" – the American idiom –
as a vehicle for serious cultural labor. Mencken, an early translator of
Nietzsche, seems to be appealing for an end to translation, and his call for
writers to be "bold enough to venture into" the American language (395)
would be reiterated throughout American modernism.[3] But Mencken's
statement cannot be taken at face value, and in fact was not. On one level,
as modernists were well aware, Mencken's gesture in some ways simply
displaces onto the "foreign" the violence of normativizing linguistic pressures that exist within any language and renders it always already "foreign," although this very quality was often seen as desirable in its capacity
for estrangement.[4] For Gertrude Stein, for example, the importance of

writing as opposed to speech lay in how the former made this fundamental disunity palpable.[5]

On another level, more in line with Mencken's concerns, it is already evident that such prohibitions on idiom already exist *within* the American scene for writers from linguistic communities whose everyday forms are deemed even less suitable for high cultural purposes than whatever sort of "American" language Mencken had in mind. Obviously, African American writers felt that sort of pressure most acutely, and in some ways this makes their position the most pressingly "American" with respect to Mencken's misgivings. But the point to be made is that Mencken's statement and ones like it cannot help but foreground the question of the positions of languages with regard to each other. For implicit here, and explicit in most modernist African American writing, is that the imperative to "translate" that so worries Mencken means not only – and perhaps not primarily – a distancing from the natural, but in addition a devaluing of certain idioms in and of themselves, along with the social praxis that goes with them. Yet to insist on their preservation intact – to refuse their assimilation or translation into the acrolect – is to assert claims about cultural specificity and singularity, as well as the relationship between language and cultural practice, that are by no means self-evident or unassailable.[6]

Translating Americans: Toward the Nightmare of Esperanto

It is, of course, one of the great ironies of the period of American modernism that while American economic and military power were increasingly dominating the world stage in a manner that was missed by few, American cultural production remained, almost axiomatically, of low prestige (or gained what prestige it had precisely by being "low," "popular," or even "primitive," as in the case of cinema or jazz, as Genevieve Abravanel has recently stressed).[7] For all of these reasons, American modernists could not fail to be aware of their linguistic "position," as Henry James – by many accounts, the first American modernist novelist – had put it. "Every language has its position, which, with its particular character and genius, is its most precious property," James wrote in 1907 in *The Question of Our Speech*.[8] And at his most disappointingly elitist, James identifies the "common school" and newspaper, as well as the mass of immigrants, as the greatest threats to the American idiom. Before this, however, in his delineation of what he calls the "high modernism of the conditions now surrounding, on this continent, the practice of our language" (53), he makes a far more interesting point: that the "American" language is *itself* in some ways an immigrant, and therefore functions differently in relation to its speakers than any other modern idiom. "It came *over*, as the phrase is," James writes of the American language, "... to find itself transplanted to spaces it had never dreamed, in its comparative humility, of covering, to conditions it had never dreamed, in its comparative innocence, of meeting" (53, original italics). For James, the American "medium of utterance" (53) finds itself thus "disjoined from all the associations" she (as James genders her) had had in England, leaving her "divested of that beautiful and becoming drapery of native atmosphere and circumstance" (53) that attends on all the other modern European tongues. For James, then, Americans have not so much a despised provincial vernacular – as in Mencken's account – as no proper language at all. As traditionally troped, a "mother tongue" is an origin and source from which one can stray through multilingualism, and which one can perhaps violate and betray, through translation or interlingual interference. But James suggests that the American language has *already* strayed – that, having "come over" with those who speak it, it has come to share their fate rather than ground them for a sojourn into the new. In other words, if for Mencken the American is unfairly asked to translate out of her mother tongue, for James, in a profound sense, the American has no mother tongue at all, but rather a catachretical language in which words have been forced from their proper meanings and "associations," just as the people who use them have been forced from their own. This is an idiom searching for the grounding that it is unable to provide itself. At the outset of the modernist period, then, for James the "position" of the American "medium of utterance" is precisely to be in some way positionless, untethered to "native circumstance" and environment in an unsettling and destabilizing manner.[9]

Interestingly, at modernism's close, a certain kind of American English finds itself in a similar predicament, if turned inside out and upside down. That is to say, for the translation theorist Antoine Berman, it is the English language that, through the international dominance of the United States, risks becoming the irresistible tidal wave submerging all forms of cultural specificity under the onslaught of global capitalist uniformity. Berman points to the "growing homogenisation of communication systems" and isolates the following as the leading elements of this phenomenon: "the destruction of dialects and local speech forms, and the leveling of the differences between national languages in the service of the model of a non-language, for which English has served as both guinea pig and victim – a model thanks to which automatic translation would become thinkable."[10] As opposed to James' "American" as an uprooted maiden that inaugurates the modernist period, in 1984 Berman characterizes English – now become the "non-language" of global domination – as "a deracinating jargon which is not even Esperanto, that naïve humanist dream, which now reveals its true face as nightmare" (289).

This gradual drift in the conceptualization of American English from deracinated immigrant to deracinating capitalist apparatus, passing through a way station as rustic embarrassment, does much to chart the varying practices of novelists such as Stein, Hemingway, McKay, Djuna Barnes, Ralph Ellison, and Pynchon and DeLillo as we move through the century. For the central period of modernism, however, it seems clear that with regard to translation two major elements hold sway. First is what Robert Crawford has described as the antinormative drive of "provincial" modernism, as seen not only in the many modernist novelists who engage with explicitly multilingual and international contexts, but also in those who stress local or regional linguistic particularity. That these two elements often figure prominently in the work of the same writers (Stein, Hemingway) only further proves Crawford's point.[11] Second, however, are the modernists who stress the divisions within the American linguistic space that go beyond regionalism, or have more pointed implications. Chief among these would be African American writers in their relationship to a vernacular that was in fact supraregional, and which was certainly perceived as having more than regional significance by both African Americans themselves and others. In addition, one must not overlook the immigrant writing that addresses the United States as a multilingual site and explores the relationship between the dominant English and other languages on both a personal and social level.

Gertrude Stein: "I can't see you any longer when I look"

Gertrude Stein is crucial for any discussion of American modernism's relationship to translational spaces, not least for her ability to link what is often read as a form of cubist "abstraction" – itself "translated" from the visual arts – to the material and historical question of the multiplicity of languages. Thus, while Stein has been credited for bringing the visual practices of cubism into the literary field for many years, more recently accounts of her style as a form of linguistic interference – whether from French, German, or even Yiddish – have become staples of criticism, along with an emphasis on her stylized evocation of both vernaculars (especially African American) and immigrant-inflected English in her early work (for example, *Three Lives* or *The Making of Americans*). But multilingual exchange is foregrounded throughout her work. *The Autobiography of Alice B. Toklas*, for example, stresses her Parisian scene as one mostly mediated by French, but largely a French spoken by nonnative speakers. That said, the book's language is very largely uniform, and despite the occasional French phrase or cited bits of dialogue, almost all of the conversation in the novel is presented through the indirect discourse of the already ventriloquized "voice" of Alice. Individual speaking styles do not tend to emerge, and Stein's strangely deterritorialized and stilted English lends precisely the same tone to conversations occurring in French and those presumed to be held in English. In this sense, Stein's prose style in *The Autobiography* is in some ways totalitarian, mostly effacing the linguistic particularities of both different languages and different people, as everyone speaks pretty much the same medium. But this in itself gives particular interest to a casual episode "Alice" recounts about halfway through:

> It was during this summer that Picasso gave us a letter to a friend of his youth one Raventos in Barcelona. But does he talk French, asked Gertrude Stein, Pablo giggled, better than you do Gertrude, he answered.[12]

This passage is striking, in that it defamiliarizes Stein's very process of defamiliarization in her prose. Stein's question, first of all, points to the fact that this conversation, like so many others between her and Picasso throughout the book, was conducted in French, and therefore that virtually none of the reported conversation that Alice gives us reports what actually was said. For example, here is the crucial scene where, after eighty or ninety sittings, Picasso paints over Stein's face in his famous portrait:

> Spring was coming and the sittings were coming to an end. All of a sudden one day Picasso painted out the whole head. I can't see you any longer when I look, he said irritably. And so the picture was left like that. (49)

In other words, the passage first cited tells or reminds us that Picasso in fact did *not* say, "I can't see you any longer when I look," but rather something in French, which we are reading in translation. Once the possibility of verisimilitude is rejected, then the question of Stein's bizarre renderings becomes only more pressing. How are we to interpret the unidiomatic elements, such as "Pablo's" omission of the preposition and indirect object pronoun we might expect after the phrase "When I look" or, in the other passage, "Gertrude" saying "talk French" rather than "speak French"? And should we regard the somewhat stilted quality of the English in *The Autobiography* as reflecting in some way the imperfect French of "Gertrude"? The simple answer to the latter question is no, because the narrative voice is not meant to be Gertrude's but rather that of Alice. A more complex answer, however, would point to how Stein refuses to normativize her idiom with regard to any speech habits that can be isolated within it. That is to say, her idiom makes no effort to mimic or specifically register the multilingual or exophonic exchanges it relays, but it also eschews a flat, universalizing style that could be seen to imply a fundamental ease of translation and a disinterest in the signifying force of linguistic specificities – and the interference they produce.

Like Stein's own face in Picasso's portrait, the linguistic scenes of *The Autobiography* are in some way painted over, but by an idiom that, while rejecting direct representation of linguistic practice, nevertheless foregrounds the structural details and questions of register and idiomatic usage that both translation and exophonic discourse tend to emphasize. Stein's language here does not translate specific linguistic events so much as allegorize a space of social exchange mediated by translation and multilingualism.

If this particular linguistic surface is fairly consistent in both *The Autobiography of Alice B. Toklas* and *Everybody's Autobiography*, it is worth noting that in later texts Stein does at times return to a more localized, stylized vernacular, notably in *Brewsie and Willie*, a text about and inspired by the young American soldiers she encountered after the liberation of France. Here, a colloquial American speech is the substratum for the familiar Steinian torsions – "You got to, said Willie, you got to Brewsie, you got to hold out a little hope"[13] – which is not surprising in a text largely concerned with going back to a "home" to which Stein would never return and of which the final words are "We are Americans" (778).

Henry Roth: "Boddeh Stritt"

Henry Roth's *Call It Sleep* is equally concerned with America, but here the question of translation arises not in the context of expatriate cosmopolitanism but rather in relation to a displaced immigrant's construction of the domestic and the maternal, in a massively overdetermined Oedipal scenario. Much of the novel navigates young David Schearl's negotiations with Yiddish, English, and Hebrew in multilingual New York, and it quite often specifies the language of the conversations it presents. A clearly paradigmatic scene occurs when David strays from home and finds himself lost amid unfamiliar streets. A kindly stranger asks him where he lives, and David answers "Boddeh Stritt,"[14] in the Yiddish accent of the grownups in his entourage. The man translates this as "Potter Street" and sends David on his way, but this translation is erroneous, and David's house is not there. Later, in a police station, the Irish officers offer a new interpretation, "Barhdee Street" (99), which leads them to David's mother, who comes to fetch him. Joshua L. Miller has pointed out that the reader is never told what the correct street name really is (239) but one must wonder if, by triangulating between the Irish and the Yiddish accents, the clever reader can identify it: Barder Street? Barday Street? Border Street? Such a procedure would certainly be in keeping with Roth's overweening master in *Call It Sleep*, James Joyce. But as Hana Wirth-Nesher has noted, Roth's drafts indicate that the locus as he conceived it in at least internal code was "Body Street," and this body is very much the mother's throughout the book.[15] Yiddish, both as independent language and as inflection of English, is so much the language of the home that when David strays from home, as in the previous scene, Yiddish cannot take him back. It is also very much the language of his mother, who, the novel reminds us at various junctures, is less easy in English than her husband, who came over before her, or her son, rapidly assimilating linguistically at school.

Yiddish is not only the boy's first language, but it is the language of the maternal cocoon. Given David's violent and abusive father and his parents' obviously unhappy marriage, at this cocoon's heart is the secret mystery of his mother's desire, along with that of others' desire for her. One of the novel's central moments, then, occurs when David's mother finally tells her sister the story of her first love affair, but makes sure to do so in Polish, rightly suspecting that young David, playing quietly in a corner, will be all too interested in what she has to say. Thus, just as the mother expresses a wholly exogamous object of desire, she additionally excludes David by violating the language of the protective hearth, as exophony echoes exogamy. In this novel, the incest taboo – the mother's necessary alterity – can only mean one thing: David is thrown out into the world of English. However, this dichotomy is triangulated by another language, Hebrew, at once foreign and – at least phantasmatically – intimate, as its mastery promises a return to a sort of Jewish core that can compensate for the social marginalization of Yiddish as well as the impossible maternal fusion. At the outset, at least, Hebrew functions in this manner entirely as a fetish, for if David's mother's shift into Polish bars his access to the content of her story, his introduction to Hebrew bars the very question of content. His initial lessons (at which he excels) consist of learning to read the Hebrew characters phonetically, with no knowledge whatsoever of their meaning. If Yiddish is the domestic language of full meaning as opposed to an English that is still partly approximate even for David, or a Polish that he cannot translate and in which his mother struggles, Hebrew appears as a magical language of Jewish identity whose power resides in its separability from content, in its somatic singularity.

Thus Roth's novel, like much of modernism, including that of Henry James, stresses translation not only as a question of cognitive transfer, or the pragmatics of signification, but of the affective investment in particular languages or semiotic systems whose import subsists above and beyond the practical questions of what can or cannot be translated into or out of them.[16] The empty signifiers of Hebrew and the rabbi who transmits them open a possible conceptualization of language as paternal in *Call It Sleep*, as opposed to the maternal Yiddish and the literally exotic English and Polish. In some respects, the American modernist prose work that most closely resembles *Call It Sleep* is *Le Schizo et les langues*, the autobiography of Louis Wolfson, a New York Jew of the next generation, written in a peculiar French that the schizophrenic Wolfson, an autodidact, felt shielded him from the English language, itself permeated with the unbarrable invasiveness of his mother, extended through her voice and idiom.[17]

Claude McKay: "ain'tchu one of us, too?"

Claude McKay's work also foregrounds questions of linguistic multiplicity, translation, and the diaspora, albeit the African one. Rather than Roth's paradigm of a variety of languages coalescing – or not – in an accented and inflected American English, McKay stresses linguistic plurality within the context of the dispersal of the peoples of sub-Saharan Africa and the fracturing of what may or may not have been a shared identity. McKay's personal history leaves his own placement especially complex in terms of nationality, region, vernacular, and identifications with available "traditions." Born in Jamaica, then a British colony, McKay first gained fame as a poet of the Jamaican vernacular – a living example of Jamaican peasant authenticity, as it were, though this authenticity was largely fabricated.[18] But if Jamaica was then legally British, McKay – especially as a fiction writer – has more frequently been received as an "American" writer than a British one, largely because of the success of his first and most famous novel, *Home to Harlem*. This work is not particularly character or plot driven – indeed, it is most "modernist" in its distance from those devices – and derives a good deal of its interest as a depiction of the manners, morals, and everyday social practice of the lower classes of the famous African American neighborhood of New York. Not least vivid among the elements it foregrounds is the African American vernacular, as well as jokes and song lyrics, which stand out with particular force against the backdrop of the neutral and discrete narrative voice. Given these elements, its critical placement at the very center of the Harlem Renaissance was all but inevitable. But if McKay did indeed spend five years of his life in Harlem, Harlem was not his home, and he was not an autochthonous native informant. In theory, its local idiom would be no more "natural" to this Jamaican author than any other in America, save on the assumption that there is an essential "African" quality or diasporic heritage that would allow him to assimilate it more easily than, say, the Jewish American English spoken a few miles away, in Henry Roth's Lower East Side. This is one reason his decision to adopt a French setting for his next novel on the African diaspora, *Banjo*, is so resonant.

Banjo relies even less on narrative structure than *Home to Harlem*, as McKay was happy to acknowledge. He subtitled it *A Story without a Plot*, and, like the former novel, its interest derives from its depictions of social practice, daily life, and also intellectual and political debate, an element given far more scope in *Banjo* than in the previous novel. But given that *Banjo* specifically focuses on Marseilles as the meeting ground for blacks from the United States, the West Indies, and colonial Africa, the novel cannot rely on regionalist approaches to local color and custom nearly so much as can *Home to Harlem*; and when it does so, the perspective is exoticism rather than that of the unveiling of the familiar. Indeed, the entire writerly project is for these reasons made to differ crucially from *Home to Harlem*: as so much of the exchange in *Banjo* is either between non-Americans, in French, or both, the African American vernacular and oral culture are not able to carry the aesthetic and ideological burden that they do in *Home to Harlem* – or in other leading novels of the Harlem Renaissance, such as *Their Eyes Were Watching God*.

That said, the novel's lead character, "Lincoln Agrippa Daily, familiarly known as Banjo,"[19] is nothing if not an incarnation of the cultural prestige of the African American within the African diaspora at this time. He is a jazz musician, and the novel insists throughout that African American jazz is now the calling card of African cultural achievement on the global stage. In this way, the black American jazz musician is on the leading edge of African diasporic cultural recognition everywhere, though this in itself is of limited worth: the novel insists on how French enthusiasm for jazz and acceptance of its players has virtually no broader impact on the country's essential racism, particularly with regard to French African colonies. Given the importance of jazz to the novel, however (one even greater than that found in *Home to Harlem*, where the music also features prominently), one might well ask why the musician at its core does not play a more typical jazz instrument – a likely choice in the twenties would be the trumpet. The answer, of course, is that the banjo is an African instrument, or at least an American translation of one. Banjo, then, is a reminder of the African essence of jazz, and his instrument itself is a literal object of the diaspora, traveling with the displaced peoples who created it.[20]

Meanwhile, with regard to how McKay placed himself in terms of native culture, region, and nation, it is fascinating to note that the autobiographical stand-in for him in both *Home to Harlem* and *Banjo* is a young Haitian intellectual and writer named Ray. Although this allows McKay to preserve his geographic identity as a West Indian, it also establishes him as Francophone, an element that is far more than an idle detail. When Jake, the central character in *Home to Harlem*, first encounters him, Ray is reading French, a language of which Jake has a rudimentary knowledge, having been stationed in France during the Great War. When Jake asks Ray why his

French is so good, Ray answers, "C'est ma langue maternelle,"[21] a phrase Jake cannot follow. After Ray translates, Jake cuts him off:

"Don't crap me," Jake interrupted. "Ain'tchu – ain'tchu one of us, too?"

"Of course I'm Negro," the waiter said, "but I was born in Hayti and the language down there is French."   (131)

It is not clear if Ray's definition of "us" corresponds to that implied by Jake, and that is entirely what is at stake: the boundaries and limits of shared diasporic identity as negotiated by differing languages and histories of assimilation, which of course include differing notions of the category of "race" that might otherwise be deployed to counter the vicissitudes of history and "culture." The implications of being entirely "Negro" yet a native French speaker with no lived relation to Africa are explored further in *Banjo*, where, again, Ray's relationship to language is foregrounded at the moment of his entrance on the scene. Seeing that Banjo has been overcharged for a meal by a café owner, Ray intervenes and makes use of his superior French to successfully argue the case that Banjo's rudimentary knowledge of the language prevented him from prosecuting. Whether there is in fact a fundamental fraternal blackness that transcends differences in language and culture, however, is a question the novel debates throughout. For example, describing the scene when Banjo plays in a raucous café, the narrator explains, "Senegalese, Sudanese, Somalese, Nigerians, West Indians, Americans, blacks from everywhere, crowded together, talking strange dialects, but, brought together, understanding one another by the language of wine" (36). This is a "language," however, that would presumably include nonblacks, and indeed in other settings in the novel does so. Meanwhile, one of the most emphatic calls for a translingual, essential African character, made by a black guitar player, is presented at once as a piece of internalized racism and as a category independent of skin color: "Niggers is niggers all ovah the wul'. . . . Always spoil a good thing. Always the same no matter what color their hide is or what langwidge they talk" (50–51). The novel explores such issues with a complexity and density impossible to summarize here.[22] Throughout, it is at once concerned with modes of transmission among differing African identities – with what translates *between* African diasporic communities – and how "African" culture in the broadest sense translates to and is mistranslated by dominant white cultures as well as globally dominated ones, specifically Arab, Chinese, and South Asian. In these respects, perhaps the central point of interest of the novel is how it implicitly parallels the transmissibilities and interferences surrounding cultural and semiotic encodings of languages and music, with those of body color, features, and styles, none of which are allowed to fall comfortably on either side of the nature/culture divide.

Ernest Hemingway: "drunken people or foreigners"

If the case of Claude McKay shows the centrality of translation and multi-lingualism for modernist investigations into cultural specificity, they were also at the heart of the most abstract modernist concerns with representation and fidelity to either inner experience or the externality of the object. Obviously, any translation implies mediation, stressing that the text one is given to read is not the "original" or the "real thing" – that a specific language has been interposed between the object and its perceiver. And in this respect, translation is inevitably at the crux of what are perhaps the two prime competing imperatives of modernist prose: on the one hand, to achieve a sort of hyper-realism, to blast through sentimentality and convention and thus bring language ever closer, if only allegorically, to what it is meant to represent (hence, stream of consciousness, stark dialogue, etc.), and on the other, to acknowledge and foreground the mediation of artistic and linguistic structures, forms, and traditions. Many of the most important works of high modernism – *Ulysses* or the *Cantos* – can be defined by their attempt to honor both those imperatives at once. In a less elaborate mode, however, one can see similar dynamics at work in an author whose role in consolidating a large swathe of modernist interventions into not only a style or a mode but almost a genre is too easily forgotten: Ernest Hemingway.

Arguably, no modernist prose writer "ventured" into the American demotic more insistently or forcefully than Hemingway; however, one of his most consistent stylistic modes insists on nothing so much as that it is the representation of a language that is not English. Unlike Stein, in Hemingway often a certain stilted, pared-down usage presents itself as an effect of translation, an estrangement of English meant to reflect foreign usage and syntax. If Hemingway often presents speech as colloquial, crucially, in such cases he also presents it in an idiom that cannot be tied to any specific regional, ethnic, or class dialect. This makes sense, as it would be absurd (for example) to present the speech of Parisian waiters by way of a New York accent, giving them a historical and geographical specificity that erases the very effect of the local that the author is at pains to capture. At the same time, however, colloquial speech is *nothing but* local usage, identifiable as such. We are presented here with a major problem of "translational mimesis," which Juliette Taylor-Batty has shown to be an important and recurrent question for modernist novelists.[23] Hemingway's frequent solution to this particular conundrum is almost a contradiction in terms: a deterritorialized colloquial – that is to say, an *allegory* of those elements of usage that are by definition untranslatable (and in this way, we find Hemingway within the general parameters of the translational problems addressed by his great stylistic master, Stein). The conversations in his story "A Clean, Well-Lighted Place" are typical of this style, giving the flavor of informal conversation but with turns of phrase and usage that are unidiomatic:

> "He must be eighty years old."
> "Anyway I should say he was eighty."
>
> "I wish he would go home. I never get to bed before three o'clock. What kind of hour is that to go to bed?"
>
> "He stays up because he likes it."
> "He's lonely. I'm not lonely. I have a wife waiting in bed for me."
> "He had a wife once too."
> "A wife would be no good to him now."
> "You can't tell. He might be better with a wife."[24]

If the short, choppy phrases and absence of complex sentences could seem to represent nonnative speakers chatting in English, one should remember that these phrases are meant to represent a conversation held by native speakers, but in Spanish. Should we conclude, then, that this sort of usage is more common to Spanish than to English? Probably not, and not only because Hemingway's "American" dialogues share some of these traits, but also because in this quite short tale, the typically laconic Hemingway narrator offers only one substantive intervention, and it touches on precisely these questions. When the younger waiter from the earlier dialogue, eager to get home to his wife, harries his last customer, a partially deaf and probably drunk older man, the scene is described this way:

> "Finished," he said, speaking with that omission of syntax stupid people employ when talking to drunken people or foreigners. "No more tonight. Close now."
> (381)

In other the words, the narrator suggests that reduced syntax is less the sign of a foreign speaker than of a speaker addressing foreigners, in a manner that denies or misunderstands their own capacity to translate. The "stupidity" of the waiter lies in his attitude toward translation, his sense that syntax is an obstacle to rather than a vector of the kernel of meaning he wishes to convey, and at the same time shows how the pretext of language difference can justify the xenophobic hostility embodied by the refusal to fully present the "native" language to the foreigner. However, in a tersely written story obsessed with the incommunicability of private experience, the story calls into question its own narrative stance by the same token: Are we, the readers, the foreigners to whom the story itself is stupidly speaking?[25] That this question is not idle might be indicated by the story's close, where Hemingway allows the surfaces to be breached and provides a glimpse of a character's consciousness. For when we are finally given the older waiter's ultimate thoughts, the language is neither a stylized allegory of Spanish nor a tonally neutral representation of some sort of transcultural and universal interiority, but something else yet again:

> It was all a nothing and a man was a nothing too. . . . Some lived in it and never felt it but he knew it all was nada y pues nada y nada y pues nada. Our nada who art in nada, nada be thy name thy kingdom nada thy will be nada in nada as it is in nada. (383)

Here, the Spanish infiltrates the decidedly uncolloquial English of the Lord's Prayer just as the "nothing" infiltrates an expression of faith, in a multilingual interior monologue that cannot be located either "inside" the Spanish-speaking character's head or within the English prose surface. In this manner, the hardened super-realism of Hemingway's prose and pose points to nothing so much as the multiplicity of languages, and by that token, to the intercession of the word. Once the authenticity of dialogue and specific language practices assert themselves as a value in their own right, as they do throughout modernist prose in English, while the mimetic framing of narration itself is also subjected to questioning, then translation slides from being a technical problem to an ontological question – and one that becomes even more pressing as modernism progresses over the twentieth century and boundaries between poetry and prose become increasingly porous. Though less explicitly than in poetry, for American prose, too, the history of modernism cannot be thought of apart from the questions of representation and transmission in the largest senses and, therefore, translation.

NOTES

1. On translation and American poetry, see above all Steven Yao, *Translation and the Languages of Modernism: Gender, Politics, Language* (New York: Palgrave, 2002). Jahan Ramazani also argues for the centrality of transnational, transcultural, and translingual exchange in *A Transnational Poetics* (Chicago: University of Chicago Press, 2009). If translation and multilingualism are less notable in American modernist prose than poetry, Juliette Taylor-Batty has nevertheless deftly shown their very strategic role in modernist fiction in English generally, in a study that interestingly contains no extended readings of American authors: *Multilingualism in Modernist Fiction* (New York: Palgrave, 2013). For an acute recent account of the theoretical interest of and in translation in modernism and modernist studies, see Rebecca Beasley, "Modernism's Translations," in *The Oxford Handbook of Global Modernisms*, eds. Mark Wollaeger and Matt Eatough (Oxford: Oxford University Press, 2012).

2. H.L. Mencken, *The American Language: An Inquiry into the Development of English in the United States*, 3rd ed. revised and enlarged (New York: Alfred A. Knopf, 1926), 4.

3. Notably, by Stein and Pound. It is worth noting that Mencken refers explicitly to poets, though his arguments seem intended to be taken as of general application. Clearly, modernist prose writers such as Sherwood Anderson and Ernest Hemingway can be seen as responding to imperatives such as those of Mencken.

4. For a theoretical discussion of the relationship between translation and modernist valorizations of defamiliarization, see Taylor-Batty, especially 19–27.

5. This paradigm emerges in a cluster of texts from the '30s and '40s that thematize writing's relation to thinking, principally *Everybody's Autobiography*, "The Coming of the Americans," and "What Is English Literature." Let me specify that I am in no way affirming the "naturalness" of spoken language as opposed to the artificiality of writing. Rather, I want to suggest, first, that systems of written literature impose *different* sorts of structural estrangement than those pertaining to spoken exchange and, second, that this difference can make palpable what might otherwise seem "natural," "spontaneous," or otherwise unconstrained in spoken discourse. Our inner language in which we talk to ourselves in our minds, at once solipsistic and never materialized, is at once spoken and written in these senses.

6. The most powerful critique of nativist American modernist cultural particularism is that found in Walter Benn Michaels' *Our America: Nativism, Modernism, and Pluralism* (Durham: Duke University Press, 1995), although the universalist position he adopts is open to question. For a brilliant recent study of the paradoxes of modernist investment in vernaculars and nonstandard idioms, and their relationship to conceptualizations of cultural authenticity, see Matthew Hart's study of "synthetic vernaculars," *Nations of Nothing but Poetry: Modernism, Transnationalism, and Synthetic Vernacular Poetry* (Oxford: Oxford University Press, 2010).

7. Genevieve Abravanel, *Americanizing Britain: The Rise of Modernism in the Age of the Entertainment Empire* (Oxford: Oxford University Press, 2012).

8. Henry James, *Henry James on Culture: Collected Essays on Politics and the American Social Scene*, ed. Pierre A. Walker (Lincoln: University of Nebraska Press), 53.

9. For a more extended account of Mencken and James in relation to these issues, and Stein's equation of writing with the foreign, see my *American Modernism's Expatriate Scene: The Labour of Translation* (Edinburgh: Edinburgh University Press, 2007). For an important recent consideration of Mencken and American modernism, see Joshua L. Miller, *Accented America: The Cultural Politics of Multilingual Modernism* (Oxford: Oxford University Press, 2011).

10. Antoine Berman, *L'épreuve de l'étranger: Culture et traduction dans l'Allemagne romantique* (Paris: Gallimard, 1984), 288 (my translation).

11. Crawford defines "provincial" modernism in his pathbreaking *Devolving English Literature* (Edinburgh: Edinburgh University Press, 2000). His argument there is that Scottish and American modernists oppose the "English cultural centre" (262) through two allied strategies: multilingual texts that relativize the importance of English generally, and the "demotic urge" (262) to represent local usage and forms. Thus, "the 'provincial' and the international are bonded, but

not in the kind of cosmopolitan sense that makes a poem's speech as international as nylon" (269).

12. Gertrude Stein, *Selected Writings of Gertrude Stein*, ed. Carl Van Vechten (New York: Vintage Books, 1972), 116–117.

13. Gertrude Stein, *Writings: 1932–1946*, eds. Catharine R. Stimpson and Harriet Chessman (New York: Library of America, 1998), 769.

14. Henry Roth, *Call It Sleep* (New York: Penguin Modern Classics, 1991), 96.

15. Hana Wirth-Nesher, *Call It English: The Languages of Jewish American Literature* (Princeton, NJ: Princeton University Press, 2006); see n. 26, p. 192, for the occurrences of "Body Street" in the manuscript notes.

16. In other words, the overinvestment in a particular set of arbitrary cultural practices and structures, as encapsulated by language. In James this often takes the form of touristic mystification and exoticism, but such terms can too easily obscure the differences within a complex panoply of attitudes and subjective stances.

17. Louis Wolfson, *Le Schizo et les langues* (Paris: Editions Gallimard, 1970).

18. McKay attended school in Jamaica, mastered standard English, and originally considered himself a writer in that language, though he dabbled in dialect verse. It was his white English patron, Walter Jekyll, who encouraged McKay to write in dialect and present himself as a living expression of the Jamaican folk. See Michael North, *The Dialect of Modernism: Race, Language & Twentieth-Century Literature* (Oxford: Oxford University Press, 1994), 100–110, for a brilliant account.

19. Claude McKay, *Banjo: A Story without a Plot* (1929; New York: Harcourt Brace, 1957), 3.

20. When another character accuses Banjo of playing the instrument of "Dixie" and "bondage," he goes on to encourage Banjo to consider alternatives such as the "piano and violin, harp and flute" (91) – the instruments of Western high cultural prestige, rather than jazzy brass or reeds, options that in this context are simply not raised.

21. Claude McKay, *Home to Harlem* (1928; Hanover: Northeastern University Press, 1987), 130.

22. The interested reader should consult Brent Hayes Edwards' pathbreaking *The Practice of Diaspora: Literature, Translation, and the Rise of Black Internationalism* (Cambridge: Harvard University Press, 2003), to which my account is happily indebted. Edwards discusses translation in some detail, including the historical importance of the translation of *Banjo* into French in 1931.

23. As Taylor-Batty stresses, she adopts this term and her initial typologies from Meir Sternberg's important article, "Polylingualism as Reality and Translation as Mimesis," *Poetics Today* 2.4 (1981): 221–239. Her illuminating close readings of Lawrence, Mansfield, Richardson, and Rhys uncover very similar questions and dynamics to those I am briefly sketching here with regard to Hemingway. Hemingway himself employs many other strategies of translational mimesis in addition to those I'm privileging here, which seem to me particularly resonant with regard to major trends in American modernist prose. One important example of other practices would be *For Whom the Bell Tolls*, which deploys the archaic English familiar second-person form to convey at once the Spanish distinction between formal and informal address and the archaic feel of

nonstandard, popular Castilian speech forms. For more on this, see Milton Azevedo, "Shadows of a Literary Dialect: *For Whom the Bell Tolls* in Five Romance Languages," *The Hemingway Review* 20, no. 1 (Fall 2000): 30–48.

24. Ernest Hemingway, "A Clean, Well-Lighted Place," in *The Short Stories of Ernest Hemingway* (New York: Charles Scribner's Sons, 1953), 381.

25. As Werner Sollors points out in an illuminating article, Delmore Schwartz had argued in 1951 that among Hemingway's stylistic devices one finds "above all the simplified speech which an American uses to a European ignorant of English" (cited in Sollors, 465). What is worth thinking about is to what extent Hemingway generalizes a structure of address that positions the reader as linguistic outsider and the narrator as stupid xenophobe. For the relation of these matters to American ethnic writing, see Werner Sollors, "Hemingway Spoken Here," *Cambridge History of American Literature, Vol. 6*, ed. Sacvan Bercovitch (Cambridge: Cambridge University Press, 2002).

13

JULIAN MURPHET

New Media Modernism

Media Trauma

It would be impossible to exaggerate the importance of the printed codex to the West's project of Enlightenment. The symbolic writing systems that covered millions of books in print constituted the West's dominant information storage technology for some centuries. As Friedrich Kittler puts it, "all data flows ... had to pass through the bottleneck of the signifier. Alphabetic monopoly, grammatology."[1] And thence, if it was not to perish, to be printed on paper, bound in a codex, stored on a shelf, and arranged systematically. One of the most successful genres internal to this "monopoly" of print capitalism over the storage of information was the novel – an upstart cultural technology battening on inherited oral forms of narration, gene-splicing those with a descriptive extensiveness made possible by movable type, and supercharging the solution with an admixture of dramatic scenography. The novel, that darling machine of the energetics of "subjectification," thrived like all literature on *repressions* endemic to the book as medium: in Lacanese, the repression of the Real in favor of the Symbolic – or more plainly, the constitutive deafness and blindness of all alphabetical print to the "noises" of reality. Literature, and with it the novel, transcodes the waves and radiation of experience into so many combinations of twenty-six letters.

So long as its monopoly was uncontested, this was not a problem. But from the moment that other data-storage systems became available (photography, telegraphy, phonography, film, etc.) and contested that monopoly, literature has been plagued by envious fantasies, nightmares, and parapraxes, testifying to the erosion of the repressive membrane between its constitutive signs and the "Real" for which they had long stood in good faith. This psychic trauma we call "modernism."

Nowhere was this cultural dynamic more pronounced than in the United States, where the new media found a favorable habitat in the relative national philistinism and cult of the inventor surrounding personae such as T.A. Edison, but where, too, the printed word had been such a foundational medium of statecraft. The first nation of the book was also the first nation of mechanized inscription, electrical connectivity, and broadcast signals. The interference patterns created by this unprecedented vortex of cultural and technological energies were etched into the cerebral cortices of the period's most inventive writers – artists of the word whose sensitivity to both the strong residual claims of the literary system and to the emergent media ecology of analog recording and playback, wireless transmission, and station-to-station connectivity gave rise to imaginative syntheses and contradictory representational pressure points in which can be detected the onset of a long and painful transition, still unfinished today, from an alphabetical to a digital-storage monopoly.[2]

The coeval usurpation of the printed word itself by powers profoundly aligned with the "mass culture" being made possible by instantaneous broadcasting and mass distribution had a parallel effect. The seizure of the literary means of production by what cultural history has labeled the "yellow" journalism of the large newspaper barons of the end of the nineteenth century was felt as a travesty and an undermining of the civilizational function of literature. Rotary press and halftone printing techniques allowed for massive print runs, subsidized by new advertising methods embedded like copy. Print capitalism's apotheosis was not exclusively American in origin, but the United States provided perhaps its optimum sphere of activity and growth; and the prognosis for the book as a medium was not promising. As Walter Benjamin put it, "Printing, having found in the book a refuge in which to lead an autonomous existence, is pitilessly dragged out onto the street by advertisements and subjected to the brutal heteronomies of economic chaos. This is the hard schooling of its new form."[3]

When the narrator of Jack London's *The Iron Heel* asks a young journalist why a grisly industrial accident is making no appearance in the newspapers, the answer is indicative:

> "We're all solid with the corporations," he answered. "If you paid advertising rates, you couldn't get any such matter into the papers. A man who tried to smuggle it in would lose his job. You couldn't get it in if you paid ten times the regular advertising rates."[4]

Print capitalism is "solid" with its entire industrial base, a fused horizon of class interests where each is "caught up in the wheels and cogs of the industrial machine" and all are "slaves of the machine" (46). And that machine is coextensive with the thriving industrial sectors associated with the newer media – recorded music, corporate radio, vertically integrated Hollywood, Bell Corporation, and so on. The uncomfortable truth of the new media ecology is that "literature" (printed matter) is henceforth just one inextricable part of an industrial cog turning to keep the capitalist system running. Two kinds of repression, then, are at stake in the period in which the modernist novel thrived: the symbolic repression of the noises of the "Real" that new media such as gramophones and photography had brought to light to the detriment of literature's monopoly over information and the ideological repression of the *economic real* (class struggle) that the corporate take-over of the media system as a totality portended. The modernist American novel found itself in the unusual and uncomfortable position of overcompensating on both fronts.

The Membrane of Style

The dystopian note was the loudest of the era, but it was not the only one being sounded. Perhaps the most extraordinary act of novelistic innovation was made by an artist whose sanguine equanimity in the face of media shock was at one with her revolutionary methods. Gertrude Stein's familial epic *The Making of Americans*, still the least read modernist masterpiece (the evaluation was her own), was crafted, she later declared, under the pressure of the new mass-production information economy being consolidated in the first years of the twentieth century. Readers of this text, purporting to be a saga of the Dehning and Hersland families, are confronted by a tar pit of prose in which sentences have less a functional than a formal purpose. Though they do communicate information, the periods do so in a manner that is colossally redundant, since most are enmeshed within a tissue of insistently similar clauses differentiated from one another by minor variations. We can separate three consecutive sentences from the very end of the work to give a sense of what is at stake (the emphases are added to clarify the syntactical method):

> Family living can be existing **and** every one can come to be a dead one **and** *not any one then is remembering any such thing.*
> Family living can be existing **and** every one can come to be a dead one **and** *some are remembering some such thing.*
> Family living can be existing **and** every one can come to be a dead one and *every one is then a dead one **and** there are then not any more being living.*[5]

Parataxis governs the way these sentences are put together; conjunctions connect parts of a repeated syntactic structure and open it up to new, variable materials. The constant, balanced two-clause formula (life vs. death, familial immortality, individual demise) is followed by three versions of an ending. This typical passage can stand for the whole.

Written intermittently between 1903 and 1922, *The Making of Americans* wasn't published in the United States until 1934, when Stein undertook a lecture tour in part to promote it. She told her bemused audiences, "in the Making of Americans, I was doing what the cinema was doing, I was making a continuous succession of the statement of what that person was until I had not many things but one thing." Declaring her literary aesthetic to be in line with the "period of the cinema and series production," Stein observed that just as in a motion picture "no two pictures are exactly alike each one is just that much different than the one before," her prose involves "no repetition," since each sentence "was just that much different from" the ones before and after it.[6] As she presents it, circa 1934, the world is a mass-mediated world jumping to the rhythms of series production. Her sentences are attempts to assimilate those rhythms at the level of form, not content. It is in the way her apparent syntactical repetition (over 1,000 insufferable pages) manages to incorporate just enough internal variation that Stein makes a moving picture, a "whole portrait."

Whatever its ultimate heuristic value, this retrospective account of one of the key developments in modernist prose sets an ambitious agenda for contemporary research into how the mass media affected the protocols of literary narrative. Rather than simply look for "representations" of the media in modernist prose and attend to their moral or political valence, a more rewarding approach may be to account for the style itself as in some sense a tactical reaction to the new media ecology, and a corresponding adjustment of the novel form to a rapidly changing cultural environment. Style can be considered a sensitive membrane between two systems coming into increasing contact and intermingling technically in the early twentieth century – the literary system and the system of new media.

Stein's most illustrious disciple – and architect of perhaps the most influential prose style of the twentieth century – Ernest Hemingway, is most often discussed in terms of the pressure exerted on him by the professional journalism he undertook before emigrating to Europe.[7] Yet, although it seems appropriate to consider the role of uninflected reportage on his signature "degree zero" style, recent research has shown that his writing for newspapers and supplements was relatively florid and verbose, in keeping with the conventions of the time.[8] It was, rather, the encounter with Stein and the Parisian avant-garde that sharpened Hemingway's literary vigilance against cliché, abstraction, redundancy, and emotionality. And that, in turn, can be understood in relation to the pivotal role of that avant-garde as bellwether for the *système des beaux-arts*' response to the new media ecology: testing the newly mechanized techniques of cinema and advertising for their aesthetic potentials and then transposing those back into the older arts.[9] The expatriate Americans (Stein, Hemingway, Fitzgerald, etc.) discovered in Paris perhaps the world's most sophisticated aesthetic reaction to their own exported mass-cultural products. And for the Parisian avant-garde, it was the "subject" itself that needed to be evacuated from the foreground of aesthetic attention, so that the more general trends toward massification and mediation could be properly confronted.

Hemingway's stories are perhaps the optimum place to consider these dynamics at work; but his early novels, too, clearly illustrate the tendency. Stanley Aronowitz has written, "It is not that Hemingway is actually a pulp fiction writer who, for some reason, the critics have mistaken for a modern master of the novel. Hemingway is the novelist of the twentieth century precisely because he has extirpated the 'extraneous' category of subjectivity."[10] He did so by way of a stylistic economy that admits of the inhumanism of the new means of communication, while placing a powerful taboo on the very sentiments and affects dissembling that inhumanism in the newer media themselves. It is worth remembering how, in its period of ascendancy, the new media system thrived by "remediating" the exhausted emotional matrix of the Victorian period: affective clichés, superannuated feelings, none of which functioned in the arts any longer but which enjoyed a spectral afterlife in the mass mediation of consumerism. Consider Benjamin's account of this undeath of sentiment in advertising and films: "in face of the huge images across the walls of houses, where toothpaste and cosmetics lie handy for giants, sentimentality is restored to health and liberated in American style, just as people whom nothing moves or touches any longer are taught to cry again by films."[11] Such was the anachronistic formula of the new media system: superannuated literary sentiments, mechanical means of production.

Hemingway's prose style is an effort to incorporate, homeopathically, the ground tone of those mechanical means of production, without recycling any of the depleted Victorian feelings for which serious literature had no further use. The principal reason it had no use for them or the subject who was supposed to hold them together was that cinema had already arguably put an end to that entire humanist regime of sense and sensibility: "cinema is what kills the soul," as Kittler has aggressively written.[12] If it is no longer literature's purpose to construct that soulful presence, what is it there for?

> Miss Gage looked. They had me look in a glass. The whites of the eyes were yellow and it was the jaundice. I was sick for two weeks with it. For that reason we did not spend a convalescent leave together. We had planned to go to Pallanza on Lago Maggiore. It is nice there in the fall when the leaves turn. There are walks you can take and you can troll for trout in the lake.[13]

There is, of course, a story here, involving love, war, frustrated desire, and illness. There are characters interacting; a diagnosis is made; plans are disappointed. But there is nothing for the cultivated sympathetic intelligence to connect with; a bland plastic coating repels all empathy. To get a real sense of what is happening in this passage, we may compare a passage from Henry James:

> The charm of the Mediterranean coast only deepened for our heroine on acquaintance, for it was the threshold of Italy, the gate of admirations. Italy, as yet imperfectly seen and felt, stretched before her as a land of promise, a land in which a love of the beautiful might be comforted by endless knowledge.[14]

In James' prose, we note the rhetorical accent on subjective potentiality and enrichment – the promise of "deepening," "stretching before," "endlessness." Metaphors ("threshold," "gate") and characterizations ("land of promise") buttress the passage's (ironic) account of a healthy symbiotic relationship between person and place, whose effect is to extend the personality inward even as it draws her out. None of this for Hemingway. Not only are the eyes of the subject yellowed over by a cynical jaundice, but what he is allowed to imagine of the Italian lakeside is bereft of all personal coordinates. Gradually, but inevitably, the grammatical focus slides away from the immediate situation and gets stranded in vapid generality. A kind of shorthand tourist rhetoric intrudes at the point of maximum intimacy in the imagined holiday. The single evaluative term, "nice," is the most evasive and empty available; even Baedeker would have phrased it more alluringly.

Hard-Boiled Subjects

This resistance to subjective inwardness is a reflex of the degree to which Hemingway understood his craft in purely reactive terms. If the truth of the new media is inhuman, mechanistic, prosthetic, then shoring up the human spirit, the soul, the rich and multifaceted subject, seems a quaint fool's game. Far better for the novel to abandon it and explore instead the literary intensities available to an aesthetic appropriation of posthuman phenomena. Nowhere was this course of action so avidly pursued as in the "hard-boiled" school of American noir writers, who perfected a brutal art of literary subtraction and cast a lean, mean shadow over twentieth-century prose. It was not just in relation to the privileged zone of the protagonist that the war against depth took place; rather, the entirety of what Alex Woloch calls the "character-system" itself – that complex network of interactions that defines novelistic narrative economy – was retrofitted.[15] We can see this in stark clarity in Dashiell Hammett's first novel, *Red Harvest* (1928), where the

Continental Op's terse narration is in part justified by the fact that there is simply no time to waste: the new media ecology obviates the need for rhetorical filler. "From a drug store in upper Broadway I telephoned Dick Foley and asked him to come over to my hotel. He arrived a few minutes after I got there."[16] Not only are the spaces abstract and impersonal, but the speed of telephonic mediation means that characters only have to connect long enough for the essential information to be relayed. This kind of narrative velocity means both that the character system can proliferate (many more personages appear in these brief pages than in a typical James novel) and that the amount of information can redouble – provided there is nothing anti-quated to encumber it. U.S. crime fiction of this period is dense with data and alive with character-systemic transference to a degree unprecedented in literary history, and it is so because of what has been emptied out: namely, literariness. A didactic matter-of-factness substantiates the thesis that litera-ture in a media ecology survived by jettisoning the very stylistic "distinction" it had evolved in the long period of its dominance. "I went out to look for Reno Starkey" could well have set the terms for a long, adventurous chapter in Dickens or Trollope; but here it is all over in the blinking of an eye: "After an hour of searching I located him, by telephone, in a Ronney Street rooming house" (144). The wasted hour need not be elaborated; a telephone has done the trick; the narrative ticks forward.

Horace McCoy's chilling *They Shoot Horses, Don't They?* (1935) arranges its narrative of mass-cultural automatisms around intermediary pages of boldface headline copy purporting to be court transcripts relating to the death sentence handed down upon the narrator-protagonist for his role in the mercy killing at the center of the novel. The past-tense recapitula-tion is interrupted by italicized present-tense reflections from the dock; note the way McCoy orchestrates their alternation:

> I got back on the dance floor as the whistle blew and the orchestra began to pay. This was not a very good orchestra; but it was better than the radio because you didn't have to listen to a lot of announcers begging and pleading with you to buy something. Since I've been in this marathon I've had enough radio to last me the rest of my life. *There is a radio going now, in a building across the street from the court room. It is very distinct. "Do you need money? ... Are you in trouble? ..."*[17]

Here the radio serves as a hinge in more than one sense. Not only does it articulate past and present around a figural constant, it underlines the degree to which this kind of narrative is itself a prolongation of radio's uncanniness in another medium. Given that the whole story is being told by a man being sentenced to death, the narrative voice is thrown out of the familiar domain of novelistic narration and into the *unheimlich* territory of the radio voice. McCoy's novel shares this feature with James M. Cain's *Double Indemnity* (1935) and *The Postman Always Rings Twice* (1934): a well-nigh posthumous narrating instance, buying into the pervasive suspicions of radio as a spirit medium. "Although most accounts of wireless celebrated communities increasingly interconnected by the technology, ... other tales brooded instead over lives and souls transmuted and dispersed into the enveloping ether. In a world now supernaturally blanketed by human consciousness afloat in the air, stories of paranormal radio as the 'voice from the void' pondered the fate of the still corporeal yet increasingly isolated individuals who found themselves bathing, often reluctantly, in the waves of the wireless sea."[18] The noir fictions of the '30s and '40s participated in this syndrome by forging a novel "oral aesthetic" in tune with "the omnipresence of a radio culture," as Fredric Jameson has remarked. "Both pulp or hard-boiled detective stories and *film noir* are indeed structurally distinguished by the fundamental fact of the *voice-over*, which signals in advance the closure of events to be narrated just as surely as it marks the operative presence of an essentially radio aesthetic which has no equivalent in the earlier novel."[19]

Of Raymond Chandler it need only be said that his commitment to the American demotic in all its vulgar inventiveness was tempered by a virtually avant-gardist sense of what commodity culture had done to experience (carved it up into reified units with no organic connection), the most creative response to which was Eisenstein's: the dialectical clash of incommensurate montage cells. Advertising would take the same route in due course, but in the meantime, Chandler's signature similes ring with the outrageousness of a multimedia dada installation:

I felt like an amputated leg.[20]
Even on Central Avenue, not the quietest dressed street in the world, he looked about as inconspicuous as a tarantula on a slice of angel food.[21]
She gave me a smile I could feel in my hip pocket.[22]
"You boys are as cute as a couple of lost golf balls ... how in the world do you do it?"[23]
I belonged in Idle Valley like a pearl onion on a banana split.[24]

This is yet another adaptation of the "literary" to a regime of sense orchestrated by new media impressionisms and the "ruthless annihilation of aura" immanent to it. As Benjamin put it, "The countless grotesque events consumed in films are a graphic indication of the dangers threatening mankind from the repressions implicit in civilization. American slapstick and Disney films trigger a therapeutic release of unconscious energies."[25] Chandler is entitled to the same praise; his prose is one of modernity's great pressure release valves. That he and the "Back Mask" school do not regularly make the canon of modernist American prose is due to a spurious notion of form that refuses to recognize style such as this as formally innovative in the manner of Joyce's interior monologues or Pound's documentary technique. Its remarkable innovations were so rich and productive that they became absorbed into a different, more marketable novelistic tradition than the High Moderns, but its achievement is modernist through and through.

Vernacular Modernism

Though Nathanael West and Anita Loos are enjoying something of a renaissance today, their obscurity for many years was a symptom of the extent to which scholastic modernism had been purged of its more "vernacular" elements. West's extraordinary 1933 novella *Miss Lonleyhearts* is a pitch-perfect allegory of the fate of literature in the new media age. A writer is obliged by economic circumstance to "become-medium" as an advice columnist for a New York newspaper. Responding in print to the alienated missives of the nameless majority, teased mercilessly by his colleagues ("How now, Dostoievski?"[26]), Miss Lonelyhearts finds himself mechanically pounding out countless column inches of inane cliché, at one point breaking off:

> He could not go on with it, and turned again to the imagined desert where Desperate, Broken-hearted and the others were still building his name. They had run out of sea-shells and were using faded photographs, soiled fans, time-tables, laying cards, broken toys, imitation jewelry – junk that memory had made precious. . . . (87)

In a world where emotions and counsel are branded by the seriality of commodity culture, this fantasy image of the modern imagination frames it as a material reflux of consumer waste. In *The Day of the Locust* (1939), Hollywood's great apocalyptic satire, West adumbrates the pure depthlessness of postmodernity in a Los Angeles where people have themselves become playback mechanisms, replaying software implanted in them by the media that invest them:

> She began to sing.
>
> > "Jeepers Creepers!
> > *Where'd you get those peepers? . . .*"
>
> She trucked, jerking her buttocks and shaking her head from side to side.
> Homer was amazed. He felt that the scene he was witnessing had been rehearsed. He was right.[27]

The consequence of privately owned media empires whose function is to broadcast corporate-sanctioned cultural materials on a mass level is one vast inhuman "rehearsal" of prefab intensities, affects, emotions, moods, scenes, intimacies, gestures, dreams, and visions peddled by the masters of capital. The human body is become a vessel for electrical signals, prerecorded sounds, and mass-projected moving images – a "jerking" conductor of nervous stimulants in mass circulation. The novel, once itself the choice technology of bourgeois "soul production," is stranded in a terminal back alley, unable to keep the pace set by waves and radiation moving at the speed of sound and light through the human biomass. Its remaining task, in West's hands as in the hands of Wyndham Lewis across the ocean, is to bear witness to the implosion.

> So then we got to talking quite a lot and I told him that I was traveling to get educated and I told him I had a girl with me who I was trying to reform because I thought if she would put her mind more on getting educated, she would get more reformed. Because after all Mr. Spoffard will have to meet Dorothy sooner or later and he might wonder what a refined girl like I was doing with a girl like Dorothy. So Mr. Spoffard really became quite intreeged. Because Mr. Spoffard loves to reform people and he loves to senshure everything and he really came over to Europe to look at all the things that American come over the Europe to look at, when they really should not look at them but they should look at all of the museums instead.[28]

Anita Loos, a veteran Hollywood screenwriter by the age of thirty, knew very well what she was doing in 1925 when she unleashed her blonde monster Lorelei Lee in a torrent of infantile clauses. Couched in radically paratactic and merely additive syntax – the odd prefatory "So" and "Because" gesturing, weakly, in the direction of hypotaxis – these clauses assail the reader with the concupiscent egotism of a prepubescent child. Loos is sure to lace the undertaking with generous amounts of irony, but in outline, her narrative is Jamesian (American ingénue goes to Europe to find a wealthy and cultured husband), and the comparison is meant to be damaging. For Loos has projected a situation where one of the gold-digging "flappers" she had helped create on the silent screen walks ignorantly into a Jamesian novelistic scenario and destroys it from within. Again, as an allegory for the role of new media on the institution of the novel form, this could hardly be improved.

Subordination or Incorporation?

If Loos had made her living as a writer for the early films prior to embarking on her career as a novelist, the reverse was the more common trajectory for a generation raised into this most tumultuous of periods in the history of the form. During the Great Depression, indeed, it could be said that Hollywood served as an industrial patron to the nation's most talented novelists.[29] So prodigious was their appetite for "story," given the standardization of the "classic Hollywood" narrative film as industrial norm and the conquest of sound (triggering a sharp rise in the need for good dialogue), that the big studios could afford to put novelists on lucrative salaries and corral them in stables, delivering piecework to order for genre pictures or "prestige" productions on the whims of executive producers. The new media ecology had not only outflanked and outwitted the *système des beaux-arts* of which the literary novel was a centerpiece, but by the late 1920s it had literally absorbed it. There was henceforth no "external" vantage point from which to stand aloof and in judgment over the mass-mediatized dehumanization of an entire population. It was from within the belly of the beast that the process was to be observed, through a glass darkly, and with powerful formal repercussions.

F. Scott Fitzgerald, far too attractive and glamorous a cultural celebrity to be "merely" an author in the Jazz Age, experienced the consequent demotion of his chosen form in terms of crisis:

> I saw that the novel, which at my maturity was the strongest and supplest medium for conveying thought and emotion from one human being to another, was becoming subordinated to a mechanical and communal art that, whether in the hands of Hollywood merchants or Russian idealists, was capable of reflecting only the tritest thought, the most obvious emotion. It was an art in which words were subordinate to images, where personality was worn down to the inevitable low gear of collaboration. ... [T]here was a rankling indignity, that to me had become almost an obsession, in seeing the power of the written word subordinate to another power, a more glittering, a grosser power ... something which tended to make my efforts obsolescent, as the chain stores have crippled the small merchant, an exterior force, unbeatable ...[30]

His choice of word for the novel form, "medium," is of course motivated by the circumambient Darwinian scenography, where the ecological ousting of one power by "another ... grosser power" leads to industrial "obsolescence" in a more poignantly economic sense: the novel is revealed as a mere "medium" by the onslaught of media that now do its work for it. This extraordinary figuration, an account of the "crack-up" of American life and culture, as of his own psychic equipoise, crystallizes Fitzgerald's relation to the new media system as adversarial, a stance made all the sharper by his most often fruitless, humiliating toil for MGM.

Yet the novels are haunted in a more ambiguous sense than his ego was. In their subtle, often openly nostalgic prose, which eschews the pointedly blank and mechanical stylistics of Hemingway and the noirs in favor of elegant periods, deft subordinations, and spacious syntax, the mechanical media obtrude both as minatory figures of decline and opportune metaphors for the narrative texture itself. So the Princeton undergraduates in *This Side of Paradise* are mocked for their habit of listening to the Graphophone, staging review theatrics, singing hit songs, and attending the cinema ("Amory decided that he liked the movies, wanted to enjoy them as the row of upper classmen in front had enjoyed them"[31]). Yet, at a critical point later on, the narrator, reaching for a convenient illustration of a hangover, offers this: "the isolated pictures began slowly to form a cinema reel of the day before" (185). Hedging its bets in this way, Fitzgerald's novelistic style attempts the implausible: it presumes that the new media are simply available for novelistic enclosure, the novel's vaguely nineteenth-century style now approving, now reproving the cultural tendencies at work in cinema, recorded music, and radio. The character-system and spatial economy of Henry James is relatively intact.

But the signs are, in general, ominous. There is a simile in *The Great Gatsby* (1925) that illustrates the new front line of the "machine in the garden" dynamic proposed by Leo Marx as endemic to the American novel. "And so with the sunshine and the great bursts of leaves growing on the trees, just as things grow in fast movies, I had that familiar conviction that life was beginning over again with the summer."[32] Michael North, noting that this description is meant to set the scene for Nick Carraway's summer of reading, observes that "Nick is already so much a member of the modern audience, an onlooker in a society of spectacle, that even the excitement of settling down to read is expressed in terms of film."[33] True, but for the natural to be qualified so cavalierly by a mechanical trope is for the novel to have capitulated in advance, such that the scene of reading must never come; it doesn't, and what follows is one of the great cautionary tales of a culture ranging over visual and auditory surfaces rather than plumbing the literary depths.

It all comes full circle in the final, unfinished novel, *The Last Tycoon*, of which it is possible to say here only that in it two media (film and the novel) circle one another warily like a predator and its prey, only for the older species finally to collapse in upon itself and expire in the jaws of the voracious, "glittering . . . grosser" force. The bitterness is all to the fore, as when Kathleen Moore tells Stahr about her dead father:

> "He wrote a book called 'Last Blessing'. Did you ever read it?"
> "I don't read."
> "I wish you'd buy it for the movies. It's a good little book. I still get a
> royalty from it – ten shillings a year."[34]

Money is the ultimate medium through which culture is now evaluated; books can be tidy little earners, but the big Studio producer doesn't read them. He hires people to do that. The substance of this little vignette lies in the form itself: a punchy stichomythic exchange with no extraneous description, just like in the movies. The novel is here caught in the process of submitting, finally, to the "exterior force" that has assumed its place in the narrative ecosystem.

Another serious novelist obliged to work for pay in the studio system was William Faulkner. His public statements of contempt for the industry that subsidized his leanest years as a novelist for a long time blocked any serious inquiry into the formal debt those novels paid to the institution he supposedly reviled. It is only recently that attention has turned to the complex negotiations at work in the notoriously verbose discursive texture of Faulkner between the lingering prestige of a nineteenth-century form and the contestations to its hegemony launched by newer media in the early twentieth century.[35] We can only scan the evidence here, but it should be sufficient to clarify the point.

Unlike Fitzgerald, Faulkner saw the extraordinary use-value of the Black Mask style as a literary approximation of America's new media-saturated depthlessness and found the wherewithal to put it to use himself. The famous description of the degenerate hoodlum Popeye in *Sanctuary* is a direct graft of Chandlerian prose:

> He saw, facing him across the spring, a man of under size, his hands in his coat pockets, a cigarette slanted from his chin. His suit was black, with a tight, high-waisted coat. His trousers were rolled once and caked with mud above mud-caked shoes. His face had a queer, bloodless color, as though seen by electric light; against the sunny silence, in his slanted straw hat and his slightly akimbo arms, he had that vicious depthless quality of stamped tin.[36]

Three sentences beginning with the masculine possessive pronoun underline the mechanical and repetitive shallowness of what is at stake here: an anaphoric colonization of literary characterization by the two-dimensionality of genre film. Popeye's visage is always and already "as though seen by electric light," and his whole body flattens into "that vicious depthless quality" that allows the figures of mass media to circulate without limit. This is a mass-produced stereotype; and Faulkner is the kind of writer not to let the point go to waste. Three more sentences beginning with "His" follow: "His skin had a dead, dark pallor. His nose was faintly aquiline, and he had no chin at all. His face just went away, like the face of a wax doll set too near a hot fire and forgotten" (183). This mechanical prose style effectively writes itself.

Later in the novel, as the action turns to legal wranglings in the town of Jefferson, we are exposed to the source of this alarming reduction of human beings to paper-thin clichés:

> The sunny air was filled with competitive radios and phonographs in the doors of drug- and music-stores. Before these doors a throng stood all day, listening. The pieces which moved them were ballads, simple in melody and theme, of bereavement and retribution and repentance metallically sung, blurred, emphasised by static or needle – disembodied voices blaring from imitation wood cabinets or pebble-grain horn-mouths above the rapt faces, the gnarled slow hands long shaped to the imperious earth, lugubrious, harsh, and sad.   (257)

Much is at stake in this descriptive passage: the throng's passive reception of mediated sound; the stupid simplicity of the mass-produced songs; the metallic "blur" of playback or broadcast; the generalized disembodiment of "voice"; and the stark contrast between these simple melodies and the now unsung, only implied songs of southern agricultural labor as living cultural expression of the "gnarled slow hands" that till the earth. The scene bears sorrowful witness to an abstract expropriation of regional culture by the imperial forces of Northern broadcast and recording technologies; an expropriation the novel is, finally, helpless to resist. Faulkner's challenge was to engineer a style that somehow took cognizance of this abstraction without surrendering to it abjectly. His solution, at least in the great early sequence of works, was to alter the stylistic physiognomy and formal agenda of each new novel just enough to show the resilient oral traditions of southern geniality pitched in desperate "vocal" battle with these newer mass-mediated signals. As I Lay Dying's "tour de force" rotation of fifteen narrators in fifty-nine fragments of monologue turns comically on a substitution of one dead mother who speaks posthumously within her coffin (like a radio voice) for another, new and improved one who comes equipped with "one of them little graphophones" on which the family can play their mail-order records and reconstitute the familial bond on a new, mass-produced basis.[37] Satire was only one option; the formal uniqueness of each novel that Faulkner wrote between 1929 and 1942 established a modernism that refused to give in to standardization or repetition.

We must at last turn to perhaps the period's most explicit and self-conscious adapter of the novel form to its new situation amid the mechanical and electrical media. John Dos Passos' novels "of the 1920s and 1930s abound in fragments of song lyrics, allusions to jazz and Tin Pan Alley melodies, and references to the movies."[38] And it is not simply that the novels "abound" in such snippets of mass culture; rather, the novel form itself can be felt increasingly to mutate around the "foreign" media matters, rebuilding itself from the ground up to accommodate them. In the event, this genuflection of the venerable "medium [best equipped] for conveying thought and emotion" went so far as to replace many of its time-honored formal verities: collective protagonists rather than singular ones; multiple intercut parallel storylines rather than a dominant and a minor plotline; a verbal saturation of "impersonal" circulating discourses rather than a cultivated and organic narrative idiom; and the explicit admission of numbered sections, in the great *U.S.A.* trilogy labeled "Camera Eye" and "Newsreel."

In *Manhattan Transfer*, a mechanical piano becomes a synecdoche of the new mechanical media system as a whole; in its distracting presence, the writer, Jimmy Herf, trying here to be "Literature," composes snatches of a story:

> He was making up the story in his mind ... In a lonely abandoned dancehall on Sheepshead Bay ... lovely blooming Italian girl ... shrill whistle in the dark ... I ought to get out and see what's going on. He groped for the front door. It was locked. He walked over to the piano and put another nickel in. Then he lit a fresh cigarette and started walking up and down again. Always the way ... a parasite on the drama of life, reporter looks at everything through a peephole. Never mixes in. The piano was playing *Yes We Have No Bananas*. "Oh hell!" he kept muttering and ground his teeth and walked up and down.[39]

Dos Passos here constructs something like a loop between the mechanical reiterations of the player piano and the clichéd drivel that pops into Jimmy's head as he "composes" his story. Moreover, the very impossibility of writing in a world wired for inane sound and driven by automatic mechanisms is made perfectly clear.

As for *U.S.A.* itself – *The 42nd Parallel* (1930), *1919* (1932), and *The Big Money* (1936) – this great epic of the new media age circles restlessly around twelve relatively independent characters scattered across the capitalist nation-state par excellence, drawing out the many ways in which class struggle defines the horizon of social existence, albeit within a sharply drawn sense of the media that both ramify that struggle and mystify it. But these loosely intertwining destinies are counterpointed by more-abstract and utterly impersonal chapters: the "Newsreel" chapters that bravely illustrate the situation by abandoning narrative altogether and constructing collage-like arrangements of found social text; occasional quasi-lyrical biographies of socially symbolic real-world citizens; and the "Camera Eye" sections that, in contravention of their name, dwell within the phenomenological intimacies of an alienated subject. The "Camera Eye" sections are the least visual and entertain only a fitful and enigmatic formal relationship to the silent Soviet film aesthetic from which they draw their name (North points out that these chapters are "predominantly or even exclusively aural, some of which might more appropriately have been named for the phonograph"[40]); but as Suárez has shown, they add up to a colossal, impersonal, politically radical *Bildungsroman* for the anonymous citizenry of a media century.[41] The trilogy's vast construction of textuality, a Frankenstein's monster of discordant, incompatible, and postliterary language games, stitched together with flagrantly visible seams, conveys an immense charge of cultural energy – as if Dos Passos had exposed the pages of his chef d'oeuvre to the radiation of media energy all around it, allowing his prose to soak it up and mutate at the level of its DNA.

NOTES

1. Friedrich Kittler, *Gramophone, Film, Typewriter*, trans. Geoffrey Winthrop-Young and Michael Wutz (Stanford, CA: Stanford University Press, 1999), 4.
2. For more on this line of approach to U.S. literature, see Joseph Tabbi and Michael Wutz, eds., *Reading Matters: Narrative in the New Media Ecology* (Ithaca, NY: Cornell University Press, 1997); Michael Wutz, *Enduring Words: Literary Narrative in Changing Media Ecology* (Tuscaloosa: University of Alabama Press, 2009); Mark Goble, *Beautiful Circuits: Modernism and the Mediated Life* (New York: Columbia University Press, 2010); and Paul Gilmore, *Aesthetic Materialism: Electricity and American Romanticism* (Stanford, CA: Stanford University Press, 2009).
3. Walter Benjamin, *One-Way Street and Other Writings*, trans. Edmund Jephcott and Kingsley Shorter (New York: Verso, 1985), 62.
4. Jack London, *The Iron Heel* (c. 1908; London: Penguin, 2006), 51.
5. Gertrude Stein, *The Making of Americans* (1925; Champaign: Dalkey Archive Press, 1995), 925.
6. Gertrude Stein, "Portraits and Repetition," in *Gertrude Stein: Writings 1934–1946* (New York: The Library of America, 1998), 294–295.
7. See above all Charles Fenton, *The Apprenticeship of Ernest Hemingway* (New York: Farrar, Strauss and Young, 1954).
8. Ronald Weber, *Hemingway's Art of Non-Fiction* (London: Macmillan, 1990), esp. 20–30.
9. For more on this, see Julian Murphet, *Multimedia Modernism: Anglo-American Modernism and the Literary Avant-Garde* (Cambridge: Cambridge University Press, 2009).
10. Stanley Aronowitz, *Dead Artists, Live Theories* (London: Routledge, 1994), 56.
11. Benjamin, *One-Way Street*, 89.
12. Kittler, *Gramophone, Film, Typewriter*, 155.
13. Ernest Hemingway, *A Farewell to Arms* (1929; London: Vintage, 1999), 128.
14. Henry James, *The Portrait of a Lady*, ed. Robert D. Bamberg, Norton Critical Edition, 2nd ed. (1881/1908; New York: Norton, 1995), 193.
15. See Alex Woloch, *The One vs. the Many: Minor Characters and the Space of the Protagonist in the Novel* (Princeton, NJ: Princeton University Press, 2003).
16. Dashiell Hammett, *Complete Novels* (New York: Library of America, 1999), 144.

17. Horace McCoy, *They Shoot Horses, Don't They?* in *Crime Novels: American Noir of the 1930s and 40s*, ed. Robert Polito (1935; New York: Library of America, 1997), 144.

18. Jeffrey Sconce, *Haunted Media: Electronic Presence from Telegraphy to Television* (Durham: Duke University Press, 2000), 64.

19. Fredric Jameson, "The Synoptic Chandler," in Joan Copjec, ed., *Shades of Noir* (New York: Verso, 1993), 36.

20. Raymond Chandler, *Trouble Is My Business*, Kindle edition (1939; London: Hamish Hamilton, 2013), loc 377 of 3487.

21. Chandler, *The Long Goodbye*, in *Three Novels* (1953; London: Penguin, 1993), 167.

22. Chandler, *The Long Goodbye*, 250.

23. Chandler, *The High Window*, in *The Lady in the Lake and Other Novels* (1942; London: Penguin, 2001), 126.

24. Chandler, *The Long Goodbye*, 443.

25. Benjamin, "The Work of Art in the Age of Its Technological Reproducibility," second version, in *The Work of Art in the Age of Its Technological Reproducibility, and Other Writings on Media*, eds. Michael W. Jennings, Brigid Doherty, and Thomas Y. Levin, trans. Edmund Jephcott et al. (Cambridge: Harvard University Press, 2008), 38.

26. Nathanael West, *Novels and Other Writings* (New York: Library of America, 1997), 87.

27. West, *Novels*, 283.

28. Anita Loos, *Gentlemen Prefer Blondes* and *But Gentlemen Marry Brunettes* (1925, 1928; London: Penguin, 1998), 78.

29. The list includes F. Scott Fitzgerald, Nathanael West, Dorothy Parker, Raymond Chandler, John Steinbeck, Anzia Yezierska, and William Faulkner.

30. F. Scott Fitzgerald, *The Crack-Up with Other Pieces and Stories* (1945; London: Penguin, 1965), 49.

31. F. Scott Fitzgerald, *This Side of Paradise* (1920; London: Penguin), 37.

32. F. Scott Fitzgerald, *The Great Gatsby* (1925; London: David Campbell, 1991), 5.

33. Michael North, *Camera Works: Photography and the Twentieth-Century Word* (New York: Oxford University Press, 2005), 112.

34. F. Scott Fitzgerald, *The Love of the Last Tycoon: A Western*, ed. Matthew J. Bruccoli (1941; Cambridge: Cambridge University Press, 1993), 113.

35. See John T. Matthews, *William Faulkner: Seeing through the South* (Oxford: Wiley-Blackwell, 2009); Peter Lurie, *Vision's Immanence: Faulkner, Film, and the Poplar Imagination* (Baltimore: Johns Hopkins University Press, 2004); Peter Lurie and Ann J. Abadie, eds., *Faulkner and Film: Faulkner and Yoknapatawpha 2010* (Jackson: University of Mississippi Press, 2014).

36. William Faulkner, *Sanctuary*, in *Novels 1930–1935* (1931; New York: Library of America, 1985), 181.

37. Faulkner, *As I Lay Dying*, in *Novels 1930–1935*, 177.

38. Juan A. Suárez, *Pop Modernism: Noise and the Reinvention of the Everyday* (Urbana: University of Illinois Press, 2007), 82.

39. John Dos Passos, *Manhattan Transfer* (1925; London: Penguin, 1986), 288.

40. North, *Camera Works*, 145.

41. Suárez, *Pop Modernism*, 80–115.

14

GAYLE ROGERS

American Modernisms in the World

A field that was viewed as too belated, derivative, and provincial even to merit its own Library of Congress subject heading until the publication of Hugh Kenner's *A Homemade World* (1975), American modernism is now studied in an astounding array of international contexts that its authors inhabited and theorized: transatlantic, black Atlantic, and transpacific; hemispheric, pan-Caribbean, postslavery, and plantation; borderlands; ethnic, immigrant, multilingual, and diasporic (African, Arabic, Middle Eastern, Jewish).[1] Global currents famously flowed through the New York arts scene, in Harlem and in Greenwich Village alike, and suffused literature, art, film, and magazines. This suffusing was so pervasive that even a "prairie" novel such as Willa Cather's *My Ántonia* (1918), far removed from modernism's metropolitan-based formal experiments, intimately links the immigrant experience in the U.S. heartland to harrowing Old World violence in Russia – through a subplot conveyed in a language the male protagonist cannot understand. American modernist novels appear to be "global" in most every way, full of foreign settings, plots, languages, and characters, and often written by expatriates or by foreign-born nationals within the United States. They frequently engage the roles of imperialism and colonialism, transnational and multilingual cultures, and exile and displacement in creating what was understood to be a distinctly "modern" mode of experience.

But to understand the novel in the contexts of such a brave new world, we must recognize first that the elements that constituted "the United States," "America," and "the world" were changing in mutually dynamic – and often bloody – ways. This was visible in sites such as the American West and the Philippines; in the protracted debates among nativists, pluralists, assimilationists, expansionists, isolationists, and others; and in pithy observations such as John Dos Passos's line on the Sacco and Vanzetti trial: "all right we are two nations."[2] "The novel" was changing rapidly too, and the narrative experiments that were isolated as "modernist" rose amid both European and

American imperialism and large-scale decolonization movements. Scholars of modernism, on the one hand, have studied the novel extensively, but traditionally in sites and languages associated with European empires. The seminal works of postcolonial modernist criticism, such as those by Fredric Jameson, Raymond Williams, and Edward Said, read modernism's "international style," fragmented forms, and tropes of "unknowability" through Euro-imperial histories. On the other hand, Donald Pease, Amy Kaplan, and John Carlos Rowe have noted that for decades academics hardly or reluctantly acknowledged that America was an imperialist nation at all, thus leaving a hole in our analysis of American modernism beyond its conventional boundaries.[3]

The "transnational turn" in American studies away from exceptionalist and essentialist models helped retheorize modernism, productively complicating Alfred Kazin's observation in 1942 that the American modernists could not stop writing about the American world they desperately tried to escape.[4] It has also brought into greater focus the works of writers who, for reasons such as race, citizenship, or ideology, did not fit (and, in fact, often threatened) the Cold War–era model of American studies. Much of this scholarship, however, has concentrated on cultural politics and critiques, poetic form, subjectivities and identities, and border crossings.[5] To some degree, these valuable elements are inseparable from novelistic form, but the worldly life of the American modernist novel extends beyond such topics and categories. Nor can we simply follow the paths of U.S. empire in this moment in order to trace a "transnational America," as that would replicate the process of territorial acquisition itself. If John Higham's claim about modernism – "Americans rebelled by extending the breadth of experiences, Europeans by plumbing its depths" – has some truth to it, we must account for this "breadth" with a critical lens that understands geographies as never constructed neutrally.[6]

Scholars including Brent Hayes Edwards, Laura Doyle, and Paul Giles, to name a few, have resituated American modernism in multinational, multilingual contexts without reifying its Americanness. Building on Houston Baker's and Paul Gilroy's work, Edwards traces the expansive international contacts and translational exchanges among black intellectuals and writers of the African diaspora in the twentieth century.[7] Doyle reads the American modernist novel in a transatlantic, imperial, and transhistorical context in which "a whole fleet of modernist protagonists arrive, after a seaside launching toward freedom, at [a] dead end in the story of desire, race, and liberty" that her study delineates.[8] Giles denaturalizes and deterritorializes the American nation in part by showing similarities between the internationalism of prenational and contemporary American literatures, and by noting that the "lineaments of US national identity were shaped and consolidated by three wars over a span of eighty years" (the Civil War and the two world wars) rather than in a singular line traceable from the Puritans to the present.[9] We could explore other connections too, such as Susan Hegeman's call to take "seriously the centrality of the ideology of *Americanism* to modernist theory and practice. For intellectuals from Italy to Russia to Japan, 'America' was taken to be synonymous with the massified modernity that presented such an object of combined horror and fascination," and with the international struggles for humanitarian justice.[10] Said's concept of Orientalism also has critical purchase in analyzing the confrontations with fractured modern life through the figure of the Other that appear in a range of American modernist novels, from Pearl S. Buck's *The Good Earth* (1931) to Native American novelist-activist D'Arcy McNickle's *The Surrounded* (1936).

I propose here a different way of exploring dialectically one of the major contributions of the U.S. modernist novel: its multivalent "new internationalism," as Alain Locke wrote, that stood at the nexus of an unprecedented convergence of historical forces.[11] Few American modernists celebrated uncritically their country's empire or its rank as the new global capital of technological modernity (and, increasingly, finance). Rather, they invested themselves complexly in empire: the global mobility, disorienting critiques, and new idioms that empire enabled were essential to their work, and so were the often anti-imperial, sometimes anti-American movements such as black internationalism, international socialism, and the battles for women's rights, sexual freedoms, and queer identities. The desire to make a contingently constructed "American" space a node in these overlapping global networks that did not ingrain the patterns of empire led modernist novelists to look contrastingly to the Old World of Europe, with its familiar sites and its forgotten corners, to the classical world of Greece, to contemporary and ancient Africa, to Mexico, the Caribbean, South America, and Asia, and beyond. In the process, modernists negotiated what it meant to be part of America in a world in which it was, for the first time, an exporter of new literatures and a global cultural force. No American writer won a Nobel Prize, for instance, until 1930, while three won between 1930 and 1938: Sinclair Lewis, Eugene O'Neill, and Buck. After World War II, American novelists found themselves recruited and their works disseminated as part of the U.S. state's goodwill or propagandistic efforts. At present, *The Great Gatsby* (1925) exists in translation in nearly forty languages and is cited by leading contemporary vanguard writers in Latin America as their model for "writing for translation," throwing into relief the double edge of the emerging U.S. globalization that many modernists resisted.[12]

To unpack that process from several angles, this essay proceeds in two parts: First, I survey three famous movements – black American modernism, the Lost Generation, and women's writing – and account for the global factors that informed their modes of literary "globalism," which were variously politicized, alliance-based, expatriate, and cosmopolitan, diasporic, and popular. The second half of this essay is a brief analysis of a figure whose internationalism has been seen freshly in recent years: William Faulkner. I follow the works of his Latin American translators and commentators, including Jorge Luis Borges, several Boom novelists, and the Martinican intellectual and writer Édouard Glissant, in order to integrate them with approaches to Faulkner in new southern and hemispheric studies, as articulated primarily in Anglophone U.S. academies. By examining the ways in which Faulkner, as both regionalist social commentator and arch-formalist mythopoetic creator, traveled farther south, we can flesh out the contingency and malleability of the American modernist novel as it was received, adapted, contested, and transformed beyond the apparently familiar linguistic and national borders of its production.

Modernist Movements, Global Exchanges

American modernism arose in a moment when internationalism itself was under attack. A powerful nativist movement pressed for the United States to be a monolingual English state, as Theodore Roosevelt urged. French was banned in Louisiana, and bilingual schools were shut down around the country, immigrant languages were suppressed, and translations were sometimes illegal to send through the mail. For many Anglophone writers who rebelled against this movement and reshaped English around collisions with foreign tongues, Paris was a critical locale, but it was not simply a liberated counterpoint to the Puritan United States. It was a place where individuals and media networks converged, where influential figures such as Jean-Paul Sartre promoted the works of Faulkner, Dos Passos, and Richard Wright, and where one might find a gateway to other cities and entire cultures. The pathways of translation in novels, journals, and newspapers among Paris, New York, Chicago, Moscow, Madrid, Berlin, Buenos Aires, and various sites in West Africa and the black Caribbean connected multiple literary economies. In many of the cases discussed below, modernist novelists collaborated on translations, publicized themselves and shaped their personae abroad, and worked forcefully to recast the foreign reception of images and ideas of the United States. Indeed, nearly all of these figures emerged in translation as a loose collection of voices representing an antidote to the uncultured materialism with which many Europeans especially associated U.S. culture.

Black American modernism – which extends beyond the Harlem Renaissance or African American writing alone and includes, for instance, Afro-Caribbean writers in New York – was a movement whose geographies, practices, and networks of cultural-political solidarity formed what we might call a globalism of alliances. Multiple senses of internationalism and translation are necessary to unravel the work of Zora Neale Hurston, who studied under the anthropologist Franz Boas and researched folklores and vernaculars in the American South across the 1920s and '30s. Hurston also traveled on a Guggenheim Fellowship to Haiti and Jamaica to study Obeah practices, and she saw multiple links between her American and Caribbean fieldwork. Her research provided material for her novel *Their Eyes Were Watching God* (1937), which she composed while in Haiti. The title of her ethnographic work, *Tell My Horse* (1938), is a translation of the Kreyòl (Haitian Creole) phrase "parlay cheval ou." Later, she created a glossary of Harlem slang, accompanied by a brief "Story in Harlem Slang" (1942), and traveled to Honduras in hopes of finding African ties to past civilizations; while there, she wrote *Seraph on the Suwanee* (1948). In Hurston's hands, modernism's oft-noted "difficulty" was forged not through recondite mythical allusions, but through vernaculars, demotic speech, and dialects translated novelistically. By contrast, Jean Toomer's collage-like work *Cane* (1923), which stretches the bounds of the category "novel" itself, was initially dismissed by some prominent critics as a provincial, regionalist portrait of a fading mode of black life in rural Georgia. Only by exploring the titular reference further – "Cane" and the international sugar trade – do we begin to notice Toomer's subtle globalism, which in turn was rooted partially in his readings of French symbolism. Toomer employs African gods and a Jewish lead character in other parts of *Cane*, and, looking forward to his studies with the worldly mystic George Gurdjieff, he suggests a line of connection to Eastern spirituality when he names a character and vignette "Carma."

For Langston Hughes, whose global thinking is perhaps captured most famously in "The Negro Speaks of Rivers" (1921), translation often was an act of leftist solidarity. His English versions of Spanish-language poets such as Nicolás Guillén and his international travels have made him a figure who exemplifies the political currents that coursed across the terrain studied by the subfield of hemispheric American studies. Hughes also translated the Haitian writer Jacques Roumain's novel *Masters of the Dew* (1944, English 1947), a now-classic text of Caribbean Marxist literature. We can juxtapose his work and his figure with those of the Jamaica-born novelist Claude McKay, who immigrated to the United States for college, then spent stretches of time in London, Russia, and France. Not only did McKay produce English-language poetry in Jamaican dialects and best-selling novels in

New York, but his essays on racism and lynching in the United States, written while he was in Russia, were actually published in Russian and then translated back into English. McKay's influences included the French Guyanese writer René Maran's novel *Batouala* (1921); later, thanks to Maran's prodding, the novelist Walter Francis White traveled to Paris to secure the translation of his own *Fire in the Flint* (1924).

Fashioning a different set of black American/European alliances were figures such as Nella Larsen, Richard Wright, and Ralph Ellison. In her semi-autobiographical novel *Quicksand* (1928), Larsen, who was born in Chicago to a Danish mother and black West Indian father, presents the story of Helga Crane, a woman who straddles and navigates the complicated worlds of racial and gendered identities in Europe, the American South, Harlem, and Chicago. Wright's influences – Proust, Tolstoy, and Dostoevsky – and his legacy were both far-reaching and global. With *Native Son* (1940), he gained fame in Europe in translation almost immediately; Frantz Fanon's "The Fact of Blackness" (1952) evinces this novel's importance to postcolonial black internationalism. Wright left the United States permanently in 1946 and became a French citizen in 1947, and his exchanges in Paris with Sartre and Albert Camus vitally informed his works, for which he also wrote accompanying notes for Francophone readers. From there, he traveled to present-day Ghana, Spain, and Indonesia, studying and lecturing on international race relations and the fate of communism during the Cold War. Ellison radically rewrote Dostoevsky's Underground Man as his unnamed narrator-protagonist in *Invisible Man* (1952). Interweaving Freudian theory, techniques from French literature, André Malraux's politics, and the existential mysticism of the Spanish philosopher Miguel de Unamuno (who also captivated Wright), Ellison crafted an international consciousness for his Invisible Man that charted a new possibility for depicting race in American prose. Jonathan Arac has brilliantly unpacked the global, cross-linguistic wordplay embedded, for example, in the novel's famous phrase "I yam what I yam."[13] Ellison also traveled and lectured abroad after World War II, including in Rome, where he was active in the postwar literary scene.

If Paris was one kind of networked site for black modernists, it was a different one for the Lost Generation, a circle congregated and headed by Gertrude Stein and including novelists such as Ernest Hemingway, F. Scott Fitzgerald, and John Dos Passos. This group's collective globalism was largely an expatriate, dislocated one. Lost Generation works, which reread American culture through foreign eyes, relied rarely on literary translations and more often on cultural defamiliarization, through which they restaged modern clashes of the Old and New Worlds. (In this way, they were also heirs to the late works and European presence of Henry James and to his laments that American arts still failed to gain a greater international reputation.) In their background, too, are works such as Sherwood Anderson's *Winesburg, Ohio* (1919), a novelesque short story cycle that bears the influences not only of Freud and of Russian novelists, but also of Anderson's own experiences in Cuba during the Spanish-American War.

Gathering a range of international techniques, Stein's novels were ground-breaking in their formal experimentation. Her interlocking stories in *Three Lives* (1909) draw on Cézanne's perspectival approach to painting by fore-grounding language as a medium, not a transparent window onto reality, through which narration cannot easily pass. Her *Tender Buttons* (1912) presents "things" – common objects in a room – in an incantatory, repetitive style that strips away familiarity and heightens the sonic experience of reading, resonating with Russian Futurist *zaum* poetry. Several of Hemingway's novels are set in Europe (and many were written abroad), and he fictionalized parts of his experiences as an ambulance driver in World War I in both *The Sun Also Rises* (1926) and *A Farewell to Arms* (1929). These novels use an array of foreign characters, foreign-language phrases, and (in the latter novel) wartime pidgins to contribute to Hemingway's well-known "iceberg" method, in which he gives the reader only a small glimpse of the action and dialogue, leaving the rest submerged. In *For Whom the Bell Tolls* (1940), he produced his most radical experiment with form and language by writing faux-archaic, estranged English dialogue filtered through Spanish (mis)translation, mimicking Spanish's syntax, rhythms, and modes of address. As he spent much time in his later life in Cuba and on safaris in Africa, Hemingway continued to cultivate his worldliness as a celebrity too.

Dos Passos, who also served as an ambulance driver in World War I, published *Manhattan Transfer* (1925), an experimental novel about the crisscrossing lives of New Yorkers (many of them immigrants) that blends Russian cinematic montage theory with Spanish and French social realist styles. He had come to know the Spanish tradition in particular when traveling in Spain in 1916, a trip that produced several important essays on and translations of leading figures of Spanish literature of the era. With his *U.S.A.* trilogy (1930–1936), Dos Passos established himself as a pioneering documentarian and commentator on the possibility of an international leftist revolution. The tensions between the Old World of Europe, especially the Europe of World War I, and the New World of America also appear frequently in Fitzgerald's novels. In his masterpiece *The Great Gatsby*, the famous final line "So we beat on, boats against the current, borne back ceaselessly into the past" refers not only to the title character's failed attempts to rewrite his history with Daisy Buchanan, but also to the American elite's disastrous desire to cling to the customs, arts, prejudices, and mythical "bloodlines" of their

European ancestors, just after Europe had undergone a cataclysmic internecine war. In Paris and just beyond the Lost Generation's circle, we also find Henry Miller. His pornographic *Tropic of Cancer* (1934), which elicited a celebrated obscenity trial, made him the American writer who adapted most fully the techniques of the continental surrealists to explore his unconscious in prose. Waldo Frank also spent much time in Spain and in South America, and his multiperspectival portrait of New York City, *City Block* (1922), is a forgotten forebear of Dos Passos' *Manhattan Transfer*.

In contrast to the Lost Generation, U.S. women novelists drew extensively on global cultures and translational practices in their experimental works in order to foster and interpret a gendered globalism. Kate Chopin was central to emergent feminist modernism and the transnational New Woman movement. Her novels, such as *The Awakening* (1899), use New Orleans' multiculturalism and her own mixed ancestry to recast the gendered American experience – indeed, to rethink whiteness and creoleness (whether French, Cajun, or Anglo-American), blackness, and mixed-race identities and womanhood together at the close of the nineteenth century. *The Awakening*'s heroine, Edna Pontellier, finds her sexuality activated not by her marriage, but by the affections of another man, Robert Lebrun, just off the coast of the Louisiana mainland on Grand Isle; because of the intensity of their passion, Robert must flee to Mexico for the majority of the novel. Furthermore, Chopin, who worked as a French-English translator when her works were too scandalous to sell robustly, was translating Guy de Maupassant while writing *The Awakening*. In a different vein, H.D. (Hilda Doolittle), known for her poetry and her translations of numerous Greek texts, authored three cycles of novels (*Magna Graeca*, *Madrigal*, and *Borderline*) that use classical Greek figures and places to refigure same-sex desire and the conflicts between masculinity and femininity in contemporary poetic production. In one of the novels, *Bid Me to Live* (written in the 1930s and '40s, unpublished until 1960), she elaborates her theory of Greek translation and its utility for the contemporary woman writer. For H.D., translation, novel-writing, and sexual politics are one practice, one assault on patriarchy and the imperialism of male authority.

Djuna Barnes' novel *Nightwood* (1936), which is both formally and topically radical, traverses the worlds of Europe's nobility and its nontraditional sexual subcultures, and American religious mores and taboos, in order to represent a vision of supranational sexual existence. As Monica Kaup has argued, Barnes also employs an "ornate, circular, obscure, and hyperbolic style" indebted to the pre-Enlightenment Baroque tradition to recuperate an "alternate modernity" before the hegemony of rationalism in Europe.[14] Barnes, who collaborated on French and German translations of her works, was influential in her own right in France. Edith Wharton, whose relationship to modernist writing was sometimes reluctant, also fashioned her late realist ironic style in Paris. Lesser-known figures belong here too: Alyse Gregory drew on her work as an arbiter of international style and taste as editor of the *Dial* when writing *King Log and Lady Lea* (1929), a novel in which lesbian desire plays a subtextual role. Anaïs Nin, one-time partner of Henry Miller in Paris, wrote a series of diaries and female erotica that drew on "deviant" sexual practices from around the world.

This survey leaves aside the modernism of the American Southwest (Willa Cather, Américo Paredes, and John Steinbeck merit attention here); numerous writers along America's shifting geographical, linguistic, and cultural borders (Carlos Bulosan, Henry Roth, Anzia Yezierska, and others); and even the internationalism of America's domestic popular culture, in which the best-selling book of 1919 was a translation of the Spanish author Vicente Blasco Ibáñez's *Four Horsemen of the Apocalypse* (*Los cuatro jinetes del Apocalipsis*, 1916). Blasco Ibáñez's novel became the basis for the early blockbuster movie starring Rudolph Valentino and even helped earn the author an honorary Doctor of Letters from George Washington University in 1920. Buck and McKay had bestsellers too, while the runaway successes of Anita Loos' comic novel of transatlantic and European travel, *Gentlemen Prefer Blondes* (1925), and the Spanish-born philosopher George Santayana's rereading of America's national mythology, *The Last Puritan* (1935), provide points of intersection between figures associated with modernism and the efforts of U.S.-based multinational institutions to capitalize on their aesthetics in popular culture. Such plans were consonant with the work of publishers such as Bennett Cerf of Random House, who popularized Joyce's *Ulysses* and organized Gertrude Stein's lecture tour of the United States in 1934, and with the attempts of several editors at Farrar, Straus and Giroux to circulate more English translations of modernist works from other countries.

Beyond Black and White: The Creole Faulkner

The case of Faulkner illuminates this multivectored worldliness. By reading him through some of his major interlocutors such as Borges, the Boom writers, and Glissant, and in the context of new U.S. southern studies, we can throw into relief the *engagements* – literary and critical – of American modernism and its foreign "lives," rather than tracking influence alone in a top-down, diffusionist manner. As the work of Deborah Cohn and others has documented extensively, Faulkner's presence in Caribbean and Spanish American literature requires us to rethink and reread the contexts of his "own little postage stamp of native soil" in Mississippi – and to ask in what ways Yoknapatawpha County was and was not an exceptional space in the Americas, not simply in the United States.[15] The "Creole Faulkner" evinces that the traditional emphasis in modernist criticism on form, myth, and method can coexist, in productive tension, with an approach to regionalisms that values global, comparative, and multilingual critique.

Historians, sociologists, and literary critics have noted that, unlike the North, the American South shares with most other parts of the world the experience of having been defeated in a war, occupied, and reconstructed both civically and culturally. By reconceiving the map of the South, one can see its multiple connections, especially before World War II, to the Caribbean, West Indian, and Central and South American worlds, dating back at least to the time of triangular trade.[16] The South was not a borderland analogous to the southwestern U.S./Mexico divide, for instance, but rather was a region, an imagined and fallen nation whose connections to its neighbors north of the Mason-Dixon line were antagonistic and oftentimes precarious. It was also a vital commercial link between the American North of factories, finance, and consumers of its products (cotton, sugar, tobacco) and the Caribbean and South American regions for which it was "the North" and an economic colonizer. These latter spheres form collectively with the American South the "plantation South," part of the international "complex," as Philip D. Curtin calls it, that provided raw materials, labor, and – despite violent policing of the borders between white and black cultures – a great deal of cultural exchange.[17] New Orleans developed its diverse, polyglot atmosphere as a slave-trading hub, a link between American cities along the Mississippi River and places such as Cuba. It was thus the site from which both jazz – the quintessential syncretistic American musical art form – and the *Plessy v. Ferguson* case (1896) arose around the same time. The city's Spanish-language journal *Mercurio* (1911–1917), with its international editorial board, remains a record of the lively and dynamic Hispanophone ambit in which the city found itself at the time. And, before he traveled to Canada to join the Royal Air Force, to Hollywood to write screenplays, or back to his native Lafayette County, Mississippi, a young William Faulkner called it home. Faulkner, who had contributed jazz-inspired drawings to a university magazine while in college, wrote and published his first two novels in New Orleans.

The pan-American contexts of the U.S. South are rendered beautifully in the opening paragraphs of Borges' short story "The Cruel Redeemer Lazarus Morell" (1935). Here, Borges begins with an expansive list of phenomena that the conquest of the New World and the importation of African slaves have spawned across the Americas, from W.C. Handy's blues to the *candombe*, from "the mythological stature of Abraham Lincoln" to "that deplorable *rumba* 'The Peanut Vendor.'" He then describes the Mississippi River as "a dark and infinite brother of the Parana, the Uruguay, the Amazon, and the Orinoco. It is a river of mulatto-hued water; more than four hundred million tons of mud, carried by that water, insult the Gulf of Mexico each year" through New Orleans.[18] For Borges, the river is an emblematic site of racial and cultural mixing that spans the Americas, over-flowing the historically recent boundaries of distinct nations and languages. Moreover, Borges wrote this story just after having translated for the Argentine journal *Sur* Langston Hughes' "I, Too" and "The Negro Speaks of Rivers," both of which resonate with his trans-American figuration of the Mississippi's real and metaphorical cultural linkages.[19] In the late 1930s, Borges wrote of Faulkner that the "peculiar world of *The Unvanquished* is of the same blood as this America and its history; it, too, is creole [*criollo*]," meaning that it has a pan-American atmosphere with an Old World cos-mopolitanism, not a nationalist or provincialist regionalism.[20] After prais-ing Faulkner in short book reviews – albeit with his typical coyness and ambivalence – he would translate Faulkner's *The Wild Palms* in 1940; this was the second and, at the time, most influential rendition of the American's work in Spanish.[21]

Borges had a large hand in fostering Faulkner's presence in the Latin American Boom. On the heels of Borges' translation came many more throughout the forties and fifties, and as critics, authors, and translators themselves had to grapple with the challenges to form, dialect, and grammar that Faulkner's works presented outside of English, they amplified his tech-niques. Indeed, some scholars have claimed that Borges' rendition of *The Wild Palms*, more than any other text, gave other Hispanophone novelists a new path beyond realism, one that used stylistic innovation as a form of internationalist social critique.[22] Gabriel García Márquez, Carlos Fuentes, Mario Vargas Llosa, José Donoso, and Julio Cortázar, among others, iden-tified to varying degrees with a number of themes in Faulkner's life and works. Coming from a defeated region, Faulkner represented a different "America" than the one of the New York–based empire, and his legacy in their writings diverges from the local and national histories that they inher-ited. They looked, as did other writers such as Juan Carlos Onetti and Juan Rulfo, to his novels' depictions of the plantation and the uneasy rise of modernization, changing social orders, neocolonialism and neofeudalism, strife in civil war, familial tragedy, grinding poverty, community decline and stagnation, and themes of death and the undead. So strong was the identifi-cation and transference that García Márquez, who constructed Macondo in *One Hundred Years of Solitude* (1967) in part by dislocating and repurpos-ing Yoknapatawpha County, wrote that not only Faulkner, but the majority of the novelists from the US South, are possessed by the demons of the Caribbean. But it was Faulkner who showed me how to decipher them. . . . Yoknapatawpha has banks on the Caribbean Sea; so in some ways, Faulkner is a writer from the Caribbean, in some ways he's a Latin American writer.[23]

Such identifications proliferated: for Fuentes, Faulkner is "both yours [the U.S. South's] and ours," while for Vargas Llosa, "the world of Faulkner was not his, in effect. It was ours. . . . He wrote in English, but he was one of us."[24]

Like the Boom writers would, Faulkner found international success in a version of modernist regionalism that turned "minor" spaces into global ones not by way of social or literary realism, but by channeling myth, allusions, cyclical or disrupted temporalities and narratives, multiple perspectives, technical experimentation, and more through an overlooked locale. García Márquez's Macondo and Derek Walcott's St. Lucia follow this model that Pascale Casanova argues originated in Joyce's Dublin – a model that brings peripheries to the center and forges arguments for literary autonomy that are not tied to realist depictions of impoverished local spaces.[25] But rather than separating Boom fiction from the social conditions of its origins, an understanding of Faulkner's presence in its formation deepens our knowledge of its translingual nature, which was conceived in a generative process of production and consumption. That is, the marriage between Faulkner and writers to the south of the United States was not simple and harmonious. The Boom writers, for instance, were primarily leftists, far from Faulkner's conservative stubbornness toward desegregation. He may seem an unlikely figure around which they constructed their literary politics, then, but their Faulkner – unlike the Faulkner of many African American or white southern writers – embodies a different fusion of form and critique; indeed, the transgressions of racial boundaries that figure prominently in his plots were hardly transgressions in societies where *mestizaje* is often the norm.

Similarly, the lines of Faulkner's legacy, influence, and contestation in the works of Caribbean authors in several languages are deep and entwined. The best-known case is that of Édouard Glissant, whose dialogues with Faulkner's works span his career. Glissant, whose conception of *créolité* revised the universalism of the *Négritude* movement to account for the fragmented histories and geographies of the Caribbean, saw in Faulkner a decentering of narrative authority, a focus on rootlessness over linearity, and a rejection of "sacred filiation." Thus, for him, the American South was "'an incalculable border' of Caribbean island consciousness," and the Mississippi River was a perfect emblem of a contorted, overflowing, multidirectional body of water that feeds into many other rhizomatic tributaries.[26] Echoing Borges, Glissant, in his creative study *Faulkner, Mississippi* (1996), calls the

Mississippi the "mythic river, Chateaubriand's exotic Meschacébé, ... the Deep River of Southern Blacks. The grand Old Man, site and booty for so many battles in the War of Secession, a channel of life and death leading from the continent's Nordic heart to its Creole delta."[27] Scraping across the sedimented layers of southern history, he finds through Faulkner's life and work, and throughout present-day Mississippi, the traces and signs of Caribbeanness and créolité across an American South still dynamically forming. Barbara Ladd writes that Glissant's Faulkner "has more in common with the writers of the Plantation/Postplantation America than with writers of the US at large, more in common with Alejo Carpentier and Jacques Roumain than with Hemingway and Fitzgerald."[28] Other Caribbean writers who take up Faulkner's works directly or indirectly range from Wilson Harris, Maryse Condé, Vincent Placoly, and Aimé Césaire to Michelle Cliff, Edwidge Danticat, Marie Vieux-Chauvet, and Patricia Powell.

These insights and contestations allow us to reinvestigate the history and signification of the Caribbean-South nexus in Faulkner's *Absalom, Absalom!* (1936). In this novel, Thomas Sutpen, born to a poor Scots-Irish family in western Virginia, recalls the moment when he realized that if he wanted to become wealthy, he first had to travel to the "West Indies." There, he works as a plantation overseer and brutally puts down a black revolt, then marries Eulalia Bon, a mixed-race French creole daughter of a plantation owner (though her "blood" is initially unknown to Sutpen). Their son, Charles Bon, is born in Haiti and reared, tellingly, in New Orleans. The "demon" Sutpen then designs his own miniature empire translated to Mississippi: Sutpen's Hundred, plotted on land he "took from a tribe of ignorant Indians" with a "Spanish coin."[29] To assist him, he lures a French architect away from Martinique and holds captive for two years this "small, alertly resigned man with a grim, harried Latin face, in a frock coat and a flowered waistcoat and a hat which would have created no furore on a Paris boulevard," forcing him to collaborate on his ill-fated enterprise (26). Sutpen also speaks with his slaves in what the local whites mistake as a "sort of French" and fail to realize is a "dark and fatal tongue of [the Haitians'] own" – presumably, Kreyòl (27). All of these details underscore the "global" South that Sutpen incorporates in a paradoxical effort to create a racially "pure" Confederate dynasty.

Thus, after abandoning his "tainted" wife and neglecting Charles, Sutpen marries a white woman in Mississippi, with whom he has two children, Henry and Judith. This attempt to occlude and suppress his own mixed past (his Irish blood keeps him from being fully "Anglo-Saxon") ultimately fails: Charles returns and wants to marry Judith, Sutpen's daughter and Charles' half-sister (unbeknownst to him). When Charles threatens his

half-brother Henry – *"I'm the nigger that's going to sleep with your sister.
Unless you stop me"* – Henry kills the racially "impure" Charles (286; italics
in original). Sutpen's desperate hope to preserve his dynasty is embodied by
the survivors of his line whom he disavows, such as Clytie (his daughter by a
slave woman); he also impregnates a poor fifteen-year-old white girl. Years
later, he is killed, Sutpen's Hundred is burned by the last of his cast-off heirs,
and only his black great-grandson Jim Bond, "the scion, the last of his race,"
described as an "idiot negro," remains (300, 301).

Thus, when miscegenation infiltrates and ruins the whiteness of Sutpen's
imagined empire and lineage, it enters first through a remote Caribbean
corner of the South and then through the gateway of New Orleans. But
geography and history cannot provide all of the answers we might seek to
understand Sutpen's project: that is, we should not look too closely for an
actual "Haiti" in the novel. Instead, as critics have pointed out, Faulkner's
Haiti is anachronistic: since slavery was abolished in 1794, John T.
Matthews points out, "no white French sugar planters remained on Haiti
in 1827," when Sutpen would have arrived.[30] Walter Benn Michaels asserts
that Faulkner thus constructs Haiti, through Sutpen's confusion at the mis-
alignment of race and power that he expected in the Caribbean, as a "place
where blacks are enslaved. . . . and at the same time free (hence the mother of
Charles)" – that is, his Haiti "retrofit[s] the free to the slave, . . . which retrofits
the social configurations of Jim Crow to the plantation."[31] If we look instead,
as Valérie Loichot suggests, for the symbolic, mythic, and coded place of Haiti/
"Haiti" in the novel, we find that "Sutpen's burned skin, the wild men's mud
covering, the French architect's fancy wardrobe, Eulalia Bon's elusive figure,
and Charles Bon's composite self bring to the surface of the novel a buried or
repressed Caribbean, otherwise skewed or evacuated from geographical
representations."[32] Furthermore, Faulkner employs a common stereotype in
which Haiti stands in for darkness, voodoo, and the Caribbean's only fully
successful slave revolt, while Martinique was the cultured "Paris of the
Antilles." And Faulkner was writing in the wake of a U.S. military occupation
of Haiti (1914–1934), when some Americans, like many Confederate southerners had a century before, were eyeing Haiti (like Cuba) as a province ripe
for natural and economic exploitation.

The duality encoded in "Haiti" as a possible site of both degeneration and
regeneration, possession and dispossession, in *Absalom, Absalom!* is borne
out most fully when we read the novel skeptically from its own historical and
imagined "Souths." That is, the translations, revisions, and critiques of
Faulkner's fiction that issued from the "Creole" Americas point to créolité
and mestizaje, doomed patriarchy, and sociopolitical upheavals from
below – Thomas Sutpen's greatest fears – as beginnings, rather than ends,

in New World contexts. This notion of creoleness, which was apparent and adaptable to Borges and others but was obscured for decades in academic criticism in the Anglophone United States, extricates a reading of the novel from Sutpen's (and largely, Faulkner's) vision of history through a Euro-American Hegelian lens: it forecasts Charles Bon and Jim Bond as possible figures of regeneration. The possibility that this novel narrates the fall of the entire "plantation South" is both within and beyond the sphere of thought created by the novel's two principal storytellers, the Mississippian Quentin Compson and the Canadian Shreve McCannon, in their dorm room at Harvard. Haiti, for them, is "the halfway point between what we call the jungle and what we call civilization, [... with] a soil manured with black blood from two hundred years of oppression and exploitation until it sprang with an incredible paradox of peaceful greenery and crimson flowers and sugar cane" (202). Shreve posits a future in which "in time the Jim Bonds are going to conquer the western hemisphere. Of course it wont be in our time and of course as they spread toward the poles they will bleach out again like the rabbits and the birds do, so they wont show up sharp against the snow. But it will still be Jim Bond; and so in a few thousand years, I who regard you will also have sprung from the loins of African kings."[33] But where Shreve's vision is a near-empty, exoticized, racialized fantasy of places such as "Porto Rico [*sic*] or Haiti or wherever it was we all came from but none of us ever lived in," Faulkner's interlocutors who *have* lived in such places have seen the ways in which the razing of Sutpen's Hundred symbolically reemplaced the South in its supranational, hemispheric, and multiracial environs (239). Here, we can denaturalize the imprint of Yoknapatawpha and see it, like Dublin, Macondo, and Haiti, as both a real place with a history of exploitation, racial tension, and unending series of destructions and reconstructions, and a modernist space of mythical, symbolic resonance through which Faulkner weaves his plot. Seeing Yoknapatawpha as an unoriginal *literary* creation also reminds us that Faulkner borrowed heavily in creating this very novel. While he rounds out his myth-making by allegorizing the novel through the Biblical the story of Absalom – David's rebellious, fratricidal, wayward son who returned to fight his father, only to be killed by David's general, Joab – he silently takes large swaths of the plot from George Cable's *The Grandissimes: A Story of Creole Life* (1880).

Old Americas, New Maps

Absalom, Absalom! as an influentially "global" American modernist novel, thus alternately offers and obscures several new maps and routes of exchange. Quentin and Shreve, in fact, do not see in their own hemispheric commonality the "geographical transubstantiation" of "that Continental Trough" traversed by the Mississippi River, the "geologic umbilical" of the "spiritual lives of the beings within its scope" (208). Other lost experiences beneath this Continental Trough and beneath Yoknapatawpha's map include those of the indigenous peoples in the Americas, by which we might comparatively link the Native Americans that figure into Faulkner's works – often in historically inaccurate ways, and in caricature – to depictions of Caribs of the Lesser Antilles in the works of a number of other modernist writers. Another map might view the U.S. South not as it had been consolidated by the time of Faulkner's settings, but through the history of Mississippi's original European conquest, which came in the explorations of Hernando de Soto. Which is to say, Mississippi was, like Mexico, like Peru, like Argentina, and like Hispaniola, once a Spanish territory. The Spanish Americas of the distant past map imperfectly but provocatively onto modernist locales.

This mode of postcolonial or global approach to the U.S. South and to Faulkner also raises numerous questions that we can ask when thinking of American modernism. Are we imagining slave-holding plantation owners with a great deal of power as colonial subjects? Do we risk reinscribing a form of colonial domination by emplacing the South in new geographical ambits reaching to *its* south? Do we diminish the Global South – which refers primarily to African, Asian, and Central and South American countries – by suggesting its commonalities with a particular region in a First World empire and a southern, white, male author who had his own imperialist tendencies? What cultural politics were articulated in various Spanish, French, Portuguese, and other translations of Faulkner that might have resisted or redirected these very questions? And how do we read the tense relationships between modernists and state-sponsored diplomacy such as the Good Neighbor program (Frank went to Latin America) or the use of authors as goodwill ambassadors (Faulkner would later go to South America)? Striking a delicate balance among these concerns is at the core of the questions many scholars of American literature, taking their cues from critiques developed in spaces both affected by and beyond the reach of their country's empire, now ask across a range of fields and temporalities.

NOTES

I am grateful to Wai Chee Dimock, Benjy Kahan, John T. Matthews, and Imani Owens for their comments on drafts of this essay, and to Jonathan Arac, Daniel Balderston, and María Julia Rossi for our exchanges on the topic.

1. See David Ball, "Revisiting the New: Recent Fault Lines in American Modernist Criticism," *College Literature* 37, no. 3 (Summer 2010): 185.

2. John Dos Passos, *The Big Money* (1936; New York: Houghton Mifflin, 2000), 371.

3. See *Cultures of United States Imperialism*, eds. Amy Kaplan and Donald E. Pease (Durham: Duke University Press, 1993).

4. See Alfred Kazin, *On Native Grounds: An Interpretation of Modern American Prose Literature* (1942; San Diego: Harvest, 1995), xxiii. For an overview and critique of this subfield, see Donald E. Pease, "Introduction: Re-Mapping the Transnational Turn," in *Re-Framing the Transnational Turn in American Studies*, eds. Winfried Fluck, Donald E. Pease, and John Carlos Rowe (Hanover, NH: Dartmouth College Press, 2011), 1–46.

5. Peter Hays' "Modernism and the American Novel," for instance, actually spends nearly as much time discussing poetry as prose (*A Companion to the American Novel*, ed. Alfred Bendixen [Malden, MA: Blackwell, 2012], 60–75). See also Bendixen's essay in the same volume, "Beyond Modernism: The American Novel Between the World Wars," 76–89.

6. John Higham, "The Reorientation of American Culture in the 1890s," in Higham et al., *The Origins of Modern Consciousness*, ed. and intro. John Weiss (Detroit, MI: Wayne State University Press, 1965), 47.

7. See Brent Hayes Edwards, *The Practice of Diaspora: Literature, Translation, and the Rise of Black Internationalism* (Cambridge, MA: Harvard University Press, 2003).

8. Laura Doyle, *Freedom's Empire: Race and the Rise of the Novel in Atlantic Modernity, 1640–1940* (Durham: Duke University Press, 2008), 394.

9. Paul Giles, *The Global Remapping of American Literature* (Princeton, NJ: Princeton University Press, 2011), 11.

10. Susan Hegeman, *Patterns for America: Modernism and the Concept of Culture* (Princeton, NJ: Princeton University Press, 1999), 21; italics in original.

11. Alain Locke, "The New Negro," in *The New Negro*, ed. Locke, intro. Arnold Rampersad (New York: Simon & Schuster, 1992), 14–15.

12. Raquel Garzón, "Letras en vuelo libre," *El País*, July 31, 2013: http://cultura.elpais.com/cultura/2013/07/31/actualidad/1375288159_941224.html

13. See Jonathan Arac, "Global and Babel: Language and Planet in American Literature," in *Shades of the Planet: American Literature as World Literature*, eds. Wai Chee Dimock and Lawrence Buell (Princeton, NJ: Princeton University Press, 2007), 19–38.

14. See Monika Kaup, "The Neobaroque in Djuna Barnes," *Modernism/modernity* 12, no. 1 (2005): 85–100.

15. See also Tanya Fayen, *In Search of the Latin American Faulkner* (Lanham, MD: University Press of America, 1995). For Cohn, see notes 20, 22–24, and 26.

16. It is worth noting that all of these regional terms – and the more broad-reaching term "Latin America" – are debated and contested for their historical accuracy and lines of inclusion/exclusion. See Michel Gobat, "The Invention of Latin America: A Transnational History of Anti-Imperialism, Democracy, and Race," *American Historical Review* 118, no. 5 (December 2013): 1345–1375.

17. Philip D. Curtin, *The Rise and Fall of the Plantation Complex: Essays in Atlantic History* (Cambridge: Cambridge University Press, 1990).

18. Jorge Luis Borges, "The Cruel Redeemer Lazarus Morell," in *A Universal History of Iniquity*, trans. Andrew Hurley (New York: Penguin, 2004), 7, 8; translation modified.

19. See Vera M. Kutzinski, *The Worlds of Langston Hughes: Modernism and Translation in the Americas* (Ithaca, NY: Cornell University Press, 2012), 106–111.
20. Qtd. in Deborah Cohn, *History and Memory in the Two Souths: Recent Southern and Spanish American Fiction* (Nashville, TN: Vanderbilt University Press, 1999), 43.
21. The Cuban writer Lino Novás Calvo translated *Sanctuary* in 1934, while the Spanish critic and translator Antonio Marichalar disseminated Faulkner's works in the *Revista de Occidente* (Madrid) throughout the 1930s. *The Wild Palms* is now known by its corrected title, *If I Forget Thee, Jerusalem* (1939).
22. See Earl Fitz, "William Faulkner, James Agee, and Brazil: The American South in Latin America's 'Other' Literature," in *Look Away!* eds. Jon Smith and Deborah Cohn, 422. The Cuban writer Lino Novás Calvo translated *Sanctuary* in 1934, while the Spanish critic and translator Antonio Marichalar disseminated Faulkner's works and figure in the *Revista de Occidente* throughout the 1930s.
23. Qtd. in Cohn, "Faulkner and Spanish America: Then and Now," in *Faulkner in the Twenty-First Century: Faulkner and Yoknapatawpha, 2000,* eds. Robert W. Hamblin and Ann J. Abadie (Jackson: University of Mississippi Press, 2003), 50.
24. Qtd. in Cohn, *History and Memory,* 2, 43.
25. See Pascale Casanova, *The World Republic of Letters,* trans. M.B. DeBevoise (Cambridge: Harvard University Press, 2004).
26. Qtd. in J. Michael Dash, "Martinique/Mississippi: Édouard Glissant and Relational Insularity," in *Look Away!* ed. Smith and Cohn, 95.
27. Édouard Glissant, *Faulkner, Mississippi,* trans. Barbara Lewis and Thomas C. Spear (New York: Farrar, Straus and Giroux, 1999), 10.
28. Barbara Barbara Ladd, "William Faulkner, Édouard Glissant, and Body in *Absalom, Absalom!* and *A Fable,*" in *Faulkner in the Twenty-First Century,* 34.
29. William Faulkner, *Absalom, Absalom!* (1936; New York: Vintage International, 1990), 10, 26; cited hereafter in text.
30. John T. Matthews, "Recalling the West Indies: From Yoknapatawpha to Haiti and Back," *American Literary History* 16, no. 2 (Summer 2004): 250.
31. Walter Benn Michaels, "*Absalom, Absalom!* The Difference between White Men and White Men," in *Faulkner in the Twenty-First Century,* 146.
32. Valérie Loichot, "Faulkner's Caribbean Geographies in *Absalom, Absalom!*" in *Faulkner's Geographies: Faulkner and Yoknapatawpha, 2011,* eds. Jay Watson and Ann J. Abadie (Jackson: University Press of Mississippi, 2015), 4.
33. Faulkner, *Absalom, Absalom!* 302; see Ladd, "William Faulkner," in *Faulkner in the Twenty-First Century,* 40.

FURTHER READING

Regionalism in American Modernism

Brooker, Peter and Andrew Thacker, eds. *Geographies of Modernism: Literatures, Cultures, Spaces*. Abingdon: Routledge, 2005.

Cappetti, Carla. *Writing Chicago: Modernism, Ethnography, and the Novel*. New York: Columbia University Press, 1993.

Dorman, Robert L. *Revolt of the Provinces: The Regionalist Movement in America, 1920–1945*. Chapel Hill: University of North Carolina Press, 2003.

Duck, Leigh Anne. *The Nation's Region: Southern Modernism, Segregation, and U.S. Nationalism*. Athens: University of Georgia Press, 2006.

Farland, Maria. "Modernist Versions of Pastoral: Poetic Inspiration, Scientific Expertise, and the 'Degenerate' Farmer." *American Literary History* 19, no. 4 (2007): 905–36.

Harvey, David. *The Condition of Postmodernity: An Enquiry into the Origins of Cultural Change*. Oxford: Wiley-Blackwell, 1991.

Hsu, Hsuan L. *Geography and the Production of Space in Nineteenth-Century American Literature*. Cambridge: Cambridge University Press, 2010.

Smith, Neil. "Contours of a Spatialized Politics: Homeless Vehicles and the Production of Geographical Scale." *Social Text* 33 (1992): 54–81.

Thacker, Andrew. *Moving through Modernity: Space and Geography in Modernism*. New York: Manchester University Press, 2003, 8, 7.

Wyatt, David. *The Fall into Eden: Landscape and Imagination in California*. New York: Cambridge University Press, 1991.

Yaeger, Patricia, ed. *The Geography of Identity*. Ann Arbor: University of Michigan Press, 1996.

Transpacific Modernisms

Bow, Leslie. *Betrayal and Other Acts of Subversion: Feminism, Sexual Politics, Asian American Women's Literature*. Princeton, NJ: Princeton University Press, 2001.

Chan, Sucheng. *Asian Americans: An Interpretive History*. Boston: Twayne, 1991.

Cheung, King-Kok, ed. *An Interethnic Companion to Asian American Literature*. Cambridge: Cambridge University Press, 1996.

Chu, Patricia P. *Assimilating Asians: Gendered Strategies of Authorship in Asian America*. Durham: Duke University Press, 2012.

Chuh, Kandice. *Imagine Otherwise: On Asian Americanist Critique*. Durham: Duke University Press, 2003.

Cruz, Denise. *Transpacific Femininities: The Making of the Modern Filipina*. Durham: Duke University Press, 2012.

Hsu, Hsuan L. *Geography and the Production of Space in Nineteenth-Century American Literature*. Cambridge: Cambridge University Press, 2010.

Kang, Laura Hyun Yi. *Compositional Subjects: Enfiguring Asian/American Women*. Durham: Duke University Press, 2002.

Kim, Elaine. *Asian American Literature: An Introduction to the Writings and Their Social Context*. Philadelphia: Temple University Press, 1982.

Koshy, Susan. *Sexual Naturalization: Asian Americans and Miscegenation*. Stanford, CA: Stanford University Press, 2004.

Lawrence, Keith and Floyd Cheung, eds. *Recovered Legacies: Authority and Identity in Early Asian American Literature*. Philadelphia: Temple University Press, 2005.

Lee, Christopher. *The Semblance of Identity: Aesthetic Mediation in Asian American Literature*. Stanford, CA: Stanford University Press, 2012.

Lee, Julia. *Interracial Encounters: Reciprocal Representations in African and Asian American Literatures, 1896–1973*. New York: New York University Press, 2011.

Lee, Rachel C. *The Americas of Asian American Literature: Gendered Fictions of Nation and Transnation*. Princeton, NJ: Princeton University Press, 1999.

Lee, Yoon Sun. *Modern Minority: Asian American Literature and Everyday Life*. Oxford: Oxford University Press, 2013.

Ling, Jinqi. *Narrating Nationalisms: Ideology and Form in Asian American Literature*. New York: Oxford University Press, 1998.

Lowe, Lisa. *Immigrant Acts: On Asian American Cultural Politics*. Durham: Duke University Press, 1998.

Lye, Colleen. *America's Asia: Racial Form and American Literature, 1893–1945*. Princeton: Princeton University Press, 2005.

Marchetti, Gina. *Romance and the Yellow Peril*. Berkeley: University of California Press, 1993.

Ngai, Mae M. *Impossible Subjects: Illegal Aliens and the Making of Modern America*. Princeton, NJ: Princeton University Press, 2004.

Nguyen, Viet Thanh. *Race and Resistance: Literature and Politics in Asian America*. New York: Oxford University Press, 2002.

Palumbo-Liu, David. *Asian/American: Historical Crossings of a Racial Frontier*. Stanford, CA: Stanford University Press, 1999.

"Theory and the Subject of Asian America Studies." *Amerasia Journal* 21, nos. 1&2 (1995): 55–65.

Park, Josephine. *Apparitions of Asia: Modernist Form and Asian American Poetics*. New York: Oxford University Press, 2008.

Ponce, Martin Joseph. *Beyond the Nation: Diasporic Filipino Literature and Queer Reading*. New York: New York University Press, 2012.

Wong, Sau-Ling. "Denationalization Reconsidered: Asian American Cultural Criticism at a Theoretical Crossroads." In *Postcolonial Theory and the United States: Race, Ethnicity, and Literature*, edited by Amritjit Singh and Peter Schmidt, 122–148. Jackson: University Press of Mississippi, 2000.

Reading Asian American Literature: From Necessity to Extravagance. Princeton, NJ: Princeton University Press, 1993.

Wilson, Rob. *Reimagining the American Pacific: From South Pacific to Bamboo Ridge and Beyond.* Durham: Duke University Press, 2000.

Yu, Timothy. "'The Hand of a Chinese Master': José Garcia Villa and Modernist Orientalism." *MELUS: Journal of the Society of Multiethnic Literature of the United States* 29, no. 1 (Spring 2004): 41–59.

Ethnic American Modernisms

Cowart, David. *Trailing Clouds: Immigrant Fiction in Contemporary America.* Ithaca, NY: Cornell University Press, 2006.

Dinnerstein, Leonard, Roger L. Nichols, and David M. Reimers. *Natives and Strangers: Ethnic Groups and the Building of America.* Oxford: Oxford University Press, 1990.

Dinnerstein, Leonard and David Reimers. *Ethnic Americans: A History of Immigration and Assimilation.* New York: New York University Press, 1977.

Early, Gerald, ed. *Lure and Loathing: Essays on Race, Identity, and the Ambivalence of Assimilation.* New York: Allen Lane, 1993.

Fernández-Armesto, Felipe. *Our America: A Hispanic History of the United States.* New York: Norton, 2014.

Ferraro, Thomas. *Ethnic Passages: Literary Immigrants in Twentieth-Century America,* Chicago: University of Chicago Press, 1993.

Giles, Paul. *The Global Remapping of American Literature.* Princeton, NJ: Princeton University Press, 2011.

Grice, Helena, Candida Hepworth, and Maria Lauret. *Beginning Ethnic American Literatures.* Manchester: Manchester University Press, 2001.

Lee, A. Robert. *Multicultural American Literature: Comparative Black, Native, Latino/a and American Fictions.* Mississippi: University Press of Mississippi, 2003.

Ostendorf, Berndt and Stephan Palmié. "Immigration and Ethnicity." In *Modern American Culture: An Introduction,* edited by Mick Gidley, 142–165. London: Longman, 1993.

Parrillo, Vincent. *Strangers to These Shores: Race and Ethnic Relations in the U.S.* New York: Pearson, 1980.

Pinder, Sherrow O. *American Multicultural Studies: Diversity of Race, Ethnicity, Gender and Sexuality.* London: Sage, 2012.

Saxton, Alexander. *The Rise and Fall of the White Republic.* London: Verso, 1991.

Singh, Amritjit, et al., eds. *Memory, Narrative and Identity: New Essays in Ethnic American Literatures.* Lebanon: Northeastern University Press, 1994.

Stavans, Ilan, ed. *Becoming Americans: Four Centuries of Immigrant Writing.* New York: Library of America, 2009.

Takaki, Ronald T. *From Different Shores: Perspectives on Race and Ethnicity.* Oxford: Oxford University Press, 1994.

Wald, Priscilla. *Constituting Americans: Cultural Anxiety and Narrative Form.* Durham: Duke University Press, 1995.

Waters, Mary. *Ethnic Options: Choosing Identities in America.* Berkeley: University of California Press, 1990.

The Worlds of Black American Modernism

Baldwin, Kate. *Beyond the Color Line and the Iron Curtain: Reading Encounters between Black and Red, 1922–1963*. Durham: Duke University Press, 2002.

Barrett, Lindon. *Racial Blackness and the Discontinuity of Western Modernity*, edited by Justin A. Joyce, Dwight A. McBride, and John Carlos Rowe. Urbana: University of Illinois Press, 2014.

Bell, Kevin. *Ashes Taken for Fire: Aesthetic Modernism and the Critique of Identity*. Minneapolis; London: University of Minnesota Press, 2007.

Braddock, Jeremy and Jonathan Eburne, eds. *Paris, Capital of the Black Atlantic: Literature, Modernity and Diaspora*. Baltimore: Johns Hopkins University Press, 2013.

Chandler, Nahum. *X – The Problem of the Negro as a Problem for Thought*. New York: Fordham University Press, 2014.

Glissant, Édouard. *Poetics of Relation*, translated by Betsy Wing. Ann Arbor: University of Michigan Press, 1997.

Hutchinson, George. *The Harlem Renaissance in Black and White*. Cambridge: Harvard University Press, 1996.

Jackson, Lawrence P. *The Indignant Generation: A Narrative History of African American Writers and Critics, 1934–1960*. Princeton, NJ: Princeton University Press, 2011.

JanMohamed, Abdul R. *The Death-Bound-Subject: Richard Wright's Archaeology of Death*. Durham: Duke University Press, 2005.

Judy, Ronald A.T. *(Dis)Forming the American Canon: African-Arabic Slave Narratives and the Vernacular*. Minneapolis: University of Minnesota Press, 1993.

Kelley, Robin. *Freedom Dreams: The Black Radical Imagination*. Boston: Beacon Press, 2002.

Mackey, Nathaniel. *Discrepant Engagement: Dissonance, Cross-Culturality and Experimental Writing*. Cambridge: Cambridge University Press, 1993.

Marriott, David. *Haunted Life: Visual Culture and Black Modernity*. New Brunswick; London: Rutgers University Press, 2007.

Moses, Wilson J. "The Lost World of the Negro, 1895–1919: Black Literary and Intellectual Life before the 'Renaissance.'" *Black American Literature Forum* 21, nos. 1–2 (Spring–Summer 1987): 61–84.

Moten, Fred. *In the Break: The Aesthetics of the Black Radical Tradition*. Minneapolis: University of Minnesota Press, 2003.

"The Case of Blackness." *Criticism* 50, no. 2 (2008): 177–218.

North, Michael. *The Dialect of Modernism: Race, Language and Twentieth-Century Literature*. New York: Oxford University Press, 1994.

Quijano, Aníbal. "Coloniality of Power, Eurocentrism and Latin America." *Nepantla: Views from South* 1, no. 3 (2000): 533–580.

Silva, Denise Ferreira da. *Toward a Global Idea of Race*. Minneapolis: University of Minnesota Press, 2007.

"No-bodies: Law, Raciality and Violence." *Griffith Law Review* 18, no. 2 (2009): 212–236.

Spillers, Hortense J. *Black White and in Color: Essays on American Literature and Culture*. Chicago: University of Chicago Press, 2003.

Thomas, Lorenzo. *Extraordinary Measures: Afrocentric Modernism and Twentieth Century American Poetry*. Tuscaloosa: University of Alabama Press, 2000.

Wilderson III, Frank B. *Red, White and Black: Cinema and the Structure of U.S. Antagonisms*. Durham: Duke University Press, 2010.

Wynter, Sylvia. "1492: A New World View." In *Race, Discourse and the Origin of the Americas*, edited by Vera Lawrence Hyatt and Rex Nettleford, 5–57. Washington, DC: Smithsonian Institution Press, 1995.

"Rethinking 'Aesthetics': Notes toward a Deciphering Practice." In *Ex-Iles: Essays on Caribbean Cinema*, edited by Mbye Cham, 237–272. Trenton, NJ: Africa World Press, 1992.

"On Disenchanting Discourse: 'Minority' Literary Criticism and Beyond." *Cultural Critique* 7 (Autumn 1987): 207–244.

Gender and Geomodernisms

Appadurai, Arjun. *Modernity at Large: Cultural Dimensions of Globalization*. Minneapolis: University of Minnesota Press, 1996.

Benstock, Shari. *Women of the Left Bank: Paris 1900–1940*. London: Virago, 1987.

Berman, Jessica. *Modernist Commitments: Ethics, Politics, and Transnational Modernism*. New York: Columbia University Press, 2011.

Dimock, Wai Chee. *Through Other Continents: American Literature across Deep Time*. Princeton: Princeton University Press, 2008.

Doyle, Laura. "Geomodernism, Postcoloniality, and Women's Writing." In *The Cambridge Companion to Modernist Women Writers*, edited by Maren Tova Linett, 129–145. Cambridge: Cambridge University Press, 2010.

Doyle, Laura and Laura Winkiel, eds. *Geomodernisms: Race, Modernism, Modernity*. Bloomington: Indiana University Press, 2005.

Felski, Rita. *Doing Time: Feminist Theory and Postmodern Culture*. New York: New York University Press, 2000.

Ferland, Anne E. "Women's Fiction, New Modernist Studies, and Feminism." *Modern Fiction Studies* 59, no. 2 (2013): 229–240.

Fleissner, Jennifer. "Is Feminism a Historicism?" *Tulsa Studies in Women's Literature* 21, no. 1 (2002): 45–66.

Friedman, Susan Stanford. "Planetarity: Musing Modernist Studies." *Modernism/modernity* 17, no. 3 (2010): 471–499.

Gaonkar, Dilip Parameshwar, ed. *Alternative Modernities*. Durham: Duke University Press, 2001.

Gikandi, Simon. "Modernism in the World." *Modernism/modernity* 13, no. 3 (2006): 419–424.

Levin, Harry, "What Was Modernism?" *Massachusetts Review* 1, no. 4 (1960): 119–131.

Linett, Maren Tova, ed. *The Cambridge Companion to Modernist Women Writers*. Cambridge: Cambridge University Press, 2010.

Scott, Bonnie Kime, ed. *Gender in Modernism: New Geographies, Complex Intersections*. Urbana: University of Illinois Press, 2007.

Williams, Raymond. "When Was Modernism?" In *The Politics of Modernism: Against the New Conformists*, edited by Tony Pinkney, 31–35. London: Verso, 1987.

Wollaegher, Mark with Matt Eatough, eds. *The Oxford Handbook of Global Modernisms*. Oxford: Oxford University Press, 2010.

Borderlands Modernism

Arroyo, Jossiana. "Technologies: Transculturations of Race, Gender, and Ethnicity in Arturo Schomburg's Masonic Writings." *Centro Journal* 17, no. 1 (2005): 4–25.

Capetillo, Luisa. *A Nation of Women: An Early Feminist Speaks Out*, edited by Félix Matos Rodríguez, translated by Alan West-Duran. Houston, TX: Arte Público, 2005.

Flores, Magón, Ricardo. *Dreams of Freedom*, edited by Chaz Bufe and Mitchell Cowen Verter. Oakland, CA: AK Press, 2000.

González, Jovita. *Dew on the Thorn*. Houston, TX: Arte Público, 1997.

Hoffnung-Garskof, Jesse. "The Migrations of Arturo Schomburg." *Journal of American Ethnic History* 21, no. 1 (Fall 2001): 3–49.

Lewthwaite, Stephanie. "Modernism in the Borderlands: The Life and Art of Octavio Medellín." *Pacific Historical Review* 81, no. 3 (August 2012): 337–370.

Lomas, Laura. *Translating Empire: José Martí, Migrant Latino Subjects, and American Modernities*. Durham: Duke University Press, 2009.

López, Sam. *Post-revolutionary Chicana Literature: Memoir, Folklore, and Fiction of the Border, 1900–1950*. New York: Routledge, 2007.

Mena, María Cristina. *The Collected Stories*, edited by Amy Doherty. Houston, TX: Arte Público, 1997.

Mitchell, Pablo. *West of Sex: The Making of Mexican America 1900–1930*. Chicago: University of Chicago Press, 2012.

Niggli, Josefina. *The Plays of Josefina Niggli: Recovered Landmarks of Latino Literature*, edited by William Orchard and Yolanda Padilla. Madison: University of Wisconsin Press, 2005.

Padilla, Yolanda. "Mexican Americans and the Novel of the Mexican Revolution." In *Open Borders to a Revolution: Culture, Politics, and Migration*, edited by Jaime Marroquín Arredondo, Adela Pineda, and Magdalena Mieri, 133–152. Washington, DC: Smithsonian Institute Scholarly Press, 2013.

"The Transnational National: Race, the Border, and the Immigrant Nationalism of Josefina Niggli's Mexican Village." *CR: The New Centennial Review* 9, no. 2 (Fall 2009): 45–72.

Ramos, Julio. *Divergent Modernities*, translated by John Blanco. Durham: Duke University Press, 2001.

Sánchez González, Lisa. "Modernism and Boricua Literature: A Reconsideration of Arturo Schomburg and William Carlos Williams." *American Literary History* 13, no. 2 (Summer 2001): 242–264.

Schedler, Christopher. *Border Modernism: Intercultural Readings in American Literary Modernism*. New York: Routledge, 2002.

Streeby, Shelley. *Radical Sensations: World Movements, Violence, and Visual Culture*. Durham: Duke University Press, 2013.

Venegas, Daniel. *The Adventures of Don Chipote, or When Parrots Breast-Feed*, translated by Ethriam Cash Brammer. Houston, TX: Arte Público Press, 2000.

Villegas de Magnón, Leonor. *The Rebel*. Houston, TX: Arte Público Press, 2007.

Zamora O'Shea, Elena. *El Mesquite*. 1935. College Station: Texas A&M, 2000.

Queering Modernism

Benstock, Shari. *Women of the Left Bank: Paris, 1900–1940*. Austin: University of Texas Press, 1986.

Boone, Joseph Allen. *Libidinal Currents: Sexuality and the Shaping of Modernism*. Chicago: University of Chicago Press, 1998.

Chauncey, George. *Gay New York: Gender, Urban Culture, and the Making of the Gay Male World, 1890–1940*. New York: Basic Books, 1994.

Duggan, Lisa. *Sapphic Slashers: Sex, Violence, and American Modernity*. Durham: Duke University Press, 2000.

Goldberg, Jonathan. *Willa Cather and Others*. Durham: Duke University Press, 2001.

Herring, Scott. *Queering the Underworld: Slumming, Literature, and the Undoing of Lesbian and Gay History*. Chicago: University of Chicago Press, 2007.

Lindemann, Marilee. *Willa Cather: Queering America*. New York: Columbia University Press, 1999.

Kent, Kathryn R. *Making Girls into Women: American Women's Writing and the Rise of Lesbian Identity*. Durham: Duke University Press, 2003.

Love, Heather. *Feeling Backward: Loss and the Politics of Queer History*. Cambridge: Harvard University Press, 2007.

Nealon, Christopher. *Foundlings: Lesbian and Gay Historical Emotion before Stonewall*. Durham: Duke University Press, 2001.

Ponce, Martin Joseph. *Beyond the Nation: Diasporic Filipino Literature and Queer Reading*. New York: New York University Press, 2012.

Roof, Judith. *Come as You Are: Sexuality and Narrative*. New York: Columbia University Press, 1996.

Schwartz, A. B. Christa. *Gay Voices of the Harlem Renaissance*. Bloomington: Indiana University Press, 2003.

Sedgwick, Eve Kosofsky. *Epistemology of the Closet*. Berkeley: University of California Press, 1990.

See, Sam. "'Spectacles in Color': The Primitive Drag of Langston Hughes." *PMLA* 124, no. 3 (2009): 798–816.

Sietler, Dana. *Atavistic Tendencies: The Culture of Science in American Modernity*. Minneapolis: University of Minnesota Press, 2008.

Somerville, Siobhan B. *Queering the Color Line: Race and the Invention of Sexuality in American Culture*. Durham: Duke University Press, 2000.

Stockton, Kathryn Bond. *The Queer Child, or Growing Sideways in the Twentieth Century*. Durham: Duke University Press, 2010.

Terry, Jennifer. *An American Obsession: Science, Medicine, and Homosexuality in Modern Society*. Chicago: University of Chicago Press, 1999.

Trask, Michael. *Cruising Modernism: Class and Sexuality in American Literature and Social Thought*. Ithaca, NY: Cornell University Press, 2003.

Vogel, Shane. *The Scene of Harlem Cabaret: Race, Sexuality, Performance*. Chicago: University of Chicago Press, 2009.

The Scientific Imagination of U.S. Modernist Fiction

Auerbach, Erich. *Mimesis: The Representation of Reality in Western Literature.* Princeton, NJ: Princeton University Press, 1953.

Blackwell, Stephen H. *The Quill and the Scalpel: Nabokov's Art and the Worlds of Science.* Columbus: Ohio State University Press, 2009.

Buell, Lawrence. "Faulkner and the Claims of the Natural World." In *Faulkner and the Natural World,* edited by Donald M. Kartiganer and Ann J. Abadie. Jackson: University Press of Mississippi, 1999.

Canavan, Gerry. "Science Fiction in the United States." In *The American Novel, 1870–1940,* edited by Priscilla Wald and Michael A. Elliott. Oxford: Oxford University Press, 2014.

Cokal, Susann. "Caught in the Wrong Story: Psychoanalysis and Narrative Structure in *Tender Is the Night.*" *Texas Studies in Literature and Language* 47.1 (Spring 2005): 75–100.

Fernilough, Anne. "Consciousness as a Stream." In *The Cambridge Companion to the Modernist Novel,* edited by Morag Shiach. Cambridge: Cambridge University Press, 2007.

Flesch, William. *Comeuppance: Costly Signaling, Altruistic Punishment, and Other Biological Components of Fiction.* Cambridge: Harvard University Press, 2007.

Hayles, N. Katherine. *The Cosmic Web: Scientific Field Models and Literary Strategies in the Twentieth Century.* Ithaca, NY: Cornell University Press, 1984.

Hejinian, Lyn. *The Language of Inquiry.* Berkeley: University of California Press, 2000.

Latour, Bruno. *Politics of Nature: How to Bring the Sciences into Democracy.* Cambridge: Harvard University Press, 2004.

Manganaro, Marc, ed. *Modernist Anthropologist: From Fieldwork to Text.* Princeton, NJ: Princeton University Press, 1990.

Martin, Ronald E. *American Literature and the Universe of Force.* Durham: Duke University Press, 1981.

Meyer, Steven. *Irresistible Dictation: Gertrude Stein and the Correlations of Writing and Science.* Stanford, CA: Stanford University Press, 2001.

Richardson, Joan. *A Natural History of Pragmatism: The Fact of Feeling from Jonathan Edwards to Gertrude Stein.* Cambridge: Cambridge University Press, 2007.

Richardson, Richard. *William James: In the Maelstrom of American Modernism.* Boston: Houghton Mifflin, 2006.

Ross, Dorothy, ed. *Modernist Impulses in the Human Sciences, 1870–1930.* Baltimore: Johns Hopkins University Press, 1994.

Seitler, Dana. *Atavistic Tendencies: The Culture of Science in American Modernity.* Minneapolis: University of Minnesota Press, 2008.

Stengers, Isabelle. *Thinking with Whitehead: A Free and Wild Creation of Concepts.* Cambridge: Harvard University Press, 2011.

Tamm, Eric Enno. *Beyond the Outer Shores: The Untold Odyssey of Ed Ricketts, the Pioneering Ecologist Who Inspired John Steinbeck and Joseph Campbell.* New York: Thunder's Mouth Press, 2005.

Thrailkill, Jane F. "Science, Medicine, Technology, and the Novel, 1860–1915." In *The American Novel, 1870–1940,* edited by Priscilla Wald and Michael A. Elliott. Oxford: Oxford University Press, 2014.

Trout, Steven. "Rebuilding the Outland Engine: A New Source for *The Professor's House*." *Cather Studies 6: History, Memory, and War*, edited by Steven Trout. Lincoln: University of Nebraska Press, 2006.

Vermuel, Blakey. *Why Do We Care about Literary Characters?* Baltimore: Johns Hopkins University Press, 2010.

Visual Cultures of American Modernism

Allred, Jeff. *American Modernism and Depression Documentary*. New York: Oxford University Press, 2010.

Biers, Katherine. *Virtual Modernism Writing and Technology in the Progressive Era*. Minneapolis: University of Minnesota Press, 2013.

Blair, Sara. *Harlem Crossroads: Black Writers and the Photograph in the Twentieth Century*. Princeton, NJ: Princeton University Press, 2007.

"The Photograph's Last Word: Visual Culture Studies Now." *American Literary History* 22, no. 3 (2010): 673–697.

Burrows, Stuart. *A Familiar Strangeness: American Fiction and the Language of Photography, 1839–1945*. Athens: University of Georgia Press, 2010.

Crary, Jonathan. *Suspensions of Perception: Attention, Spectacle, and Modern Culture*. Cambridge: MIT Press, 1999.

Entin, Joseph. *Sensational Modernism: Experimental Fiction and Photography in Thirties America*. Chapel Hill: University of North Carolina Press, 2007.

Finnegan, Cara A. *Picturing Poverty: Print Culture and FSA Photographs*. Washington, DC: Smithsonian Books, 2003.

Goldman, Jonathan, and Aaron Jaffe, eds. *Celebrity Star Maps: Celebrity, Modernity, Culture*. Farnham: Ashgate, 2010.

Jacobs, Karen. *The Eye's Mind: Literary Modernism and Visual Culture*. Ithaca, NY: Cornell University Press, 2001.

Jay, Martin. *Downcast Eyes: The Denigration of Vision in Twentieth-Century French Culture*. Berkeley: University of California Press, 1993.

Kalaidjian, Walter B. *American Culture between the Wars: Revisionary Modernism and Postmodern Critique*. New York: Columbia University Press, 1993.

Lears, T.J. Jackson. *Fables of Abundance: A Cultural History of Advertising in America*. New York: Basic Books, 1994.

Lurie, Peter. *Vision's Immanence: Faulkner, Film, and the Popular Imagination*. Baltimore: Johns Hopkins University Press, 2004.

Mao, Douglas. *Fateful Beauty: Aesthetic Environments, Juvenile Development, and Literature 1860–1960*. Princeton, NJ: Princeton University Press, 2008.

Marchand, Roland. *Creating the Corporate Soul: The Rise of Public Relations and Corporate Imagery in American Big Business*. Berkeley: University of California Press, 1998.

Mitchell, W.J.T. *What Do Pictures Want? The Lives and Loves of Images*. Chicago: University of Chicago Press, 2005.

North, Michael. *Camera Works: Photography and the Twentieth-Century Word*. New York: Oxford University Press, 2005.

"Visual Culture." In *The Cambridge Companion to American Modernism*, edited by Walter B. Kalaidjian, 177–194. Cambridge Companions to Literature. Cambridge: Cambridge University Press, 2005.

Saab, A. Joan. *For the Millions: American Art and Culture between the Wars.* Philadelphia: University of Pennsylvania Press, 2004.

Scholes, Robert A., and Clifford Wulfman, eds. *Modernism in the Magazines: An Introduction.* New Haven, CT: Yale University Press, 2010.

Smith, Shawn Michelle. *American Archives: Gender, Race, and Class in Visual Culture.* Princeton, NJ: Princeton University Press, 1999.

Smith, Terry. *Making the Modern: Industry, Art, and Design in America.* Chicago: University of Chicago Press, 1993.

Jazz and Blues Modernisms

Anderson, Paul Allen. *Deep River: Music and Memory in Harlem Renaissance Thought.* Durham: Duke University Press, 2001.

Batker, Carol. "'Love Me Like I Like to Be': The Sexual Politics of Hurston's *Their Eyes Were Watching God*, the Classic Blues, and the Black Women's Club Movement." *African American Review* 32, no. 2 (Summer 1998): 199–213.

Benston, Kimberly. *Performing Blackness: Enactments of African-American Modernism.* London: Routledge, 2000.

Biers, Katherine. *Virtual Modernism: Writing and Technology in the Progressive Era.* Minneapolis: University of Minnesota Press, 2013.

Brooks, Daphne A. *Bodies in Dissent: Spectacular Performances of Race and Freedom, 1850–1910.* Durham: Duke University Press, 2006.

Brown, Jayna. *Babylon Girls: Black Women Performers and the Shaping of the Modern.* Durham: Duke University Press, 2008.

Chauncey, George. *Gay New York: Gender, Urban Culture, and the Making of the Gay Male World, 1890–1940.* New York: Basic Books, 1995.

Davis, Angela Y. *Blues Legacies and Black Feminism: Gertrude "Ma" Rainey, Bessie Smith, and Billie Holiday.* New York: Vintage, 1998.

Douglas, Ann. *Terrible Honesty: Mongrel Manhattan in the 1920s.* New York: Noonday Press, 1995.

Edwards, Brent Hayes. *The Practice of Diaspora: Literature, Translation, and the Rise of Black Internationalism.* Cambridge: Harvard University Press, 2003.

Graham, T. Austin. *The Great American Songbooks: Musical Texts, Modernism, and the Value of Popular Culture.* New York: Oxford University Press, 2013.

Griffin, Farah Jasmine. *Harlem Nocturne: Women Artists and Progressive Politics during World War II.* New York: Basic Civitas, 2013.

Gussow, Adam. "'If Bessie Smith Had Killed Some White People': Racial Legacies, the Blues Revival, and the Black Arts Movement." In *New Thoughts on the Black Arts Movement*, edited by Lisa Gail Collins and Margo Natalie Crawford, 227–252. New Brunswick: Rutgers University Press, 2008.

Jacques, Geoffrey. *A Change in the Weather: Modernist Imagination, African American Imaginary.* Amherst: University of Massachusetts Press, 2009.

Mackey, Nathaniel. *Discrepant Engagement: Dissonance, Cross-Culturality, and Experimental Writing.* Tuscaloosa: University of Alabama Press, 1993.

O'Meally, Robert G., ed. *The Jazz Cadence of American Culture.* New York: Columbia University Press, 1998.

Omry, Keren. *Cross-Rhythms: Jazz Aesthetics in African-American Literature.* New York: Bloomsbury, 2009.

Pavlic, Ed. *Crossroads Modernism: Descent and Emergence in African-American Literary Culture*. Minneapolis: University of Minnesota Press, 2002.

Reed, Anthony. "'A Woman Is a Conjunction': The Ends of Improvisation in Claude McKay's Banjo: A Novel without a Plot," *Callaloo* 36.3 (Summer 2013): 758–772.

Simawe, Saadi A., ed. *Black Orpheus: Music in African American Fiction from the Harlem Renaissance to Toni Morrison*. New York: Routledge, 2000.

Smethurst, James. *The African American Roots of Modernism: From Reconstruction to the Harlem Renaissance*. Chapel Hill: University of North Carolina Press, 2011.

Vazquez, Alexandra T. *Listening in Detail: Performances of Cuban Music*. Durham: Duke University Press, 2013.

Weheliye, Alexander. *Phonographies: Grooves in Sonic Afro-Modernity*. Durham: Duke University Press, 2005.

Williams, Sherley Anne. "The Blues Roots of Contemporary Afro-American Poetry." In *Chant of Saints: A Gathering of Afro-American Literature, Art, and Scholarship*, edited by Michael S. Harper and Robert B. Stepto. Urbana: University of Illinois Press, 1979. 123–135.

Translation and the American Modernist Novel

Berman, Antoine. *L'épreuve de l'étranger: Culture et traduction dans l'Allemagne romantique*. Paris: Editions Gallimard, 1984. Translated by S. Heyvaert under the title *The Experience of the Foreign: Culture and Translation in Romantic Germany*. Albany: State University of New York Press, 1992.
La traduction et la lettre ou l'auberge du lointain. Paris: Editions du Seuil, 1999.

Crawford, Robert. *Devolving English Literature*, revised second edition. Edinburgh: Edinburgh University Press, 2000.

Dow, William. "John Dos Passos, Blaise Cendrars, and the 'Other' Modernism," *Twentieth Century Literature* 42, no. 3 (Fall 1996): 396–415.

Hart, Matthew. *Nations of Nothing But Poetry: Modernism, Transnationalism, and Synthetic Vernacular Writing*. New York: Oxford University Press, 2010.

Lennon, Brian. *In Babel's Shadow: Multilingual Literatures, Monolingual States*. Minneapolis: University of Minnesota Press, 2010.

MacCannell, Dean. *The Tourist: A New Theory of the Leisure Class*. Berkeley: University of California Press, 1999.

Michaels, Walter Benn. *Our America: Nativism, Modernism, and Pluralism*. Durham: Duke University Press, 1995.

North, Michael. *The Dialect of Modernism: Race, Language, and Twentieth-Century Literature*. New York: Oxford University Press, 1994.

Ramazani, Jahan. *A Transnational Poetics*. Chicago: University of Chicago Press, 2009.

Sallis, John. *On Translation*. Bloomington: Indiana University Press, 2002.

Schulte, Rainer and John Biguenet, eds. *Theories of Translation: An Anthology of Essays from Dryden to Derrida*. Chicago: University of Chicago Press, 1992.

Sternberg, Meir. "Polylingualism as Reality and Translation as Mimesis." *Poetics Today* 2, no. 4 (1981): 221–239.

Taylor-Batty, Juliette. *Multilingualism in Modernist Fiction*. New York: Palgrave Macmillan, 2013.

Venuti, Lawrence. *The Translator's Invisibility: A History of Translation*. London: Routledge, 1995.

Will, Barbara. *Unlikely Collaboration: Gertrude Stein, Bernard Faÿ, and the Vichy Dilemma*. New York: Columbia University Press, 2013.

Yao, Steven G. *Translation and the Languages of Modernism: Gender, Politics, Language*. New York: Palgrave Macmillan, 2002.

New Media Modernism

Gilmore, Paul. *Aesthetic Materialism: Electricity and American Romanticism*. Stanford, CA: Stanford University Press, 2009.

Gitelman, Lisa. *Scripts, Grooves, and Writing Machines: Representing Technology in the Edison Era*. Stanford, CA: Stanford University Press, 1999.

Goble, Mark. *Beautiful Circuits: Modernism and the Mediated Life*. New York: Columbia University Press, 2010.

Hayles, N. Katherine. *How We Became Posthuman: Virtual Bodies in Cybernetics, Literature and Informatics*. Chicago: University of Chicago Press, 1999.

Kittler, Friedrich. *Gramophone, Film, Typewriter*, translated by Geoffrey Winthrop-Young and Michael Wutz. Stanford, CA: Stanford University Press, 1999.

Lurie, Peter. *Vision's Immanence: Faulkner, Film, and the Poplar Imagination*. Baltimore: Johns Hopkins University Press, 2004.

Murphet, Julian. *Multimedia Modernism: Anglo-American Modernism and the Literary Avant-Garde*. Cambridge: Cambridge University Press, 2009.

North, Michael. *Camera Works: Photography and the Twentieth-Century Word*. New York: Oxford University Press, 2005.

Peters, John Durham. *Speaking into the Air: A History of the Idea of Communication*. Chicago: Chicago University Press, 1999.

Sconce, Jeffrey. *Haunted Media: Electronic Presence from Telegraphy to Television*. Durham: Duke University Press, 2000.

Stewart, Garrett. *Between Film and Screen: Modernism's Photo Synthesis*. Chicago: Chicago University Press, 1999.

Suárez, Juan A. *Pop Modernism: Noise and the Reinvention of the Everyday*. Urbana: University of Illinois Press, 2007.

Tabbi, Joseph and Michael Wutz, eds. *Reading Matters: Narrative in the New Media Ecology*. Ithaca, NY: Cornell University Press, 1997.

Trotter, David. *Literature in the First Media Age*. Cambridge: Harvard University Press, 2014.

Wutz, Michael. *Enduring Words: Literary Narrative in Changing Media Ecology*. Tuscaloosa: University of Alabama Press, 2009.

American Modernisms in the World

Chu, Patricia. *Race, Nationalism and the State in British and American Modernism*. Cambridge: Cambridge University Press, 2006.

Dash, J. Michael. *The Other America: Caribbean Literature in a New World Context*. Charlottesville: University of Virginia Press, 1998.

Dimock, Wai Chee and Lawrence Buell, eds. *Shades of the Planet: American Literature as World Literature*. Princeton, NJ: Princeton University Press, 2007.

Doyle, Laura and Laura Winkiel, eds. *Geomodernisms: Race, Modernism, and Modernity*. Bloomington: Indiana University Press, 2005.

Duck, Leigh Anne. *The Nation's Region: Southern Modernism, Segregation, and US Nationalism*. Athens: University of Georgia Press, 2006.

Edwards, Brent Hayes. *The Practice of Diaspora: Literature, Translation, and the Rise of Black Internationalism*. Cambridge: Harvard University Press, 2003.

Edwards, Brian T. and Dilip Parameshwar Gaonkar, eds. *Globalizing American Studies*. Chicago: University of Chicago Press, 2010.

Fishkin, Shelley Fisher. "Crossroads of Cultures: The Transnational Turn in American Studies – Presidential Address to the American Studies Association, November 12, 2004." *American Quarterly* 57, no. 1 (March 2005): 17–57.

Gilroy, Paul. *The Black Atlantic: Modernity and Double-Consciousness*. Cambridge: Harvard University Press, 1995.

Greeson, Jennifer Rae. *Our South: Geographic Fantasy and the Rise of National Literature*. Cambridge: Harvard University Press, 2010.

Gruesz, Kirsten Silva. *Ambassadors of Culture: The Transamerican Origins of Latino Writing*. Princeton, NJ: Princeton University Press, 2002.

Handley, George B. *Postslavery Literature in the Americas: Family Portraits in Black and White*. Charlottesville: University of Virginia Press, 2000.

Kaplan, Amy and Donald E. Pease, eds. *Cultures of United States Imperialism*. Durham: Duke University Press, 1993.

Lavender, Caroline F. and Robert S. Levine, eds. *Hemispheric American Studies*. New Brunswick: Rutgers University Press, 2008.

Michaels, Walter Benn. *Our America: Nativism, Modernism, and Pluralism*. Durham: Duke University Press, 1995.

Miller, Joshua L. *Accented America: The Cultural Politics of Multilingual Modernism*. New York: Oxford University Press, 2011.

Morrisson, Mark. "Nationalism and the Modern American Canon." In *The Cambridge Companion to American Modernism*, edited by Walter Kalaidjian, 12–35. Cambridge: Cambridge University Press, 2005.

Scott, Rebecca. *Degrees of Freedom: Louisiana and Cuba after Slavery*. Cambridge: Harvard University Press, 2005.

Smith, Jon and Deborah Cohn. *Look Away! The US South in New World Studies*. Durham: Duke University Press, 2004.

Spillers, Hortense. *Black, White, and in Color: Essays on American Literature and Culture*. Chicago: University of Chicago Press, 2003.

Trefzer, Annette and Ann J. Abadie, eds. *Global Faulkner: Faulkner and Yoknapatawpha, 2006*. Jackson: University of Mississippi Press, 2009.

Wilson, Sarah. *Melting-Pot Modernism*. Ithaca, NY: Cornell University Press, 2010.

Zamora, Lois Parkinson. *Writing the Apocalypse: Historical Vision in Contemporary US and Latin American Fiction*. New York: Cambridge University Press, 1999.

INDEX

Abravanel, Genevieve, 195
Absalom, Absalom! (Faulkner), 24, 239–242
Adams, Ansel, 2
Adams, Henry, 160
Adolescence (Hall), 125
Adorno, Theodor, 162, 169
aesthetic movements, 5, 8. *See also specific movements*; African American culture and literary traditions, 12–13; canon formation and, 182; double consciousness and, 75–76; Ellison and, 181; folk cultures, 53, 182; language and, 195; oral culture and, 53, 182; vernacular culture and, 192n15. *See also specific writers*
African American literary studies, 178–179
African American modernism(s), 8, 13, 22–23, 122, 178–191, 197, 230, 232–233. *See also* Afromodernism; black modernism
African American musical forms, 13, 178–191. *See also* blues; jazz
African American performance studies, 183
African Americans, 12–13, 112, 186–187, 197. *See also specific writers*
African emigration, 93
Africanism, 102
Afro-diasporic culture and literary traditions, 69, 71, 179–180, 201, 203–204
Afromodernism, 4
Against the Day (Pynchon), 151–152
Agee, James, 2, 171, 172
alienation, 35, 40–42
The Ambassadors (Henry James), 125
America: A Family Matter (Gould), 54
America Is in the Heart (Bulosan), 36–43, 45
American Civil War, 53
American dream, 40
American English, 194, 195–196
American identity, 14–15, 26, 40–41, 54, 60, 66n18
Americanization, 59, 60

American literature. *See* U.S. literature
The American Scene (Henry James), 12–13, 159–161, 162
An American Tragedy (Dreiser), 138
And China Has Hands (Tsiang), 43
Anderson, Paul, 183
Anderson, Sherwood, 138, 145–146, 149–150, 207n3, 233
Anthony, Susan B., 1–2
Arac, Jonathan, 232
Ariès, Philippe, 125
Armstrong, Louis, 181
Aronowitz, Stanley, 214
Arrowsmith (Lewis), 137, 138
Asian Americanists, 36
Asian American literary canon, cultural nationalism and, 36–37
Asian American modernism, 9, 22–23, 35–48; alienation and, 40–42; canon formation and, 36–37; capitalism and, 42–44; exile and, 40–42; literary resistance and, 42–44; race and, 41–42; systems and, 42–44; transpacific contexts of, 38–39; transpacific elite and, 40–42; U.S.-Asian relations and, 38–39; women and, 44–47
Asian American narrative: "belatedness" of, 37; realism and, 37
Asian Americans: American dream and, 40; Asian butterfly trope and, 45; citizenship of, 38; double consciousness and, 36; exclusions from immigration, 35, 40–41; identity politics and, 36–37; immigration and, 40, 47; immigration of, 35, 36; labor and, 40; as model minority, 47, 48; objectification of, 42; race and, 35, 40, 42, 47, 48; representations of, 35, 39, 44–47. *See also* Asian Americans; Asian women
As I Lay Dying (Faulkner), 131–132, 133, 223

Cambridge Companions to ...

AUTHORS

Edward Albee edited by Stephen J. Bottoms

Margaret Atwood edited by Coral Ann Howells

W. H. Auden edited by Stan Smith

Jane Austen edited by Edward Copeland and Juliet McMaster (second edition)

James Baldwin edited by Michele Elam

Beckett edited by John Pilling

Bede edited by Scott DeGregorio

Aphra Behn edited by Derek Hughes and Janet Todd

Walter Benjamin edited by David S. Ferris

William Blake edited by Morris Eaves

Boccaccio edited by Guyda Armstrong, Rhiannon Daniels, and Stephen J. Milner

Jorge Luis Borges edited by Edwin Williamson

Brecht edited by Peter Thomson and Glendyr Sacks (second edition)

The Brontës edited by Heather Glen

Bunyan edited by Anne Dunan-Page

Frances Burney edited by Peter Sabor

Byron edited by Drummond Bone

Albert Camus edited by Edward J. Hughes

Willa Cather edited by Marilee Lindemann

Cervantes edited by Anthony J. Cascardi

Chaucer edited by Piero Boitani and Jill Mann (second edition)

Chekhov edited by Vera Gottlieb and Paul Allain

Kate Chopin edited by Janet Beer

Caryl Churchill edited by Elaine Aston and Elin Diamond

Cicero edited by Catherine Steel

Coleridge edited by Lucy Newlyn

Wilkie Collins edited by Jenny Bourne Taylor

Joseph Conrad edited by J. H. Stape

H. D. edited by Nephie J. Christodoulides and Polina Mackay

Dante edited by Rachel Jacoff (second edition)

Daniel Defoe edited by John Richetti

Don DeLillo edited by John N. Duvall

Charles Dickens edited by John O. Jordan

Emily Dickinson edited by Wendy Martin

John Donne edited by Achsah Guibbory

Dostoevskii edited by W. J. Leatherbarrow

Theodore Dreiser edited by Leonard Cassuto and Claire Virginia Eby

John Dryden edited by Steven N. Zwicker

W. E. B. Du Bois edited by Shamoon Zamir

George Eliot edited by George Levine

T. S. Eliot edited by A. David Moody

Ralph Ellison edited by Ross Posnock

Ralph Waldo Emerson edited by Joel Porte and Saundra Morris

William Faulkner edited by Philip M. Weinstein

Henry Fielding edited by Claude Rawson

F. Scott Fitzgerald edited by Ruth Prigozy

Flaubert edited by Timothy Unwin

E. M. Forster edited by David Bradshaw

Benjamin Franklin edited by Carla Mulford

Brian Friel edited by Anthony Roche

Robert Frost edited by Robert Faggen

Gabriel García Márquez edited by Philip Swanson

Elizabeth Gaskell edited by Jill L. Matus

Goethe edited by Lesley Sharpe

Günter Grass edited by Stuart Taberner

Thomas Hardy edited by Dale Kramer

David Hare edited by Richard Boon

Nathaniel Hawthorne edited by Richard Millington

Seamus Heaney edited by Bernard O'Donoghue

Ernest Hemingway edited by Scott Donaldson

Homer edited by Robert Fowler

Horace edited by Stephen Harrison

Ted Hughes edited by Terry Gifford

Ibsen edited by James McFarlane

Henry James edited by Jonathan Freedman

Samuel Johnson edited by Greg Clingham

Ben Jonson edited by Richard Harp and Stanley Stewart

James Joyce edited by Derek Attridge (second edition)

Kafka edited by Julian Preece

Keats edited by Susan J. Wolfson

Rudyard Kipling edited by Howard J. Booth

Lacan edited by Jean-Michel Rabaté

D. H. Lawrence edited by Anne Fernihough

Primo Levi edited by Robert Gordon

TOPICS